59.95

Handbook of Cross-Cultural Psychology ,

PSYCHOPATHOLOGY

VOLUME 6

EDITED BY

Harry C. Triandis
University of Illinois at Urbana-Champaign, USA

Juris G. Draguns
The Pennsylvania State University, USA

ALLYN AND BACON, INC.

Boston   London   Sydney   Toronto

Library of Congress Cataloging in Publication Data   (Revised)

Main entry under title:

Handbook of cross-cultural psychology.

   Includes bibliographies and index.
   CONTENTS: v. 1. Triandis, H. C. and Lambert, W. W., editor. Perspectives.—v. 2. Triandis, H. C. and Berry, J. W., editors. Methodology.—v. 3. Triandis, H. C. and Lonner, W. Basic processes.— [etc.]—v. 6. Triandis, H. C. and Draguns, J. G., editors. Psychopathology.

   1. Ethnopsychology—Collected works. I. Triandis, Harry Charalembos, 1926–   [DNLM: 1. Ethnopsychology. 2. Cross-Cultural comparison. GN270 H2361]
GN502.H36   155.8   79-15905
ISBN 0-205-06497-3 (v. 1)

Printed in the United States of America.

Production editor: Shirley Davis
Preparation buyer: Linda Card

Contents

Volume 3. BASIC PROCESSES

Volume 4. DEVELOPMENTAL PSYCHOLOGY   (in press)

Volume 5.   SOCIAL PSYCHOLOGY

Volume 6.   PSYCHOPATHOLOGY

Preface

Cross-cultural psychology has been expanding in the past twenty years[1] to the point that there is now a need for a source book more advanced than a textbook and more focused than the periodical literature. This is the first handbook of cross-cultural psychology. It is an attempt to assemble in one place the key findings of cross-cultural psychologists. In addition to serving the needs of graduate instruction, the *Handbook* will be useful to advanced undergraduates and to professional social and behavioral scientists.

This *Handbook* will do more than summarize the state of cross-cultural psychology in the 1970s. It should provide a bridge that will allow more traffic in the direction of a new kind of psychology. One of the key facts about psychology is that most of the psychologists who have ever lived and who are now living can be found in the United States. About 50,000 psychologists live in the United States and several thousand more graduate each year. The rest of the world has only about 20 percent of the psychologists that are now or have ever been alive. Moreover, psychology as a science is so overwhelmingly the product of German, French, British, Russian, and North American efforts that it is fair to consider it an entirely European-based enterprise (with American culture considered the child of European culture). Yet, science aspires to be universal. Cross-cultural psychologists try to discover laws that will be stable over time and across cultures, but the data base excludes the great majority of mankind who live in Asia and the Southern Hemisphere. Are so-called "psychological laws" really universal? Are theories merely parochial generalizations, based on ethnocentric constructions of reality? This *Handbook* assembles reports of the methods, procedures, and findings that ultimately will give definitive answers to such questions, answers that are crucial for the development of psychology. If psychology must be changed to understand the behavior and experience of the majority of mankind, then this is a fact of profound importance. If not, it is still good to know that no changes are needed. The reality probably lies between these two extremes, and different psychological laws can be held as "true" with varying degrees of confidence.

We engage in cross-cultural psychology for many reasons, which are enumerated in the Introduction to Volume 1. Volume 1 examines the field in broad perspective and examines how it relates to some other fields. Volume 2 focuses on methodology, since the cross-cultural enterprise poses formidable methodological difficulties. The remaining volumes concentrate on basic psychological processes such as learning, motivation, and perception (Volume 3); developmental processes (Volume 4); social psychological (Volume 5); and psychopathological (Volume 6) phenomena.

One key policy decision for a handbook is whether to cover the material exhaustively, saying a word or two about every study, or in depth, saying rather more about a few key studies. Our decision for greater depth resulted in incomplete coverage. However, much of the work in cross-cultural psychology is methodologically weak. Rather than attacking such studies, we decided to de-emphasize them in favor of those studies that are methodologically defensible. However, this was not a decision that was applicable to all the methodologically weak areas. In some areas of cross-cultural psychology, there has been so *much* weak work that any student starting to work on related problems is likely to find dozens of studies and hence get the impression that this is a respectable area of inquiry. In such cases we could not ignore the weak studies. But while we had to quote them and criticize them, we could not sacrifice much space in this effort. For instance, most of the work using versions of the prisoner dilemma game in different cultures results in uninterpretable findings. In Volume 5 Leon Mann and Gergen, Morse, and Gergen discuss this work and show why it is weak.

Some work was left out simply because space limitations did not allow complete coverage. Other work was omitted on the grounds that it really is not cross-cultural psychology, and may more appropriately be included in comparative sociology, cultural anthropology, or some other field. Some of these decisions are inevitably arbitrary. Obviously, a *Handbook* like this one is likely to *define* the field, both by what it includes and by what it excludes. We are distinctly uncomfortable about some of the exclusions. For instance, our coverage of Freudian, neopsychoanalytic, and related cross-cultural studies is extremely limited. However, other theoretical systems, such as a "liberated cognitive behaviorism" (Triandis, 1977) will encompass the insights derived from this tradition. We have very little discussion of ethnoscience, ethnomusicology, and ethnolinguistics; we believe these materials now belong to other neighboring disciplines. It is of course obvious that this judgment may be wrong. A revision of this *Handbook*, which may be necessary in a decade or two, could well give a central position to one of these topics.

In writing this *Handbook* we have been very much aware of the probability that psychologists from non-European-derived cultures will find it among the most useful books that they may obtain from European-derived cultures. Much of what psychologists teach in their own cultures is based on studies done with subjects from European-derived cultures. They cannot be sure that such information is culture-general. This *Handbook* faces this question and could become a companion volume of any European-derived psychology book. Since many psychologists do not have English as their first language, we have tried to keep the language as concise as possible. If the style appears telegraphic at times, it is intentional.

We allowed the authors of the chapters considerable freedom in expressing themselves. We felt that an international enterprise such as this *Handbook*, should not impose narrow, possibly ethnocentric standards. Thus, authors have been allowed to use the style and spelling that is more appropriate in their own country. English now exists in many versions; the language of Scotland is not identical to Indian English. Rather than obliterate such differences with a heavy editorial hand, we have preserved them.

Volume 1 includes background material that any serious student of cross-cultural psychology would want to know. It examines the history, the major theoretical frameworks, and the relationship between cross-cultural psychology and some other closely related disciplines.

Volume 2 concentrates on methodological problems. Cross-cultural psychology has all the methodological problems of research done by psychologists in a homogeneous culture, plus additional ones that arise because it is cross-cultural. The authors describe the particular technique and emphasize the special difficulties—the particular methodological dilemmas that one faces in cross-cultural work—stressing those strategies developed to deal with those dilemmas. For example, since the reader is assumed to know about experimental methods, the chapters on experiments deal only with special concerns of cross-cultural psychologists doing experiments.

Volume 3 focuses on basic psychological processes—perception, learning, motivation, and so on. Here we tried to give the experimental psychologists who investigate such processes a chance to expand their perspective. We focused on what appears to be universal, but also emphasized ways in which cultural factors may intrude and change some of the processes.

Volume 4 examines developmental perspectives. Some of the key areas discussed are the development of language, personality, and cognition. Since the major effort in the past twenty years in cross-cultural developmental psychology has been on testing aspects of Piaget's theoretical system, a major focus is on this topic.

Volume 5 deals with cross-cultural social psychology. It examines the major traditional topics—attitudes, values, groups, social change—and some of the newer topics—environmental psychology and organizational psychology.

Volume 6, the last one, is of greatest interest to clinical psychologists or psychiatrists. The focus is on variations of psychopathology, on methods of clinical work, as well as on the cultural and family antecedents of psychopathology.

Our expectation is that the committed student of cross-cultural psychology will want to own all six volumes. However, in this age of specialization and high costs we know that many will buy only Volume 1 plus one other. Finally, certain specialists will want a single volume to enlarge their perspective on their own discipline, by examining the related cross-cultural work. These different patterns of acquisition produce a serious policy problem concerning coverage. A key theory or key cross-cultural finding may have to be mentioned in each volume for those who purchase only one volume, which may create considerable overlap across volumes. However, the authors have cross-referenced chapters in other volumes. Also, we have allowed minimum coverage of a particular topic that has been covered extensively in another volume, so that purchasers of only one volume will acquire some superficial familiarity with that topic.

In some cases, the topics are sufficiently large and diffuse that coverage by two different authors does not result in redundancy. When this was the case, I simply sent copies of the relevant sections of other chapters to these authors and asked them, when revising, to be fully aware of coverage in other chapters.

The idea to publish a *Handbook of Cross-Cultural Psychology* originated with Jack Peters of Allyn and Bacon, Inc. He asked me at the 1972 meetings of the American Psychological Association, in Hawaii, whether I would be interested in editing such a handbook. The idea appealed to me, but I was not sure of the need. We wrote to a sample of distinguished psychologists for their opinions. They were almost unanimous in thinking that such a handbook would be worth publishing. At the conference on "The Interface between Culture and Learning," held by the East-West Center, in Hawaii, in January 1973 we asked a distinguished, international sample of cross-cultural psychologists for their opinion. They were also supportive. By the summer of 1973 a first outline of a handbook was available, but it also became very clear that I alone could not handle the editing. The handbook should reflect all of psychology; I was not competent to deal with such a vast subject. Hence the idea emerged of having several Associate Editors, who would cover different aspects of the topic.

The Society for Cross-Cultural Research, at its 1975 Chicago meetings, heard a symposium in which G. Kelly, G. Guthrie, W. Lambert, J. Tapp, W. Goodenough, H. Barry, R. Naroll, and I presented our ideas about the shape of the *Handbook,* and we heard criticism from both anthropologists and psychologists in the audience about our plans.

In January 1976 we were fortunate to be able to hold a conference sponsored by the East-West Center, Hawaii, in which about two-thirds of the chapters were thoroughly discussed. We are most grateful to the Center for this support. The East-West Center held a course for post-doctoral level, young social scientists from Asia, the Pacific, and the United States, using the drafts of the *Handbook* chapters as a textbook. Richard Brislin, Stephen Bochner, and George Guthrie were the faculty. Fifteen outstanding young social scientists[2] were thus able to give us feedback from the point of view of the consumer, but even more important, they pointed out statements that may have been ethnocentric, incorrect, confusing, and outdated.

From the very beginning, we were committed to producing a handbook with authors from every continent. This was not possible. However, the *Handbook* includes chapters by authors from nine countries. To avoid as much ethnocentrism as possible, I appointed a board of twenty Regional Editors. These editors were asked to supply abstracts of publications not generally available in European and North American libraries. These abstracts were sent to those chapter authors who might find them useful. Thus, we increased the chapter authors' exposure to the non-English international literature. By summer 1975, fourteen of these twenty Regional Editors had supplied abstracts listed by cultural region. They were:

Africa

> R. Ogbonna Ohuche (University of Liberia, Monrovia, Liberia)
> The late M. O. Okonji (University of Lagos, Nigeria)
> Christopher Orpen (University of Cape Town, South Africa)
> Robert Serpell (University of Zambia, Lusaka, Zambia)

Circum-Mediterranean

> Yehuda Amir (Bar-Ilan University, Israel)
> Terry Prothro (American University, Beirut, Lebanon)

East-Eurasia

> S. Anandalakshmy (Lady Irwin College, New Delhi, India)
> John L. M. Dawson (University of Hong Kong)
> Wong Fong Tong (Jamaah Nazir Sekolah, Kuala Lumpur, Malaysia)
> S. M. Hafeez Zaidi (University of Karachi, Pakistan)

Insular Pacific

> Subhas Chandra (University of South Pacific, Fiji)

South America

> Eduardo Almeida (Mexico City)
> Gerardo Marin (Universidad de los Andes, Bogotá, Colombia)
> Jose Miguel Salazar (Universidad Central de Venezuela, Caracas, Venezuela)

It should be mentioned that with such an international group of authors, chapters required particularly skillful editing of the style so that all chapters would be excellent not only in content but in language. My wife, Pola, and Doris S. Bartle supplied this expertise and were among those who contributed to the realization of a truly international undertaking.

A number of colleagues functioned as special reviewers for individual chapters. Thanks are due to S. M. Berger, Charles Eriksen, Lucia French, Lloyd Humphreys, and Fred Lehman for their critical comments. In addition, the final version of each volume was read by a scholar, and I would also like to acknowledge their valuable suggestions and comments: Volume 1, Daniel Katz; Volume 2, Uriel Foa; Volume 3, Lee Sechrest; Volume 4, Barbara Lloyd and Sylvia Scribner; Volume 5, Albert Pepitone; and Volume 6, Ihsan Al-Issa.

Harry C. Triandis

NOTES

1. Documentation of this point would include noting that several journals (the *International Journal of Psychology*, the *Journal of Social Psychology* and the *Journal of Cross-Cultural Psychology*) publish almost exclusively cross-cultural papers; there is a *Newsletter*, first published in 1967, that is largely concerned with this area; there are *Directories* of the membership of cross-cultural psychologists, first published by Berry in the *International Journal of Psychology* in 1969, then revised and extended and published as a booklet by Berry and Lonner (1970) and Berry, Lonner, and Leroux (1973); and finally, there is the International Association for Cross-Cultural Psychology, which has held meetings in Hong Kong (1972), Kingston, Canada (1974), Tilburg, Holland (1976), Munich, West Germany (1978), which now has a membership of about 350 active researchers from about fifty countries. Psychology has been an international enterprise for almost a century, and the Union of Scientific Psychology, and the International Association of Applied Psychology have been meeting every two or so years, since the turn of the century. But the emphasis on collecting *comparable* data in several cultures is relatively new, and has expanded particularly after the mid 1960s. A number of regional international organizations, such as the Interamerican Society of Psychology, and the Mediterranean Society of Psychology, have become active in the last twenty years.

2. Listed by country the participants were:
   Australia: Brian Bishop (Perth, Institute of Technology), Margaret M. Brandl (Darwin, Department of Education), Betty A. Drinkwater (Townsville, James Cook University), Michael P. O'Driscoll (Adelaide, Flinders University).
   Fiji: Lavenia Kaurasi (Suva, Malhala High School)
   Indonesia: Suwarsih Warnaen (Jakarta, University of Indonesia)
   Japan: Yuriko Oshimo (University of Tokyo) and Toshio Osako (Tokyo, Sophia University)
   Pakistan: Sabeeha Hafeez (Karachi University), Abdul Haque (Hyderabad, University of Sind)

Philippines: Liwayway N. Angeles (Rizal, Teacher Education)
Thailand: Jirawat Wongswadiwat (Chaingmai University)
United States: Angela B. Ginorio (New York, Fordham University), Howard Higginbotham (University of Hawaii), Caroline F. Keating (Syracuse University), and James M. Orvik (Fairbanks, University of Alaska)

At the conference, the following authors and editors, in addition to Brislin, Bochner, and Guthrie, were also present: Altman, Barry, Berry, Ciborowski, Davidson, Deregowski, Draguns, Heron, Holtzman, Hsu, Jahoda, Klineberg, Lambert, Longabaugh, Lonner, R. and R. Munroe, Michik, Pareek, Price-Williams, Prince, Sanua, Sutton-Smith, E. Thompson, Tseng, Triandis, Warwick, Zavalloni.

Biographical Statements

HARRY C. TRIANDIS, the General Editor, was born in Greece, in 1926. During childhood he received several cross-cultural influences: German and French governesses, French and Italian high school years. After three years of engineering studies at the Polytechnic Institute of Athens, he attended McGill University in Montreal, Canada, where he graduated in Engineering. He worked in industry for three years, during which he obtained a master's degree from the University of Toronto. But engineering was not as interesting to him as studying people. He returned to McGill to learn basic psychology, and studied with Wallace E. Lambert and Don Hebb. From there he went to Cornell University, where he studied with W. W. Lambert, W. F. Whyte, T. A. Ryan, Alexander Leighton, and others. From Cornell in 1958 he went to the University of Illinois, where he is now Professor of Psychology. He conducted cross-cultural studies in Greece, Germany, Japan, and India, and worked in collaboration with black psychologists on the perceptions of the social environment among blacks and whites. His books include *Attitude and Attitude Change* (1971), *The Analysis of Subjective Culture* (1972), *Variations in Black and White Perceptions of the Social Environment* (1975), and *Interpersonal Behavior* (1977). He was Chairman of the Society of Experimental Social Psychology (1973–74), President of the International Association of Cross-Cultural Psychology (1974–76), President of the Society for the Psychological Study of Social Issues (1975–76), President of the Society of Personality and Social Psychology (1976–77), and Vice-President of the Interamerican Society of Psychology (1975–77).

JURIS G. DRAGUNS was born in Riga, Latvia. He completed his primary schooling in his native country, graduated from high school in Germany, and obtained his B.A. and Ph.D. degrees in the United States. He was trained as a clinical psychologist at the University of Rochester and has held a succession of clinical, research, and academic positions in New York, Massachusetts, and Pennsylvania. His research in psychiatric symptom expression in relation to culture developed out of a more general interest in social influences upon psychopathology and in conceptual models of psychological disturbance. He has been involved in comparing Japanese and Argentine psychiatric patients with their counterparts in the United States and has investigated the manifestations of psychopathology within ethnically and socially heterogeneous groups of patients in Israel, Massachusetts, and Hawaii. His writings include a number of research reports and reviews on psychopathology in relation to culture and on other subjects, published by the General Learning Press, in the *Journal of Cross-*

of Abnormal Psychology, and other journals. He is a coeditor of *Counseling across Cultures* (1976), published by the University Press of Hawaii. He has taught at the University of Mainz in West Germany, has held a fellowship at the East-West Center in Honolulu, Hawaii, has participated in several Interamerican Congresses of Psychology in various countries of Latin America, and has been a consultant to an international project involving the cross-cultural comparison of values and philosophies of life. He is Professor of Psychology at The Pennsylvania State University where he teaches a variety of courses on abnormal psychology, personality, psychological assessment, and the role of cultural factors in behavior.

GEORGE M. GUTHRIE was born in Canada. After receiving an undergraduate degree in psychology at the University of Western Ontario in London, Canada, and a graduate degree at the University of Minnesota, he accepted an appointment at The Pennsylvania State University. His training was in clinical psychology, an interest that led him to seek experience abroad to gain some understanding of the effects of different cultural backgrounds on behavior. He held a Fulbright appointment in the Philippines in 1959–60, which led to a book with a Filipina, Pepita Jimenez Jacobs, *Child Rearing and Personality Development in the Philippines* (Pennsylvania State University Press, 1966). Later, he spent sabbatical years at the East-West Center in Honolulu, Hawaii, in 1966–67 and 1975–76. From 1966 to 1969 he was director of a study of modernization in the Philippines, from which came *Psychology of Modernization in the Rural Philippines* (Ateneo de Manila, IPC Paper No. 8, 1970). He has continued cross-cultural research in the Philippines and research on social factors and personality in the United States.

PATRICIA PICKETT TANCO completed a bachelor's degree at Hood College in Maryland and an M.A. at Wellesley College. She lived for twelve years in the Philippines and traveled extensively in Asia and Europe. Ms. Tanco taught social studies with a cross-cultural orientation at an international high school in Manila. She also directed the Philippine portion of a three-country research project evaluating supplemental feeding programs for children. In addition, she worked on evaluation studies of the U.S. Peace Corps in the Philippines and edited social science research reports prepared by members of USAID Philippines and by the Philippine Commission on Population.

WEN-SHING TSENG was born in Taiwan in 1935. He and his wife JING HSU, who was born in Harbin, China, in 1937, both obtained their medical education at the School of Medicine, National Taiwan University, and received their psychiatric training at the Department of Neuro-Psychiatry, National Taiwan University Hospital, at Taipei. Subsequently, Wen-Shing Tseng, as a World Health Organization Fellow, and Jing Hsu, as an

American Association of University Women and Fulbright Fellow, went abroad for further training at Massachusetts Mental Health Center of Harvard Medical School in Boston. Through such experiences of encountering another culture and dealing with psychiatric patients of different cultural backgrounds, they developed a keen interest in the field of transcultural psychiatry. After their return to Taiwan, besides regular teaching activities and clinical service, they engaged in the study of shaman, fortune-telling, and other folk psychotherapy in Taiwan. In 1971 they served as East-West Center Fellows with the Culture and Mental Health Program of Asia and the Pacific at the Social Science Research Institute of the University of Hawaii. They published several articles together in the past regarding the analysis of Chinese children's stories, Chinese opera, and the experience of intercultural psychotherapy. Presently, both are faculty members of the Department of Psychiatry at the University of Hawaii School of Medicine, continuing their teaching and research in the multiethnic society of Hawaii.

JING HSU (see Wen-Shing Tseng).

VICTOR D. SANUA was raised in Belgium. His parents were of Sephardic origin (Spanish Jews) and had Italian citizenship. He spent World War II in Egypt, where he attended the American University at Cairo and graduated with a B.A. degree in the social sciences in 1945. He worked for the Indian Red Cross, the British Army, and later with the Office of War Information of the United States. He received his Ph.D. in clinical psychology from Michigan State University in 1956. His clinical internship was at New York University–Bellevue Medical Center, where, because of his familiarity with several languages, he was assigned to psychological evaluations of foreign-born patients. At New York University–Bellevue, he conducted research with Puerto Ricans and wrote a monograph on the vocational rehabilitation problems of disabled Puerto Ricans in New York City (1957).

He has done research at Cornell Medical School—where he participated in the Midtown Manhattan study—and at Harvard University, has taught at Yeshiva University and at The City College–City University of New York, and now is Professor in the School of Social Work of Adelphi University, Garden City, Long Island, New York. He was a Fulbright Scholar at the University of Paris (Sorbonne). He has written in the field of sociocultural aspects of social stress, schizophrenia, minority groups, and cross-cultural psychology. He wrote "The Sociocultural Aspects of Schizophrenia: A Review of the Literature," in *The Schizophrenic Syndrome*, edited by L. Bellak and L. Loeb, and "Immigration, Migration and Mental Illness: A Review of the Literature with Special Emphasis on Schizophrenia," in *Behavior in New Environments: Adaptation of Migrant Populations*, edited by Eugene Brody, both published in 1969. He is a past President of the International Council of Psychologists (1970–72), and Secretary General (1960–65) and Vice-President (1973–75) of the Interamerican Society of Psychology.

ANTHONY J. MARSELLA was born in Cleveland, Ohio, in 1940. He received his Ph.D. degree in clinical psychology from The Pennsylvania State University in 1968. Following a clinical psychology internship at Worcester State Hospital, Worcester, Massachusetts, Dr. Marsella was awarded a Fulbright-Hays Research Scholar appointment to the Philippines for the study of social stress and psychological adaptation. He also was awarded a post-doctoral appointment as an NIMH Research Fellow in the Culture and Mental Health Program. He has conducted research in the Philippines, Korea, and Sarawak and has also studied several ethnocultural groups residing in Hawaii. At the present time, he is Associate Professor, Department of Psychology, University of Hawaii, and Director, WHO/NIMH Schizophrenia Research Center. He also is Associate Director of an NIMH grant for developing interculturally skilled counselors and psychotherapists. Dr. Marsella has published more than fifty journal articles, book chapters, and monographs. Many of these publications have been concerned with ethnocultural aspects of depression and with social stress and psychological adaptation. He has coauthored two books: *Perspectives in Cross-Cultural Psychology* (Academic Press, 1979) and *Cross-Cultural Counseling and Psychotherapy* (Pergamon Press, in press).

RAYMOND PRINCE is Professor of Psychiatry, McGill University, and Research Director, The Mental Hygiene Institute, Montreal, Canada. Born in Ontario in 1925, his interest in the relationships between psychiatric disorders and social class and in the psychotherapeutic effects of religious practices may be related to his rigidly Baptist, working-class family milieu during childhood. He qualified in Medicine (1950) and in Psychiatry (1955) at the University of Western Ontario. His first cross-cultural experience was in Nigeria, where he spent three years as a government psychiatrist, and he subsequently studied the treatment practices of indigenous Yoruba healers. He also spent two years as mental health consultant for the World Health Organization in Jamaica. He worked on mental health surveys in Nigeria and Nova Scotia with A. H. Leighton, and on H. B. M. Murphy's cross-cultural survey of schizophrenia in rural Quebec. For many years he has been an active member of the Section of Transcultural Psychiatric Studies at McGill and on the editorial board of *Transcultural Psychiatric Research Review* and *Ethos*. He is president of the R. M. Bucke Memorial Society for the Study of Religious Experience, and is coeditor with D. H. Salman of its *Newsletter-Review*. He has published some eighty papers in the fields of social psychiatry and the cultural dimensions of religious experience and psychotherapy. He is editor of *Trance and Possession States* (1968) and, with D. Barrier, of *Configurations: Biological and Cultural Factors in Sexuality and Family Life* (1974).

1

Introduction to *Psychopathology*

Juris G. Draguns

The topic of this volume has at various times been designated ethnopsychiatry (Devereux, 1956; Ellenberger, 1968; Pélicier, 1968; Seguin, 1972), transcultural psychiatry (Kiev, 1972; Pfeiffer, 1970; Wittkower & Rin, 1965), comparative psychiatry (Kraepelin, 1904; Lenz, 1964; Yap, 1974), or psychopathology across cultures (Draguns, 1973).[1] The core meaning shared by these several overlapping labels is the concern with the manifestations of psychologically disturbed, abnormal behavior on a worldwide basis. The question immediately arises as to the purpose, meaning, and justification of studying psychological disturbance of diverse cultures.

Historically, this area of investigation goes back to the first decade of the twentieth century (Kraepelin, 1904) and is anticipated in the sporadic reports of travelers, colonial administrators, and anthropologists concerning the strange disturbances episodically observed in a variety of remote lands. For a long time, however, the study of psychological disturbance in alien cultures led a rather modest existence as an extension of descriptive psychiatry beyond the cultural domain in which it originated, providing a quaint catalogue of symptoms and syndromes never or rarely seen at the primary sites of Western psychiatrists' professional activity.

By contrast with this peripheral role, the description, investigation, and treatment of psychological disorder within Western cultures quickly evolved into a significant, if contested, source of information for the understanding of complex human behavior, of difficult personal decisions and choices, and of their consequences. Beginning with Freud, psychodynamic theorists drew heavily upon the verbal productions of people entangled in their subjective distress, as did a variety of modern personality theorists of cognitive, phenomenological, existential, and humanistic persuasions. All of them generalized from observations of disturbed human functioning to shed light on human behavior in its individuality and complexity.

The study of abnormal behavior in diverse cultural milieus has a simi-lar potential for providing some of the underpinnings for a comprehensive cross-cultural psychology. The observer of abnormal psychological reactions outside of his own cultural setting has the opportunity for glimpsing the subjective world of another culture that to other observers of the same culture is oftentimes denied. The systematic utilization of this source of information is a promise which at this time is not yet systematically fulfilled. One of the reasons is that the study of variations of normal behavior across cultures and the study of its disturbed aberrations are carried on autonomously.

There are signs, however, that the invisible barrier separating these two domains of cross-cultural psychology is finally being penetrated. The basic link between these two areas concerns the plasticity of abnormal behavior. Is psychological disturbance essentially uniform all over the world, different only in the trivial trappings of custom, language, imagery, and information? Or does each culture independently shape manifestations of behavior at the lowest limits of social appropriateness and personal effectiveness? Between these extreme positions, articulated in the historical and contemporary literature, a host of nuances and graduations is found. Yet the question remains: What share of variance in psychopathological expression is accounted for by cultural influences? To put it differently, to what extent—if any—is the model of psychiatric classification and diagnosis historically evolved in Paris, Leipzig, and New York appropriate for the description and comparison of psychopathology across the world?

The questions just broached are related to the ferment approaching the proportions of a paradigm clash, which the parent disciplines of psychiatry and clinical psychology have been experiencing through the sixties and seventies. Much heat has been generated by the arguments for and against the "medical model"—the broad notion that abnormal behavior equals, resembles, or can usefully be construed as a number of diseases, in the sense in which this term is used in internal and physical medicine. This view has been stridently and persuasively attacked (e.g., Sarbin & Mancuso, 1972; Szasz, 1969) and spiritedly and sophisticatedly defended (e.g., Grinker, 1969; Kendell, 1975; Roth, 1963; Wishner, 1972). The key concepts of the medical model have been analyzed and differentiated (Sarason & Ganzer, 1968; Wishner, 1972), and the controversy surrounding the medical model has been reviewed and evaluated (Draguns & Phillips, 1971; Phillips & Draguns, 1971; Price, 1978). Alternatives to the medical model in the form of labeling theory (e.g., Scheff, 1966), social learning theory (Ullmann & Krasner, 1975), the organismic adaptational point of view (Phillips, 1968) and a variety of existentialist and humanist positions (Laing, 1967; Maslow, 1968) have been proposed. Different though they are in their conceptual origins and thrusts, they emphasize such features as the continuity of behavior through the normal and disturbed phases of adaptation and the social process of becoming "mentally ill" and of emerging from such a state. Moreover, these points of view converge toward the recognition that psychopathology can be neither fully described nor explained unless the social transactions in which the disturbed person participates with other members of his community are taken into account.

The data and formulations of cross-cultural psychology of abnormal behavior can potentially be brought to bear upon the arguments for or against the medical model. It is perhaps paradoxical, however, that the few volumes with transcultural or comparative psychiatry in their titles explicitly or implicitly (Kiev, 1972; Pfeiffer, 1970; Yap, 1974) proceed from the assumption that the most useful and realistic way of conceptualizing abnormal behavior is in terms of disease entities. The competing points of view have not yet systematically penetrated the cross-cultural study of psychological disturbance, with the possible exception of the labeling theory (see Murphy, 1976). Yet the several nontraditional views of abnormal behavior have points of contact with the cultural relativist positions of Benedict (1934), Devereux (1956), and others who held that each culture creates, defines, and shapes psychological disorders in its own image. These formulations blended in with the broader functionalist tradition in cultural anthropology according to which it is essential to describe—but sterile to compare—cultural characteristics and manifestations. One of the key objectives of this volume is to examine the accumulated evidence on psychological disturbance in various cultures in relation to the substantive issue of its cultural plasticity and the methodological problem of cross-cultural comparability.

To emphasize continuity between normal and abnormal behavior, in the chapter that follows, Guthrie and Tanco deal with the interface between social and abnormal behavior. Their discussion of alienation and anomie is, broadly speaking, concerned with the lack of fit between the individual and his or her milieu, the state of being in—but not of—a society, and the diverse frustrations (some of them productive of abnormal behavior in the restricted sense of the term) that result from social disorientation, a lack of belonging, and a general malaise partaking of both unhappiness and loneliness. As Guthrie and Tanco point out, the concept of alienation is both broad and vague, and the burden is variously placed upon the individual or the society for experiencing it. One possible way of attempting to pin it down in an empirically oriented undertaking is to attempt identifying those social and cultural antecedents that produce or inhibit alienation. On the basis of evidence that is far from complete, the authors attempt to sketch the links between various kinds of social unraveling and individual distress. One of their conclusions is that the relationship between social change and individual suffering is far from direct or axiomatic; people in various cultures are more robust than, in some writings at least, they have been given credit for.

Moving gradually toward the core areas of psychopathology, Tseng and Hsu explore a variety of conditions that, while they cause impairment in efficiency, deviance in social behavior, and subjective distress, do not lead to the recognition of disability or disorder on its own terms. These borderline states concurrently pose the question: Where and on what basis are limits of pathological behavior drawn in cross-cultural perspective? Is the yardstick of normality and abnormality internal to each culture? Can criteria of psychopathology be defined and applied in a universal, pancultural manner? At what point does suboptimally effective and efficient behavior shade off into a generally shared characteristic of the culture in which it is found? What are the limits of usefulness of psychiatric nomenclature and nosology when applied to functioning groups that, from the point of view of the outside observer, exhibit impairment and distress? These questions have been discussed, although not definitively answered, in a host of psychiatric, psychological, and anthropological writings (e.g., Benedict, 1934; Devereux, 1956; Draguns, 1977; Endleman, 1967; Jacoby, 1967). In any case, abnormal behavior is not the exclusive hallmark of psychologically disabled or disturbed individuals. Tseng and Hsu describe the range of disturbing and distressing, although not disabling, phenomena recorded at various points of the globe. In the process, they describe the interplay of stress and the response to it from the cultural vista.

In the chapter following, Draguns deals with the cross-cultural panorama of psychological disturbance of clinical severity and attempts to integrate the available evidence in relation to the issue of plasticity of psychopathological expression. The views of the proponents of the absolutist medical and cultural relativistic points of view are presented, as is the evidence—at different degrees of rigor and solidity—that bears on these contrasting positions. The author's conclusions steer clear of the two extremes. Worldwide *commonalities* are detected in the specific expressions and patterns of disturbance around the globe; yet, *variations* in experience, behavioral expression, and social response to abnormal behavior are undeniable and so intertwined that they defy separation. Culture itself is deeply embedded in human confusion, loss of efficiency, and distress.

There is a danger inherent in presenting and organizing cross-cultural information on disturbed behavior. A curiously static air is conveyed by the examination of the descriptive and comparative data; it is as though this information were captured at a frozen moment. Moreover, devoting a chapter to major psychopathology inadvertently creates the impression that the patterns of abnormal behavior described by Draguns are distinct, sui generis, the property of abnormal individuals and none else.

The chapter on depression by Marsella has been included in part to dispel this misconception. As Marsella points out, depression runs the gamut of severity from a mild and fleeting mood to which few people, in whatever culture they may be reared, are strangers to an all-engulfing aversive psychological state that interferes with accomplishing tasks, cultivating social relationships, and indeed with life itself. There is a twofold justification for including a chapter on depression in this volume. For one, as a syndrome, symptom, and mood state it has been more intensively studied across cultures and by a greater variety of approaches and methods than any other phenomenon of abnormal interest. For another, its ubiquitous nature, evoked by a sad song in one case, by a tragic personal loss in another, makes depression an ideal point of departure for the simultaneous and comparative study in visibly normal and unambiguously impaired individuals. Such work has been done by a number of investigators and is described by Marsella.

The other possible misconception produced in the chapter by Draguns is counteracted in the chapters by Sanua and Prince. As all of us know, behavior—whether functional or aberrant—is in a constant state of flow; it changes, evolves, and terminates. The chapters by Sanua and Prince are directly based upon this recognition. Sanua brings together what disparate and scattered information is extant on the antecedent conditions of psychopathology in relation to culture. His chapter proceeds from two points of departure: (1) child-rearing and socialization experiences differ across cultures and (2) child-rearing and socialization experiences of psychologically disturbed individuals are often deviant. Is there a way to integrate these two bodies of knowledge? Sanua's task is made all the more difficult by the continuing and unresolved controversy concerning the impact of childhood experiences even in a culturally unitary milieu. Moreover, what culturally relevant information exists is disproportionately concentrated on one psychological disorder—schizophrenia. With these difficulties in the background, the chapter attempts to present and sift what is currently known on this as yet amorphous and inchoate topic.

In the final chapter, Prince concentrates on the events that transpire upon the social recognition of a disorder, and his focus is on the culturally patterned experiences designed to help the sufferer return to his or her normal level of functioning. Cultures, as a rule, do not helplessly stand by while their members experience psychological disturbance. They try to counteract the disorder; they intervene. Can any common threads be discerned in the rich panorama of culturally shaped therapeutic techniques? What light do available descriptive accounts shed upon the arguments of what are the "active ingredients" of psychotherapeutic experience on a culturally uniform ground? Prince believes that the therapist has a catalytic role to play in mobilizing the individual's endogenous resources and in helping him or her overcome the confusion, distress, and ineffectuality of psychological distress. How these resources are mobilized is a matter of culturally shared frames of reference, and the resulting panorama of therapists' modi operandi is dazzling in its variety.

It is not surprising that so far we are essentially in a recording rather than investigative stage of studying cross-cultural psychotherapy. What remain to be separated are the wheat and the chaff—the irrelevant trappings and the therapeutically potent components of therapists' interventions. The problems of doing systematic therapy and process-outcome research in modes of therapy other than that of one's culture are briefly alluded to by Prince, who sees many practical and methodological obstacles to realizing this goal. He does not believe that it cannot be implemented in principle; the history of research on psychotherapy on its home grounds in North America and Western Europe is barely thirty years old. The transfer and adaptation of the accumulated experience and sophistication to other cultures should require a lot less than three decades.

The common thread that is sometimes submerged, yet recurrently rises to the surface in each of the chapters in this volume, is the role that culturally descriptive and comparative information may play in the formulation of general principles of psychology. As pointed out elsewhere (Jahoda, 1975), the conceptual justification of cross-cultural psychology is ultimately provided by the generally valid psychological formulations that have been developed with the help of cross-cultural data. Thus, the chapters in this volume are presented as stepping stones toward this endeavor, still at a rather early stage in the development of the study of abnormal behavior across cultures. As such, the data extant lend themselves more easily to the formulation of relevant questions than to the provision of definitive answers. Although final responses to such global questions as those concerning the nature and degree of the relationship between psychopathology and culture are not yet in, it is possible to take stock of the results for or against particular conceptual positions on this issue and on other broadly significant problems. What the authors in this volume demonstrate is that the field of cross-cultural study of abnormal behavior is ripe for transcending its purely empirical, fact-gathering stage. The data available—though rarely conclusive—can be organized around a number of reference points, and these reference points, in turn, may serve as foundations for more ambitious, systematic, and sophisticated research. As pointed out above, this research holds the promise of contributing answers not only to questions concerning the generic relationship of psychopathology to its milieu but to the even more global issue of what constitutes psychopathology and what is the best model for capturing its crucial features.

Note

1. A terminological complication, traceable to the multidisciplinary nature of endeavor in this field, must be introduced at this point. Wittkower (1969), who has made notable contributions in standardizing terminology in the field of the study of psychiatric disorder and culture, favors the use of transcultural psychiatry as a term to encompass all study of disturbed behavior in relation to culture. He proposes to restrict the term cross-cultural to actual comparisons of psychological disturbance in two or more cultures (see Wittkower and Rin, 1965). His proposals are systematically followed in the psychiatric literature but less so in psychological and anthropological writings. In the context of this *Handbook* it may be confusing to use the term "cross-cultural" in its broad, generic sense throughout the preceding volumes and to employ the designation "transcultural" in reference to abnormal behavior.

References

BENEDICT, R. Culture and the abnormal. *Journal of Genetic Psychology*, 1934, *1*, 60–64.

DEVEREUX, G. Normal and abnormal. In Anthropological Society of Washington, *Some uses of anthropology: Theoretical and applied*. Washington: Anthropological Society of Washington, 1956.

DRAGUNS, J. G. Comparisons of psychopathology across cultures: Issues, findings, directions. *Journal of Cross-Cultural Psychology*, 1973, *4*, 9–47.

————. Problems of defining and comparing abnormal behavior across cultures. *Transactions of the New York Academy of Sciences*, 1977, *285*, 664–675.

DRAGUNS, J. G., & PHILLIPS, L. *Psychiatric classification and diagnosis: An overview and critique*. Morristown, N.J.: General Learning Press, 1971.

ELLENBERGER, H. Intérêt et domaines d'application de l'ethno-psychiatrie. *Proceedings of the Fourth World Congress of Psychiatry*. Amsterdam: Excerpta Medica, 1968.

ENDLEMAN, R. Toward a transcultural psychodynamic. In R. Endleman (Ed.), *Personality and social life*. New York: Random, 1967.

GRINKER, R. R. Emerging concepts of mental illness and models of treatment: The medical point of view. *American Journal of Psychiatry*, 1969, *125*, 865–879.

JACOBY, J. The construct of abnormality: Some cross-cultural considerations. *Journal of Experimental Research in Personality*, 1967, *2*, 1–15.

JAHODA, G. Presidential address. In J. W. Berry & W. J. Lonner (Eds.), *Applied cross-cultural psychology: Selected papers from the Second International Conference of IAACP*. Amsterdam: Swets and Zeitlinger, 1975.

KENDELL, R. E. The concept of disease and its implications for psychiatry. *British Journal of Psychiatry*, 1975, *127*, 305–315.

KIEV, A. *Transcultural psychiatry*. New York: Free Press, 1972.

KRAEPELIN, E. Vergleichende Psychiatrie. *Zentralblatt für Nervenheilkunde und Psychiatrie*, 1904, *15*, 433–437.

LAING, R. D. *The politics of experience.* New York: Pantheon, 1967.

LENZ, H. *Vergleichende Psychiatrie.* Vienna: Maudrich, 1964.

MASLOW, A. H. *Toward a psychology of being* (2nd ed.). Princeton, N.J.: Van Nostrand, 1968.

MURPHY, J. M. Psychiatric labeling in cross-cultural perspective. *Science,* 1976, *191,* 1019–1028.

PÉLICIER. Y. La psychologie des peuples et la psychiatrie. *Revue de psychologie des peuples,* 1968, *23,* 288–302.

PFEIFFER, W. M. *Transkulturelle Psychiatrie: Ergebanisse und Probleme.* Stuttgart: Thieme, 1970.

PHILLIPS, L. *Human adaptation and its failures.* New York: Academic Press, 1968.

PHILLIPS, L., & DRAGUNS, J. G. Classification of the behavior disorders. *Annual Review of Psychology,* 1971, *22,* 447–482.

PRICE, R. H. *Abnormal behavior: Perspectives in conflict* (2nd ed.). New York: Holt, Rinehart & Winston, 1978.

ROTH, M. Neurosis, psychosis, and the concept of disease in psychiatry. *Acta psychiatrica scandinavica,* 1963, *39,* 128–145.

SARASON, I. G., & GANZER, V. J. Concerning the medical model. *American Psychologist,* 1968, *23,* 507–510.

SARBIN, T. R., & MANCUSO, J. C. Paradigms and moral judgments: Improper conduct is not a disease. *Journal of Consulting and Clinical Psychology,* 1972, *39,* 6–8.

SCHEFF, T. J. *Being mentally ill: A sociological theory.* Chicago: Aldine, 1966.

SEGUIN, C. A. Ethno-psychiatry and folklore psychiatry. *Revista Interamericana de Psicologia,* 1972, *6,* 75–80.

SZASZ, T. S. *Ideology and insanity.* New York: Doubleday, 1969.

ULLMANN, L. P., & KRASNER, L. *A psychological approach to abnormal behavior* (2nd ed.). Englewood Cliffs, N.J.: Prentice-Hall, 1975.

WISHNER, J. Convergent trends in psychopathology. *Proceedings of the Seventeenth International Congress of Applied Psychology.* Brussels: Editest, 1972.

WITTKOWER, E. D. Perspectives of transcultural psychiatry. *International Journal of Psychiatry,* 1969, *8,* 811–824.

WITTKOWER, E. D., & RIN, H. Transcultural psychiatry. *Archives of General Psychiatry,* 1965, *13,* 387–394.

YAP, P. M. *Comparative psychiatry: A theoretical framework.* Toronto: University of Toronto Press, 1974.

2

Alienation[1]

George M. Guthrie
Patricia Pickett Tanco

Contents

Abstract

In theory, the study of alienation in other societies should clarify the nature of the process, should point to necessary and sufficient causes, and should suggest methods by which alienation might be overcome or avoided. These expectations have not, however, been fulfilled.

Major shortcomings of the research cited lie in ambiguous definitions of alienation and in unreliable and naive measurement. In spite of the fact that Seeman has demonstrated that alienation has at least a half dozen different meanings, investigators continue to treat it as a unitary process. Even though some speak of the complexity of alienation, almost all investigators use unidimensional scales that obscure any complexity that might be present. Another shortcoming of the measurement procedures has been the common reliance on short scales of as few as five dichotomous items. Not only would such scales fail to measure the complexity attributed to alienation but they would also be of very low reliability.

In almost all research on alienation, the process has been response-defined; that is, the concept of alienation has been used as a summary and explanation of the behavior patterns that have been observed. Causes have been inferred from conditions, whereas a more productive approach would have been to specify conditions or causes and determine whether alienation followed.

The pervasive changes associated with modernization and the massive migration from the countryside to the cities of the Third World have not resulted inevitably in alienation in spite of the fact that members of many societies are rapidly exchanging old values for new.

Anyone undertaking cross-cultural research on alienation should specify his or her definition of alienation, adopt measurement techniques that reflect the definition and minimize response biases, and interpret results within the context of the cultural patterns of the people being examined. We cannot assume that our conceptualization of alienation is as appropriate in an alien society as it is in North America. Culturally induced differences in alienation are, after all, part of the domain of study of cross-cultural psychology.

Introduction

The study of alienation in this volume is cross-cultural, not only with respect to behavior in different societies but also in the attempt to draw on the literature of both psychology and sociology. Just as tribal groups have different languages, deities, and rituals, so do academic disciplines. Although we share with sociologists similar goals of survival through scholarship, we worship different ancestors, Wundt, Freud, and Watson or Durkheim, Weber, and G. H. Mead; we utter different incantations of empiricism and theoretical analysis; we worship numbers or words; and we bow to the power of experimental data or field research. Occasionally one group raids the other, seizing some of the victims' fairest ideas and carrying them off to enrich an ideological pool grown weak from too much inbreeding.

The concept of alienation and the social processes from which alienation is inferred have been primarily the concern of sociologists. Alienation has been for clinical sociologists, if such there be, what anxiety has been for clinical psychologists: both a symptom and a cause of behavior deemed undesirable by the victim and by society at large. Alienation has been invoked to account for such diverse activities as crime, alcoholism, racial prejudice, labor unrest, delinquent children, and mental illness, until it seems to be the root of all evil just as the devil was a century ago. The problem is that alienation, anxiety, and the devil are all inferred from responses and remain remarkably impervious to experimental manipulation. We have not shown what circumstances will increase alienation nor what will cast it out.

Early research and theory having to do with alienation have been influenced by the popular American belief in the moral superiority of rural life to the social disorganization, confusion, and loss of primary group controls of the city. White and White (1962) have reviewed statements of this belief from Thomas Jefferson to Frank Lloyd Wright of recent times. As Inkeles and Smith (1970) point out, this concern for the disruptive effects of mass society and industrialization has been repeated by Sorokin and Park—one does not need to go back to Charles Dickens. One reads of the breakdown of traditional values and the loss of the sense of community, but too little of escape from old repressive and erroneous beliefs and of establishment of new social skills and self-confidence. But departure from the rural way of life is a less convincing explanation of alienation when the alienated are rich and young members of powerful rather than minority groups and from families who have lived in cities for generations.

Because alienation has most frequently been defined in terms of its manifestations rather than in terms of manipulable antecedent circumstances, there has been a great deal of unproductive controversy concerning the real nature of alienation. Inevitably, the manifestations of alienation vary from one social group to another, depending on the discrepancy between their current social situation and what they have expected to encounter. With equal certainty, definitions of alienation vary from researcher to researcher, depending on which aspects of behavior the investigator chooses to emphasize. Throughout the literature there is frequently the implication that alienated individuals are out of tune with their society and are not getting much satisfaction from living in their current situation. There is also usually the implication that they would be happier if society changed or if they changed so as to conform more to the shared expectations of the majority.

Seeman (1959) has suggested a clarification in the use of *alienation* that is especially congenial to psychologists:

Alienation is here taken from the social-psychologists' point of view. Presumably a task for subsequent experimental and analytical research is to determine (a) the social conditions that produce these five variants of alienation, or (b) their behavioral consequences. . . . I seek a more researchable statement of meaning.

Seeman suggested that alienation has been used with at least five separate meanings that need to be distinguished:

1. *Powerlessness*—the expectancy or probability held by the individual that his own behaviors cannot determine the occurrence of the outcomes, or reinforcements he seeks.
2. *Meaninglessness*—the individual is unclear as to what he ought to believe, when the individual's minimal standards for clarity in decision making are not met.
3. *Normlessness*—high expectancy that socially unapproved behaviors are required to achieve given goals.
4. *Isolation*—the experience of those who assign low reward value to goals or beliefs that are typically highly valued in a given society.
5. *Self-estrangement*—loss of intrinsic meaning or pride in current work so that the individual performs only for anticipated rewards.

In a later paper, Seeman (1972a) suggested that *isolation* be called *cultural estrangement* and that a sixth category, *social isolation*—the sense of exclusion or rejection versus social acceptance—be added.

Seeman's analysis in terms of reinforcements and expectations, which has been greatly influenced by Rotter's (1966) social learning theory, immediately suggests to psychologists an experimental approach to alienation or at least a basis for making predictions of where alienation will appear or will be alleviated in naturally occurring circumstances when rewards are withdrawn or returned for activities of some or all of the citizens. Following Rotter, Seeman has pointed out that the powerlessness aspect of alienation resembles Rotter's external locus of control; in both cases the outcomes an individual experiences are determined by processes beyond his control.

Not all authors take the social psychological orientation of Seeman, however, so that the meanings of *alienation* continue to proliferate and the reader's patience is likely to be severely tested by extended discussions of all the shades of meaning which one investigator wishes to discriminate from those suggested by earlier authors. In our opinion, as long as social scientists persist in defining alienation in terms of consequences without reference to antecedents they will continue to quibble about meanings for the concept but will not advance our understanding of the process by which alienation, however defined, comes about.

In a book devoted entirely to the analysis of the concept of alienation Johnson (1973) states:

Alienation is an atrocious word. In its use as a general concept, scientific term, popular expression, and cultural motif, alienation has acquired a semantic richness (and confusion) attained by few words of corresponding significance in contemporary parlance. Few concepts have been subjected to as long a history of association with diverse disciplines, each contributing its own emphases and meanings. Moreover, although popularization of technical terms is common, the plethora of contexts in which alienation is cited on a colloquial level seems extravagant when compared to other vogue expressions.

Most terms which possess scientific bite are characterized by a reasonable specificity of denotation, a clarity of meaning within particular disciplines, and an absence of serious internal paradox or ambiguity. None of these adhere to the word, alienation. Alienation is used to denote a great variety of often quite dissimilar phenomena.* (p. 3)

Most people who have read some of the literature on alienation would agree with Johnson, but what is surprising about his statement is that it is from the first two paragraphs of his opening chapter. Those who study alienation either have a high tolerance for ambiguity, or write their introductions last.

We find Seeman's definitions of alienation most satisfactory among the many that have been offered. He has taken into account the fact that alienation may have different manifestations and has avoided the mistake of placing all expressions on one dimension either in conception or in measurement.

Alienation from a Cross-Cultural Perspective

In this chapter we want to examine alienation from a cross-cultural, psychological perspective. Because alienation is considered to result from social processes, one would expect that different social processes found in different societies would modify the manifestations of alienation. In this sense we are using different societies as a natural laboratory to study alienation—the cross-cultural perspective. As psychologists, we will look at manifestations of alienation and try to identify the steps by which individuals and groups of individuals acquire the behavior patterns of alienation. In this emphasis we will pay little attention to two extensive domains of research on alienation processes: alienation within our own society and the social-political conflict between Marxist and other ideologies. We will assume that the reader has some acquaintance with alienation in North America and Western Europe. We omit the Marxist literature because it is primarily political and polemical and because the research on alienation in Third World countries is concerned more with

* From F. Johnson, ed., *Alienation: Concept, Term and Meanings* (New York: Seminar Press, 1973). Reprinted by permission.

the effects of social change and migration than with the effects of conditions of labor.

Neither limitation will be easy to observe nor be clear-cut, because the majority of references to alienation refer to members of North American society and those of other industrial countries. Leaving Marx out is about as difficult as discussing psychopathology without Freud. Marx's emphasis on the role of the capitalist system of industrial production as a source of alienation has had, and continues to have, profound social and political implications in many parts of the world.

The cross-cultural perspective in psychology is more than the application of psychological concepts to behavior in societies different from the societies in which the concepts were formulated. Social processes and the products of social processes, such as language and personality, affect many aspects of behavior, but the contributions of these antecedent conditions are difficult to observe within one cultural tradition. Cross-cultural data may enable us to sort out the effects of differences in linguistic systems, child-rearing practices, sex roles, and other antecedents of current behavior. In this sense other cultures provide a natural laboratory in which important independent variables are already modified, variables that it would not be feasible or even ethically acceptable to modify in our own society. We must use cross-cultural data if we wish to study the effects of extended families on personality development, which may be different from the effects of nuclear families that are almost universal in our own society. Polynesian fosterage, in which the majority of children may experience two or more sets of parents, is a good example of the modification of an important variable, one we cannot manipulate in our own society. American mothers will not give their children to their neighbors to keep, even in the interests of science.

But other variables change at the same time as the ones that interest us. Polynesian children who experience fosterage also experience all the other aspects of Polynesian society, which may differ from our own. Differences cannot, therefore, be attributed to fosterage. The Polynesian pattern does, at least, lead us to call into question our belief that uncertainty and shifting of relationships between children and their parents inevitably leads to instability in children. At the same time it leads us to question the older belief in an almost instinctual bond between a mother and her child. As one Polynesian mother said to one of the authors, "If I love my neighbor and she asks me for my baby, why shouldn't I give it to her?"

In addition to comparisons of circumstances that may precipitate alienation, the study of alienation in other societies may enable us to broaden our perspectives on the patterns of behavior prompted by the experience of alienation and the various ways members of different societies cope with the phenomenon.

Unfortunately, as we shall see, most studies of alienation in non-

Western settings have not been undertaken from the perspective we have outlined above. They have used the concept of alienation to understand the people who may be experiencing difficulties, rather than using the people with their different cultural backgrounds to understand alienation.

We can gain another perspective on alienation when we subject members of one society to a marked change of social structure by immersing them in an alien society. We will examine this as it has been reported by Peace Corps volunteers and other Americans who have lived for limited periods of time surrounded by markedly different social structures.

Finally, as psychologists we will look at attempts to measure alienation and will explore the possibility of interpreting the effects of changes in social structure in terms of changes in reinforcement schedules. There is a growing literature with animal and human subjects which suggests that many of the phenomena attributed to alienation can be induced under laboratory conditions by changing a reinforcement schedule or by subjecting a subject to unavoidable pain or failure. In contrast to many descriptive formulations of alienation, a formulation in terms of reinforcement variables is, in theory at least, testable.

Some History of the Concept of Alienation

Because there are many excellent reviews of the history of the concepts of alienation and anomie we will offer a very selective historical perspective. More general reviews include those of Schact (1970) and Johnson (1973), while Israel (1971) has summarized Marx's original formulation and its subsequent elaborations. For our purposes there are four important names to bear in mind: Marx, Durkheim, Merton, and Seeman.

From what was an early and excellent model of cross-cultural research, Durkheim (1897/1951) offered the concept of anomie. Compared with more recent definitions, anomie appears to be close to Seeman's (1959) normlessness. The term anomie has continued to appear in the literature where it is used more or less interchangeably with alienation. *Le Suicide* is also among the first reports of the consistent and organized use of statistical methods in social research. Using data from many European countries and spanning the half century from 1840 to 1890, he sought to develop a classification of suicides and then to infer the social processes associated with each type. The effort at typing developed after he found no consistent relationships between suicides and such factors as psychopathology and alcoholism, nor were there consistent relationships with race, age, sex, height, or season of the year. On the contrary, different social groups had specific tendencies toward suicide.

Present-day social scientists would report relationships as correlation coefficients and would try to order the contributions of various factors by multiple regression analyses. Without these methods, Durkheim simply presented tables showing, for instance, the frequency of insanity and of suicide for various European countries and pointed out that those countries with many insane did not necessarily have many suicides, nor did those with few insane show few suicides. Furthermore, in other tables he demonstrated that, while there were marked differences between Catholics and Protestants in suicide, there were few differences in insanity rates. He showed also that because suicide rates for Protestants varied from one province to another, one could not account for suicide in terms of religious affiliation. This is cross-cultural research at its best—checking to see if a relationship between two variables found in one society holds in other societies.

When demographic explanations could not be supported, Durkheim turned to explanations in terms of social processes, such as economic disasters or prosperity. In addition, he recognized the role of social traditions in some societies such as Japan. From these and many other sources he deduced three types of suicide: egoistic, due to lack of integration of the individual into society; altruistic, a fulfillment of higher commandments; and anomic, which is due to a failure of regulation by society.

Durkheim's book is especially interesting to a cross-cultural psychologist because he gathered suicide data from France, Italy, Germany, and Switzerland and was able to classify subjects for age, sex, religion, and occupation. From what are today simple tabulations he discovered relationships that led him to formulate the concept of *anomie* or the loss of law or control. He concluded that suicide occurred more frequently when individuals underwent a pronounced change, such as a loss or great prosperity.

Merton (1964, 1968) extended Durkheim's analysis in essays on social structure and anomie in which he examined the differential ability of people to achieve the goals of society. With different degrees of access, individuals make different adaptations:

1. *Conformity*—using approved means to achieve approved goals
2. *Innovation*—unconventional means for approved goals
3. *Ritualism*—approved means for unusual goals
4. *Retreatism*—a rejection of both the goals and the means approved by the individual's society
5. *Rebellion*—a substitution of new values in which the current social structure is seen as a barrier to the achievement of these new goals

Merton's papers have been tremendously influential among sociologists and other social scientists, but they did not reduce the proliferation of meanings for either alienation or anomie.

It remained for Seeman (1959, 1967, 1972a, 1972b, 1972c) in a series of papers to suggest some order in the use of terms, for as Seeman (1972a) remarked:

> The idea of alienation has shown remarkable endurance and an embarrassing versatility. It survives despite recurring invitations to abandon the concept on varied grounds, including the fact that it explains too much by far. The invitation seems especially tempting when it is invoked to explain particular troubles and their opposites: alienation accounts, at once, for conformity and deviance, for political passivity and urban riots, for status-seeking and social retreat, for "other-directed" styles of life and the "hippie" phenomenon, for surburban malaise and do-it-yourself activism.

> The list of phenomena explained is ultimately discouraging. The critics may be right; to explain everything is to explain nothing, and if that is the best we can do we should, indeed, abandon the notion of alienation. We should recognize that we seem unable to escape an array of mutually reinforcing troubles involved in its use: hidden ideological commitments about the good society, romantic assumptions about human nature, confusions between alienation and related concepts, plus some plain vagueness for good measure.* (p. 467)

Alienation has been for sociologists what anxiety has been for psychologists and libido for psychoanalysts, an inferred process invoked to account for observed events, and intervening variable that has little, if any, predictive value and one that has few testable implications. Sometimes alienation was present, sometimes it was not, but it did refer to some important aspects of the relationships between social structure and behavior.

This would appear to be a situation in which cross-cultural data would be especially desirable because observations in other societies may enable us to extend the range of antecedent conditions and observe new consequences that are not available in our own society. What happens to the alienation process when changes occur in the social structure of members of societies with cultures markedly different from our own? How universal is the process? What are the general and what are the culture-specific manifestations?

Overview of Recent Theory
and Research

There is now a vast literature on alienation as witness Geyer's (1972, 1974) bibliography of more than 1,800 books, articles, dissertations, and papers

---

* From "Alienation and Engagement" by M. Seeman. In Angus Campbell and Philip E. Converse, eds., *The Human Meaning of Social Change* (New York: Russell Sage, 1972). © 1972 by Russell Sage Foundation, New York. Reprinted by permission.

as of July 1974. Much of this material is very recent. The inventory of Cole and Zuckerman (1964) of a decade earlier listed fewer than 10 percent of the sources cited by Geyer. The comparison, however, is merely suggestive because, working in Amsterdam, Geyer searched journals in many European languages including Eastern European, while the earlier tabulation was confined largely to American authors writing in English.

Cole and Zuckerman (1964) have provided a very valuable inventory of empirical studies of alienation, beginning with Durkheim's classic on suicide in 1897, down to 1964. The inventory is followed by an annotated bibliography of theoretical studies dating from Durkheim's speculation on the division of labor in 1893 down to the date of their publication. There is in each tabulation a considerable gap following the original Durkheim report. Empirical studies do not pick up again until 1941, while theoretical studies are cited beginning in 1928. It would appear that the theory is older than the data. The earlier empirical studies were predominantly concerned with alienation and various indices of delinquency, while later studies were more concerned with differences associated with socioeconomic status. Throughout the years from 1940 to 1964 there was a heavy reliance on either interviews or questionnaires. Almost all the research was done in the United States. The bulk of the studies classified subjects by socioeconomic status and additionally by a measure of alienation, while the most common dependent variables were various antisocial activities or more measures of alienation and anomie.

In addition to the extensive bibliographies prepared by Geyer (1972, 1974), which is not annotated and which we have referred to above, there have appeared both an annotated bibliography of 225 items and a review paper by Lystad (1969, 1972). The breadth of the use of the concept of alienation is illustrated by her topical classification, which includes theory and method, and alienation among workers, voters, young people, old people, blacks, and the poor. Everyone has at least a touch of alienation except prosperous white Angle-Saxon Protestants in the United States; maybe they should be examined too.

Part of Lystad's summary included:

> The modern focus on alienation involves a concerted effort to clarify the meaning of the term, a broader conceptualization of the causes and consequences of alienation, and considerable empirical research on its prevalence in our time. This extended approach has led to the study of man's feelings of estrangement from not only economic structures but also other major social structures as well. It has facilitated the study of alienation in nonindustrialized societies and in societies whose social institutions are undergoing rapid social change.

> Seeman's studies on alienation as seen through mass society theory have provided the beginnings of an orderly theoretical scheme for prediction studies. His findings indicate, however, that mass society theory underestimates

the social psychological processes mediating between man and his social structure. Seeman found in the social learning theory of Rotter an opportunity to include the study of pertinent psychological variables of expectancy and reinforcement in the analysis of the social situation. In cross-cultural studies he was able to establish that these variables are important not only in the laboratory or with simulated tasks but also among people who are exposed to a variety of control-relevant information that bears on everyday life. These studies demonstrate how two seemingly unrelated theories, mass society and social learning, actually involve related propositions about knowledge processes.

There are still basic methodological issues to be resolved. There is no clearcut definition of alienation in the literature; the concept must be operationally defined very carefully. A common fault of researchers is failure to present the scaling methods used in their published works; they need further to explain exactly how they distinguish between the alienated and the non-alienated in their samples. There is a further need for the study of degree of alienation of the individual from his social structure. Dichotomous categories of "alienated" and "not alienated" are not adequate.* (Lystad, 1972, p. 102–103)

A recent review of alienation is Seeman's (1975) chapter in the *Annual Review of Sociology*. Not surprisingly, Seeman has ordered studies under his six variants of alienation outlined at the beginning of this chapter. Seeman's analysis is important, not because it is based on empirical evidence that there are six distinct categories of alienation, but because his analysis clarifies considerably the many meanings the word *alienation* may connote in various expressions of theory and in reports of research. It is a set of rules about the meanings that may be attached to the word. Much tedious debate would be reduced if authors began with his categories and then specified exceptions and changes they felt were necessary for their research setting.

In a later review of technology, alienation, and job satisfaction, Shepard (1977) has emphasized the complexity of the relationships between different levels of technology and various expressions of alienation. As was demonstrated by Blauner (1964), within an industrial society, technology can be found at three stages: a craft production system with low job specialization, mechanized, mass, or assembly line production with high specialization, and automated production where low job specialization is again the rule. It would appear that work alienation is greatest in assembly line situations and less for craft or automated production settings. Alienation may take any or all of Seeman's original forms and may be specific to the work situation or generalized to many aspects of the worker's life. Shepard (1977) suggests that not only should alienation be conceptualized and measured as a multidimensional condition but that technology or the industrial setting also be seen as a pattern of variables

* From "Social Alienation: A Review of Current Literature" by M. H. Lystad, *Sociological Quarterly*, 1972, *13*, 9–113. Reprinted by permission.

such as pacing of workload, mode of supervision, and level of supervision. We infer that it is no longer acceptable to speak simply of workers alienated by an industrial setting.

Measurement of Alienation

It may seem unusual to treat measurement before one describes in detail the phenomenon to be measured and the theory within which the measurement is suggested. In this case, however, there has been a considerable interplay between measurement and theory building in which investigators have inferred the phenomenology of the alienated, developed statements expressive of alienation, and combined these items into scales. These scales in turn have become the operational definition of alienation and have contributed to theory development and further analysis of the phenomenon. In other words, we are not certain whether scales have feathers or a shell. In their sourcebook of measures of social psychological attitudes Robinson and Shaver (1973) have assembled no fewer than fourteen scales which are named anomy, anomia, powerlessness, alienation, and helplessness. According to our count, thirteen of the fourteen scales are made up of statements expressive of one or more of the above states of mind, all of them in much the form of the following examples drawn from the most widely used scale, the Anomia Scale of Srole (1956).
Here are some examples:

2. Nowadays a person has to live pretty much for today and let tomorrow take care of itself.
4. It is hardly fair to bring children into the world with the way things look for the future.
5. These days a person doesn't really know what he can count on.

In thirteen of the fourteen scales, one gets points for alienation by agreeing with the statements. In only one scale, the powerlessness scale of Neal and Seeman (1964) is a forced-choice format used. Here are some examples:

1. a. I think we have adequate means for preventing runaway inflation.
   b. There is very little we can do to keep prices from going higher.
3. a. A lasting world peace can be achieved by those of us who work toward it.
   b. There is very little we can do to bring about a permanent world peace.

In both of the above pairs the subject receives a score for alienation, in this case powerlessness, if he or she chooses the second alternative as the one more strongly believed in.

The format of these items, other than the forced choice, is most unfortunate because they are influenced greatly by acquiescence, or the tendency by the subject to agree with any statement. Extensive research by Jackson (1971) and by many others has shown that many self-report inventories of attitudes and adjustment are measures of response style as much as, or more than, measures of the dispositions implied by the labels. Thus, it has been found that those who are lower in education and/or income are more likely to agree with statements. This can be demonstrated by reversing the meaning of the statement, in which case many subjects will agree both with the original statement and with its opposite. This has been found with respect to the Srole Scale by Lenski and Leggett (1960). Furthermore, the tendency to agree inflates the correlation between pairs of items in a provisional form of a scale regardless of the content of the items. The usual methods of scale construction, which rely on measures of internal consistency, do not cope with this problem of response acquiescence, and the result is the frequent finding that those with lower income and/or education are more alienated. It is also important to realize that the usual methods of reliability assessment do not differentiate test-taking sets. The tendency to agree manifested by the poor and uneducated (alienated) merely raises the reliability and reproducibility of alienation scales.

Because theories of alienation have emphasized determinants within the social structure, little attention has been given to such characteristics as anxiety and hostility, which may be closely associated with alienation. This has important theoretical considerations—because explanations in terms of interpersonal processes constitute plausible rival hypotheses—and measurement implications—because we need to demonstrate that measures of alienation and of hostility and anxiety are not highly correlated. McClosky and Schaar (1965) found that scores on self-report scales of anomy or normlessness were highly related to self-report scales on such variables as hostility, anxiety, and inflexible defensiveness. They concluded that anomy results from "impediments to interaction, communication, and learning, and is a sign of impaired socialization." In light of the evidence on acquiescence as a determinant of responses to all attitude measures, there is also the possibility that much of the covariation they found is due to method variance or response style. The implication is clear, therefore, that in studies of alienation multiple measures are necessary in order to demonstrate discriminant validity.

In an assessment of the discriminant validity of work alienation and work satisfaction measures, Seybolt and Gruenfeld (1976) carried out separate analyses for men and women at professional and managerial, cleri-

cal, service, and manual occupational levels. Correlations ranging from
−.52 to −.70 indicate that, given the limited reliability of short scales, their
indices were measuring the same thing. The authors, however, are unwilling to surrender a separate status for alienation:

> Because of the generally low discriminant validity found between the two
> variables as operationalized here in self-report terms, perhaps to measure this
> phenomenon of work alienation accurately we must leave the realm of attitu-
> dinal research. . . . It is not an attitudinal reaction to the work, but the work
> itself which is the central factor to be considered. Alienation is a structural,
> objective concept and not an attitudinal reaction to that structure. (Seybolt &
> Gruenfeld, 1976, p. 201)

To illustrate further the role of acquiescence as a determinant of
scores on the Srole Scale, Carr (1971) generated a second set of items that
were the obverse of the original Srole items. For instance, the item,
"Nowadays a person has to live much for today and let tomorrow take
care of itself," was presented in an alternative form: "Nowadays a person
can't just live for today. You have to plan ahead for tomorrow." The argument is that if subjects agreed with the first form they would logically have
to disagree with the second. Giving all items, both the original and obverse
form, Carr found a correlation between the original scale and its obverse
of .79 indicating that the scale is measuring the subject's tendency to agree
rather than his personal beliefs. While psychologists have interpreted acquiescence as a personality trait, Carr suggests that it be seen as a social
tactic by which the weak protect themselves from those who are stronger.

The weakest element in most studies of alienation would appear to be
the measure of alienation that is a short scale of five to ten items, sometimes only one or two, and thus is as much a measure of test-taking attitudes as of alienation. Seeman (1975) observed that alienation studies in
general "have remained entirely too dependent upon what is basically the
'quick fix'—one-shot survey results, with inadequate measures (one or
two items is not rare)." Fortunately for our concerns, when data are collected in alien groups there is less reliance on short scales and greater use
of nonreactive measures.

In the same vein we must observe that while authors repeatedly emphasize the complex multidimensional nature of alienation they proceed
to use unidimensional, single-score scales, or worse still, collect a variety
of items purported to indicate powerlessness, meaninglessness, and so on,
and add those relatively independent attitudes together for a single score.
They may not have heard of Thurstone but they should have heard of
Guttman. There is clearly a need for the greater application of multivariate
procedures to this field of study.

A significant attack on the problem of whether there is one overall
alienation or several, e.g., Seeman's six, has been made by Neal and Rettig
(1967) who found a large first factor in an analysis of twenty-nine alien-

ation items designed to measure powerlessness and normlessness. But because items to measure social isolation, meaninglessness, and so forth were not included, their results do not answer the question of how many independent or correlated alienations there may be.

Cummings and Manring (1977) took care of some of the difficulties just mentioned. Ninety-six blue collar workers took a set of twenty alienation items which on factor analysis yielded five factors of powerlessness (eight items), normlessness (three), instrumental work orientation (four), meaninglessness (three), and self-evaluative involvement (two items). They shortened the scales further to from one to three items and found significant correlations with tardiness and with self-rated effort on the job for powerlessness, normlessness and meaninglessness but not with the ratings of effort by supervisors. We agree with their closing sentence. "Additional research using larger sample sizes, more diverse populations and settings, and longitudinal research designs is needed to provide more definitive knowledge on the organizational impacts of alienating work" (Cummings & Manring, 1977, p. 177). We would add that longer, and thus more reliable, and validated measures of each dimension of alienation are also needed.

For our purposes, there is a strong reason to suggest that scale construction should be repeated in cross-cultural studies in a society different from the one in which the scale was initially developed. A new factor analysis would be most desirable in order to clarify the organization of attitudes of alienation and also to determine what sort of response biases are operating.

We will also see in some studies to be reviewed that authors are carried away with correlation coefficients based on large numbers of subjects that are close to but significantly different from zero. It would seem especially appropriate for those who toil in the alienation vineyard to be aware of the statisticians' coefficient of alienation. This alienation has nothing to do with our chapter but is an indication of how much variance remains unaccounted for in a relationship. For our purposes the square of a correlation coefficient indicates the percentage of variance accounted for. A correlation of .20 indicates that four percent of the variance has been accounted for by the measure of alienation. This finding can be trivial even though, with many cases, .20 is highly significant. There would be few findings to report if we held out for correlations above .50 or 25 percent of the variance. The correlations reported in research on alienation could be spuriously low due to short, unreliable measures or indices of alienation, or to the factorial complexity of the measures, or spuriously high due to response biases in self-report measures.

Finally, a rather interesting contradiction is suggested when one examines the content of Alienation and Modernization Scales. Alienation, it is argued, comes about with the breakdown of traditional values and the incomplete adoption of industrial values. An important component of alienation is powerlessness, yet scales of modernity score admissions of powerlessness as traditional. Thus, a subject who takes both of these measures will appear traditional and alienated or modern and low in alienation, which is not in accord with most theories of modernization or alienation.

Studies of Alienation in Other Societies

Although studies of alienation in societies other than North America and Western Europe are numerous, they are widely scattered with respect to theoretical orientation and journal of publication. Just as is the case in the West, members of many disciplines—sociology, political science, public health, law, and anthropology, and even a few psychologists—have approached their research on alienation from different perspectives and have selected data consonant with their theories and with their problems as they defined them. Cross-cultural comparisons, therefore, are well nigh impossible except at a very qualitative level. The causes of alienation in the studies we cite are most varied, as are the indices of alienation; the latter is in contrast to North America where there has been excessive reliance on short questionnaires to measure the presence or absence of alienation.

Most of the reports we will review are cross-cultural only in the sense that they deal with alienation in other than industrial societies. Only infrequently do the authors analyze their results from a cultural perspective, pointing out the role that foreign cultural factors may play in the development and manifestations of alienation as they have defined it. On the contrary, the typical study we have reviewed applies theories and indices developed in the West to social phenomena in a non-Western setting. Such an approach may enhance comparability of both theories and measures, but it may obscure some of the ways in which the cultural patterns of other societies modify behavior.

In one of the most significant reports of cross-cultural research on alienation that has come to our attention, Seeman (1971) has summarized his studies of the "urban alienations" of Sweden, France, and the United States—"the purported effects of the emerging industrial and mass society on the character and quality of social life." In parallel studies in these three societies Seeman demonstrated that alienation from work, or self-estrangement, was independent of the powerlessness component of alienation and that the latter—not work alienation but powerlessness—was significantly related to ethnic prejudice, low levels of political information, and political unrest. Seeman's demonstration in three societies of the lack of relationship between work alienation and usual social indicators of alienation casts doubt on the widely held notion that mass society and industrialization inevitably lead to loss of community.

Incidental to their study of the psychology of becoming modern, Inkeles and Smith (1974) examined aspects of alienation among respondents at levels of modernization from cultivators to urban workers in large-scale enterprises in Argentina, Chile, India, Israel, Nigeria, and Bangladesh. In order to determine whether modernization disrupted the life pattern of their respondents so that they experienced more personal stress, Inkeles and Smith (1970) administered a Psychosomatic Symptoms Test consisting of a list of five to fifteen physical symptoms commonly considered indicative of emotional stress. Items were not the same in each country because informants indicated that their citizens did not suffer one or more of the complaints. Respondents were asked such questions as whether they had trouble sleeping, whether they were bothered by nervousness, or shortness of breath, or headaches, or frightening dreams. Inkeles concluded, "Of the modernizing influences frequently identified as likely to induce individual disorganization through disruption of personality, creation of strain, introduction of disturbing stimuli, and the like, none consistently and significantly brings about increased maladjustment as measured by the Psychosomatic Symptoms Test." The modernizing influences examined included education, urban residence, exposure to mass media, industrial versus agricultural employment, and duration of factory employment.

In addition, Inkeles and Smith (1974) considered *efficacy*, a sense that one has some control over his material and social environment and an essential characteristic of modern as opposed to traditional men. Items measuring this sentiment were included in his Overall Modernity Scale, a scale that differentiated clearly between traditional cultivators and industrial workers in each country. Efficacy is, of course, the opposite of powerlessness so that Inkeles's data indicate quite clearly that modernization and urban residence reduce the powerlessness component of alienation.

In the review that follows we will examine reports of alienation among North American Indian and Eskimo groups and in the major areas of the developing world: Africa, Latin America, and Southeast Asia. Most of the research we will summarize is not explicitly cross-cultural in the sense that the investigators have looked for differences in behavior of alienated people and have related the differences to broader cultural patterns. On the contrary, they are, for the most part, applications of the concepts of alienation and various measurement techniques to members of a non-Western society. The findings are interpreted as though the people being studied were members of the society in which theories of alienation were developed. When we have reviewed these reports we will attempt to draw some implications from cross-cultural comparisons. This is admittedly a weak approach. We will discuss later the desirability of designing research on alienation so that the role of cultural factors can be recognized and assessed.

Native American Populations

Indian and Eskimo groups in the United States and Canada have attracted increasing attention from governmental and social agencies as the white majority has become increasingly aware of their relative economic deprivation. Problems of poor health, poverty, and high rates of alcoholism have proven to be widespread and resistant to amelioration both on tribal reservations and in urban areas to which Indians particularly have migrated. In one way or another the concept of alienation has been invoked to account for the demoralization of those who continue on the periphery of the more affluent society and for the various forms of social stress and failure of those who attempt to join the larger industrial world.

Graves (1970) studied 259 male Navajos who migrated to Denver over a decade. As earlier investigators have reported, Graves found that "Indian arrests are ten or more times those for whites, and at least three or four times those of other migrant groups." Of their arrests, 86 percent were alcohol related, in contrast to 51 percent for the total population. When he removed the arrests for drunkenness, he found that Indians are no more likely to be arrested than other groups. In fact the rate of arrest for serious crimes is lower than with non-Indian groups. In a direct application of Merton's (1964) goals-means analysis, Graves reported that those who were strongly oriented toward the dominant society and its material rewards and who had poor and irregular jobs were most likely to show high rates of drinking. The feeling of long-term relative deprivation was seen as a relevant factor for this pattern. Graves, however, showed that the migrant Navajo's economic position is only one factor of many, which include his parental models, education, and the extent of his relationships with non-Navajos in Denver. The Navajo who had friends outside the Navajo community in Denver and who was married was much less likely to be arrested for being drunk. Conversely, the most vulnerable were single men who had no place to go with their Navajo friends except to bars. The behavioral indications of alienation have many more roots than just conflicts between new cultural demands and old habits alone.

There are, of course, explanations other than alienation that have been offered to account for high rates of alcohol consumption by native Americans. As reviewed by Brod (1975) these alternatives include drinking as a social institution found in some tribes prior to contact with Europeans, a physiological predisposition to a low tolerance for alcohol (which is shared with mongoloid populations), individual motivations as reported in members of middle-class society, and sociocultural stresses. This fourth explanation sounds at first like alienation, but Brod has given it a more psychodynamic interpretation as the following quotation indicates:

> In transition, traditions necessarily depreciate faster than the value-systems they represent, because it is the increasing cost (of any sort) of maintaining a tradition that initiates the depreciation of the underlying communal value. Thus, in an individual, a choice to disregard a costly tradition leaves guilt or self-deprecatory feelings. Alcohol intoxication at once displaces those residual uncomfortable feelings, and contributes to the furtherance of transition by rendering tradition cumbersome and difficult in comparison to its immediate gratification. Drunkenness (an extreme form of intoxication) is identity with a state of blissful irresponsibility where the demands of life are omnipotently dealt with by relinquishing consciousness of achievement, autonomy, and responsibility. (Brod, 1975, p. 1390)

Levy and Kunitz (1971) examined the relationships between social disorganization and homicide, suicide, and alcoholism among Indians of the Navajo and Hopi reservations in order to determine the relative contributions of aboriginal culture patterns and the disruptions of acculturation and social disorganization. In some of the reports they reviewed, about the effects of culture contacts, it is implied that primitive societies were highly integrated, stable, homogeneous, and possessed of coherent moral orders that enabled the individual to withstand physical privation. Modern industrial societies are heterogeneous, less well integrated, less stable, and, with confused and conflicting moral codes and tend to be more anomic and to exhibit more personal disintegration in the form of social and mental pathologies. Primitive societies conquered by modern industrial societies are in acute states of social disintegration because of very rapid change, radically different moral orders competing for allegiance of the population, and virtually no satisfactory means to achieve either the traditional or the new goals. In consequence, levels of personal disintegration ought to be high (Levy & Kunitz, 1971).

It is impossible, of course, to obtain data on precontact social pathology indicators, but an examination of the homicide rate in selected tribes for the period 1883 to 1889 indicated high homicide rates that ranged from 2 to 165 per 100,000 with a median on the order of 25, which indicates that they "were murdering each other at an adequate rate without benefit of moral confusion or rapid social disintegration." Data on suicide are more difficult to obtain, but the authors conclude that they are consistent with recent homicide data. "Navajo suicide and homicide rates are currently comparable with those of the nation and have been stable for long periods of time" (Levy & Kunitz, 1971).

Their data on Navajo drinking is also interesting in view of the widely held opinion that alcoholism is a problem among all Indian populations.

Deaths due to cirrhosis of the liver are not different from national figures, a finding that led Levy and Kunitz to conclude that the Navajo may not suffer so much from addictive alcoholism as is believed but rather drink in highly visible ways that offend white sensibilities. In fact Graves (1970) hypothesized that this form of drinking might indicate a venting of hostility against the white population.

The Hopi, who are considered much less prone to alcoholism than the Navajos, showed a higher death rate due to cirrhosis than their heavily drinking Navajo neighbors. In spite of their reputed nonaggressive demeanor, the Hopi showed suicide and homicide rates as high as those of the Navajo. Although earlier authors have acknowledged that traditional societies generate stress, they blame the disorganization engendered by contact with dominant white culture for the signs of alienation among current Indian groups. In contrast to this view, Levy and Kunitz suggest that when seen in a more accurate perspective "the prevalence and patterning of these behaviors are largely explainable in terms of persisting elements of aboriginal culture."

In another look at alienation among American Indians, Stull (1972) found that modern Papago Indians had higher accident rates than traditional individuals and that rates were higher for all in modern than in traditional villages. The moderns were defined as those who held regular employment other than agricultural or domestic service. Because the distribution of causes was essentially the same for traditionals and moderns, one is led to conclude that higher rates are due to stresses associated with modernization. This inference is further supported by the fact that differences are greater between employed and unemployed in modern than in traditional communities.

Shore and Stone (1973) related their finding of a high prevalence rate—some four times greater than for non-Indian women—of duodenal ulcer among Northwest coastal Indian women to the stress of a matrilineal society compounded by the poverty of the group. Poverty adds stresses to women in many societies. We should also note that in each of these four studies nonreactive measures were used: arrests, accidents, and ulcers.

In order to reduce these and other manifestations of stress, Bigart (1972) has suggested that factories be organized to fit into Indian value patterns. Presumably, alienation would be reduced if ownership and time scheduling corresponded more closely to tribal ways, but the full implications of this proposal can be realized only by careful experimentation.

In the foregoing studies a rather simplified relationship has been implied in which cultural changes lead to alienation, which manifests itself in alcoholism, antisocial behavior, physical symptoms, and various forms of subjective distress. Jessor, Graves, Hanson, and Jessor (1968) sought to develop and test a theory that would incorporate both sociocultural and personality factors in an attempt to account for deviance, especially alcoholism, in a community in the American Southwest populated by Anglos, Mexican Americans, and American Indians. They suggested that one consider the sociocultural environment as a system made up of an opportunity structure, a normative structure, and a social control structure. In a parallel conceptual approach to personality they construed personality as a system made up of perceived opportunity, personal belief, and personal control structures. Measures of sociocultural and personality structures, primarily of the self-report variety, were developed and relationships with five indices of alcoholism and deviance were examined. While individual indices correlated with deviance measures in the predicted direction, a combination of sociocultural and personality measures yielded much higher correlations. Indians were found to be characterized by limited opportunities, high normlessness or anomie, and weak social controls, conditions predisposing them to high deviance rates. It was these factors rather than their ethnic status per se that predisposed them to more frequent delinquencies.

In Northern Canada and Alaska, alienation has not become so apparent among industrial settings (which barely exist) but rather in the boarding schools established for Indian and Eskimo youth. Clifton (1972) compared the adjustment of Eskimo, Indian, and métis students at a residential school in the Northwest Territories that served students from the Mackenzie River and the Arctic coast. The métis showed higher grade placement for age, but equal percentages over fourteen years of age dropped out during the year. In a rather novel index of conformity, Clifton found that the percentage of students who were arrested for liquor violations or who became pregnant was zero for Eskimos, 28 for Indians, and 20 for métis.

In a well-reasoned study of Indian métis and non-Indian students in the Northwest Territories, Franklyn (1974) found no differences in alienation for sex or ethnic group. There were some slight differences in favor of the non-Indians in academic achievement. These findings, keeping the limitations of an alienation questionnaire in mind, indicate that not all Indian and part-Indian groups are more alienated than non-Indians. It would seem that the long period of residential schooling reduced ethnic differences, at least in this case.

Barger and Earl (1971) reported that Eskimos made a more complete adjustment to town life than did Cree Indians in a new community on the East shore of Hudson Bay. The former seemed to learn technical skills more readily while the latter were reluctant to give up the hunting life. This is an area that needs more study because it presents two groups making differing degrees of transition in essentially the same environment. Alienation may be increased where the option to go back to the old lifestyle remains open. In a community of Hare Indians on the Arctic Circle in the Northwest Territories, Savashinsky (1971) suggested that stress was apparently controlled by the high mobility of the group, which dispersed to and returned from hunting and trapping areas two times each year.

In a frequently cited paper, Berreman (1964) illustrated the process of alienation, mobility, and acculturation among the residents of an Aleutian village, exposed to increasing contact with whites who had established a DEW line radar station nearby. This paper is significant insofar as it shows the processes by which the Aleuts, to varying degrees over a decade, embraced the norms of the dominant outside group.

Subsaharan Africa

The imposition of colonial status and later achievement of independence have severely disrupted Africans' cultural patterns. Education and industrialization, both of which introduced many alien elements, are believed to change traditional societies profoundly, but whether they increase alienation or not is uncertain. In Kano, Nigeria, Armer (1970) tested two theoretical arguments concerning the effects of formal Western education in producing a sense of alienation among individuals in traditional, non-Western societies. The value-conflict thesis leads to the hypothesis that education and alienation are positively associated. The goal frustration thesis suggests that education and alienation are negatively associated among individuals with modern value orientations and positively associated among those with traditional orientations.

An eight-item general alienation scale was developed with two items for each of meaninglessness, normlessness, estrangement, and powerlessness. Unfortunately, all items were keyed so that agreement indicated alienation. A twenty-two-item scale of modernity was also developed, again primarily with measures of internal consistency. When a check indicated that more than half of his 582 respondents were highly acquiescent, Armer carried out his analysis on nonacquiescent respondents only. Data on these respondents indicated that education increased alienation among traditional respondents but not among those with more modern outlooks. This study is extensive and well reasoned; it is unfortunate that, in our opinion, the measures of alienation and of modernity are so loaded with response acquiescence and the scales are so factorially complex that the results must be viewed with great caution.

Gutkind (1973) has used a title that serves as a summary, "From the energy of despair to the anger of despair: The transition from social circulation to political consciousness among urban poor in Africa." Forty of seventy Nigerians interviewed in 1966 were interviewed again in 1971 after the Civil War. Employment had been uncertain for many of them, and they had become quite disillusioned with the ability of their political leaders to keep their promises of improved economic conditions. In spite of their continuing frustration they remained unorganized and, though angry, unable to develop any unified action. Gutkind is puzzled that more strenuous expressions of resentment have not appeared among educated and urban men who are denied the goal of employment.

In contrast to the situation in Nigeria, the Ghanaian government has made elaborate efforts to forestall difficulties for the thousands who were displaced by the Volta River dam that was built in the early 1960s. Eighty thousand people had to be resettled from 700 villages into fifty new towns with surrounding agricultural land. The social disorganization that must inevitably follow such resettlement is as intense as that which follows other extensive changes; indeed it is more intense because everyone, and not just the educated or the old or the young, is affected. In this case, some of the points of impact are not of the sort ordinarily associated with alienation, but they do gravely distort the lives of the people. A major factor, like that experienced by migrants to the city, is the vastly increased scale of life, loss of privacy, and greater exposure to scrutiny of each citizen.

Lumsden (1973) observed the processes of accommodation of Ghanaians resettled at one of the new communities organized by the Volta River Authority. The new housing posed problems because, for instance, settlers were forbidden to bring their domestic animals, which would have dirtied the planners' "model town" appearance. As a result the animals were lost or stolen. New day-to-day problems of living were added: women of one village mocked those of another who were unable to wear good clothes; major family quarrels were heard more widely with the houses close together; and one's retarded and handicapped village mates were less easily hidden. These problems were offset in part by an increase in social and religious events.

There were other problems which could be appreciated only by those who understood something of the belief systems of the settlers. Traditional burying grounds were flooded and new sites had to be defined. The spirits were also flushed out of their sacred sites, an emergency that had to be resolved. And the taboos on the sleeping place and activities of menstruating women were not provided for in the design of the new houses.

Lumsden's is a fascinating paper and shows the benefits gained from an in-depth understanding of an alien society and a sensitivity to others' beliefs and experiences. One can imagine the gentle fog of ignorance that would have settled on this research had he gone in with the usual Alienation Scale.

Latin America

The citizens of Central and South America have been experiencing many of the changes of other developing areas, changes that include migration from rural areas to the cities, the replacement of subsistence agriculture by industry, and the rapid change in speed and content of communications media, especially radio and television. One would expect and one does find many situations conducive to and productive of alienation.

In what is in many ways a classic cross-cultural study, Simpson (1970) asked whether occupational mobility had a different impact on the mobile individual in different cultural contexts. Costa Rica and Mexico, with their more ascriptive status systems, and with marked distinctions between white-collar and blue-collar occupations, were contrasted with the United States where there is relatively more status accorded to achievement and less to family standing. Simpson hypothesized that in ascriptive societies upwardly mobile individuals will experience more normlessness than nonmobile individuals; whereas in an achievement-oriented society upwardly mobile individuals will experience no more normlessness than nonmobile individuals of their class of origin or class of destination. Downwardly mobile individuals in both ascriptive and achievement systems will experience more normlessness than the nonmobile. This is an intriguing design, in the opinion of these reviewers, because it is one of the few we have encountered in which culture is seen as a moderating variable, a variable that changes the relationships between antecedents and effects. It is an impressive design also because, with more than 1,000 respondents in each country, we can expect stable findings.

However, in our opinion, the study is seriously flawed because the measures of normlessness and powerlessness consist of only two items. Normlessness was indicated by agreement with (1) "I often wonder what the meaning of life really is" and (2) "People's ideas change so much that I wonder if we'll ever have anything to depend on." Powerlessness was indicated by agreement with (1) "Sometimes I have the feeling that other people are using me" and (2) "There is little chance to get ahead in this life unless a man knows the right people." In view of the unreliability of a two-item scale and the problem of response acquiescence, it is not surprising that there were few significant differences. This study has at least one great strength and one great weakness in our opinion. It is one of few that is cross-cultural in the sense that culture is incorporated as a variable when the ascriptive and achievement orientations are contrasted. The weakness, which is shared with many studies of alienation but exaggerated here, is the use of two-item measures that have inevitably low reliability and are seriously subject to response acquiescence.

Zurcher, Meadow, and Zurcher (1965) also incorporated a cultural variable, in this case universalism-particularism, in their study of alienation among Mexican, Mexican-American, and American bank employees. The cultural variable in this case referred to the impersonal human relationship patterns of industrial societies versus the personalized modes of a folk society. Alienation, measured by a four-item scale, was slightly higher for the Mexican than the American respondents but, in separate correlation matrices for each ethnic group, alienation correlated significantly with particularism (.21) only for the Americans; the correlations were .07 and .02 for the Mexicans and Mexican Americans respectively. Although all correlations were so low as to be socially insignificant, this finding suggests that maybe Americans are more troubled by universalism with its impersonal emphasis than are those who are members of a society that is said to act on more personalized considerations.

Alienation and its products are often assumed to be strongest among the children of migrants caught between parents' and peers' different values. Rosen (1973) examined family interaction patterns in rural families of Brazil and in recent migrants, established migrants, and native poor of Sao Paulo. Parents and children were observed in their homes working on a series of standardized problems such as block stacking, tinker toy constructions, and pick-up-sticks. He found that "with a longer period of residence in the city, migrant families become more egalitarian, family relations become more open and responsive, and parents place greater emphasis on achievement and independence for their sons" (Rosen, 1973). The significance of this study for our purpose lies in its use of a different method of data collection and in the attempt to assess changes in interpersonal behavior patterns that may enable participants to cope more adequately with a new social setting.

Watson (1972) also used data collection procedures more familiar to psychologists. Aspects of self-identity were assessed using interviews, life histories, and responses to TAT cards with small carefully selected samples of tribal Guajiro (N = 14) and urban Guajiro (N = 15) who were living in Maracaibo, Venezuela. Self-images of tribal respondents emphasized the virtues of compliance, economic responsibility to the group, nurturance, and nonaggressiveness while urban subjects appraised their behavior in terms of being civilized, educated, powerful, assertive, and clever, and they feared being uncivilized, helpless, and stupid. Watson inferred a good deal of dissonance between real and ideal identities among the urban Guajiro which he attributed to defective socialization in the city.

> The typical urban Guajiro who is shaped by these socialization patterns is id-dominated and lacking in strong ego resources. He is not only incapable of devising strategies to achieve ideal standards, he is unable to make the defensive adjustments that would seem necessary to subjectively resolve the conflict engendered by the disparity between his real and his ideal identity,

such as repressing strong dependency and aggressive urges, or finding acceptable object substitutes. (Watson, 1972, p. 1204)

We are not sure what this interpretation proves about urban Guajiro, but we are impressed with the degree to which all findings are explicable if one plays the psychodynamic game.

Finally, in a paper that is cross-cultural in emphasis and that bears on alienation, Sanford (1970) has examined the applicability in Mexico of Maslow's theory that man is characterized by a hierarchy of needs. Individuals have five categories of needs, each of which must be satisfied before the next higher need can be attended to. These include physiological, safety, social, esteem, and, finally, needs for self-realization. In Mexico, however, Sanford argues that while physiological and safety needs are primary, there is also a very powerful need for esteem that often seems strongest of all. Work, and by implication, the products of work do not appear to satisfy higher needs, a fact which, if true, has important implications for industrial management. For our purposes one would then expect that separation from work would not be as alienating as is the case where one's work satisfied esteem as well as more physiological needs.

Other Geographic Areas

Studies of alienation have been reported from many other countries which do not cluster as conveniently as the foregoing. The collective farms or kibbutzim of Israel provide an interesting social experiment in which industrialization and urbanization are separated. Eden and Leviatan (1974) compared farm and factory workers on kibbutzim of similar size, organization, and income. They hypothesized that if industrial work has the harmful effects attributed to it then scores of industrial workers on mental health, job-satisfaction, and alienation measures would be different from those of farm workers.

Data were obtained by questionnaire from 476 industrial and 175 farm workers at 27 different kibbutzim. They found:

> Factory workers rated their jobs significantly lower than did farm workers on plant manager's leadership, opportunities for self-realization on the job, participation, control, peer relations, and information about the job. However, factory jobs were rated cleaner, easier, and more mental. Factory and farm workers were similar in outcome measures, including supervisory ratings of performance, job satisfaction, mental health, and alienation. (Eden & Leviatan, 1974, p. 596)

For our purposes, the alienation score was based on two items for each of Seeman's five dimensions, making a single index of ten items. Because alienation scores were virtually identical for industrial and agricultural workers, the authors concluded that one must "seek the sources of the malaise of modern industrial man somewhere beyond the workplace."

Rettig (1972) interviewed 700 kibbutz members on various collectives, classifying the collectives for political orientation, size, affluence, homogeneity, and distance from a city. Alienation was measured by 144 questions of the 306 Rettig used in each interview. The 144 were made up of 51 items concerned with political participation, 27 with areas of work, and 66 with social relations. Scoring was on face validity considerations of the yes-no answer each item called for. The author concluded that overall there was a remarkably low level of alienation found; the most alienated kibbutz appeared to be heterogeneous in membership, close to a city, and not Marxian in organization.

Rettig summarized:

> In concluding the present report, it is fair to state that there are powerful influences in the kibbutz system which contribute to discontinuity and change, such as the age-graded peer group system, the deemphasis of kinship structure, the partial industrialization and employment of hired labor, the absorption of immigration, and the ever-increasing urbanization of the surrounding Israeli society. Despite these influences, however, the kibbutz appears to have been able to erect a social structure which is highly flexible and responsive to these pressures for change, thus presenting effective barriers against anomie and high levels of alienation. One important source of flexibility lies in the nonbureaucratization of kibbutz society, especially by the election and rotation of all office holders. Other barriers to anomie may, of course, lie in the very emphasis of the peer group system, which tends to diminish such expressions of anomie as social isolation, meaninglessness, powerlessness, and normlessness because there always are other members at hand to redefine norms, give meaning to kibbutz existence, and to relate compassionately when one experiences threat or isolation.* (Rettig, 1972, p. 52)

The city of Hong Kong with its recent immigrants provides an excellent setting for the cross-cultural study of alienation. Hong (1973) found that kin visitation and extended households were equally common among families in downtown Kowloon and in Sheung Shui-Fanling in the New Territories, a traditional Chinese village. His subjects were Form IV students, seventeen to eighteen years of age, attending grant-aided secondary schools. There were differences, however, on the Srole Anomia Scale, with the urban group receiving higher scores. Hong argued that this difference was due to urban living because race, educational level, age, and income level (through school eligibility) were controlled.

Iga (1971) examined the histories of seventy-two male students at Kyoto University who committed suicide between 1955 and 1968, seeking to classify them in Durkheim's types. Of the sixty-nine cases with suffi-

---

* From S. Rettig, "Anomie in Kibbutz," *International Journal of Group Tensions*, 1972, 2(4), 37–52. Reprinted by permission.

cient information, none were classified egoistic, three as altruistic, thirteen as fatalistic, and the remaining fifty-three as anomic. An additional forty-five students who had been considered suicidal were contrasted with sixty-eight controls. The suicidal subjects had aspirations as high as those of nonsuicides, but they had less effective means for goal attainment. In addition to their economic, health, and family problems, they were characterized by a short time perspective, rigidity, unrealistic definition of the situation, nonrationality, and dependence. Their personality traits were more conducive to an alienated conception of the self, and they tended to define a failure situation as irrecoverable. Unfortunately, cross-cultural comparisons were not provided.

Examining high school students of Japanese descent in the United States, people who were subjected to markedly conflicting expectations and values, Okano and Spilka (1971) found that there were no differences in reported feelings of alienation associated with high or low identification with their Japanese heritage nor with achievement motivation. A single study, with a relatively small number of sixty-one subjects, should not call for an immediate revision of our theories, but it does question a common assumption that strong ethnic identity protects against alienation.

Classically, alienation has been considered with reference to the person or group who moves from the rural area to the industrial setting. However, Strathern (1972) found that the parents and relatives who remained at home in Mount Hagen were distressed when their sons went to live and work in Port Moresby. The reactions must be seen within the cultural context of New Guinea. The migrants cause distress at home by failing to share their earnings, by not being at home and available for marriage at the appropriate age, and by being absent when parents were sick or near death. In Mount Hagen, if parents die separated from offspring, their ghosts may retaliate against the absent ones. The situation is made more difficult because, while the migrant is tempted to spend his earnings in Port Moresby, he is pressured to use them for social obligations when he returns to Mount Hagen, yet the only socially approved pattern is to use his earnings to establish a business in the mountains. His relatives at home are as disrupted by his absence as he is by his migration, a facet of alienation that is usually ignored.

Preliminary results from one portion of an ongoing study by Verma and Moskowitz (1975) indicate a sense of alienation by educated Moslems in a North Indian town. The purpose of the project was to study Hindu-Moslem relations in India. The town, chosen for its harmonious relations and overall stability in terms of population and economy, will later be contrasted to a riot-prone town. A college was established in this town in 1960 and for the first time higher education was made easily accessible to residents. Respondents were asked to identify influential persons within the Moslem community. What resulted was an outpouring of dissatisfaction and disaffection at the perceived ineffectual leadership of the traditionally oriented elite. It is the contention of the authors that "the presence of the college in this town indirectly resulted in the development of an alienated sub-group within the Moslem community by directly fostering a rise in aspirations which exceeded the available opportunities for fulfilling them."

A study of some forty female students in India resulted in the tentative conclusion that "alienation can be regarded as an abortive response to avoid anticipated loss of support from the peer groups due to deviations of socialized and interiorized norms" (Srivastava, Sinha, & Jain, 1971).

Fischer (1973) studied urban alienation and anomie in the United Kingdom and the United States along two dimensions: powerlessness and social isolation. He found that there was no relationship between community size and a sense of powerlessness, that there was very little relationship between size of community and a sense of social isolation, that attendance at social meetings was not associated with urbanism, but that the larger the size of the community, the less chance that an individual will know his neighbors or have relatives living nearby. Having voluntary associations outside the neighborhood minimized feelings of social isolation even though anonymity could be maintained within the immediate area of residence. The heterogeneity of an urban population with the social problems that result can cause distrust and result in withdrawal of the individual from intimate exposure to conflicting lifestyles. Instead, he develops an associative network made up of social contacts made on a selective basis. Fisher concluded that "attribution of alienation to 'urbanism as a way of life' seems incorrect."

Form (1972) examined social behavior and anomie among automobile factory workers in India, Argentina, Italy, and the United States, the selection designed to cover the continuum from personalistic to industrialized societies. Within each factory, workers were sampled from four identical work operations that offered differing opportunities for social interaction. Data were collected from the workers concerning their social contacts on and off the job. They also answered a scale of anomie. He found no differences in anomie related to industrialization, and he showed that social patterns were determined by the factory situation and not by the traditions of the society. He concluded:

> Evidence mounts that, whatever the level of industrialization and whatever their past exposure to industry, workers' responses to the work situation are strongly conditioned by technology. Even where industry is young and workers are newly exposed to industrial discipline, factory social life is apt to be similar to that in mature industrial societies. This study's limited findings prompt one to reexamine two fashionable explanations of worker behavior: the human relations approach which emphasizes management's effort to humanize the environment, and the cultural approach which emphasizes con-

flicts in values between the factory and the traditional community. This study suggests that the social world of the factory worker everywhere is conditioned primarily by the factory's technological environment. Historically, automobile technology has been singled out by both the left and the right as providing ideal conditions for alienation and anomie. This study of automobile workers in four countries shows no direct relation between social relations in the factory and feelings of anomie. Evidence mounts that we should modify or abandon technological explanations of alienation and anomie.* (Form, 1972, p. 737)

Form's findings are in sharp contrast to social scientists' widely held beliefs that there are disruptive effects when those who have been socialized in the intimate, personalistic system of a traditional society are subjected to industrial discipline. We infer from his results that people can make the transition from the village to the factory much more readily than many believe, provided, of course, that employment is regular.

The folk-urban dichotomy in styles of life, and many parallel dichotomies, have played an important role in theories of social change and social structure. One who passed from folk to urban was expected to experience alienation. Why so few "go back to the farm" has not been thoroughly examined or explained, nor has it been made clear why industrial life wipes out rural character. Some of our assumptions, however, are called into question by an unusual study by Willems (1970). A native of the village, he examined adaptations of citizens of Neyl to the growth of the nearby German city of Cologne. Records spanning 1,000 years indicate that the villagers were able to enter marketing and wage-earning relationships to the city while preserving their cultural identity. He suggested that we should attend to the cultural continuity of urban lower class and peasantry rather than the village-city dichotomy. The community did not succumb to the attractions of industrial civilization but did fall a victim to the physical expansion of Cologne and the loss of land to industries.

We have attempted to review research on alienation, in non-Western societies primarily, with the ultimate purpose of improving our understanding of the processes of alienation. It is the hope and purpose of those who take a cross-cultural perspective that data from other cultures, where antecedents and consequences of behavior patterns are different, will improve our understanding of cause-and-effect sequences in human behavior. Cultures provide differences in antecedent conditions, and these differences are more profound and of greater duration than those that can be achieved in better controlled laboratory experiments within our own society. One would predict, for instance, on the basis of the many formulations dating back to Durkheim's anomie that alienation would be widespread among people who migrated from the kinship-dominated

* From W. H. Form, "Technology and Social Behavior of Workers in Four Countries," *American Sociological Review*, 1972, 37, 728–738. Reprinted by permission.

subsistence economy of a rural area to an impersonal urban setting and cash economy. But our reading of the evidence is that such a result is not necessary, nor even likely. Social scientists with their romanticized view of rural life may find this hard to believe. We do not have data explaining why alienation fails to appear where we expect it. A partial answer is provided by Stone (1968a) who asked a Manila squatter, "Would you not be happier back in the province where you could see the rice fields and the coconut trees and feel the breeze from the sea?" And the emigrant replied, "But life in the province is dull." They cannot go back to the farm once they have seen Paris.

Rather than experience a loss of control, it would appear that migrants to urban areas establish new affiliations and alliances to replace those they left. The fact that they and almost all of their fellow squatters continue to fail to achieve the goals of society does not appear to generate alienation. We speculate that two reasons they do not become alienated—as do minority group migrants in American cities—are that they see and hear about some members of their group who do become prosperous, and they do not see themselves as permanently excluded because of racial factors. Squatters in Manila, Jakarta, or Calcutta are members of the same ethnic groups as those that dominate government and industry in their cities.

But few firm conclusions about alienation can be drawn from these studies in other societies because alienation as a process was conceptualized ambiguously in most studies and was often measured in most unsatisfactory ways.

Alienation in the Philippines

Because both authors have had experience in the Philippines and because that country is an excellent source of cross-cultural data, we would like to examine some Philippine research on modernization and urbanization. Both of these changes should lead to conditions conducive to alienation because they lead to the loss of the systems of support and control that characterize a traditional society.

As in the case with many other developing countries, in the last quarter century the Philippines has achieved political independence and experienced a massive change in communication patterns with new roads and airlines, transistor radios and television. Schools have multiplied so that almost all children receive at least four to six years of education. There has also been a massive migration from the crowded countryside to the even more crowded cities, which has resulted in the growth of extensive squatter areas. As many as one-fourth of the people in the larger cities live in makeshift houses on land they do not own or rent, with limited or absent water, sanitation, or electric services. They survive on very low incomes with high rates of unemployment and underemployment. These migrants, surrounded by the evident prosperity of the city, are prime candidates for alienation because they have seen what others have and have come to the city to improve their own lot but have been denied access to many of the benefits of the city because of lack of skills and training and because there are many applicants for every job.

Manila squatters or slum dwellers have been studied by Filipinos Jocano (1975), Hollnsteiner (1973, 1975), Laquian (1968), Abueva, Guerrero, and Jurado (1972), and by an American, Stone (1968b, 1973). Outsiders, both Filipino and foreign, have looked upon squatter areas as aggregations of desperate and/or demoralized people who have accepted a miserable existence and who look upon the outsider with envy and resentment. Squatter areas are dangerous because the residents have appropriated land illegally and because they have everything to gain and little to lose from the practice of theft and violence. Social scientists who have gained access to the squatters and earned their confidence find poverty, to be sure, but they also find a coherent social organization and a kind of optimistic fatalism rather than sullen demoralization. This is epitomized by the finding of Abueva et al. (1972, p. 186) that 99 percent of 200 low-income respondents agree with the statement, "Any man with ability and willingness to work hard has a good chance of being successful." They have moved from the provinces or from another squatter area in the hope of bettering their lot. Jocano (1975) found that the apparent lawlessness of the area was due to the fact that squatters would not or could not be protected by police if they informed on wrongdoers. Social order was maintained by pressures within the group. The squatters also performed many services for the surrounding, more prosperous city dwellers, from house cleaning, to driving, to prostitution. Stone (1968b, 1973) also found a social organization that sustained and controlled the majority of squatters.

Hollnsteiner's (1973) summary is in agreement with the findings of each of these studies:

> This study reveals that Magsaysay Village squatters are generally an optimistic group that wants to work and improve their family's level of living. To do this they have moved to Manila where work and education opportunities abound, at least compared to their provincial hometowns. Living in a squatter area, especially the Tondo foreshore, holds the added advantage of land ownership if existing laws are implemented. With some exceptions the MV squatters diverge greatly from the stereotyped picture present in non-squatters' minds of a thieving, shiftless, dangerous slum dweller. The real squatter is the product of a poor society where rising aspirations through the development of some sectors encourages the economically disadvantaged to try their luck where the chances of success are greater.

The squatter is no more enthralled by his unkempt surroundings, dilapidated house, or lack of facilities than are appalled outsiders. He does what he can to make his house livable, but is always hampered by the lack of water to keep his house, his community, and himself clean. When he knows his tenure status is permanent, as is often the case with the house itself, he invests a great deal of time, energy, and available funds for improving it. The same would apply to his lot if he owned it.

His attachment to Magsaysay Village comes not only from his potential lot ownership or accustomed residence there but from the close ties he has developed in the neighborhood. Relatives cluster nearby, and friends are all around. The helping norm of neighbors and others gets him through the inevitable difficulties that arise especially in a poor community. Where cash is limited to pay people for various services, the norm of interdependence and reciprocal favor doing for free is functional. (p. 10–11)

In addition to the foregoing studies of Manila citizens who are squatters and very poor and logically prime candidates for alienation, two reports should be cited that deal directly with their level of contentment. Guerrero (1973) found in interviews with 200 respondents that most low-income residents think of themselves as struggling to keep going while only 20 percent describe their situation as miserable. In part, they console themselves with the thought that they are no worse off than others around them, but the secret of their condition may be their aspirations and hopes for their children. While two-thirds specify no aspirations for themselves, 70 percent want education for their children—a college education in more than half the cases. Guerrero concluded that "the findings indicate minimal feelings of hopelessness and despair, together with great expectations for the next generation, particularly by means of education."

Bulatao (1973) found that 941 Manila residents rated themselves on a three-step scale of happiness as 15 percent "very happy," 56 percent "pretty happy," and 30 percent "not so happy." These figures are quite similar to responses obtained in studies of American samples. On a twelve-step ladder rating of happiness, a similar 57 percent chose middle rungs. Of equal significance, a high percentage estimated that they would be much happier five years hence. Pessimism and despair about the future, classically a component of alienation, simply does not appear to any appreciable degree in studies of Filipinos for whom alienation might reasonably be predicted.

Similar observations have been made in other countries. In contrast to the social isolation that is believed to result when people uproot themselves from rural areas to take up residence in an urban center, Safa (1968) described a warm, friendly shantytown community in San Juan, Puerto Rico, that is characterized by a pattern of sharing and cooperation. The community draws its migrants from various regions in the country, unlike the tendency in many Asian and African cities for families from the same region to settle in one neighborhood. Since this is a long-established area, any initial concentration from one area has been replaced by more recent migrants from other areas. There are many features of rural living that have been retained. Houses remain the single-family, one-story dwellings with open windows and porches (now closely packed together, fostering constant contact). Relatives usually help newcomers find housing and employment, make introductions to friends and neighbors, and help establish the newcomers in the network of support and interaction that prevails here as in the areas from which the migrants come. It is common for the extended family to continue to reside in close proximity. Despite crowded conditions, cleanliness of both person and home are maintained. The community is a self-contained unit with a sense of group cohesion and belonging. It is the focal point of social life for all of its inhabitants, and there is only peripheral contact with the larger city. Because of this, the impersonal nature of interaction that typifies urban living is minimized, and the adverse results of the low-status position of the poor are cushioned.

There are striking likenesses between the Puerto Rican community described by Safa and similar slum and squatter communities in the Philippines. The prevailing norms and values of sharing, cooperation, and reciprocity are evident. The physical setting is also strikingly similar. It might be hypothesized on the basis of these studies that being poor and living in high-density, open-windowed, one-story homes typical of warm climates tends to facilitate the complex web of social interaction and support that mitigates feelings of alienation. By the same token, being poor but living in closed apartment buildings with little occasion for intimate social contact would tend to aggravate feelings of anonymity and isolation. What contact there is tends to be impersonal and may often be with persons in a superior socioeconomic position. Without a counterbalance of support from a secure sense of belonging to a subgroup, the individual is adrift and alienation results.

In much the same vein, Guthrie (1970) found that the modernizing forces of transistor radios, television, schools, and improved roads that appeared in the rural areas of the Philippines did not prove to be particularly disruptive influences. Aspirations were very high; tenant farmers, for instance, wanted their children to complete college and a majority expected things to be better economically over the next ten years. Modern as opposed to traditional attitudes had been adopted by the majority of tenant farmers as well as a larger majority of landowners and professional people. In spite of a literacy level of 60 to 75 percent and an awareness of the standard of living achieved by urban residents, the people of the rural areas gave little evidence of normlessness, powerlessness, meaninglessness, or isolation. Clinging to the belief that they might someday be lucky or that one of their children would prosper after completing his or her education, they did not develop the symptoms of alienation one would reasonably expect in their condition.

In the 1970s the Philippines experienced increased social turmoil in Manila with demonstrations by college students and a noisy deadlock of opposing political factions. Martial law was declared in 1972 and continues as of this writing. We would not interpret these indications of social unrest as results of alienation because the conflict was largely among factions of prosperous people, with the squatters and recent migrants as innocent or cynical onlookers.

Alienation and Health

Health authorities in addition to social scientists have reason to be concerned with the welfare of groups subjected to social change and resulting disorganization of established living patterns. A landmark review of research in this area is that of Fried (1964), which dealt with the effects of social change on mental health.

Although he makes little use of the concept of alienation, much of the work of Leighton (1959) in Nova Scotia, Leighton, Hughes, Leighton, Murphy, and Macklin (1963) in Nigeria and even Srole (1975) in New York City is carried out with the explicit theory that social disorganization predisposes to higher rates of psychiatric and psychosomatic disorders. The Leighton et al. study of the Yoruba is a good example of cross-cultural confirmation of the theory that a breakdown of traditional social patterns leads to a higher incidence of neurotic and psychosomatic disorders.

In contrast to the consistent relationships reported by Leighton and his team, Cawte and his group failed to confirm a relationship between symptoms and cultural identity. In a study of Australian aborigines, Bianchi, Cawte, and Kiloh (1970) found that ratings on acquisition of Western culture, emulation of Western attributes and lifestyle, and retention of traditional activities did not correlate significantly with symptoms on a modified Cornell Medical Index Health Questionnaire. Retention of traditional beliefs correlated positively with symptoms. These findings are contrary to Leighton's and to the general orientation of most speculation about the effects of social change. It must be noted, however, that their five- to seven-item scales had relatively low coefficients of reproducibility.

Change, with its potentiality for alienation and problems of health, can also come as a result of migration with people moving out rather than new ideas moving in. The move from rural to urban living may not be as stressful as some studies and as common sense would suggest. Parker, Kleiner, and Needleman (1969) found that the prevalence of mental illness among Negro migrants from rural areas to Philadelphia was lower than among those who migrated to the city from other cities.

In a study of the effects of stress, Aakster (1974) demonstrated some highly interesting relationships between failure to adjust to stress and illness on a random sample of 1,500 Dutch citizens. In addition, his paper offers some valuable base rate data on eighteen frequent health disturbances, data that would provide a useful frame of reference for those studying similar problems in other societies.

Migration from rural areas to urban centers is occurring on a large scale in almost all developing countries, a development that occurred two or more decades earlier in many industrialized countries. The arrival in the city of vast numbers of untrained migrants poses social, political, and health problems, but it should not be assumed that they have left a peaceful, socially integrated traditional setting to enter the turmoil of a squatter area. Stromberg, Peyman, and Dowd (1974) sampled 19,000 respondents in Teheran inquiring whether anyone had been sick in the past two weeks. Twenty percent responded positively to this question of nonspecific morbidity. Seventeen percent of both males and females who had lived four or more years in Teheran reported recent sickness. Recent male migrants (those who had been in Teheran three years or less) reported 18 percent, while 27 percent of recent female migrants had been sick in the preceding two weeks. Migrants reported problems obtaining and preparing food and difficulties with housing but not with transportation or finding work. The higher incidence of illness among women migrants appeared to be due to the loss of opportunities for productive work in the city in contrast to their many agricultural tasks in rural areas.

Finally, Wittkower and Dubreuil (1973) reviewed some aspects of the relationships between psychocultural stress and mental illness. Cultural factors may determine not only the incidence of mental illness but its manifestations as well, as is demonstrated in culture-bound syndromes. With respect to our area of concern they observe:

> Anomie refers to a lack of integration—of social organization—and is sometimes used synonymously with social disorganization. A relationship between anomie and increased frequency of mental disorders has been established. It has been demonstrated that unemployment and poverty in the slums of the big North American cities and migration to urban areas in Africa and South America are associated with high rates of mental illness. For instance, some studies would suggest that the inhabitants of the barriada of Lima are subjected to tensions which could raise their proneness to mental illness. However, the correlation between anomie and mental disease is not as simple as may appear because a variety of factors combine in determining anomie and frequency of mental disorders. (Wittkower & Dubreuil, 1973, p. 696)

The most extensive research, however, on the effect on health of changes in life experiences is that of Holmes and Masuda (1974) and Rahe, Gunderson, Pugh, Rubin, & Arthur (1972). These physicians have developed an inventory of Life Change Units designed to assess a wide variety of changes in the respondent's recent past. Changes include moving to a new house, change of employment, loss of a loved one, marriage, separation, and the birth of a child. Reviewing the research on life change and illness susceptibility Holmes and Masuda (1974) concluded:

> These data suggest that the greater the life change or adaptive requirement, the greater the vulnerability or lowering of resistance to disease, and the more serious the disease that does develop. The concept of a variable threshold of resistance and the necessity of having a special pathogen present may help to account for the differences observed in the acute infectious diseases. Thus, the concept of life change appears to have relevance to the causation of disease, time of onset of disease, and severity of disease. It does not seem to contribute much to an understanding of specificity of disease type.

It should be noted that this is cited from a book, *Stressful Life Events: Their Nature and Effects*, edited by Dohrenwend and Dohrenwend (1974), a book that deals with the effect of stressful life events on physical illness and psychiatric disorders. Although the editors and many contributors are social scientists, there is only one reference to alienation in the index and none to anomie, and the research on alienation was not cited by any other authors.

Brody (1969) has edited a very useful volume on the psychiatric disorders that follow migration or other extensive cultural changes. As was the case with the Dohrenwend book referred to above, those who study stress symptoms pay little attention to the theory or research having to do with alienation, and those interested in alienation treat it as a state of mind rather than a disorder of mind or body.

There are a number of reasons that anyone interested in the study of alienation, either in a cross-cultural setting or at home, should include data on health among his dependent variables. Because sickness is a socially significant event and is accepted as such by those who suffer, a researcher is likely to receive much more cooperation and candor than he would if he asks only about powerlessness or meaninglessness. Unobtrusive measures of medicines consumed, clinics visited, and sick leaves taken can all be obtained with some perseverance and imagination. Finally, and unfortunately, the base rate of illness is sufficiently high—as was found in the research in Teheran, Netherlands, and Australia cited above—that counts should have some desirable statistical properties. This is in contrast to suicide, for instance, which is inevitably rare. There are marked folk differences in the names for, and particularly in theories of, the causes of illness, but there is a certain cross-cultural validity about a

headache, stomach pains, and rheumatic disorders. The relationships between stresses and illnesses, however, remain obscure; longitudinal multivariate designs are needed.

Moving to a New Society

A different cross-cultural perspective on alienation can be gained by examining the experiences of Americans who have gone to live among the
members of an alien society. This is a particularly interesting situation
because it offers an informal ABA design (baseline–treatment–no treatment) in which we may be able to see how selected Americans function at
home, how they perform when they go abroad, and how they react when
they return home to the previous set of social controls and supports.
Going abroad constitutes a greater physical and social change than moving
within one's own country. The latter generates many problems as described in many popular summaries such as Packard's *A Nation of Strangers*
(1972) and portions of Toffler's *Future Shock* (1970).

An American army psychiatrist, Kojak (1974) called the American
community in Bangkok a model of social disintegration. In one year 21
percent of the more than 3,000 American couples were seen for marital
difficulties and 9 percent of American adolescents were almost certainly
using heroin. He contended that, because the Americans were scattered
throughout the city, and exposed to strikingly different social and moral
values of the city's inhabitants, they experienced severe social disintegration. This was in marked contrast to a similar group of Americans at a U.S.
Army base in Japan, who had on-base housing and maintained American
culture patterns. There was little evidence of marital discord in Japan and
no heroin addiction among adolescents. (He might have mentioned that
the Thais grow poppies while Japan has very strict drug controls that are
rigidly and successfully enforced.) Kojak concluded:

> Social disintegration can be seen as a result of and concomitant occurrence
> with unavoidable rapid cultural change and transience, but such commu-
> nities need not remain disintegrated. In addition, these data strongly indicate
> that it is difficult for families to function in a healthy way without both ac-
> cepting community responsibility and being part of a responsible com-
> munity.

Much the same situation was reported concerning American military
personnel assigned to Vietnam. In the latter years of that war there were
many newspaper reports of the use of heroin by U.S. soldiers and there
were fears that many would return with severe problems of addiction.
This has not occurred, a fact which suggests that even this severe symp-

tom of alienation—drug addiction with its physiological components of dependency—is largely situational and subject to change with a marked change of social milieu.

Peace Corps volunteers also experienced culture shock (Guthrie, 1966) or a loss of ability to function effectively and with satisfaction after they had been on the job for four to eight months. In the years after it was organized, the Peace Corps experienced a marked decline in the number who completed their two-year assignments. This decline coincided with Americans' waning enthusiasm for foreign involvements and increasing disillusionment with the aims and methods of U.S. foreign policy. This increase in dissatisfaction with the experience suggests that experiences of isolation and meaninglessness are influenced by the degree to which one's reference groups approve one's activities.

Spradley and Phillips (1972) compared cultural stress in samples of Peace Corps volunteers, Chinese students in the U.S., and American students without cross-cultural experience. In ranking a number of stress-producing situations all three groups ranked language as the area causing the greatest amount of anxiety. The PCV's ranked temporal factors second, while the Chinese found differences in interpersonal relations difficult to cope with. The authors noted that "readjustment is more difficult in those areas where the range of appropriate behavior is less restricted in the new cultural environment." Since each society seeks to socialize its members to conform to certain norms and values, it is suggested that what is implicit should be made explicit so that one would have a clear understanding of his own culture. This should serve to minimize stress when confronted by norms and values at variance with one's own.

A final example of what would appear to be alienation resulting from a marked change of social controls can be found in the Alaska pipeline project. As described by a journalist (Griffith, 1975) a sudden and dramatic increase in work opportunities and wages has brought many people to Alaska and has pulled many native Alaskans out of their traditional living patterns. The picture in many ways resembles Kojak's account of Bangkok: marriages failing, increased alcoholism, adolescents neglected and delinquent, and native women inducted into the oldest profession. Because of rigid regulations the environment of grizzly bears, caribou, and tundra will be minimally disrupted, but there is no agency that protects the people.

Because human difficulties of this sort are costly in many ways, it is not surprising that attempts have been made to reduce them through careful prior selection and training. At its inception Peace Corps officials introduced a rigorous selection and training program, but they made virtually no provision to evaluate the effectiveness of these steps. As years passed, training diminished and was moved to host country sites, and selection became largely a matter of self-selection. In one of the few evaluations of selection, Guthrie and Zektick (1967) reported that there was no relationship between evaluations at the end of training and ratings by host nationals of Peace Corps volunteers. One is led to conclude that the quality of performance in a new setting of those selected for foreign assignment is determined by contemporaneous events and influences rather than the previous personality and work habits of the participant. These data point to a greater contribution to processes of alienation of concurrent sociocultural factors than long-term psychological or psychodynamic factors.

The role of social environmental factors is also vividly demonstrated in Zimbardo's experimental prison (Haney, Banks, & Zimbardo, 1973). Undergraduates assigned randomly as jailers and prisoners showed marked changes of behavior and reported acute changes of affect. The prisoners experienced the powerlessness and isolation of alienation so that they became apathetic and unable to improve their situation. In other experiments on deindividuation (as he calls it), Zimbardo (1970) has shown that anonymity increases the frequency of antisocial behavior and that, in the absence of reference group controls, people are more likely to imitate immediate models of behavior regardless of the social merit of the model's activities. Acts of violence are sustained not so much by pent-up resentments, or alienation, as by the satisfaction and excitement one obtains immediately from a violent act.

These data from field observations and experiments with American subjects suggest interpretations of alienated behavior in terms of social learning, an interpretation that can be both tested and applied in action programs to cope with the socially undesirable consequences of alienation.

An Experimental Analysis of Alienation

Possibly because early theorists were seeking to establish an independent place in the sun for sociology, there were few attempts to analyze alienation in terms of processes within the alienated individual. Throughout the literature there appears also to be some vacillation between speaking of groups as alienated—and therefore subject to processes at the level of the group—and individuals within groups being alienated from the larger collective. At the same time there has been relatively little attention devoted to the question of how alienated behavior is acquired or reduced. Recently a psychological analysis of alienation has been offered by Stokols (1975), but no implications were drawn for cross-cultural study.

Ball (1968) has offered an analysis of the powerlessness of the people of the Southern Appalachian Mountains of the United States in terms of

Maier's (1949) experiments in which he differentiated between frustration-induced and motivation-induced behavior in rats. Animals confronted by insoluble problems developed, according to Maier, stereotyped behavior that persisted even in the face of punishment. Ball suggested that the poor residents of Southern Appalachia had evolved a subculture that could be understood best as frustration-instigated behavior. As with the rats, the people of this poverty-stricken region manifested patterns of fixation, regression, aggression, and resignation. Ball has dubbed the whole pattern of behavior of these people an "analgesic subculture."

We would like to suggest also that recent research on the effects of modifying schedules of reinforcement, the effects of extinction, and the studies of learned helplessness can provide many insights into behavior changes that appear in individuals when their relationships with their society are altered to a substantial degree.

As Homans (1961) and Scott (1971) have pointed out, the influence of the larger social group upon the behavior of an individual can be analyzed in terms of the reinforcement contingencies that an individual faces for his various acts at the hands of other members of his society. Others approve (reinforce) certain behaviors, ignore (extinguish) other activities, and disapprove (punish) still other kinds of behavior. Thus we have social and self-approval by life's M&M's, a fact of which we become most aware when approval is terminated and especially when that which has been approved is now disapproved and vice versa. This is what happens when an individual undergoes a marked change in his social structure.

As we have pointed out above, Seeman, more than others who have studied alienation, has sought to apply in his studies of alienation the theories of social learning. He has noted a remarkable parallel between the powerlessness of alienation and the external locus of control of Rotter's research.

Seeman (1972a, p. 501) observed certain congruences between his analysis of aspects of alienation and Rotter's social learning theory:

[Powerlessness] can be useful in making traditional learning theory more responsive to the specifically human features of the learning situation. Prominent among these features is the attribution that persons make concerning the causal texture of their circumstances. Along that line, Rotter and his colleagues have shown that such differences in causal attribution make a very large difference in the pattern of learning in laboratory settings. The pattern of extinction is quite different under "chance" versus "skill" circumstances, and subjects are generally less responsive to success and failure cues in the "chance-luck" situation than in a situation defined as being dependent on individual skills. In a sense, they learn less from their past experience in the situation when they feel they have low control.*

* From "Alienation and Engagement" by M. Seeman. In Angus Campbell and Philip E. Converse, eds., *The Human Meaning of Social Change* (New York: Russell Sage, 1972). © 1972 by Russell Sage Foundation, New York. Reprinted by permission.

Seeman followed by pointing out that, in challenging the experimental paradigm of traditional learning experiments where there is high experimental and low subject control, Rotter is simulating aspects of the social structure that are believed to produce alienation. In both Rotter's (1966) laboratory and in Seeman's (1967) field studies low subject control (powerlessness) led to poor learning. Seeman extends his argument to indicate that these findings suggest an explanation of the poor school performance of the poor and others low in social structure.

But there are other components in addition to powerlessness that have very persuasive laboratory analogs. In laboratory experiments Azrin, Hutchison, and Hake (1966) have demonstrated that laboratory animals, which have been previously reinforced and which have developed a stable rate of responding in an operant learning situation, will become markedly aggressive toward members of their own as well as members of other species when they are no longer reinforced. For example, a pigeon in a Skinner box has learned that twenty pecks on a button will produce a pellet of food. Over a number of trials the animal develops a very stable rate of responding and will largely ignore another untrained pigeon or other untrained animal introduced into the box. However, when the pellet-dispensing device is turned off the pigeon continues to peck for a period of time, showing increasingly disruptive patterns from its previous smooth movements, and then turns and attacks his fellow occupants. Note that the experimental animal has not attacked previously but does so only when placed on an extinction schedule. Many who are alienated are aggressive toward others against whom they have no apparent grievance.

Solomon, Seligman, and others at the University of Pennsylvania have carried out over more than a decade a series of studies, first of avoidance learning and later of learned helplessness. In their experiments a dog is placed in a large box with a low barrier in the middle of the box. A signal is given, a few seconds later the dog receives a shock through the grid in the floor on the side of the box in which he is standing. He yelps, jumps around and finally escapes by going over the barrier to the nonelectrified side. A minute later another signal and then electricity in the floor where he is standing now, more yelps, and finally an escape. The dog learns to escape quickly in a very few trials; later he learns that if he jumps as soon as the signal is given he will not receive a shock at all. This avoidance response turns out to be a rather remarkable bit of behavior because the shock apparatus can now be turned off completely and the dog will jump at the signal back and forth, back and forth, without ever having experienced another shock. This avoidance behavior is remarkably resistant to extinction.

In pursuing this work Seligman and others found that if, in the early stages of training the dog received a series of shocks from which he could not escape, a new behavior pattern appeared. The victim of inescapable (painful but not tissue damaging) shock could not learn to escape when the opportunity was made available. This was called learned helplessness. The concept has been developed by Seligman (1975) to account for many of the phenomena of clinical depression and also for the effects of cultural deprivation. The learned helplessness of Seligman's dogs and of his depressed patients resembles in many ways apathetic, powerless peasants found in many societies, a group who have few resources to be sure but who appear to ignore opportunities to improve their lot by their own efforts. Guthrie (1972) has pointed out the parallels between the dog in the shuttlebox who is failing to respond and the peasant who often appears to ignore opportunities and to resist accepting new patterns of behavior.

One of the problems we encounter, however, in an attempt to carry out an experimental analysis of alienation phenomena, is that those who have worked on the effects of various reinforcement schedules have striven for consistency in reinforcement in order to generate a stable pattern of behavior. We find most useful for our purposes those studies in which stable reinforcement contingencies are modified and unpredictability rather than predictability is maintained. We do suggest, though, that the powerlessness, apathy, hostility, and social isolation of alienation can be simulated in the laboratory situation. We must move to human subjects, of course, before we can speak of self-isolation and culture isolation. The merit of this analysis is that it suggests more explicitly the antecedent conditions and even introduces the possibility of some experimental manipulation of the phenomenon and, possibly, methods to prevent or reduce alienation.

Implications for Alienation Theory and Research

In many instances those who have studied alienation in non-Western settings have paid relatively little attention to the possibility that different social processes might give rise to different reactions to the purported antecedents of alienation. When they have paid attention to social behavior, many researchers have found that manifestations of alienation did not appear or appeared in different forms. For instance, migrants from rural areas to rapidly growing cities showed fewer symptoms of alienation when housing styles permitted frequent and close contact with neighbors. Those who had moved from rural to industrial living styles showed fewer physical symptoms that might be attributed to stress (Inkeles and Smith, 1974). In the future it is hoped that those who examine alienated behavior in non-Western cultural settings will pay more attention to social factors within the new settings and will not assume an identity of processes.

For those contemplating cross-cultural research on this topic we recommend a careful examination of the work of Seeman, which we have cited frequently, and consideration of the context-specific approach to alienation spelled out in a very lucid paper by Wegner (1975). He concluded:

> More specifically, this paper suggests that alienation be defined as negative feelings and cynical beliefs toward a particular social context, where disenchantment is based on an incompatibility between the individual's personal characteristics and the social role he is performing. Since people may be disenchanted for different reasons, the study of alienation must first identify the multiple bases of discontent, which are important in the particular role situation. After identifying the different bases for alienation, further study should focus on the characteristics of persons alienated for one reason rather than another in order to understand various types of alienation. (p. 189)

With respect to design we endorse strongly the statement by Neal and Rettig (1967):

> As guidelines for alienation research, we suggest the criteria: (1) that each alienation construct have a single, identifiable referent; (2) that researchers operationalize their concepts and assume responsibility for showing the congruence of their concepts with their empirical referents; and (3) that the alienation constructs be related empirically to either their generative social conditions or their social consequences. (pp. 61–62)

Finally, we are convinced that the measurement of alienation must be improved through the use of readily available scale construction procedures on data collected in the society to be studied and through greater use of nonreactive measures. The present excessive reliance on self-report attitude scales is a serious source of error because of the degree to which various response biases distort the results. In short, we contend that those who would study alienation need to be well informed concerning both the measurement of alienation and the culture of the people being studied.

Summary

The concept of alienation has developed from the early formulations of Marx, based on observations of the effects on individuals of industrialization, and of Durkheim, who tabulated the social context of suicide. Durkheim's anomie has come to be regarded as normlessness, one of the six faces of alienation as analyzed by Seeman (1959, 1972a). Although there is little agreement about the essential elements of alienation, in most usages it refers to an inability to achieve satisfaction in one's social or personal activities, feelings of and behavior indicative of apathy, resentment, and even rebellion, and many forms of failure to conform to the expectations of the majority of other citizens. Thus alienation has been offered as an explanation of alcoholism, addiction, delinquency, and unconventional sexual behavior. As many have observed, it explains too much.

Alienation has also been invoked to account for many socially disruptive phenomena in countries outside Western Europe and North America where there have been rapid changes of industrialization, urbanization, mass education, and expanded communication through radio and television. In many instances alienation has been applied as a diagnostic label with few implications about causes or methods of alleviation. In few cases has the cross-cultural question been asked, "How have the cultural patterns of this society modified the effects of the social changes believed to have produced these indications of alienation?"

Poor measurement of alienation is a second serious shortcoming in many of the studies we have reviewed. The scales are too short to be reliable, are subject to great distortion from response biases, and often are made up of mixed sets of items that assess relatively unrelated aspects, all said to be indicative of alienation. Multiple measures—some behavioral—and multivariate analyses of the results are needed in order that the research methods be consonant with the formulations expressed by most investigators.

In many cross-cultural studies the opportunity to observe the impact of cultural factors has been virtually excluded by the sole use of translated alienation scales. In those instances, however, where observational techniques have also been used, many additional patterns appear that were not observed in industrialized societies, such as stresses on religious practices, health practices, and financial obligations to relatives. In the Philippines where we have more data, there is, among those who could be expected to be alienated, evidence of optimism, a preservation of norms, and a cultural continuity that is counter to the behavior one would expect. Their society, at least, would appear to disprove the inevitability of alienation under conditions of severe disruption of traditional patterns. Data from the Philippines and elsewhere would also suggest that we may have exaggerated the integrity and balance of social processes within traditional communities.

Finally, to these reviewers at least, the integration of alienation theories with Rotter's (1966) research on locus of control, done by Seeman (1971), appears to be a most productive development and it suggests a model for analysis and for action programs. Later work, such as that by Seligman (1975) on learned helplessness and the studies of deindividuation by Zimbardo (1970), should help us to advance beyond the stage of counting self-reports and may also provide the conceptual tools that will enable us to see how different cultural processes modify the strength and manifestations of the many forms of alienation.

Note

1. The authors acknowledge with sincere thanks the careful and detailed critique of an earlier draft of this chapter contributed by the committee of participants at the Conference of Contributors to the *Handbook of Cross-Cultural Psychology* in January 1976 at the Culture Learning Institute, East-West center, Honolulu, Hawaii. Sabeeha Hafeez, Michael O'Driscoll, Caroline Keating, and Liwayway Angeles were members of this committee. The authors are thankful for their constructive comments.

References

AAKSTER, C. W. Psycho-social stress and health disturbances. *Social Science and Medicine*, 1974, *8*, 77–90.

ABUEVA, J. W., GUERRERO, S. H., & JURADO, E. P. *Metro Manila today and tomorrow.* Quezon City: Ateneo de Manila University, Institute of Philippine Culture, 1974.

ARMER, M. Formal education and psychological malaise in an African society. *Sociology of Education*, 1970, *43*, 143–158.

AZRIN, N., HUTCHISON, R., & HAKE, D. Extinction-induced aggression. *Journal of the Experimental Analysis of Behavior*, 1966, *9*, 191–204.

BALL, R. A. The analgesic subculture of the Southern Appalachians. *American Sociological Review*, 1968, *33*, 885–895.

BARGER, K., & EARL, D. Differential adaptation to northern town life by the Eskimos and Indians of Great Whale River. *Human Organization*, 1971, *30*, 25–30.

BERREMAN, G. D. Aleut reference group alienation, mobility and acculturation. *American Anthropologist*, 1964, *66*, 231–250.

BIANCHI, G. M., CAWTE, J. E., & KILOH, L. G. Cultural identity and the mental health of Australian aborigines. *Social Science and Medicine*, 1970, *3*, 371–387.

BIGART, R. J. Indian culture and industrialization. *American Anthropoligist*, 1972, *74*, 1180–1188.

BLAUNER, R. *Alienation and freedom.* Chicago: University of Chicago Press, 1964.

BROD, T. M. Alcoholism as a mental health problem of native Americans. *Archives of General Psychiatry*, 1975, *32*, 1385–1391.

BRODY, E. B. (Ed.). *Behavior in new environments.* Beverly Hills, Calif.: Sage, 1969.

BULATAO, R. A. Measures of happiness among Manila residents. *Philippine Sociological Review*, 1973, *21*, 229–238.

CARR, L. G. The Srole items and acquiescence. *American Sociological Review*, 1971, *36*, 287–293.

CLIFTON, R. A. The social adjustment of native students in a northern Canadian hostel. *Canadian Review of Sociology and Anthropology*, 1972, *9*, 163–166.

COLE, S., & ZUCKERMAN, H. Inventory of empirical and theoretical studies of anomie. In M. B. Clinard (Ed.), *Anomie and deviant behavior*. New York: Free Press, 1964.

CUMMINGS, T. G., & MANRING, S. L. The relationship between worker alienation and work-related behavior. *Journal of Vocational Behavior*, 1977, *10*, 167–179.

DOHRENWEND, B. S., & DOHRENWEND, B. P. (Eds.). *Stressful life events: Their nature and effects*. New York: Wiley, 1974.

DURKHEIM, E. *Suicide* (J. A. Spaulding and G. Simpson, trans.). Glencoe, Ill.: Free Press, 1951. (Originally published, 1897.)

EDEN, D., & LEVIATAN, U. Farm and factory in the kibbutz: A study of agroindustrial psychology. *Journal of Applied Psychology*, 1974, *59*, 596–602.

FISCHER, C. S. On urban alienations and anomie: Powerlessness and social isolation. *American Sociological Review*, 1973, *38*, 311–326.

FORM, W. H. Technology and social behavior of workers in four countries. *American Sociological Review*, 1972, *37*, 728–738.

FRANKLYN, G. J. Alienation and achievement among Indian-métis and non-Indians in the Mackenzie District of the Northwest Territories. *Alberta Journal of Educational Research*, 1974, *20*, 157–169.

FRIED, M. Effects of social change on mental health. *American Journal of Orthopsychiatry*, 1964, *34*, 3–28.

GEYER, R. F. *Bibliography alienation*. Amsterdam: Netherlands Universities' Joint Social Research Centre, 1972.

———. *Bibliography alienation*. Amsterdam: Netherlands Universities' Joint Social Research Centre, 1974. (Supp. to 2nd, enlarged ed.)

GRAVES, T. D. The personal adjustment of Navajo Indian migrants to Denver, Colorado. *American Anthropologist*, 1970, *72*, 35–54.

GRIFFITH, W. Blood, toil, tears and oil. *New York Times Magazine*, July 27, 1975.

GUERRERO, S. H. The "culture of poverty" in Metro Manila: Some preliminary notes. *Philippine Sociological Review*, 1973, *21*, 215–222.

GUTHRIE, G. M. Cultural preparation for the Philippines. In R. B. Textor (Ed.), *Cultural frontiers of the Peace Corps*. Cambridge, Mass.: MIT Press, 1966, 15–34.

———. *Psychology of modernization in the rural Philippines*. Quezon City: Ateneo de Manila University, IPC Papers, No. 8, 1970.

———. The shuttle box of subsistence attitudes. In B. T. King and E. McGinnies (Eds.), *Attitudes, conflict and social change*. New York: Academic Press, 1972, pp. 191–210.

GUTHRIE, G. M., & ZEKTICK, I. N. Predicting performance in the Peace Corps. *Journal of Social Psychology*, 1967, *71*, 11–21.

GUTKIND, P. C. From the energy of despair to the anger of despair: The transition from social circulation to political consciousness among the urban poor in Africa. *Canadian Journal of African Studies*, 1973, *7*, 179–198.

HANEY, C., BANKS, W. C., & ZIMBARDO, P. G. Interpersonal dynamics in a simulated prison. *International Journal of Criminology and Penology*, 1973, *1*, 69–97.

HOLLNSTEINER, M. R. Metamorphosis: From Tondo squatter to Tondo settler. Ateneo de Manila University, Institute of Philippine Culture, 1973. (Mimeograph)

———. Metamorphosis: From Tondo squatter to Tondo settler. *Ekistics*, 1975, *238*, 211–215.

HOLMES, T. H., & MASUDA, M. Life change and illness susceptibility. In B. S. Dohrenwend & B. P. Dohrenwend (Eds.), *Stressful life events: Their nature and effects*. New York: Wiley, 1974.

HOMANS, G. C. *Social behavior: Its elementary forms*. New York: Harcourt, Brace & World, 1961.

HONG, L. K. A comparative analysis of extended kin visitations, cohabitations, and anomia in rural and urban Hong Kong. *Sociology and Social Research*, 1973, *57*, 43–54.

IGA, M. A concept of anomie and suicide of Japanese college students. *Life Threatening Behavior*, 1971, *1*, 232–244.

INKELES, A., & SMITH, D. H. The fate of personal adjustment in the process of modernization. *International Journal of Comparative Sociology*, 1970, *11*, 81–114.

————. *Becoming modern*. Cambridge, Mass.: Harvard University Press, 1974.

ISRAEL, J. *Alienation: From Marx to modern sociology*. Boston: Allyn and Bacon, 1971.

JACKSON, D. N. The dynamics of structured personality tests: 1971. *Psychological Review*, 1971, *78*, 229–248.

JESSOR, R., GRAVES, T. D., HANSON, R. C., & JESSOR, S. L. *Society, personality and deviant behavior*. New York: Holt, Rinehart & Winston, 1968.

JOCANO, F. L. *Slum as a way of life*. Quezon City: University of the Philippines Press, 1975.

JOHNSON, F. (Ed.). *Alienation: Concept, term and meanings*. New York: Seminar Press, 1973.

KOJAK, G. The American community in Bangkok, Thailand: A model of social disintegration. *American Journal of Psychiatry*, 1974, *131*, 1229–1233.

LAQUIAN, A. *Slums are for people*. Manila: University of the Philippines, College of Public Administration, 1968.

LEIGHTON, A. H. *My name is legion*. New York: Basic Books, 1959.

LEIGHTON, A., LAMBO, T., LEIGHTON, D. C., MURPHY, J. M., & MACKLIN, D. B. *Psychiatric disorder among the Yoruba*. Ithaca, N.Y.: Cornell University Press, 1963.

LENSKI, G. E., & LEGGETT, J. C. Caste, class and deference in the research interview. *American Journal of Sociology*, 1960, *65*, 463–467.

LEVY, J. E., & KUNITZ, S. J. Indian reservations, anomie, and social pathologies. *Southwestern Journal of Anthropology*, 1971, *27*, 97–128.

LUMSDEN, D. D. The Volta River project: Village resettlement and attempted rural animation. *Canadian Journal of African Studies*, 1973, *7*, 115–132.

LYSTAD, M. H. *Social aspects of alienation: An annotated bibliography*. Washington: U.S. Government Printing Office, 1969.

————. Social alienation: A review of current literature. *Sociological Quarterly*, 1972, *13*, 9–113.

MAIER, N. R. *Frustration*. New York: McGraw-Hill, 1949.

MARKS, S. R. Durkheim's theory of anomie. *American Journal of Sociology*, 1974, *80*, 329–363.

McCLOSKY, H., & SCHAAR, J. H. Psychological dimensions of anomy. *American Sociological Review*, 1965, *30*, 14–40.

MERTON, R. K. Anomie, anomia, and social interaction. In M. B. Clinard (Ed.), *Anomie and deviant behavior*. New York: Free Press, 1964, pp. 213–242.

————. Social structure and anomie. In R. K. Merton, *Social theory and social structure*. New York: Free Press, 1968.

NEAL, A., & RETTIG, S. On the multidimensionality of alienation. *American Sociological Review*, 1967, *32*, 54–56.

NEAL, A., & SEEMAN, M. Organizations and powerlessness: A test of the mediation hypothesis. *American Sociological Review*, 1964, *29*, 216–225.

OKANO, Y., & SPILKA, B. Ethnic identity, alienation and achievement orientation in Japanese-American families. *Journal of Cross-Cultural Psychology*, 1971, *2*, 273–282.

PACKARD, V. *A nation of strangers*. New York: McKay, 1972.

PARKER, S., KLEINER, R. J., & NEEDLEMAN, B. Migration and mental illness. *Social Science and Medicine*, 1969, *3*, 1–9.

RAHE, R. H., GUNDERSON, E. K. E., PUGH, W. M., RUBIN, R. T., & ARTHUR, R. J. Illness prediction studies; use of psychosocial and occupational characteristics as predictors. *Archives of Environmental Health*, 1972, *25*, 192–197.

RETTIG, S. Anomie in kibbutz. *International Journal of Group Tensions*, 1972, *2*(4), 37–52.

ROBINSON, J. P., & SHAVER, P. R. *Measures of social psychological attitudes*. Ann Arbor, Mich.: University of Michigan, Institute for Social Research, 1973.

ROSEN, B. C. Social change, migration, and family interaction in Brazil. *American Sociological Review*, 1973, *38*, 198–212.

ROTTER, J. B. Generalized expectancies for internal versus external control of reinforcement. *Psychological Monograph*, 1966, *80*(Whole No. 609).

SAFA, H. I. The social isolation of the urban poor. In I. Deutscher and E. J. Thompson, *Among the people: Encounters with the poor*. New York: Basic Books, 1968, pp. 335–352.

SANFORD, A. C. A cross-cultural study of industrial motivation. *Southern Quarterly*, 1970, *8*, 145–161.

SAVASHINSKY, J. S. Mobility as an aspect of stress in an Arctic community. *American Anthropologist*, 1971, *73*, 604–618.

SCHACT, R. *Alienation*. New York: Doubleday, 1970.

SCOTT, J. F. *Internalization of norms*. Englewood Cliffs, N.J.: Prentice-Hall, 1971.

SEEMAN, M. On the meaning of alienation. *American Sociological Review*, 1959, *24*, 783–791.

————. Powerlessness and knowledge: A comparative study of alienation and learning. *Sociometry*, 1967, *30*, 105–123.

————. The urban alienations: Some dubious theses from Marx to Marcuse. *Journal of Personality and Social Psychology*, 1971, *19*, 135–143.

————. Alienation and engagement. In A. Campbell and P. E. Converse (Eds.), *The human meaning of social change*. New York: Russell Sage, 1972a, 467–527.

————. The signals of '68: Alienation in pre-crisis France. *American Sociological Review*, 1972b, *37*, 385–402.

————. Alienation and knowledge-seeking: A note on attitude and action. *Social Problems*, 1972c, *20*, 3–17.

————. Alienation studies. *Annual Review of Sociology*, 1975, *1*, 91–123.

SELIGMAN, M. E. P. *Helplessness*. San Francisco: Freeman, 1975.

SEYBOLT, J. W., & GRUENFELD, L. The discriminant validity of work alienation and work satisfaction measures. *Journal of Occupational Psychology*, 1976, *49*, 193–202.

SHEPARD, J. M. Technology, alienation, and job satisfaction. *Annual Review of Sociology*, 1977, *3*, 1–21.

SHORE, J. H., & STONE, D. L. Duodenal ulcer among Northwest Coastal Indian women. *American Journal of Psychiatry*, 1973, *130*, 774–777.

SIMPSON, M. E. Social mobility, normlessness and powerlessness in two cultural contexts. *American Sociological Review*, 1970, *35*, 1002–1013.

SPRADLEY, J. P., & PHILLIPS, M. Culture and stress: A qualitative analysis. *American Anthropologist*, 1972, *74*, 518–529.

SRIVASTAVA, P. K., SINHA, S. N., & JAIN, U. C. Some correlates of alienation among Indian female students. *Indian Journal of Psychology*, 1971, *46*, 395–398.

SROLE, L. Social integration and certain corollaries: An exploratory study. *American Sociological Review*, 1956, *30*, 709–716.

———. *Mental health in the metropolis: The midtown Manhattan study*. New York: Harper, 1975.

STOKOLS, D. Toward a psychological theory of alienation. *Psychological Review*, 1975, *82*, 26–44.

STONE, R. L. Personal communication, 1968a.

———. *Mahirap: A squatter community in a Manila suburb*. Quezon City: Ateneo de Manila University, IPC Papers, No. 6, 1968b.

———. *The politics of public and private property in greater Manila*. DeKalb, Ill.: Northern Illinois University, Center for Southeast Asian Studies, 1973.

STRATHERN, M. Absentee businessmen: The reaction at home to Hageners migrating to Port Moresby. *Oceania*, 1972, *43*, 19–39.

STROMBERG, J., PEYMAN, H., & DOWD, J. E. Migration and health: Adaptation experiences of Iranian migrants to the city of Teheran. *Social Science and Medicine*, 1974, *8*, 309–323.

STULL, D. D. Victims of modernization: Accident rates and Papago Indian adjustment. *Human Organization*, 1972, *31*, 227–240.

TEEVAN, J. J. On measuring anomia: Suggested modification of the Srole Scale. *Pacific Sociological Review*, 1975, *18*, 159–170.

TOFFLER, A. *Future shock*. New York: Random, 1970.

TURNER, J. H. Patterns of value change during economic development. *Human Organization*, 1971, *30*, 126–136.

VERMA, S. K., & MOSKOWITZ, S. B. Alienation and identity crises among Moslems in a North Indian town, 1975. (Mimeograph)

WATSON, L. C. Urbanization and identity dissonance: A Guajiro case. *American Anthropologist*, 1972, *74*, 1189–1207.

WEGNER, E. L. The concept of alienation: A critique and some suggestions for a context specific approach. *Pacific Sociological Review*, 1975, *18*, 171–192.

WHITE, M., & WHITE, L. *The intellectual versus the city: From Thomas Jefferson to Frank Lloyd Wright*. Cambridge, Mass.: Harvard University Press, 1962.

WILLEMS, E. Peasantry and city: Cultural persistence and change in historical perspective, a European case. *American Anthropologist*, 1970, *72*, 528–544.

WITTKOWER, E. D., & DUBREUIL, G. Psychocultural stress in relation to mental illness. *Social Science and Medicine*, 1973, 7, 691–704.

ZIMBARDO, P. G. The human choice. In W. J. Arnold and D. Levine (Eds.), *Nebraska symposium on motivation*. Lincoln: University of Nebraska Press, 1970.

ZURCHER, L. A., MEADOW, A., & ZURCHER, S. L. Value orientation, role conflict and alienation from work: A cross-cultural study. *American Sociological Review*, 1965, 30, 539–548.

3

Minor Psychological Disturbances of Everyday Life[1]

Wen-Shing Tseng
Jing Hsu

Contents

Abstract

Psychological and cultural elements are highlighted in minor psychological disturbances of everyday life. Based on available information, the lesser pathologies of behavior observed in common daily life are reviewed under several categories including: religion-related psychological disturbances, suicidal behavior, substance abuse, alcohol-related problems, psychosexual disturbances, aggressive/homicidal behavior, achievement-related disturbances, and epidemic psychological disturbances.

The nature of stress is defined from a cross-cultural perspective and the stresses and vulnerabilities inherent in particular sociocultural systems are noted to illustrate the possible relations between culture and stress. Finally, the means of psychopathology are discussed in terms of cultural influences on the manifestation of pathology.

Introduction

Minor psychological disturbances refer to the lesser pathologies of behavior observed in common daily life. In contrast to major psychiatric disorders, the nature of the psychopathology of such behavior is mild and less disturbing; it is seldomly dealt with as a psychiatric problem in a clinical setting and, therefore, may be referred to as "subclinical"; the nature of such behavior is more or less psychological in nature and occurs as reaction to stress rather than as a disease process with biological/endogenous predisposition; and finally, such phenomena may occur so commonly in daily life, and may involve so many people, that they may be viewed as normal individuals' suboptimal reactions to stresses and frustrations. When such behavior occurs as a part of everyday phenomena in a society, psychological and cultural elements are always highlighted in these minor disorders in comparison to major psychiatric disorders. Thus, the cross-cultural study of such disorders becomes very useful for obtaining knowledge and insight concerning cultural aspects of human behavior, particularly in relation to the issues of abnormality.

In this chapter, an initial attempt is made to define the concept of pathology and to describe the relationship between major psychopathology and minor psychological disturbances. Then, a series of examples including various types of everyday psychological disturbances from various cultural groups are presented to illustrate the cultural aspects of such minor abnormal behavior. Finally, culture-related stress and vulnerability are elaborated upon, followed by an analysis of the cultural aspect of the choice of psychopathology as a coping mechanism.

Definition of Pathology

The concepts of normality and pathology need careful clarification, particularly when we are dealing with the minor psychopathology of behavior of daily life and especially when we are doing cross-cultural studies. Most of the behavioral scientists agree that pathology of behavior can be defined from multiple perspectives (Offer, 1973; Rinder, 1964).

Pathology by definition.   Any mental condition or behavior that, from medi-cal-psychiatric-psychological points of view is dysfunctional and/or dis-organized, is defined as pathological. The human being, as a living organism, is assumed to be equipped with a certain psychological condi-tion and capacity for mental function, such as balance of psychic forces, autonomy, competence, resistance to stress, and the ability for adjust-ment. If a person lacks such capacity, manifesting a disorganized psycho-logical condition resulting in inefficient function or maladjustment, that condition is described as pathological.

Pathology as related to statistical norms.   Behavior is a departure, quantita-tively or qualitatively, from the norm of a particular society in a disap-proved, negative direction. Without doubt, this approach for determining pathology is arbitrary, relative, and may be subject to modification or change.

Pathology as socioculturally defined negative phenomena.   Based on its value sys-tem—or common belief—a society may view certain kinds of behavior as "wrong," "queer," or "sick" and label such behavior as pathological. Sometimes a behavior may be viewed by the society as pathological and labeled as "different," "eccentric," or "deviant" simply because it is an unfamiliar behavior to the society.

Since the criteria for normal and abnormal are applied subjectively, the concept of pathology may change at different times, may vary in dif-ferent circumstances, and may not be shared by different groups. A be-havior may be seen as abnormal within the culture (autopathology) but may be seen as normal by an outsider; or the reverse, i.e., a behavior may be seen as abnormal by an outsider (heteropathology) but as normal within the culture. In the process of cross-cultural study, it is very impor-tant for us to raise the question: "On what basis are we defining pathology and to what extent is this definition susceptible to cultural variation?" By so doing, we can deal with the issues of normality and abnormality more objectively.

Regarding major psychopathology and minor psychological distur-bances there is a need for clarification. Major psychopathology usually refers to the group of psychiatric disorders (commonly called psychoses) that is characterized by severe psychological disorganization and is mani-fested by the symptoms of confusion, hallucination, or delusion, with de-tachment from reality and gross impairment of sociopersonal function. Such disorders are understood as being predominantly related, with bio-logical or endogenous predisposition as causal factors; can frequently be conceptualized as disease, in terms of its process and outcome; and are suffered by a relatively limited group of people. For such disorders, professional attention and care is necessary, and somatic treatment has been considered to be useful as one of the choices of therapy.

In contrast to this, minor psychological disorders may include a variety of disorders that tend to be less disorganized or impaired in terms of the severity of pathology. They usually occur as a reaction to stress or frustration and can be comprehended as psychological in nature. Many people in a population may be involved in such disturbances, and they could, therefore, be considered as part of everyday life phenomena. The distinction between major and minor disturbances is arbitrary, but it helps us to conceptualize grossly the variations of psychopathology.

The relationship of major psychopathology, minor psychological disturbances, and normal behavior may be considered as a linear one, i.e., pathology is observed as a continuous distribution from normal behavior through minor psychological disturbances to major psychopathology. Based on the influence of early analytic theories, many scholars hold this view, believing that psychoses and neuroses represent a degree of the same pathological condition but in different stages of adaptation (Fenichel, 1945). Thus, from a clinical point of view, paranoid psychosis, neurotic suspiciousness, and normal suspiciousness; or psychotic depression, neurotic depression, and "normal" depression are very close in the nature of manifestation except in the degree of severity. As the extention of this, the nature of psychopathology is viewed essentially the same except that increased intensity or degree of pathology is distributed as a lineal spectrum across the three groups of people: the well-adjusted group, the suboptimally adjusted group, and the severely maladjusted group.

However, psychiatrists have recently learned that most major psychopathology, such as schizophrenic disorders, differ from minor psychiatric disturbances in that multiple etiological factors contribute to the formation of major psychiatric illness, with biological factors as the most prominent influence. Many clinical studies also indicate that psychoses manifest certain unique pathological findings that have not been observed in the ordinary population even for the suboptimal group (Katz & Sanborn, 1973; Grinker & Holzman, 1973). Thus, major psychopathology exists as a set of different entities, and the previous concept of linear relationship between major and minor disturbances and normal behavior does not apply.

Review of Minor Psychological Disturbances

Since the scope of human life is so wide, minor degrees of psychological disturbances are observed in various aspects, and it is practically impossible to review all of them inclusively. Based on available information, such disturbances are described under several categories of convenience.

Religion-related Psychological Disturbances

Although religious behavior is observed the world over—and is universally considered as normal—psychological disturbances may be associated with such behavior. In a study of Burmese monasticism, Spiro (1965) reported pathological Rorschach findings for the monks and pointed out their use of their religious system as a culturally constituted defense mechanism to resolve their inner conflicts. Sidewalk ashram devotees were interviewed by Deutsch (1975), who reported that virtually all devotees gave histories of chronic unhappiness, but they experienced increased well-being and periods of bliss after their involvement with the guru, who satisfied their strong underlying wish for union with a powerful object.

Many investigations have been carried out centering on the issues of religion and personality adjustments (Boisen, 1942; Casey, 1945), the sociocultural function of religion (Halifax & Weidman, 1973), as well as evaluations of mental illness among members of particular religious bodies (Giel, Kitaw, Workneh, & Mesfin, 1974; Kiev, 1964; Clark, 1944). Studies are always available on the dynamics and implications of the emergence of new religious cults such as the Holy Roller sects (Boisen, 1939) and the cargo cult (Burton-Bradley, 1973).

Religious behavior may become "pathological" if the belief becomes so fanatical and the religious practice so unusual as to disturb regular patterns of life. Some examples are some forms of faith healing, the refusal of ordinary medical treatment, or the practice of self-immolation among Vietnamese monks.

Snake handling has been described as a religious cult that spread through certain lower-class Protestant groups in the American Southeast (La Barre, 1964). In spite of the occasional deaths from snake bite—and its prohibition by law—this cult was reported as widespread. Some of the participants danced and entered trance states (associated with sexually tinged behavior), but the main picture shown by the cult was the attempt to engage in a "dangerous act"—the handling of serpents as a manifestation of supernatural powers. Most of the cult practitioners were poor whites who migrated from their rural farms to work in the cotton-mill towns. Life for the mill worker was "routinized and monotonous," "joyless and denying," and the goings-on at the Sunday morning snake-handling session have been interpreted as avenues of release and excitement for these people.

Some rural Taiwanese may practice "fire walking" as a means of worshipping their god, to prove that they are blessed by the god, and to prove they can cope with any difficulty they may have. This practice is usually undertaken whenever there is any particular difficulty in the village, such as conflict with other villagers, an epidemic of illness, or when important decisions need to be made. The participants feel the need to rely on their god for guidance and also to increase their self-confidence. The men of the village gather together at evening time in the courtyard in front of the temple. They set fire to a mountain of charcoal, and when the charcoal is very hot it is spread as a carpet over a large area. A group of eight or ten men, carrying sedan chairs containing a statue of their god, swing these chairs around the courtyard and then, barefooted, dash across the hot coals. This ritual is usually necessary for them to prove that their god is looking after them, to prove the existence of the supernatural power of the god and his blessings on them, and, finally, to activate them into solving problems they are facing. Frequently, some men are badly burned, but occasionally, probably due to tough feet and swift running, the burns are not severe.

A sociocultural review of "new religions" in Korea (Kim, 1972), reveals that most of these were usually founded during periods of historical turmoil (after the Japanese occupation, the Independence, the Korean War, the student revolution). Kim estimates that about 240 new religious organizations exist in present-day Korea. Even though each new religion has its own theoretical background, the common characteristics among them are: syncretism—claiming to be the union of Christianity, Buddhism, Taoism, Confucianism, and so forth; eschatology— believing that the present world will end and that the believers will start a new world; and the concept of the chosen people—Korea will be the political and religious center of the world. All these new religions are the manifestation of wish fulfillment on the part of deprived people who are frustrated by existing conditions. What makes these new religions relevant to psychopathology is the sexual practices associated with these beliefs. Direct sexual intercourse is frequently practiced between male leaders and female believers, or between male and female believers themselves, with the belief that through such "blood exchange" or "holy marriage" they can be rescued and become holy. Apparently, the new cults provide a way for sexually frustrated believers, particularly females who in such a traditional society seldom have alternative channels, to obtain gratification.

Suicidal Behavior

Self-destructive behavior in the form of suicide is found everywhere around the world. However, suicide rates vary greatly among different countries. Figures compiled by the World Health Organization (1973) showed that in developed countries for the period of 1950–1969, suicide rates were high in Japan, Denmark, Germany, and Switzerland (about 18 to 25 per 100,000 population); moderate in the USA, Belgium, France, and Australia (about 10 to 15 per 100,000 population); and relatively low in Canada, Venezuela, Italy, Netherlands, Norway, and New Zealand (about 5 to 10 per 100,000 population). As for the underdeveloped or developing countries, suicide rates also varied greatly. For example, rates were reported low for Thailand, 3.5 per 100,000 population (Eungprabhanth, 1975); and Uganda, 7.0 per 100,000 population (Fallers & Fallers, 1960); but high for Mandurai, India, 43.0 per 100,000 (Ganapathi & Rao, 1966), and Tikopia, Western Pacific, 37.0 per 100,000 (Firth, 1961), indicating that suicide is not necessarily a product of civilization and development.

The methods utilized for self-killing in different cultures vary greatly. For example, in Thailand (Eungprabhanth, 1975) and India (Ganapathi & Rao, 1966) insecticide is the most popular way, while hanging is the most frequent method of suicide in Africa. In general, a society tends to adopt a certain preferred method or methods during a given period of time for reasons of availability and familiarity, but such methods of suicide are as subject to change as the fashion of one's dress.

The sociologist Durkheim, back in 1897, described three basic types of suicide, concerning man and his relationship to his society: altruistic, egoistic, and anomic suicide. From a psychological point of view, it is useful to distinguish sociocultural suicide, which takes place primarily to fulfill sociocultural functions such as suttee or kamikaze mission, from personal-psychiatric suicide, which occurs primarily for an individual emotional reason.

The underlying cause for suicide varies in different cultures. For example, according to Hendin (1967), the suicidal patient is quite different in three Scandinavian countries, reflecting the vastly different cultural attitudes and psychosocial pressures of those countries. In Sweden, with its people of rigid performance expectations and a great self-hatred for failure, a "performance" type of suicide is prevalent; in contrast, the Danes, who maintain strong dependency needs, frequently attempt a "dependency-loss" suicide; for the Norwegians, less susceptible to suicide alternatives, a suicide is usually a "moral" form of suicide.

Suicide in Japan (Ohara, 1963) is of special interest, not because of its general frequency but because of its unique patterns. One pattern is the occurrence of family suicide. Family suicide is described as suicide-homicide behavior and involves two or more family members—particularly parent-child suicide. For some reason, the father and mother may wish to take their own lives as a way to cope with their depression, but at the same time they decide to kill their children to accompany them along their journey of death. The motive for such "pathological" acts appears to be the common believe that children share the goals, joys, and sorrows of their parents and would prefer death to living without them. Therefore, the society is in sympathy with such events and does not reproach parents who kill their children as part of a family suicide.

In Taiwan, even as recently as twenty years ago, when people still practiced the custom of matchmaking and the parents' permission was absolutely necessary for young people to get married, it was often reported in the newspapers that a young couple had committed suicide together—binding their bodies together and jumping into a lake or taking an overdose of drugs together in a hotel. Since there was a strong social taboo against being married without parents' permission, the young couple would have to wait patiently for the parents to change their minds, give up their hope of getting married, or, as a last alternative, decide to die together, with the hope that they would at least become husband and wife after death.

Substance Abuse

Substance abuse refers to the "abnormal usage" of a chemical substance in such a way that the subject who abuses it may develop physiological addiction, actual medical damage, or may suffer from the psychosocial impairment that may occur with it (Holzner & Ding, 1973). The phenomena of substance abuse can be observed as a part of the traditional life pattern within a society or can occur as an epidemic episode arising during certain situations and later fading away.

In general, the "abuse" of a substance is physiochemically defined because the substance has an addicting nature (such as opium) or an intoxicating potentiality (such as amphetamines). However, the abuse can be defined merely by sociocultural point of view without such physiochemical complication. For example, the excessive-compulsive consumption of "sweets" and "salty-spicy snacks" has been perceived and defined by the people of Northern India as an abuse condition—*chat* or *pan* (Vatuk & Vatuk, 1967). According to their culture, man must remain master of his food; he must not let the food master him. If a person loses his control and becomes "addicted" to sweets, even if there is no physiological complication, culturally it is defined as addiction.

The choice of intoxicants by different groups is not clearly known yet. Some investigators have considered that cultural factors may contribute to the choice of substance (Carstairs, 1954; Singer, 1974). Others take the view that availability is the determining factor, such as the usage of kratom leaf by the gardeners and peasants in Thailand (Suwanlert, 1975).

Opium-smoking behavior among the Meo of Laos is a good example of substance abuse observed as a part of traditional life (Westermeyer, 1974). The Meo are a tribal people who inhabit the mountains of several Southeast Asian countries. For most Meo, the primary importance of opium is its economic usefulness. Opium has been readily available as a cash crop, so that each household grows opium to trade for silver and iron. A few Meo occasionally use opium or are chronically addicted, but the majority refuse to use it. In contrast to the phenomenon of opium addiction in other societies, addiction among the Meo is primarily rural in origin, and a much greater proportion of women than men are addicted. Perhaps because of this, criminality in Laos among the Meo is not associated with addiction, according to Westermeyer, and opium addiction may not be uniformly correlated with decreasing social competency even though addicted behavior itself is not considered socially desirable.

The postwar epidemic use of central stimulants in Japan serves as an example of how substance abuse can occur as a transient epidemic episode (Hemmi, 1971). Japan was faced with the problem of social and economic reconstruction immediately after World War II. Everyone was forced to work hard to obtain food, housing, and the other essentials for daily living. In this situation, amphetamine, a central stimulant said to have been used by the kamikaze pilots for their suicidal attacks, appeared on the market and was sold with such advertising phrases as "get rid of slumber and be full of energy." Such slogans and drugs were quite fitting at that particular time. At first, the stimulants were used by such night workers as bartenders, waitresses, college students, artists, entertainers, and some writers because of their special situations and needs. However, when such drugs became widespread, many people reacted strongly against drug abuse, and the society as a whole imposed controls and restrictions. In time, the phenomenon of central stimulants disappeared, except among runaways and juvenile delinquents. Amphetamine abuse in Japan was transient, a reflection of the social atmosphere at that time (Hemmi, 1971).

The polydrugs abuse epidemic of the 1970s, which involved the youth of the United States and other developed countries, is a complicated social phenomenon. It has been interpreted as a complication of rapid modernization/urbanization, a reaction to the Vietnam War, a part of youth's rebellious movement, and so on. An individual study of drug abuse patients (Burke, 1971) revealed that almost half of them indicated their initial motivation for using drugs was "curiosity," while the other half emphasized the pleasant or thrilling experience. As for the underlying causes, almost half of them used drugs to "escape" from reality, one-third for a means of "belonging," and only one-tenth for the sake of "rebellion." Another psychological study of the young drug user (Kendall & Pittel, 1971) showed that their MMPI profiles indicated the predominance of character pathology as opposed to either neurotic or psychotic manifestations, i.e., inadequate impulse control, the relative absence of internalized values, and essentially narcissistic orientation toward others.

Many reports around the world support the view that there are always basic underlying psychosocial problems associated with substance abuse. Hashish consumption in Egypt (Soueif, 1967) was found to occur among the youth who were rejected by parents, had a history of quarreling in the family, and the presence of a father who took drugs. Petral inhalation among Australian aborigine adolescents was interpreted as the reaction to the breakdown of parental values, as well as a hunger for stimulation. Drug addicts in Israel (Tramer & Bentovim, 1961) were described as having the traits of low frustration tolerance and anxiety.

Alcohol-related Problems

Alcoholics are precisely described by the World Health Organization (1974) as "those excessive drinkers whose dependence upon alcohol has attained such a degree that it shows a noticeable mental disturbance or an interference with their bodily and mental health, their interpersonal relations, and their smooth social and economic functioning." However, from a cultural point of view, the problems of alcohol have different meanings and need to be viewed more broadly than merely as "alcoholism" in the ordinary clinical sense. For example, as pointed out by Jellinek (1962), in Finland the most serious alcohol problems are the violence and other damage caused by occasional release of heavy drinkers; in France, a large proportion of drinkers may incur some of the physiologically damaging characteristics of chronic alcoholism without their having ever shown intoxication or any behavior characteristic of "addictive drinking" as may be observed among Anglo-Saxon drinkers.

Since the cross-cultural comparison of actual alcohol problems is difficult, the observation of overall alcohol consumption in the population is usually utilized as an index for the prevalence of alcoholism. Data published by the World Health Organization (1974) have indicated that the annual alcohol consumption per head of adult population varies vastly among different countries, ranging from 26 liters per head for France, 17 liters for Yugoslavia, 13–14 liters for Chile and Australia, through 5–6 liters for Finland, Japan, and the United Kingdom, to only 2.4 liters for Israel. In order to explain the possible reasons for the different alcohol problems among different ethnic groups, recent studies have focused upon alcoholic sensitivities (Ewing, Rouse, & Pellizzari, 1974) or hereditary tendencies (Goodwin, 1971).

It is a well-known fact that the drinking patterns vary in different cultures. Bales (1949), using an anthropological basis, distinguished between four different types of attitudes that are present in various cultural groups and seem to have different effects on the rates of alcoholism, i.e., complete abstinence, a ritual attitude, a convivial attitude, and a utilitarian attitude.

As for the motivational factors in drinking, Horton (1943) used a sample of primitive societies to reveal that there is a positive relation between the degree of male insobriety and the level of "subsistence insecurity" in the society, thus supporting the view that alcohol consumption is related to the reduction of anxiety. Field (1962) reanalyzed Horton's data and pointed out that social organization is related to sobriety, i.e., increased social organization is associated with increased control of drinking behavior and, thereby, a decreased tendency toward drunkenness. Bacon (1973) stated that he and his colleagues, Barry and Child, using similar methods, validated another factor—dependency conflicts—as one of the motives for drunkenness.

McClelland, Davis, Kalin, and Warner (1972) examined in a sample of forty-four cultures the relationship between themes in folktales and the extent of drinking and concluded that heavy drinking is associated with the preoccupation with power. In another analysis, they identified a number of social and structural factors that foster drunkenness. These typically include a loose and vague hierarchy and absence of tight social control. Corroborating Field (1962), McClelland et al. (1972) concluded:

> Sober societies ... are better organized, hierarchical, solidary, often agricultural and settled communities which give wide and strong support to a man and which stress inhibition and respect. Societies which do not provide a man with the solid support apparently often put him in a situation of conflict, where he wants or is expected to be assertive and yet must be obedient. He solves the conflict by dreams of being powerful in a primitive, non-instrumental impulsive way, and finds in alcohol a means of promoting these dreams—of buying, at least temporarily, the strength he needs. (p. 72-73)

It is obvious that there is a great diversity in the views on the motivational sources of heavy alcohol usage. McAndrew and Edgerton (1969) used a rich panorama of ethnographic data to establish the bases for different patterns of drunken behavior across cultures. Their analysis emphasizes the continuity between culturally sanctioned modes of need expression and the characteristic patterns of inebriated behavior of a given milieu. Culture then molds and guides the expression of behavioral disinhibition that the ingestion of alcohol powerfully stimulates. By stressing the cultural plasticity of behavior that comes into play under the influence of alcohol, McAndrew and Edgerton imply that alcohol consumption may serve a variety of motives: joyful abandon here, a morose withdrawal there. The attempts to trace varying degrees of alcohol consumption to a single need or motive must, at this point, be examined with caution.

Psychosexual Disturbances

Based on differences in child-rearing practices, socioculturally defined sex roles, and a society's attitude toward sex, various patterns of sexual expression exist in different cultural settings (Honigmann, 1947). Certain kinds of sexual practices such as nudism, prostitution, wife-swapping, and the like may be considered as part of a "fringe element" in society, depending on how and by whom they are analyzed or viewed. In an anthropological survey of human sexual behavior among 150 societies, Ford (1949) revealed common phenomena that can be observed cross-culturally, such as the occurrence of sexual activity prior to sexual maturity, the presence of regulation concerning conception before marriage, the avoidance of coitus in certain circumstances such as menstruation, the active role of the male in courting and initiating intercourse, and others. On the other hand, he also reported that homosexual behavior among male children, adolescents, and adults is widespread. Sexual relations with animals are reported to be common among males in quite a number of societies, and while polyandrous societies are relatively rare, an overwhelming number of societies recognize the practice of polygamy. Thus, Ford's study illustrates the great variety of sexual behavior patterns that may exist in different societies.

Churchill (1968) systematically investigated male homosexual behavior from cross-cultural and cross-species points of view. He surmised that an inherent capacity on the part of all mammals, both human and subhuman, to become sexually aroused by the same sex and homosexual responsiveness is far more frequent among males than females. According to him, Ford and Beach (cited in Churchill, 1968) have observed that, among societies in which adult homosexual activities are said to be rare, definite and specific social pressure is directed against such behavior. Opler (1965) pointed out that homosexual behavior is far less pronounced among nonliterate people than among those at higher levels of economic development, although heterosexual experimentation often has greater social sanction.

From his observation of homosexuality in Tahiti, Levy (1971) speculated that from the standpoint of the community, allowing the presence of one homosexual in a village served the function of stabilizing a precarious and undesirable aspect of identity by providing a clearly negative image of this male role. This is an especially interesting phenomenon in a culture that has relatively little differentiation between the sexes in the process of child development. Concerning the social regulation of sexual behavior, Murdock (1949) emphasized that sexual regulation normally reflects social necessity, not mere cultural phrasing, and whenever social restraints become too ambitious, a marked discrepancy appears between the cultural ideal and actual observable behavior. In general, most studies support the view that sexual behavior pattern is very much influenced by sociocultural factors and that the concept, definition, and restriction of sexual deviation are likewise heavily subject to sociocultural influences.

Perhaps one of the most interesting psychosexual disturbed behaviors observed in common daily life is the practice of *couvade*, a custom of some primitive tribes such as those in the coastal region of British Honduras (Belize), in which the father goes to bed as if he is experiencing labor pains when his wife is having a baby (Munroe, 1973). This behavior of a male physically participating in female behavior of delivery is considered pathological by psychiatric definition, illustrating a confusion in gender roles. By utilizing data gathered from systematic analysis of the Ethnographic Atlas, Munroe , Munroe, and Whiting (1973) demonstrated that such sexual identification problems are closely related to matriresidential patterns and mother-infant sleeping arrangements, as well as to the absence of male figures in a residential living pattern, supporting the notion that such culturally shared psychosexual disturbed behavior is related to the culturally related psychosexual development.

It is a common folk belief among people in South China (Yap, 1965; Rin, 1965), Malaya, and also Northern India (Carstairs, 1956) that excessive loss of semen causes bodily weakness for the male. These people believe that semen is not easily formed. As an example, the traditional Indian believes that it takes forty days and forty drops of blood to make one drop of semen. Men are warned to regulate sexual life carefully and to control intake of certain "hot" foods, which are considered to be related to the production of semen. Consequently, many men who had indulged in sexual activity would react sensitively to any physical symptoms of malaise and loss of energy, were very much concerned with real or imagined spermatorrhea, and sought strength-giving medicine. Such culturally patterned and shared anxiety may reflect the basic insecurity feelings a man may have associated with a prolonged intimate relationship with his mother, which may be reinforced by existing child-rearing practices in such cultures. Nevertheless, it certainly creates and aggravates the man's fear for sexual gratification and produces culturally conditioned pathology.

Closely related to the problems of spermatorrhea—fear of an excessive loss of semen—is another psychosexual disturbance—*koro*, or impotence panic—as observed among the Southern Chinese (Rin, 1965; Yap, 1965). It is a syndrome observed among people who consider sexual excess harmful and believe that penile shrinkage due to sexual excess can be fatal. Usually precipitated by masturbation or intercourse, a man suddenly develops acute anxiety or panic, centered around the fear of shrinkage of penis and his frantic efforts to prevent it from happening. Psychiatric case studies revealed that the victim usually had a characteristic premorbid personality, associated with a lack of paternal identification, overprotection by the mother, and anxiety in achieving masculinity. However, undoubtedly the culturally related folk sexual belief led the victim to manifest this psychosexual disturbance in such a culturally specific form. Although *koro* has been found predominantly among the Southern Chinese, it is by no means an uncommon disturbance in groups other than the Chinese. Ngui (1969) reported a transient epidemic of *koro* in Singapore in 1967 that involved about 500 cases. The outbreak was caused by a rumor that eating pork from diseased pigs would cause "shrinkage of the penis." The majority of those who appeared at area clinics for treatment were Southern Chinese, but there were also several Malays, Indians, and Eurasians.

Aggressive Homicidal Behavior

In general, even though violently aggressive behavior is disapproved of in most cultures, we do not observe the same forms of violence in every society. Several societies actually enjoy institutionalized aggressive behavior, such as bullfighting, wrestling, and speedway racing, even though such behavior may be considered as pathological by an outsider. By studying the personality development of the Dogon of Mali and the Agni of the Ivory Coast from a psychoanalytic point of view, Parin (1972) speculated that different cultures produce different psychic structures according to the manner in which aggressive energy is handled at different developmental phases. Jones (1971) described how aggression was dealt with in a group of Australian Western Desert aborigines: disputes between male members of a tribe were handled by ritualized combat in which only minor wounds were inflicted, while in disputes among women a combatant would often club in the vertex of her opponent's skull.

Boyer and Boyer (1965) pointed out that the aggressive drives for Mescalero and Chiricahua Apaches cannot be properly handled after the process of acculturation in modern reservation life, the social conditions being such that hostility can no longer be discharged against an enemy or outsider, nor can it be dissipated by the dangers of the raid or hunt as it was in the past. Finally, witches, ghosts, and bogeys no longer serve as unambivalently sanctioned beings upon whom aggression can be projected.

Focusing upon the situation in Puerto Rico, Rothenberg (1964) reported that the rate of murder and nonnegligent manslaughter was 7.1 per 100,000 in 1961 (4.7 per 100,000 for the USA), and the death rate due to motor vehicle accidents was more than twice that of the United States. In spite of the traditional cultural ideals emphasizing the qualities of dignity, hospitality, and friendliness, he felt that Puerto Ricans lacked the ability to adapt or channel aggressive energy.

Many reports indicate that there is a frequent occurrence of "morbid rage reaction" in some societies that is characterized by the fact that a relatively quiet person, without any warning, suddenly flies into a blind rage and, using a dangerous weapon readily available, injures or kills many people in a public place. Such phenomena, instead of being described as a bizarre, culture-bound syndrome, have been described as a common psychosocial occurrence with certain epidemic characteristics (Westermeyer, 1973a).

Several reports from Malaysia, Laos, Thailand, and the Philippines describe common features of this phenomenon (Ellis, 1893; Zaguirre, 1957). The individual involved is usually a young, uneducated man, faced with severe frustration such as loss of money, job, or friends, and is publicly insulted, thereby suddenly developing a morbid hostility with a diffuse target. Such phenomena tend to occur as epidemics, particularly when there is rapid social change resulting in economic or political upheaval (Westermeyer, 1973a). The culture contributes to the occurrence of such phenomena by providing awareness of such violent alternatives as a means of deliverance from an unbearable situation.

Reviews of literature indicate that the amok runner of Malaya was originally referred to as a hero who sacrificed himself in battle against an enemy (Murphy, 1971; Teoh, 1972). Later, the rage resulted in a homicidal act within his family, with the individual in a dissociated condition. Recently, it has been happening only among chronically mentally disordered persons, indicating the historical evolution of this behavior, a modification associated with the change of cultural attitude toward rage.

In spite of the general impression that the Lao people are gentle, unambitious, and nonaggressive, murder in Laos has been relatively frequent (Westermeyer, 1973c). Case studies indicate that the assassination victims were habitual criminals who killed others, stole, and severely threatened a community's safety. They were considered dyssocial persons whose behavior was odious and who were an increasingly intolerable burden to the village group. In some cases, the victims were political authorities who abused their position and power and were harmful to the people. The act of assassination might take place as a group behavior or as an individual, secret act. The Laotian society tended to understand and accept such instances of murder as a means of removing people who were a threat to the existence of the group. Actually, from a psychosocial point of view, assassination, even if it is a pathological behavior, serves as a negative sanction in the governance of interpersonal relations in a society where no other regulatory or legal systems exist.

Achievement-related Disturbances

Although seeking achievement is ubiquitous, the intensity of the need or the pressure for such achievement may vary in different societies and may bring about different kinds of complications.

While the problem of gaining admission to good academic institutions is not peculiar to Japan, the severity and intensity of this problem and the high frequency of psychological disturbance connected with gaining admission to academic institutions are (Vogel, 1962). Many middle-class parents, even if they are short of funds, struggle to provide their children with desks and hire a tutor for a year or two to work regularly with the child in preparation for the entrance examination for junior high school. The student has to give up various other activities, recreational, athletic, and so forth to study several hours a day after school. The examination season is a climax after long months of preparation, and many students manifest tension, anxiety, and fear of the examination. Psychiatric consultation is sought by some of the parents to ascertain the cause of the child's academic underachievement and any remedy to improve it.

Historically, Vogel (1962) further remarks, the best way to obtain competent people for government positions has been to select them from certain institutions of higher learning. Japanese firms generally make a life commitment to the employee at the time of hiring, therefore it is necessary to select carefully men and women of considerable competence. Since the best students will almost invariably try to get into the best universities, the most reliable single factor for judging competence in a prospective employee is the university attended by the student. This is the sociocultural background behind the tension involved in seeking entrance to a higher ranked academic institution.

Such an achievement-related disturbance is manifested differently after the student actually enters college. Because of the excess gratification of the dependence need in early life (Doi, 1973), many Japanese youths have difficulty with university graduation as a transition to independence and responsible adulthood. It is particularly true for those who have difficulty obtaining better jobs in a better company after graduation to secure their future. Many students develop a fear of leaving the university and purposely fail final examinations to stay on year after year for a long period, thus postponing their graduation and continuing their dependence on their parents. According to Kasahara (1974a), a survey at Kyoto University in 1970 revealed that, in spite of the ordinary four-year curriculum, over one-quarter of the senior class had postponed graduation for more than one year and nearly 4 percent for more than three years. They address such phenomena as graduation phobia.

Epidemic Psychological Disturbances

The term epidemic psychological disturbance refers to a sociocultural-psychological phenomenon in which a group of people, through social contagion, collectively manifest psychological disorders within a brief period of time. Although it may take various forms such as group panic or collective delusion, its most common manifestation is an outbreak of hysteria. As it may involve a large number of ordinary people, it deserves special attention as a kind of everyday psychopathology.

Many collective manifestations of "peculiar behavior" have been known historically in the West, such as dancing manias (tarantism) or Salem witch trials—all of which are related to epidemic hysteria.

According to Teoh, Soewondo, and Sidharta (1975), twenty-nine episodes of "peculiar behavior" involving school students were reported between 1962 and 1971 in Malaysia, indicating that it occurs as a frequent phenomenon in that area (Tan, 1963). They described in detail one episode in which fifty adolescent Malaysian girls within a period of a couple of weeks, developed acute attacks of disturbance, such as difficulty in breathing, hyperventilation, tetanic spasm (or trance state) as a reaction to an unpopular schoolmaster's actions—his frequent intrusion into the students' private lives in the dormitory. The outbreak of such an epidemic was interpreted as a culturally accepted and effective way to advise an authority figure to alter the source of problems.

Similar occurrences of mass hysteria have been reported in developed countries, such as England (Moss & McEvedy, 1966), America (Schuler & Parenton, 1943; Nitzkin, 1976), and Japan (Ikeda, 1966). Those involved are usually females in institutionalized settings such as schools, hospitals, even factories. There is usually a preexisting stress or apprehension, such as academic stress, among the group (Muhangi, 1973). The ideas or beliefs transmitted or shared by members of the group are always familiar or seem so probable to them that they readily accept such ideas or information without hesitation. It does not matter whether the information concerns a "scientific" explanation such as gas intoxication or radiation from an H-bomb test as the cause of "pitting marks" on car windshields (Medalia and Larsen, 1958) or a "supernatural" explanation, such as being possessed by the angered spirits as the reason of misbehaving (Teoh, Soewondo, & Sidharta, 1975)—as long as it meets their understanding, the group accepts it and reacts collectively.

From a sociopsychological point of view, such epidemics may serve as a coping defense for the group to deal with the problems they are facing, usually in the form of group protest.

Culture, Stress, and Vulnerability

From a psychological point of view, stress may be defined as a force which, when exerted upon a person, disturbs the psychological homeostasis, producing a feeling of discomfort and rendering the person incapable of activity and performance. The kinds of stress are numerous, occurring as *conflict, loss, threat, deprivation, uncertainty, restriction,* and so on. In general, it is conceptualized as an external force even though it may originate intrapsychically. In contrast, *vulnerability* is defined as the constitutional factor that renders a person less tolerant or ill-equipped to cope with stress.

Clarification of Concepts

1. Up to two decades ago, most behavioral scientists tended to derive their theories of pathology from the fundamental principle that a pathological response is a reaction to stress, and the greater the stress the more severe the pathological response (Fenichel, 1945; Coleman, 1964). Since psychopathology is classified clinically as a major disorder (psychosis) or a minor disorder (neurosis, personality disorder, and so forth), in that order, most psychologists and psychiatrists believe that psychosis occurs as a reaction to "severe" stress, while neurosis or personality disorder occurs as a reaction to "minor" stress. However, psychiatrists have recently taken the view (Grinker, 1975) that multiple etiological factors (biological, psychological, and sociocultural) contribute to the formation of psychopathology and that the proportion of etiological factors varies between severe mental illness and mild mental illness, i.e., relatively more emphasis on biological factors is placed in psychoses, and more emphasis on psychological and sociocultural factors in the case of minor disororders. Consequently, the assumption of a simple parallel relationship between the intensity of psychological stress and the severity of psychopathology is applicable.

2. Some behavioral scientists have attempted to describe and conceptualize stress as a uniform entity and have tried to measure and compare the intensity of stress of groups of people by a single method (Leighton, 1972; Lauer, 1973). However, in actuality the nature of stress is quite variable and complicated. Stress is the state manifested by a specific syndrome that consists of all the nonspecifically induced changes within a biologic system. Thus, stress has its own characteristic form and composition but no particular cause. In its medical sense, stress is essentially the rate of wear and tear on the body (Selye, 1956). The term "stress" has been used to signify environmental agents that disturb structure and

function, as well as responses to such agents (Lazarus, 1971). It has physiological, psychological, and sociological referents. Even the definition of psychological stress depends on how the person interprets the significance of a harmful, threatening, or challenging event. Thus, there is no single index available to identify and measure stress as a single entity in a society. There is a need to recognize and to differentiate various kinds of stress (such as stress of conflict, loss, threat, or deprivation, and so on) and to study the various kinds of reaction or pathology associated with each specific stress. Despite a common autonomic nervous system, there are differences in the reported psychophysiological reactions to stressful situations among culturally different groups of people (Guthrie, Verstraete, Deines, & Stern, 1975). Based on differences among cultures, various forms of psychopathology may occur as a reaction to the same stress (Tseng & Hsu, 1970). For example, when facing an economic depression, people may react with different psychophysiological symptoms. Members of one society may respond to it by indulging in substance abuse, while members of another may become depressed (Sartorius, 1973). It would be a mistake to try to study the total intensity of stress existing in a society by simply measuring one facet of manifested psychopathology and neglecting other portions of it (Murphy & Hughes, 1965; Lynn, 1971). In sum, it is important to consider the whole picture of psychopathology as a profile rather than as a single indicator.

3. Even though it is generally assumed that human beings experience emotional reactions more or less in the same way, many investigators in recent cross-cultural studies have begun to discover cultural variations in negative emotions, such as depression and anxiety, as a reaction to stress.

Cross-national studies of depressive symptomatology among a normal adult population, as measured by the Self-Rating Depression Scale (Zung, 1972), have indicated that the scale means are highest for Czechoslovakia, followed by Sweden, Germany, Spain, England, and the United States. A similar study among normal college students carried out in Hawaii (Kinzie, Ryals, Cottington, & McDermott, 1973) showed that the score is highest for Asian (Japanese and Chinese) females, followed by Asian males and Caucasian females. These results suggest that, based on such self-reported measurement, there is a quantitative difference in baseline depressive symptomatology from country to country in the normal adult population.

Regarding the qualitative difference of emotional experience, it was found through word association studies (Tanaka-Matsumi & Marsella, 1976) that college students in Japan tend to associate with depression words that refer to the physical environment and somatic states, such as rain and dark, or disease and weariness, while Japanese-American college students in Hawaii and Caucasian-American college students tend to associate with words that are related to internal mood states, such as sadness or loneliness, indicating that there are cross-cultural variations in the subjective experience and meaning of depression among a normal population.

There have been some studies on anxiety (Cattell & Warburton, 1961; Tsujioka & Cattell, 1965) to suggest that people can be meaningfully compared across culture lines by paper-and-pencil anxiety measures. A systematic multicultural series of projects on the translation and revalidation of the State Trait Anxiety Inventory has been coordinated by Spielberger (Spielberger & Diaz-Guerrero, 1976). This instrument provides information on both the individual experience of anxiety at the moment and on the person's habitual level of anxiety. This scale has been translated into a number of languages including Spanish, Portuguese, French, Swedish, Turkish, and Hindi. The focus of the multicultural network of Spielberger and his collaborators has been on the revalidation of maximally equivalent versions of this scale in several cultural milieus. To this end, the measure was translated, back-translated, and administered to bilingual groups of individuals prior to its use with large and reasonably representative samples of the populations in question. Thus, the groundwork has been laid for the comparative cross-cultural use of this instrument.

So far, only few comparisons across culture lines have been reported. These results point to the specificity of cross-cultural differences in anxiety. In the case of Swedish and Canadian university students (Endler & Magnusson, 1976), it was found that anxiety was higher among Swedes for physical danger and ambiguous situations; Canadians were found to exhibit higher levels of self-reported trait anxiety. In a comparison of Mexican and American school children—conducted by means of the Test Anxiety Scale for Children (Diaz-Guerrero, 1976)—Mexican subjects exceeded Americans in total scores as well as in scores for defensiveness and dissimulation. On the basis of the pattern of findings obtained, Diaz-Guerrero hypothesized that Mexican children would score higher than Americans for test anxiety; the opposite would obtain for social anxiety.

The full potential of the revalidated state trait anxiety scales for cross-cultural comparisons remains to be realized. Sharma (1977) advocates supplementing such comparisons by the local development of anxiety scales based on culture-specific preoccupations, worries, and concerns. In this manner, emic sensitivity can be combined with etic comparability. Independent of this work, there has been an attempt to infer anxiety levels from a variety of social indicators (Lynn, 1971). Such studies are aimed at exploring the possible cultural variations in the expression of negative emotional reaction among normal populations.

On a more general plane, Langner (1962) developed a scale that was designed to test a variety of responses to stress. It consists of twenty-two items and includes both psychological and psychophysiological symptoms. It was used intensively in the Midtown Manhattan investigation of psychiatric epidemiology (Stole, Langner, Michael, Opler, & Rennie,

1962; Langner & Michael, 1963) and has since seen extensive application in a variety of sociocultural investigations. The Langner Scale yields information on the general degree of impairment and distress, as a kind of "emotional thermometer" (Prince, 1967) and is applicable to both clinical and nonclinical groups. In particular, it has been used to assess the effects of major sociocultural stresses such as migration (Lasry, 1975) and to compare the level of impairment and the locus of response of groups differing in ethnicity or culture. Engelsmann, Murphy, Prince, Leduc, and Demers (1972) factor-analyzed this instrument and extracted from it what they called three "weak factors," which accounted for only a small share of the variance and not all of which were present in all the populations investigated. These factors were labeled depression, anxiety, and psychosomatic complaints. Based on a review of the findings of a number of studies, Lasry (1975) concluded that Latin groups in Europe and America generally tended toward somatization, as did North Africans, while English-speaking populations expressed their distress to a greater extent through anxiety and depression.

4. Stress may be perceived differently by people from different cultural backgrounds. Even though life change events such as death of a spouse, marriage, or loss of a job are potential sources of stress for everybody, people of different sociocultural backgrounds may perceive each life change event as being productive of different degrees of stress. For example, life change events were ranked slightly differently by Japanese and Americans in terms of their degrees of perceived stress (Masuda & Holmes, 1967). Japanese tended to judge "detention in jail" and "going to a bank to borrow money" as items signifying distress in life, while Americans rated "a conflict with the spouse" as a more serious problem.

When stressful films were employed in the laboratory with the intention of studying stress-reaction patterns cross-culturally, it was found that the Japanese experimentee, in contrast to the American experimentee, was unusually sensitive to the disturbing aspects of the experimental situation and reacted, not only to the content of the film, but with marked apprehension to the experimentation itself (Lazarus, Tomita, Opton, & Kodama, 1966).

The Indians who live on the Berons River in Canada believe that animals, like man, have a body and soul (Hallowell, 1938). For them, the approach of a wild animal of any sort to their camp or habitation is an ill omen; it is a sign that someone is trying to bewitch them. The animal is thought to be the malevolent agent of the sorcerer. Therefore, if they encounter any animal, or snakes swimming in the water, or a toad hopping toward them, this might induce panic and arouse an exaggerated affective response to such an animal. People from most other societies, because of differing views about animals, would probably not perceive this as a potential source of danger, though they might well respond to other situations. For example, in the world of cities, violence inflicted or witnessed brings fright and panic at the time; later, angry voices or looks or a midnight knock on the door seem threatening and induce stress. Just as a small toad was to the Indians the "sign" of sorcery, the hostile voice or manner or the late night visitor seem to be the "signs" of violence. Both signal stress reactions. But they are perceived differently.

5. Phenomenologically similar psychopathology manifested in different societies may have a different meaning and implication. The "hippie" movement originally started in the Western World with an emphasis on freedom from sociocultural restrictions and the reversal of social norms of achievement (Distler, 1970). The whole movement started with the implied rejection of industrialized culture and reflected a cultural shift. However, when this movement was transmitted to Oriental countries, it lost its original meaning and merely became a fashion for youth to follow. There was a desire to identify with the Western World, but only in dress, hair style, and music, with relatively little intention of rebelling against industrialized culture.

Alcoholism observed in different societies shares the core picture of chemical intoxication and psychological addiction. However, the psychosocial symptomatology of alcoholism varies according to the patient's cultural affiliation. Poor social functioning such as unemployment, marital maladjustment, and law breaking are experienced more in a so-called "dry" society, while such psychosocial impairment is less marked among the alcoholics in the "alcoholic" society (Negrete, 1973).

Another example is narcotic addiction. In Laos, in spite of the ready availability of narcotics as a cash crop, and with only limited social opprobrium, the problem of narcotic addiction is not necessarily associated with severe social incapacity as in the West (Westermeyer, 1974). Most of the abusers still live and function in their family and society—although suboptimally—without any severe social impairment or complication such as criminality. This is different from other countries, where the substance is expensive, difficult to obtain, and is almost always connected with crime (Westermeyer, 1974).

Theoretically, stress and vulnerability have physiological, psychological, and sociocultural referents. In the following section, an attempt will be made to review cultural aspects of stress and vulnerability.

Stress Inherent in a Particular Sociocultural System

1. Stress produced in a culture demanding achievement. Based on its value system, a culture may make strong demands on people to achieve in certain areas, such as personal training (education), psychosexual performance, or in business. If the cultural demand for such achievement is very strong, it may create a stress for the people to perform, to compete and to be successful and may disturb their mental health. If a society values open competition for mate selections, the young have to learn how to demonstrate their masculinity or femininity in order to be attractive heterosexually, so that they can win an appropriate mate. If a society emphasizes personal training in the form of education despite limited opportunities for providing education for all, then naturally this will cause a great deal of competition. If a culture practices the patrilineal system and overemphasizes the need for a male child to succeed the family clan, it may become a stress and a demand for the woman to bear a male baby. If a mother is successful in having a son, her social status in the family is secure, but if not, her status declines and she may be replaced by another woman. Thus, stress may be produced as a result of excessive cultural demand for achievement (Wittkower & Dubreuil, 1973).

2. Stress created by culturally determined, limited behavior range.   In every society there are always certain rules and regulations in the forms of taboos, etiquette, or law that govern certain dimensions of the lives of its people. Some societies have few rules and are lenient, while some others have many strict rules. When there is excessive confinement or strictness of rules, great stress is created for those who have to behave and respond in a very limited behavioral range.

In many conservative societies, such as in traditional China, many rules of etiquette regulated the behavior of men and women. At one time, girls were supposed to bind their feet, starting at the age of four or five so that their feet would remain small and look attractive to men. Young girls were not allowed to appear in public or to meet visitors at home. Marriages were arranged by parents or matchmakers, so that young people seldom saw their spouses until the wedding night. If the husband died, the wife was expected to live the rest of her life as a widow even if she was still very young. Usually people benefit from social customs, etiquette, and laws that regulate behavior and increase the orderliness of life in a society. However, at the same time, people may suffer if the rules are too strict and interfere too much with an individual's life.

3. Stress created by culturally defined anxiety.   Many societies define certain situations as dangerous, such as breaking of certain taboos or rules. Usually the anxiety situation that is so defined is a projection of the fear or anxiety of that particular group of people or is based on the particular group experience they have had in the past associated with the anxiety situation. Since the group believes in the particular fear system, it suffers from a culturally structured anxiety.

People in the Wellesley Islands in the Gulf of Carpentaria believed that a person who entered the sea, without washing his hands after handling land-grown food, ran the risk of succumbing to sickness (Cawte,

1976). Such a belief may be interpreted as the projection of the islanders' preoccupation with the sea-land antinomy—the fear of leaving one's own territory and fear of the danger inherent in breaking rules on foreign ground. At any rate, it demanded that the people rub off any trace of land-grown food from their hands with sand and water before entering the sea. Otherwise they would become victims of *malgri*, the sickness of intruders associated with abdominal pain.

4. *Stress created by sociocultural discrimination.* Tension, hidden antagonisms, or open conflict may exist in a society if the society is made up of a majority group and a minority group, both of which form very different subcultures whose relationships are strained and characterized by discrimination. Generally, such discrimination is practiced against a minority group but, as is the case in South Africa, it may be discrimination practiced by a minority group that is in power against a majority group that is not. The discrimination may originate in differences in race, ethnic groups, or social class but may sometimes merely be the result of the difference of an image created by others. For example, the Burakumin (an outcast group in Japan), are not racially different from the majority of Japanese (DeVos & Wagatsuma, 1969), but many Japanese believe that the people of this group are visibly identifiable, and they are considered mentally inferior, immoral, aggressive, and impulsive and are discriminated against in education, occupation, and social relations. There is no intermarriage between them and other Japanese. Even the Burakumin see themselves in the same way. They thus limit their own opportunities in education, occupation, and social status, and they also have a higher incidence of antisocial attitudes expressed in behavior defined as delinquent or criminal. The most important issue is that the discrimination occurs not because of ethnic factors but because of the image of a majority group concerning a minority group.

Vulnerability Inherent in Particular Sociocultural Systems

Stress and vulnerability are related. Stress may be produced, not because of the existence of a particularly stressful situation, but because of susceptibility or a defect within the subject.

1. Through certain culturally patterned child-rearing practices, specific personality traits or types may develop, ones that are especially vulnerable to a particular kind of stress. In Japanese society (Doi, 1973), a baby is permitted to be close, intimate, and dependent upon its mother for a relatively long period of time to fulfill and indulge in the need of *amae*—the desire to be passively loved. As a result of such a child-rearing practice (Kasahara, 1974b), a child, even if it is no longer an infant at

the breast, sometimes makes no move to leave its mother and tends to shy away from strangers, leading to problems of overdependency. A special kind of neurosis—anthrophobia, a fear of others and anxiety in dealing with other people—is interpreted as the consequence of such over-dependence.

2. Vulnerability may be produced by a change of roles and the depri-vation of the source of support within the sociocultural system. For exam-ple, the sudden change of family system from the extended family to the nuclear family may bring about problems for the aged (Hsu and Tseng, 1974). Throughout their lives, they spent most of their energy and in-vested most of their emotion in raising their children with the expectation that when they got old, they could rely both financially and emotionally on the young generation. Now, suddenly the sociocultural system has changed. The married sons and daughters, instead of continuing to live with the parents in the same household, prefer to live by themselves as a nuclear family unit. The elderly people who are unprepared to live by themselves could become a lost generation, not knowing how to live the rest of their lives, susceptible to insecurity, loneliness, and depression.

3. Vulnerability may exist in the nature of the sociocultural system itself. Either due to external environmental factors or internal cultural systems, a group of people may adopt a style of life with a certain social organization and coping pattern that makes them vulnerable to certain kinds of stress.

This is well illustrated by a comparison of the adjustment of Ameri-can military communities in two different foreign settings—Thailand and Japan (Kojak, 1974). The American community in Bangkok suffers from sociocultural disintegration. The Americans are scattered throughout the city and do not form American neighborhoods per se. Many families live on streets that are not lighted, they have no cars, and they find telephone systems quite unreliable. There is a shortage of communication and trans-portation and a lack of an easily visible community leader. Above all, they find themselves questioning many of their own cultural values. The ideas of work, responsibility, and discipline are not stressed in the Thai culture. The "it does not matter" attitude of Thai society is threatening to Ameri-cans. As a result, psychopathology is more prevalent as reflected in fre-quent marital problems and failures of adjustment of adolescents. This is quite a contrast to the American community in Japan, whose existence is a model of sociocultural integration (Kojak, 1974).

Stress Produced by Rapid Sociocultural
Change and/or Disintegration

Either due to internal demand, or as the result of contact with another culture, a society usually undergoes sociocultural change. Such a change can be useful and does not necessarily produce adverse effects on the mental health of the society's members, especially if it is characterized by a certain degree of cultural elasticity. As a matter of fact, change provides stimulation for growth and is essential for health. However, if sociocultural change occurs at a very rapid rate without obvious goals, motivation, or organization, it will result in ambiguities within the basic value systems; and with few existing guides or models for change, it usually becomes a stress for the members of the group (Zaidi, 1969; Hippler, 1968).

The degree and nature of stress produced by sociocultural change varies. A sampling from communities of American Indian peoples across an ecocultural range showed that the greater the cross-cultural discontinuities, the greater the acculturative stress (Berry & Annis, 1974). Some behavioral scientists (Caudill & Scarr, 1962) analyzed value orientations systematically and were able to predict particular areas of difficulty in the process of cultural change.

The noxious effects of sociocultural disintegration are more evident in groups that used to have a highly stable, traditional, and achievement-oriented culture. With the process of industrialization and urbanization, many developing countries in the world, whose traditional agricultural and rural values present a contrast to modern industrial society (Lin, 1959), are facing value conflicts. Such value conflicts may occur in the area of family relations, loyalty to the land and habitat, personal versus community orientation in achievement, patterns of authority and leadership, as well as in the status of women (Zaidi, 1969).

Young people are particularly likely to be affected by sociocultural change and by changing value systems, since they are in the process of forming their own identity and are vulnerable to situations filled with ambiguity and confusion. Contemporary Western society is characterized by a cultural shift along a continuum from a "patristic-instrumental" culture to a more "matristic-expressive" culture (Distler, 1970). In a patristic culture, the male role is ascribed the greater value. The cultural ideal is socialization to instrumental roles. The emerging matristic culture values expressive roles, feelings, intimacy, sensory experience, and self-exploration (Carey, 1969). This is a major change, and its impact is most marked among young people.

Choice of Psychopathology:
Cultural Aspects

The manifest psychopathology may be understood as a sign of a defect or deterioration, as a way of dealing inadequately with stress, or as an adaptive alternative way of coping with problems. The nature of psychopathology is broadly determined by biological, psychological, and sociocultural factors. An attempt will be made here to elaborate on the cultural aspect in the choice of psychopathology as a coping mechanism.

Related to or Determined by the Nature of Culture

Psychopathology is related to or predetermined by the nature of the culture, specifically by its degree of complexity, the structure of the society, or the culture's way of dealing with emotion. Several studies support the existence of such correlations.

A systematic analysis of "trance" and "possession trance" observed among a world sample of societies (drawn from Murdock's *Ethnographic Atlas*, 1967) revealed that the less complex the society, the more likely it is to have only trance, while the more complex the society, the more likely it is to have possession trance (Bourguignon, 1976). From a psychopathological point of view, trance is an intrapersonal event, while possession trance constitutes an interpersonal event involving the impersonation of another being and the playing of a role in that event, which is a relatively more differentiated phenomenon. Thus, the occurrence of trance, or possession trance, as a psychic phenomenon (disregarding the question of whether it is a pathological phenomenon or an institutionalized behavior) is related to the degree of sociocultural complexity.

Excessive self-depreciation as a result of compliance to strong external control may become one of the reasons for depression. A systematic review (Chance, 1964) showed that highly cohesive groups—either highly traditional and culturally "stable" or of middle and upper socioeconomic status—tend to have more frequent symptoms of self-depreciation resulting in depression; while groups low in cohesion—characterized by extensive "flexibility" of social relations, rapid cultural change, social disorganization, low socioeconomic status, and extensive migration—have less frequent feelings of guilt and depression. Thus, the manifestation of depression in a community is speculatively related to its level of cohesion.

It is a general impression among clinicians that the phenomenon of "classic" hysterical reaction, in the dramatic form of dissociation or conversion, is gradually disappearing from some societies—mostly from the developed countries, where people are better educated and are experienced in communicating their opinions directly and in expressing their feelings through verbalization. This same psychopathology is still predominant in some societies—mostly in the so-called developing or underdeveloped countries, where people are still conservative and are used to communicating their ideas indirectly and acting out their problems or expressing their emotions through bodily reaction. Thus, the occurrence of psychopathology in the form of dramatic hysterical dissociation or conversion is related to the nature of culture, particularly in terms of how people handle and express their negative feelings.

Related to the Nature of Stress or
Vulnerability Inherent in the Culture

The nature of psychopathology manifested is specifically related to the nature of the stress or vulnerability existing in the society. If a society is excessively oriented toward action, efficiency, and achievement, one group of symptoms may occur as a reaction to such a high-tension situation (Appels, 1973). Achievement motivation scores derived from an analysis of children's stories from sixteen countries have predicted death rates from ulcers and hypertension, and power motivation scores have predicted death rates due to murder, suicide, and liver cirrhosis (Rudin, 1968). Through culturally sanctioned child-rearing practices, a certain personality trait may develop that is especially vulnerable to particular stress and conducive to the development of a specific pathology. Psychosexual problems in the form of *couvade* and *koro* (Rin, 1965) provide examples of such vulnerability. *Couvade*, mentioned earlier, is a practice in which the husband goes to bed seeming to experience labor pains while his wife is experiencing them. *Koro* is a severe anxiety state in which the victim will develop an acute somatic delusion believing that the penis will retract into the abdomen, ultimately causing the death of the victim. Such phenomena are described among the males in Southeast Asia who suffer from sexual identity problems.

Solution Patterns Modeled by the Context of Culture

Based on a particular value system, a culture defines certain ways of dealing with problems. Depending on the culturally determined attitude towards authority, the universally observed intrafamily, father-mother-child triangular conflict may be resolved in various ways. In Western children's stories, the child-hero usually wins the battle of competition, resulting in the sacrifice of parental authority, while in Oriental stories, the child becomes the victim of the conflict (Tseng and Hsu, 1972). In actual life, youth movements and student riots against authority will be the solution of choice for a society in which challenge to authority is permitted, while passive-obedience and compliance at best—and withdrawal or suicide at worst—will be among the consequences if the authority is powerful and unchallengeable.

Culturally Recognized, Provided, or
Interpreted Sick Role

The way to express a signal of distress or illness to obtain attention or to be relieved of responsibility varies in different societies. For example, in one society (Rubel, 1964), to cut a wrist in a suicidal attempt may be a powerful message for another's sympathy and help, while in another society, to complain that one is bewitched may be a useful message for obtaining the concern of others. Thus, a person may react to the stressful situation by taking the sick role that is culturally recognized, interpreted, or provided. As an example, Hispanic Americans (Spanish-speaking inhabitants of California, Colorado, New Mexico, and Texas), as well as inhabitants of the Andean countries of South America, believe that an individual is composed of a corporeal being and an immaterial soul that may become detached from the body and wander free—resulting in a condition called *susto*, manifested through listlessness, loss of appetite, disinterest in daily life, loss of strength, and depression. Any person in these groups of people may become *susto* when he or she faces frustration and is in a depressed state of mind. Consequently, the person will be recognized as suffering from *susto* and will obtain certain regimens for healing it (Rubel, 1964).

In Chinese society, somatic illness is an effective and legitimate excuse for requesting rest and care from others, while psychological strain is not (Tseng, 1975). For a person to complain about his feelings of loneliness or anxiety may be regarded as a trivial daily matter and not worthy of attention. However, if he complains about a headache, stomach discomfort, or palpitation, it may be different. Therefore, in Chinese society, somatic complaints are relatively frequent even among psychiatric patients.

Culturally Available, Tolerated, or Expected
Alternative Solutions

A pattern of resolving problems may be viewed as negative or undesirable; nevertheless, a pathological solution may be undertaken if it is known by the group to be available. The morbid rage reaction in the form of amok frequently occurs among susceptible individuals in societies where it is recognized as a behavioral alternative that provides a means of deliverance from an unbearable situation (Burton-Bradley, 1968).

Due to the nature of the culture, many forms of deviant behavior are well tolerated by a society, thus insuring their continued existence. As an example, the long-delayed graduation from a university in Japan is well tolerated by the faculty, the university, and society as a whole. As a result, these conditions do not elicit particular efforts to change or stop them (Kasahara, 1974a).

It was generally hypothesized (Stainbrook, 1954) that the incidence of depression and suicide was low among preliterate peoples, as they were protected by extended family patterns, elaborate mourning rituals, and culturally patterned outlets for hostility. However, a survey of the Kandrian district of Southwest New Britain (Hoskin, Friedman, & Cawte, 1969) indicates that there is a high incidence of suicide, and it is speculated that the familiarity of the suicide option as a response to life's difficulties is contributory to such phenomena.

*Pathology of Behavior Occurs as a Reaction to
the Problems of the Culture Itself*

Many deviant reactions, some of which may be considered pathological depending on the context of their occurrence and the perspective of the observer, occur as reactions to the "problems" of the culture itself. They may represent attempts to compensate for something needed in that culture such as (1) bringing in excitement to a monotonous life—as in the cult of snake handling or providing assurance in an uncertain situation as in the fire-walking ceremony; (2) to express resentment against one's culture—such as student riots against authority, the hippie movement against a rapidly changing society, or mass hysteria in intolerable situations; (3) to provide cultural "time out"—as in the form of nudism as a vacation from the "ordinary" life; or (4) to provide cultural adaptation—as in the case of religious conversion as part of transcultural adaptation (Lebra, 1970).

Comment

An attempt has been made to review the material from various cultural settings on minor psychological disturbances. It is believed that severe clinical psychopathology manifested in psychoses is caused by multiple factors with a greater weight of biological influence, which makes the study of the cultural contribution relatively difficult. By contrast, the minor pathologies observed in daily life are more closely related to the psychological aspect, as well as the sociocultural aspect, and such behavior is worth studying as a projection of cultural traits.

Unfortunately, a systematic cross-cultural study of such minor psychological disturbances is still in the beginning stages. We are at present observing and collecting as much data as possible from various individual cultural settings and discussing the implications presented by such data.

It has been emphasized that the nature of stress—the psychological cause of emotional disturbance—is a very complicated issue. There is a need to differentiate more specifically the kinds of stress with which we are dealing. The same efforts should be applied to the study of psychopathology—the psychological manifestation as a reaction to the stress. This is particularly true in the field of cross-cultural study, since the nature of stress and psychopathology may have different implications in various sociocultural settings needing dynamic interpretation.

The culture of a society should be seen as a complex entity composed of multiple traits or numerous dimensions. There is no single way to describe the nature of the stress and psychopathology occurring in a society. In practice, a particular dimension of it may be studied. Then the information regarding every dimension should be integrated so that the entire picture concerning the relationship between stress and psychopathology can be understood from the cultural point of view.

Note

1. An earlier version of the chapter was presented at the Conference of Contributors to the *Handbook of Cross-Cultural Psychology*, held under the auspices of the East-West Center in Honolulu, Hawaii, January 1976. The authors would like to express special thanks to Maria Brandl who contributed a sensitive and useful critique of the chapter.

References

APPELS, A. Coronary heart disease as a cultural disease. *Psychotherapy and Psychosomatics*, 1973, 22, 320–324.

BACON, M. K. Cross-cultural studies in drinking. In P. G. Bourne & R. Fox, (Eds.), *Alcoholism: Progress in research and treatment*, New York: Academic Press, 1973.

BALES, R. F. Cultural differences in rates of alcoholism. *Quarterly Journal of Studies on Alcohol*, 1949, 6, 480–499.

BERRY, J. W. & ANNIS, R. C. Acculturative stress, the role of ecology, culture and differentiation. *Journal of Cross-Cultural Psychology*, 1974, 5, 382–406.

BOISEN, A. T. Economic distress and religious experience: A study of the Holy Rollers. *Psychiatry*, 1939, 2, 185–194.

————. Religion and personality adjustments. *Psychiatry*, 1942, 5, 209–218.

BOURGUIGNON, E. "Possession" and "trance" in cross-cultural studies of mental health. In W. P. Lebra (Ed.), *Culture-bound syndromes, ethnopsychiatry, and alternate therapies*, Honolulu: University Press of Hawaii, 1976.

BOYER, L. B. & BOYER, R. M. [Some effects of acculturation on the vicissitudes of the aggressive drive.] *Acta Psiqiátrica y Psicológica de América Latina*, 1965, pp. 37.

BURKE, E. L. Drug usage and reported effects in a select adolescent population. *Journal of Psychedelic Drugs*, 1971, 3(2), 55–62.

BURTON-BRADLEY, B. G. The amok syndrome in Papua and New Guinea. *Medical Journal of Australia*, 1968, 1, 252–256.

———. The psychiatry of cargo cult. *Medical Journal of Australia*, 1973, 2, 388–392.

CAREY, J. T. The ideology of autonomy in popular lyrics: A content analysis. *Psychiatry*, 1969, 32, 150–164.

CARSTAIRS, G. M. Daru and bhang: Cultural factors in the choice of intoxicant. *Quarterly Journal of Studies on Alcohol*, 1954, 15, 220–237.

———. Hinjra and juryan: Two derivatives of Hindu attitudes to sexuality. *British Journal of Medical Psychiatry*, 1956, 29, 128–138.

CASEY, R. P. Religion and personal adjustment. *Psychiatry*, 1945, 8, 13–17.

CATTELL, R. B., & WARBURTON, F. W. A cross-cultural comparison of patterns of extraversion and anxiety. *British Journal of Psychology*, 1961, 52, 3–15.

CAUDILL, W., & SCARR, H. A. Japanese value orientation and culture change. *Ethnology*, 1962, 1, 53–91.

CAWTE, J. E. Malgri: A culture-bound syndrome. In W. P. Lebra (Ed.), *Culture-bound syndromes, ethno-psychiatry, and alternate therapies*. Honolulu: University Press of Hawaii, 1976.

CHANCE, N. A. A cross-cultural study of social cohesion and depression. *Transcultural Psychiatric Research Review and Newsletter*, 1964, 1, 19–21.

CHURCHILL, W. *Homosexual behavior among males.* New York: Hawthorn, 1968.

CLARK, R. A. Theosophical occultism and mental hygiene. *Psychiatry*, 1944, 7, 237–243.

COLEMAN, J. C. *Abnormal psychology and modern life* (3rd ed.). Chicago: Scott, Foresman, 1964.

DEUTSCH, A. Observations on a sidewalk ashram. *Archives of General Psychiatry*, 1975, 32, 166–175.

DEVOS, G. A., & WAGATSUMA, H. Minority status and deviancy in Japan. In W. Caudill and T.-Y. Lin (Eds.), *Mental health research in Asia and the Pacific*. Honolulu: East-West Center Press, 1969.

DIAZ-GUERRERO, R. Test anxiety in Mexican and American school children. In C. D. Spielberger & R. Diaz-Guerrero (Eds.), *Cross-cultural anxiety*. Washington, D.C.: Hemisphere, 1976.

DISTLER, L. S. The adolescent "hippie" and the emergence of a matristic culture. *Psychiatry*, 1970, 33, 362–371.

DOI, L. T. *The anatomy of dependence.* Tokyo: Kodansha International, 1973.

DURKHEIM, E. *Suicide* (J. A. Spaulding & G. Simpson, trans.). New York: Free Press, 1951. (Originally published, 1897.)

ELLIS, G. The amok of the Malays. *Journal of Mental Science*, 1893, 39, 325–338.

ENDLER, N. S., & MAGNUSSON, D. Multidimensional aspects of state and trait anxiety: A cross-cultural study of Canadian and Swedish college students. In C. D. Spielberger & R. Diaz-Guerrero (Eds.), *Cross-cultural anxiety*. Washington: Hemisphere, 1976.

ENGELSMANN, F., MURPHY, H. B. M., PRINCE, R., LEDUC, M., & DEMERS, H. Variations in responses to a symptom check-list by age, sex, income, residence, and ethnicity. *Social Psychiatry*, 1972, 7, 150–156.

EUNGPRABHANTH, V. Suicide in Thailand. *Forensic Science*, 1975, 5, 43–51.

EWING, J. A., ROUSE, B. A., & PELLIZZARI, E. D. Alcohol sensitivity and ethnic background. *American Journal of Psychiatry*, 1974, *131*, 206–210.

FALLERS, L. A., & FALLERS, M. C. Homicide and suicide in Busoga. In Paul Bohannan (Ed.), *African homicide and suicide*. Princeton, N.J.: Princeton University Press, 1960.

FENICHEL, O. *The psychoanalytic theory of nuerosis*. New York: Norton, 1945.

FIELD, P. B. A new cross-cultural study of drunkenness. In D. J. Pittman and C. R. Snyder (Eds.), *Society, culture, and drinking patterns*. New York: Wiley, 1962.

FIRTH, R. Suicide and risk-taking in Tikopia society. *Psychiatry*, 1961, 24, 1–17.

FORD, C. S. A brief description of human sexual behavior in cross-cultural perspective. In P. H. Hoch & J. Zubin (Eds.), *Psychosexual development in health and disease*. New York: Grune & Stratton, 1949.

GANAPATHI, M. N., & Rao, A. V. A study on suicide in Madurai. *Journal of Indian Medicine Association*, 1966, 46, 18–23.

GIEL, R., KITAW, Y., WORKNEH, F., & MESFIN, R. Ticket to heaven: Psychiatric illness in a religious community in Ethiopia. *Social Science & Medicine*, 1974, 8, 549–556.

GOODWIN, D. W. Is alcoholism hereditary? *Archives of General Psychiatry*, 1971, 25, 545–549.

GRINKER, R. R., SR. Neurosis, psychosis, and the borderline states. In A. M. Freedman, H. I. Kaplan, & B. J. Sadock (Eds.), *Comprehensive textbook of psychiatry II*. Baltimore: Williams & Wilkins, 1975.

GRINKER, R. R., SR., & HOLZMAN, P. S. Schizophrenic pathology in young adults. *Archives of General Psychiatry*, 1973, 28, 168–175.

GUTHRIE, G. M., VERSTRAETE, A., DEINES, M. M. & STERN, R. M. Symptoms of stress in four societies. *Journal of Social Psychology*, 1975, 95, 165–172.

HALIFAX, J., & WEIDMAN, H. Religion as a mediating institution in acculturation: the case of santeria in Greater Miami. In R. H. Cox (Ed.), *Religious Systems and Psychiatry*. Springfield, Ill.: Thomas, 1973.

HALLOWELL, A. I. Fear and anxiety as cultural and individual variables in a primitive society. *Journal of Social Psychology*, 1938, 9, 25–47.

HEMMI, T. Social-psychiatric study of drug abuse in Japan. *Proceedings of the Fifth World Congress of Psychiatry*. Amsterdam: Excerpta Medica, 1971.

HENDIN, H. Suicide. In A. M. Freedman & H. I. Kaplan (Eds.), *Comprehensive textbook of psychiatry*. Baltimore: Williams & Wilkins, 1967.

HIPPLER, A. E. Some unplanned consequences of planned culture change. In *Higher latitudes of North America: Socio-economic studies in regional development*. University of Alberta, Boreal Institute, Occasional Publication 6:11–21, 1968.

HOLZNER, A. S., & DING, L. K. White dragon pearls in Hong Kong: A study of young women drug addicts. *International Journal of the Addictions*, 1973, 8, 253–263.

HONIGMANN, J. J. Cultural dynamics of sex: A study in culture and personality. *Psychiatry*, 1947, 10, 37–47.

HORTON, D. The functions of alcohol in primitive societies: A cross-cultural study. *Quarterly Journal of Studies on Alcohol*, 1943, 4, 200–210.

HOSKIN, J. O., FRIEDMAN, M. I., & CAWTE, J. E. A high incidence of suicide in a preliterate-primitive society. *Psychiatry*, 1969, 32, 200–210.

HSU, J., & TSENG, W.-S. Family relations in classic Chinese opera. *International Journal of Social Psychiatry*, 1974, 20, 159–172.

IKEDA, Y. An epidemic of emotional disturbance among leprosarium nurses in a setting of low morale and social change. *Psychiatry*, 1966, 29, 152–164.

JELLINEK, E. M. Cultural differences in the meaning of alcoholism. In D. J. Pittman & C. R. Snyder (Eds.), *Society, culture and drinking patterns*. New York: Wiley, 1962.

JONES, I. H. Stereotyped aggression in a group of Australian Western Desert aborigines. *Transcultural Psychiatric Research Review*, 1971, 8, 138–140.

KASAHARA, Y. "Graduation phobia" in the Japanese university. In T. S. Lebra & W. P. Lebra (Eds.), *Japanese culture and behavior: Selected readings*. Honolulu: University Press of Hawaii, 1974a.

―――. Fear of eye-to-eye confrontation among neurotic patients in Japan. In T. S. Lebra & W. P. Lebra (Eds.), *Japanese culture and behavior: Selected readings*. Honolulu: University Press of Hawaii, 1974b.

KATZ, M. M., & SANBORN, K. O. Multi-ethnic studies of psychopathology and normality in Hawaii. In B. S. Brown & E. F. Torrey (Eds.), *International collaboration in mental health*. Rockville, Md.: National Institute of Mental Health, 1973.

KENDALL, R. F., & PITTEL, S. M. Three portraits of the young drug user: Comparison of MMPI group profiles. *Journal of Psychedelic Drugs*, 1971, 3, 63–66.

KIEV, A. Psychotherapeutic aspects of Pentecostal sects among West Indian immigrants to England. *British Journal of Sociology*, 1964, 15, 129–138.

KIM, K. New religions in Korea: The sociocultural consideration. *Journal of Korean Neuropsychiatric Association*, 1972, 11, 31–36.

KINZIE, J. D., RYALS, J., COTTINGTON, F., & McDERMOTT, J. F. Cross-cultural study of depressive symptoms in Hawaii. *International Journal of Social Psychiatry*, 1973, 19, 19–24.

KOJAK, G. The American community in Bangkok, Thailand: A model of social disintegration. *American Journal of Psychiatry*, 1974, 131, 1229–1233.

LA BARRE, W. They shall take up serpents—psychology of the southern snake-handling cult. *Transcultural Psychiatric Research Review*, 1964, 1, 154–157.

LANGNER, T. S. A twenty-two-item screening score of psychiatric symptoms indicating impairment. *Journal of Health and Human Behavior*, 1962, 3, 269–276.

LANGNER, T. S., & MICHAEL, S. T. *Life stress and mental health*. New York: Free Press, 1963.

LASRY, J. C. Multi-cultural comparisons of a mental health scale. In J. W. Berry & W. J. Lonner (Eds.), *Applied cross-cultural psychology: Selected papers from the Second International Conference of the International Association for Cross-Cultural Psychology*. Amsterdam: Swets and Zeitlinger, 1975.

LAUER, R. H. The social readjustment scale and anxiety: A cross-cultural study. *Journal of Psychosomatic Research*, 1973, 17, 171–174.

LAZARUS, R. S. The concepts of stress and disease. In L. Levi (Ed.), *Society, stress and disease* (Vol. I). London: Oxford University Press, 1971.

LAZARUS, R. S., TOMITA, M., OPTON, E., & KODAMA, M. A cross-cultural study of stress-reaction patterns in Japan. *Journal of Personality and Social Psychology,* 1966, *4,* 622–633.

LEBRA, T. S. Religious conversion as a breakthrough for transculturation: A Japanese sect in Hawaii. *Journal of Scientific Study of Religion,* 1970, *9,* 181–196.

LEIGHTON, D. C. Measuring stress levels in school children as a program-monitoring device. *American Journal of Public Health,* 1972, *62,* 799–804.

LEVY, R. I. The community function of Tahitian male transvestitism. *Transcultural Psychiatric Research Review,* 1971, *8,* 51–53.

LIN, T.-Y. Effects of urbanization on mental health. *International Social Science Journal,* 1959, *11,* 24–33.

LYNN, R. *Personality and national character.* Oxford: Pergamon, 1971.

MASUDA, M., & HOLMES, T. H. The Social Readjustment Rating Scale: A cross-cultural study of Japanese and Americans. *Journal of Psychosomatic Research,* 1967, *11,* 227–237.

McANDREW, C., & EDGERTON, R. B. *Drunken comportment: A social exploration.* Chicago: Aldine, 1969.

McCLELLAND, D. C., DAVIS, W. N., KALIN, R., & WARNER, E. *The drinking man.* New York: Free Press, 1972.

MEDALIA, N. Z., & LARSEN, O. N. Diffusion and belief in a collective delusion: The Seattle windshield pitting epidemic. *American Sociological Review,* 1958, *23,* 180–186.

MOSS, P. D., & McEVEDY, C. P. An epidemic of overbreathing among schoolgirls. *British Medical Journal,* 1966, *2,* 1295–1300.

MUHANGI, J. R. A preliminary report on "mass hysteria" in an Akole school in Uganda. *East African Medical Journal,* 1973, *50,* 304–309.

MUNROE, R. L., MUNROE, R. H., & WHITING, J. W. The couvade: A psychological analysis. *Ethos,* 1973, *1,* 30–74.

MURDOCK, G. P. The social regulation of sexual behavior. In P. H. Hoch & J. Zubin (Eds.), *Psychosexual development in health and disease.* New York: Grune & Stratton, 1949.

MURPHY, H. B. M. History and the evolution of syndromes: The striking case of latah and amok. In M. Hammer, K. Salzinger, & S. Sutton (Eds.), *Psychopathology: Contributions from the biological, behavioral and social sciences.* New York: Wiley-Interscience, 1971.

MURPHY, J. M., & HUGHES, C. C. The use of psychophysiological symptoms as indicators of disorder among Eskimos. In J. M. Murphy & A. H. Leighton (Eds.), *Approaches to cross-cultural psychiatry.* Ithaca, N.Y.: Cornell University Press, 1965.

NEGRETE, J. C. Cultural influences on social performance of alcoholics: A comparative study. *Quarterly Journal on the Study of Alcoholism,* 1973, *34,* 905–916.

NGUI, P. W. The koro epidemic in Singapore. *Australian and New Zealand Journal of Psychiatry,* 1969, *3,* 263–266.

NITZKIN, J. L. Epidemic transient situational disturbance in an elementary school. *Journal of Florida Medical Association,* 1976, *63,* 357–359.

OFFER, D. The concept of normality. *Psychiatric Annals,* 1973, *3,* 20–29.

OHARA, K. Characteristics of suicides in Japan—especially of parent-child double suicide. *American Journal of Psychiatry*, 1963, *120*, 383–385.

OPLER, M. K. Anthropological and cross-cultural aspects of homosexuality. In J. Marmor (Ed.), *Sexual inversion*, New York: Basic Books, 1965.

PARIN, P. A contribution of ethno-psychoanaltyic investigation to the theory of aggression. *International Journal of Psycho-Analysis*, 1972, *53*, 251–257.

PRINCE, R. H. Abbreviated techniques for assessing mental health in interviewing surveys: An example from central Montreal. *Laval Medical*, 1967, *38*, 58–62.

RIN, H. A study of the etiology of koro in respect to the Chinese concept of illness. *International Journal of Social Psychiatry*, 1965, *11*, 7–13.

RINDER, I. D. New directions and an old problem: The definition of normality. *Psychiatry*, 1964, *27*, 109–115.

ROTHENBERG, A. Puerto Rico and aggression. *American Journal of Psychiatry*, 1964, *120*, 962–970.

RUBEL, A. J. The epidemiology of a flok illness: Susto in Hispanic America. *Ethnology*, 1964, *3*, 268–282.

RUDIN, S. A. National motives predict psychogenic death rates 25 years later. *Science*, 1968, *160*, 901–903.

SARTORIUS, N. [Culture and the epidemiology of depression.] *Psychiatria, Neurologia, Neurochirugia*, 1973, *76*, 479–487.

SCHULER, E. A., & PARENTON, V. J. A recent epidemic of hysteria in a Louisiana high school. *Journal of Social Psychology*, 1943, *17*, 221–235.

SELYE, H. *The stress of life*. New York: McGraw-Hill, 1956.

SHARMA, S. Cross-cultural comparisons of anxiety: Methodological problems. *Topics in Culture Learning*, 1977, *5*, 166–173.

SINGER, K. The choice of intoxicant among the Chinese. *British Journal of Addiction*, 1974, *69*, 257–268.

SLABY, A. E., & SEALY, J. R. Black liberation, women's liberation. *American Journal of Psychiatry*, 1973, *130*, 196–200.

SOUEIF, M. I. Hashish consumption in Egypt, with special reference to psychosocial aspects. *Bulletin on Narcotics*, 1967, *19*, 1–12.

SPIELBERGER, C. D., & DIAZ-GUERRERO, R. (Eds.). *Cross-cultural anxiety*. Washington, D.C.: Hemisphere, 1976.

SPIRO, M. E. Religious systems as culturally constituted defense mechanisms. In M. E. Spiro (Ed.). *Context and meaning in cultural anthropology*. New York: Free Press, 1965.

SROLE, L., LANGNER, T. S., MICHAEL, S. T., OPLER, M. K., & RENNIE, T. A. C. *Mental health in the metropolis*. New York: McGraw-Hill, 1962.

STAINBROOK, E. A cross-cultural evaluation of depressive reactions. In P. H. Hoch & J. Zubin (Eds.), *Depression*. New York: Grune & Stratton, 1954.

SUWANLERT, S. A study of kratom eaters in Thailand. *Bulletin on Narcotics*, 1975, *27*, No. 3.

TAN, E. S. Epidemic hysteria. *Medical Journal of Malaya*, 1963, *18*, 72–76.

TANAKA-MATSUMI, J., & MARSELLA, A. J. Cross-cultural variations in the phenomenological experience of depression: I. Word association studies. *Journal of Cross-Cultural Psychology*, 1976, *7*, 379–396.

TEOH, J. I. The changing psychopathology of amok. *Psychiatry*, 1972, 35, 345–351.

TEOH, J. I., SOEWONDO, S., & SIDHARTA, M. Epidemic hysteria in Malaysian schools: An illustrative episode. *Psychiatry*, 1975, 38, 258–268.

TRAMER, L., & BENTOVIM, L. Clinical psychological study on eastern drug addicts. *Confina Psychiatrica*, 1961, 4, 194–213.

TSENG, W.-S. The nature of somatic complaints among psychiatric patients: The Chinese case. *Comprehensive Psychiatry*, 1975, 16, 237–245.

TSENG, W.-S., & HSU, J. Chinese culture, personality formation and mental illness. *International Journal of Social Psychiatry*, 1970, 16, 5–14.

———. The Chinese attitude toward parental authority as expressed in Chinese children's stories. *Archives of General Psychiatry.*, 1972, 26, 28–34.

TSUJIOKA, B., & CATTELL, R. B. A cross-cultural comparison of second-stratum questionnaire personality factor structures—anxiety and extraversion—in America and Japan. *Journal of Social Psychology*, 1965, 65, 205–219.

VATUK, V. P., & VATUK, S. Chatorpan: A culturally defined form of addiction. *Transcultural Psychiatric Research Review*, 1967, 4, 27–30.

VOGEL, E. F. Entrance examinations and emotional disturbances in Japan's "new middle class." In R. J. Smith & R. K. Beardsley (Eds.), *Japanese culture, its development and characteristics*. Chicago: Aldine, 1962.

WESTERMEYER, J. On the epidemicity of amok violence. *Archives of General Psychiatry*, 1973a, 28, 873–876.

———. Grenade-amok in Laos: A psychosocial perspective. *International Journal of Social Psychiatry*, 1973b, 19, 251–260.

———. Assassination in Laos: Its psychosocial dimensions. *Archives of General Psychiatry*, 1973c, 28, 740–743.

———. Opium smoking in Laos: A survey of 40 addicts. *American Journal of Psychiatry*, 1974, 131, 165–170.

WITTKOWER, E. D., & DUBREUIL, G. Psychocultural stress in relation to mental illness. *Social Science and Medicine*, 1973, 7, 691–704.

World Health Organization. *World Health Statistics Report*, 1973, 26(3).

———. *Problems and programmes related to alcohol and drug dependence in 33 countries*, Publ. 6. Geneva: WHO, 1974.

YAP, P. M. Koro—a culture-bound depersonalization syndrome. *British Journal of Psychiatry*, 1965, 111, 43–50.

ZAGUIRRE, J. C. "Amuck." *Journal of Philippine Federation of Private Medical Practitioners*, 1957, 6, 1138–1149.

ZAIDI, S. M. Sociocultural change and value conflict in developing countries: A case study of Pakistan. In W. Caudill & T. Y. Lin (Eds.), *Mental health research in Asia and the Pacific*. Honolulu: East-West Center Press, 1969.

ZUNG, W. K. A cross-cultural survey of depressive symptomatology in normal adults. *Journal of Cross-Cultural Psychology*, 1972, 3, 177–183.

4

Psychological Disorders of
Clinical Severity[1]

Juris G. Draguns

Contents

Abstract

This chapter deals with the "core areas" of psychopathology across cultures that, as a rule, are recognized as disturbed by the sufferer's peers in the milieu in which they occur as well as by outside professional observers. In the rough sense, the patterns of disturbance covered in this chapter correspond to the psychoses, neuroses, and personality disturbance, as they are labeled and conceptualized in Europe and North America, with particular emphasis upon the first of these three categories.

Upon the examination of a great many monocultural, bicultural, and multicultural investigations, it is concluded that culture exerts a noteworthy influence upon manifestations of psychopathology in its overtly observed expressions and subjectively reported experiences. The specific avenues of this influence are outlined on the basis of the evidence thus far accumulated; in particular, the notion that psychopathology represents a self-defeating caricature of the culture in which it occurs is critically examined. Much less information is extant on the differences across cultures in rates of psychopathology, and suggestions for further investigation of this difficult issue are offered.

The foregoing considerations do not argue against the existence of a number of broad, and culturally structured, dimensions of psychopathological experience on which human disturbed behavior can be universally placed. Four such axes are tentatively proposed in the chapter as pancultural elements of psychological confusion, distress, and ineffectuality.

Introduction

This chapter is concerned with what are traditionally considered the core areas of abnormal psychology and clinical psychiatry: the socially visible and grossly disabling patterns of maladaptive behavior. The objectives of the chapter are to review what is known about the constancy and variation of such states across the world and, in the process, to share with readers the conceptual and methodological complexities of this area of investigation. Inevitably, the boundaries of the topics are not neatly delineated. This is particularly the case in relation to the ground covered by Tseng and Hsu in Chapter 3 and by Marsella in Chapter 6 and, to a lesser extent, by Guthrie and Tanco in Chapter 2. In all of these cases, some overlap in the information given and topics covered is inevitable. By way of an attempt at explicit delimitation, the scope of this chapter can be specified as pertaining to the psychological disturbances that in the traditional psychiatric nosology are encompassed in the categories of psychosis, neurosis, and personality disturbance. Such a delineation, of necessity, remains approximate, especially as the relevance of these diagnostic categories—and of their more specific components—remains an open issue in relation to the examination of abnormal behavior in cross-cultural perspective.

Perhaps a more appropriate way of introducing the objectives is to list some of the basic questions around which a major share of empirical and conceptual work in this area is organized:

1. What is the nature and extent of culture's influence upon abnormal behavior?
2. Within what limits do manifestations of psychological disturbance remain culturally invariant, both in their overall frequency and in their various specific modes of expression?

3. In what ways and to what degree do cultures differ in making sense of, construing, and reacting to abnormal behavior?
4. What are the boundaries of "normal" and "abnormal" behavior in various cultures?

Transcending these concerns, the cross-cultural investigation inquires into the *culture's role* in pathogenesis and pathoplasticity (Yap, 1974; Zutt, 1967). In paraphrase, these issues respectively focus on the roles of culture in causing and shaping abnormal behavior. In the former case, what is at issue is the variation in frequency of psychological disorders as a function of cultural characteristics. In the latter instance, the question is directed to the influence of the culture in channeling, patterning, or coloring the manifestations of psychological disturbance.[2]

As mentioned in the Introduction to this volume, this chapter is being written against the background of a paradigm clash (Kuhn, 1962) in the parent discipline. Widely invoked terms such as mental illness, psychopathology, symptom, treatment, and cure can no longer be used without self-consciousness. They are likely to be automatically interpreted against the background of the clash of models and metaphors in the domain of disturbed behavior. On the one hand, traditionalists hold that the basic patterns of psychological disturbance have been discovered, differentiated, and named. In their view, this concept of mental illness provides the best available metaphor for encompassing all the manifestations of psychological disturbance. Within the confines of this position, the task of the cross-cultural investigator is relatively clear-cut and circumscribed: to observe, compare, and tabulate the various patterns of disturbance. Such procedures are guided by the assumption that the objects of cross-cultural investigation of abnormal behavior exist in a stable and comparable way across space and time.

Juxtaposed to this perspective—oftentimes descriptively or polemically identified with the medical model—is the orientation of the more socially minded investigators in the field of psychopathology in general and of cross-cultural study in particular. Proponents of this position (e.g., Scheff, 1966; Szasz, 1961, 1969; Ullmann & Krasner, 1975) hold that the very acts of identifying, labeling, and classifying behavior as abnormal are inescapably subject to cultural shaping—that psychopathology is not something that occurs but is a construction that is cognitively imposed upon certain kinds of behavior. It is, moreover, highly likely that these constructions are not identically invoked across geographical or social barriers.

For these reasons, this chapter cannot confine itself to the problem of examining psychological disturbance around the world within a comprehensive, generally applicable frame of reference. Rather, the consideration of psychopathology from the perspective of its own culture must be taken into account as well. Specifically, among the subjects considered will be the culturally indigenous conceptions of, classificatory schemes on, and attitudes toward, psychological disorder. Under the umbrella of a widely used dichotomy in cross-cultural disciplines (Brislin, Lonner, & Thorndike, 1973; Triandis, Malpass, & Davidson, 1972, 1973), this chapter will attempt to balance the etic—or universal—and emic—or culturally unique—perspectives in considering psychopathology around the world.

The issues with which the student of abnormal behavior and culture is confronted are not unique to this area of inquiry. They overlap with such problems as the relationship of society to its deviant members, the socially shared conceptual models for making sense out of behavioral deviation, and the thresholds of tolerance for various kinds of atypical, bizarre, or threatening actions. These issues are also germane to the extent and limits of social shaping of psychopathology. The consideration and comparison of what constitutes abnormal behavior, or how it is manifested in various cultural settings, potentially provides a revealing "laboratory of nature," full of conditions that cannot be practically or ethically imposed or manipulated by social scientists. The topics and findings of psychopathological phenomena in relation to culture are of possible interest to both social and clinical psychology and may shed light on some of the basic questions raised by these disciplines.

Origins of Investigation into
Cross-Cultural Psychopathology

In its relatively brief history, coextensive with the development of the disciplines of psychiatry, psychology, and cultural anthropology, the field of psychopathology in relation to culture arose rather casually and inconspicuously. Its origins can be traced to subsidiary interests of some of the pioneers of descriptive psychiatry, notably Kraepelin (1904), in the distribution and modes of expression of the disorders as observed by them in cultures very different from their own. Even antedating this trend, there began appearing the reports by medical, anthropological, and other Western observers on syndromes of psychiatric disturbance, encountered outside European and Western settings, that were alien and unfamiliar to Western psychiatric experience (see Arieti & Meth, 1959; H. B. M. Murphy, 1972a; and Yap, 1972). These reports began the fascination with culture-specific patterns of psychological disturbance, such as *amok, latah, windigo*, and *susto*. These two developments marked a direction in transcultural psychiatric effort that has not been fully overcome to this day: the equating of the transcultural with the exotic and the study of cultural effects upon psychopathology in the form of their most dramatic and conspicuous manifestations (cf. Draguns, 1977a; Favazza & Oman, 1978). Even modern textbooks on transcultural and comparative psychiatry (Kiev, 1972; Pfeiffer, 1970; Yap, 1974) continue to reflect this trend. The bulk of information contained in these volumes pertains to the psychological disturbance of non-Western groups generally and to the traditional, archaic, or "primitive" groups specifically. Africa, South East Asia, and Latin America loom large in these accounts, especially in reference to rural and tribal population groups. By contrast, relatively little information is presented that would bear directly on cultures closer to the investigators' own base: the variations in psychopathology as they are found in the several pluralistic societies of the New World, including the United States, or any differences and similarities among the psychiatrically impaired members of several Western cultures.

Psychiatrists, however, have not been the only contributors to the investigation of psychopathology across cultures. Early results of field work undertaken by anthropologists as well have included—on the empirical level—the description of abnormal behavior in the cultures investigated (cf. Linton, 1956; Kennedy, 1973) and—on the conceptual plane—the raising of the issue concerning the application of relative or absolute standards in the identification of abnormal behavior in several cultures (Devereux, 1956). Parallels were drawn between the grandiose orgiastic destruction of property during the potlatch by the Kwakiutl Indians of the Pacific Northwest and the megalomaniac behavior of psychiatric patients, between the widespread preoccupation with malevolent social influences among the Dobuans of Melanesia and the predominant ideation in clinical paranoid conditions, and between the socially withdrawn demeanor of many Balians and the asocial orientation of schizoids (Benedict, 1934). Yet, the very authors who drew these parallels were also aware of the extreme complexity of the links between culture and psychopathology. They specifically cautioned against the automatic and mindless imposition of our standards of abnormal behavior upon the functional network of very different cultural units. The contribution, then, that has characterized the efforts of cultural anthropologists has been twofold: they enriched our documentation of psychopathology in the natural milieus of its occurrence, and they raised the question concerning the applicability and nature of any etic standards of psychopathology to all human groups. As a more specific facet of this general issue, they introduced the problem of the "sick society" or culture and asked the question: Is psychopathology, as a matter of definition, infrequent in any cultural milieu (see Draguns, 1977b; Jacoby, 1967; and Chapter 3) or can the modal characteristics of the members of a culture be realistically and meaningfully described by such terms as "neurotic," "paranoid," or "hysterical," as Montague (1961), for example, has done?

Psychologists, both clinical and social, have been relative latecomers to the interdisciplinary enterprise of attempting to link abnormal behavior and culture. If there is any common denominator that characterizes their heterogeneous efforts in this field, it is in their concern with the generic relationship between psychological disturbance and its cultural milieu. Anthropologists have carefully documented the psychological disturbance of specific cultural settings, but they have been cautious about generalizing and have, for the most part, refrained from advancing comprehensive formulations on the specific terms of the relationship between abnormal behavior and culture. Psychologists, it seems, have worked more in the area of intergroup comparison than have anthropologists or psychiatrists. Both of these groups have emphasized the description of pathological phenomena within their respective contexts; psychiatrists have focused upon clinical settings and anthropologists, upon cultural milieus.

These interprofessional differences are less marked today than they once were. Instances could be easily advanced of anthropologists conducting research like psychologists, psychiatrists like anthropologists, and psychologists like psychiatrists. There is also an increased tendency toward teamwork and interdisciplinary collaboration. Nonetheless, the influences of these three professional traditions continue to mark, albeit in a diluted way, the empirical and conceptual contributions of each to this field. Indirectly, these differences in the historical points of departure increase the difficulty of surveying and integrating the disparate observations and findings that have been accumulating, at an accelerating rate, throughout this century.

Methodological Considerations

An Attempt at a Typology of Investigations:
Monocultural, Bicultural, Multicultural

The empirical studies that fall within the scope of abnormal behavior in relation to culture are exceedingly diverse. They differ in format, populations, and context of investigation. In reference to the first parameter, the studies extant can be divided into monocultural, bicultural, and multicultural, the last category shading off at its extreme into pancultural, a standard that, as yet, no empirical investigation of abnormal behavior has achieved.

Monocultural research.   The majority of the publications accumulated pertain to monocultural studies, i.e., to reports of observation or research of psychopathological phenomena that from the point of view of the observer—usually a Westerner—are culturally noteworthy or atypical. The account by a United States psychiatrist of the psychiatric problems presented by a predominantly lower-class Brazilian clientele in Rio de Janeiro would be one example (Brody, 1973). Others include: a description of a culture-specific syndrome encountered among the Canadian Ojibwa Indians (Parker, 1960), a report on the concept of madness among the Moro-Ayoreo Indians of Paraguay and Bolivia (Pagés Larraya, 1973), an investigation of patients who seek out healers at religious shrines in Ghana (Field, 1960), and the numerical tally of the psychological disorders identified and diagnosed in an Iranian province (Bash & Bash-Liechti, 1969). What all of these instances have in common is their orientation toward, and sensitivity to, cultural factors. While no explicit comparisons of groups across culture lines were undertaken in any of these studies, implicitly their results were interpreted in light of cultural factors and variations. Typically, although not invariably, there is another transcultural aspect to these investigations: the investigator and the subjects of the study come from two different cultures. In these instances, there is at least an informal comparison between the culture that the investigator knows and the one that he encounters.

Both anthropologists and psychiatrists have extensively practiced the type of study just described. Anthropologists, however, have gravitated toward the community context while the psychiatrists have often focused upon institutional settings. Thus, two subcategories of studies have come into being: those of patients in asylums, hospitals, and other kinds of therapeutic or custodial institutions and those of disturbed people in their "natural habitat": the communities in which they have spent their lives. The current trend, independent of disciplines, favors studies that are not restricted to the institutional settings. It is widely recognized that abnormal behavior is to some degree the function of the milieu in which it occurs (Paul, 1969; Scheff, 1966), although the extent of this influence continues to be a matter of controversy (Gove, 1975). Moreover, it should be borne in mind that the very institutions in which abnormal behavior is studied are culturally extraneous—imported as they are from, or imposed by, the West—in a great many non-Western and developing countries (Berne, 1956; Dawson, 1964; Singer, Aarons, & Aronetta, 1967). This recognition carries with it the implication that individuals confined within these institutions are not representative of the entire disturbed segment of the population and not comparable to their counterparts in those Western countries where the role of the mental hospital is more solidly and traditionally established.

Increasingly then the trend has been to go beyond the institutional walls and to investigate people who exhibit some kind of psychological impairment or disturbance while they continue to reside in their communities. This objective is most systematically pursued in psychiatric census or epidemiological studies that endeavor to assess the psychiatric status of an entire geographically specified population or a random or representative sample within it. A host of such studies have been conducted in different parts of the world, from Iceland (Helgason, 1964) to Taiwan (Lin, 1953; 1969). Not many of these studies are explicitly cultural in their orientation, and even fewer have been designed with the possibility of a cross-cultural comparison in mind (e.g., D. C. Leighton, Harding, Macklin, Macmillan, & A. H. Leighton, 1963; J. M. Murphy, 1972). As a result, their conceptual and operational definitions of psychopathology differ widely and unsystematically as do their data-gathering and processing procedures. These findings constitute the raw materials for the eventual comparison of epidemiological data, provided that the complexities and difficulties of using them for cross-cultural purposes are recognized and faced (Dohrenwend & Dohrenwend, 1969, 1974).

Bicultural studies. Within the relatively recent past, these monocultural research efforts have been supplemented by a variety of comparisons of psychopathology between two cultures. The goal has been to compare psychiatrically disturbed individuals with their counterparts across the culture gulf. This objective has often been unattainable because of the many potential noncultural sources of difference that obtrude upon the implementation of these comparisons. The various modes of overcoming these hurdles will constitute the topic of a later section of this chapter.

Multicultural studies. Finally, there is a small but increasing number of multilateral investigations, aspiring in some instances to worldwide representativeness, although not inclusiveness. The surveys of symptomatology of depression and schizophrenia conducted among psychiatrists by means of questionnaires are examples of this type of investigation (Murphy, Wittkower, & Chance, 1967; Murphy, Wittkower, Fried, & Ellenberger, 1963), as are the instances of the use of various kinds of social indicators related to psychopathology, such as rates of psychiatric hospitalization (Lynn, 1971), suicide (Rudin, 1968), or death from specific psychophysiological diseases (Rudin, 1968). As a byproduct of their validation, or specifically for cross-cultural purposes, the scores on some depression scales (Zung, 1969) and anxiety scales (Cattell & Warburton, 1961) have been multiculturally compared. Finally, the Human Research Area Files (see chapters by Barry and by Naroll, Michik, and Naroll in Volume 2) have so far seen little use that directly pertains to psychopathology. Naroll (1969) used this repository of data to derive a complex indicator of the prominence of suicide in the various ethnographies. He then relied upon this index in a cross-cultural test of the thwarting-disorientation theory of suicide, i.e., the view that suicide thrives in cultures that are high in the level of frustration imposed and in the assignment of responsibility for such frustration. Denko (1964, 1966), in two studies based upon the Human

Research Area Files, concerned herself with the taxonomy of culture-bound disorders and with indigenous explanations of psychological disturbance. Limitations in the use of this source are traceable to the rather modest amount of primary information available on disturbances of behavior in the original ethnographic sources. In many cases, sophisticated indirect measures, along the lines of Naroll (1969), will need to be developed and judiciously and cautiously used.

Current investigators of psychopathology in relation to culture have several options: they can immerse themselves in a single cultural network or maze way (Wallace, 1961) in order to understand its psychopathological expressions and relate them to other cultural features; they can compare psychopathology of two cultural milieus; or they can take a bird's eye view of psychopathological manifestations around the globe. When one of these courses of action is chosen, a number of other decisions must be faced. Specifically, it must be decided whom to compare, by what methods, on the basis of what units, and by means of what instruments. Once these choices are made, another set of questions—more conceptual in nature—must be answered: to whom are the findings applicable, with what limitations and what safeguards and in the light of what theories? These questions on generalization are overshadowed by a more general dilemma: when and on what basis is the relationship between culture and psychopathology established? The sections that follow take up this question.

Dilemmas and Choices for the Investigators

Who is to be studied?   This question is tantamount to the quest for an operational definition of psychopathology that would be applicable across cultures. Such a definition can be narrow or broad, conceptually derived or dictated by practical considerations, indigenous to the culture studied or imposed from the outside. Typically, investigators in this area have proceeded on the basis of the judgments of abnormality already made for them at the sites of their research. Operationally, the concept of abnormality has in many studies been equated with psychiatric hospitalization and/or the use of other psychiatric services. This procedure has resulted in the application of narrow or minimal criteria of psychopathology. Consequences of applying these criteria include their uncontrolled variability across cultures—an issue of special import when attempts are made to compare cultures at high degrees of contrast. Moreover, there are the unresolved questions of who constitutes the psychologically impaired, but psychiatrically unrecognized, segments of the population and how these people are handled in their cultural context. Another consequence of relying only on hospitalization or use of psychiatric services has been the disproportionate accumulation of information on extreme and dramatic disturbance across cultures, and as a result, our knowledge on abnormal behavior in other cultures is selectively concentrated upon psychoses. Relatively little is known about cultural variations in major ambulatory psychological disorders such as neurosis and personality disturbance.

If the typical cultural investigation of psychopathology has been based on such narrow criteria of psychopathology, the epidemiological studies have often tended toward a broad and inclusive definition of psychological disorder, often based upon the presence of psychiatric symptoms, sometimes with derivative judgments of the degree of psychological impairment. Application of these norms of psychopathology resulted in the widely publicized finding that only 18 percent of the participants in the Midtown Manhattan project were psychiatrically unimpaired and symptom free (Srole, Langner, Michael, Opler, & Rennie, 1962). While such a finding may be of interest and even valid within its own frame of reference, it pertains to something other than psychological disorder, mental illness, or psychiatric disturbance as these terms are generally used and practically applied. It is widely recognized among researchers in psychopathology that discrete symptoms are both widespread and of limited differential diagnostic value (see Phillips, 1968; Phillips & Draguns, 1971). Obviously, presence of discrete symptoms constitutes both a very broad—and conceptually questionable—criterion of psychopathology.

Another broad-band notion of psychological impairment is implicit in some anthropological and other writings that capitalize on parallels between modal personality attributes of various cultural groups and the characteristic features of various psychiatric syndromes. These judgments have variously been applied to small and remote traditional groups (DuBois, 1944), and modern nation states (Montague, 1961), including our own society (Fromm, 1955). While the idea of "society as a patient" or "the sick society" has a certain degree of intellectual appeal, it usually rests upon a rather loose and vague extension of the concept of psychopathology, resulting in reasoning based on analogies rather than on categorization. Jacoby (1967) in his taxonomy of absolute and relative criteria of psychologically aberrant states leaves room for "transcultural insanity," a state of disturbance shared by an entire culture, but he admits that the criteria for such a diagnosis are unknown and unspecified. Most writers in this field would agree that psychological disturbance is of necessity a minority phenomenon in its social milieu, and many would argue that a society of neurotics, let alone of psychotics, is a practical impossibility (e.g., Bastide, 1965; Draguns, 1977b; Yap, 1974).

Between the excessively broad and the extremely narrow criteria of abnormality, attempts have been made to find both a conceptually defensible and a cross-culturally applicable standard. Stepping stones to this end have been provided in the studies of various indigenous conceptions of abnormal behavior and of the classifications within them (e.g., Beiser, Ravel, Collomb, & Egelhoff, 1972; Murphy & Leighton, 1965; Resner & Hartog, 1970). Some sophisticated studies (e.g., A. H. Leighton, Lambo, Hughes, D. C. Leighton, J. M. Murphy, & Macklin, 1963) incorporated this information into their data gathering and compared it with their own research definitions of abnormality.

These attempts hold the promise of providing a corrective to the implicit assumption that still guides many investigators—that abnormal behavior everywhere is similar in scope and in kind and, as a consequence, the criteria of abnormality prevalent in one's own culture can be applied without revision or modification in another cultural milieu. To proceed on this assumption is an instance of a pseudoetic rationale (Brislin, Lonner, & Thorndike, 1973; Triandis, Malpass, & Davidson, 1972, 1973). Such a rationale is predicated upon confusing the observer's own culturally limited perspective with humanly universal experience.

More sophisticated proponents of the universalistic approach to delimiting psychological disturbance in cultural settings other than their own draw a sharp distinction between *adjustment* and *adaptation* (DeVos, 1965, 1976; Kluckhohn, 1962). The former refers to individual process, related to experiencing satisfaction with self and others and fulfilling one's needs and attaining one's goals. The latter pertains to the individual's meeting the criteria of appropriate behavior posited by one's culture. Maladjustment can be judged on a pancultural, universal basis; maladaption is always related to specific cultural standards. This distinction is paralleled by the lines drawn between abnormality and psychopathology (Jacoby, 1967) or "social abnormality" and "psychiatric abnormality" (Honigmann, 1953, 1954). The former concept refers to the judgment of fitness of behavior against standards of the group, the latter to an objectively specifiable disturbance regardless of the context of its occurrence. Honigmann (1953) went further and pinpointed such universal criteria of abnormality as anxiety, pervasiveness of defenses, sensory or motor dysfunction, disorders of affect, distortion of reality, regression, and disintegration. The application of any one of these standards to specific cases in a variety of settings presents problems because an objective, specific, and uniform standard of abnormality is difficult to formulate.

How are the manifestations of abnormal behavior to be grouped and classified? Closely related to the issue just discussed is the problem of applying a classificatory grid to the diverse expresssions of disturbance both within and across the various cultures studied. The earliest historical efforts of cross-cultural investigators rested on the assumption of the universal validity and applicability of the Kraepelinian nosological scheme. Disorders might vary in their specific modes of manifestation, but they were present everywhere in their basic features. As Berne (1959, p. 108) more recently put it:

> Clinically, cultural differences can be treated as mere dialects or accents of a common language; the Italian schizophrenic speaks schizophrenic with an Italian accent, the Siamese manic speaks manic with a Siamese accent.

Indeed, reports have multiplied attesting to the presence of such disorders as schizophrenia and depression in widely different cultures in all parts of the globe (e.g., Kiev, 1972; Pfeiffer, 1970).

Other investigators, however, have been impressed by the heterogeneity of the manifestations of disturbance around the world, with the attendant need for a classification system that would do it justice. The World Health Organization (Lin, 1959, 1967, 1969) has been aware of the divergent diagnostic practices of psychiatrists in its member states and has labored to provide a universally acceptable catalogue of psychiatric disturbance. These efforts, however, have taken the form of reconciling differences among diagnosticians and offering generally acceptable compromises—often with political overtones—rather than a more thorough revision of the classificatory scheme on an empirical and/or conceptual basis.

Other proposals, however, have been made by individual experts or groups of them (e.g., Muñoz, Marconi, Horwitz, & Neveillan, 1966; Savage, Leighton, & Leighton, 1965; Seguin, Castro, Valdivia, & Zapata, 1961) and have generally been in keeping with the dictum of the noted investigator of psychopathology in Africa, Margetts (1965): "The simpler, the better." Thus, these revisions represent a streamlined version of a nosological scheme whose Kraepelinian, traditional features remain recognizable.

As already mentioned in an earlier context, an alternative to a universal scheme of classification is the use of a system of classification that already exists in the culture being investigated. A general conclusion from the studies of such systems is that even cultures very much outside the mainstream of modernization possess fairly detailed, if implicit and casual, classificatory grids for grouping and differentiating psychological disturbance in their own midst. With a few exceptions (e.g., A. H. Leighton et al., 1963) these schemes have been investigated in their own right, rather than being fitted into the research on the empirical manifestations of disorder in various cultures. Yet, recent advances in establishing the equivalence of the components of various national diagnostic systems (Engelsmann, Vinař, Pichot, Hippius, Giberti, Rossi, & Overall, 1971; Kendell, Pichot, & von Cranach, 1974; Pichot, 1967) might point the way for a more systematic comparison of formal and informal, scientific and prescientific, and Western and indigenous systems of classification. These schemes vary in details, but generally result in the establishment of "translations" from one scheme to another of categories that are differently labeled but are found to correspond to the same constellations of symptoms. These procedures have so far been applied within the relatively narrow range of disparities among the several national variants of essentially the same nosological system as is used in various countries of Europe and America. Potentially, these techniques are applicable to systems more widely divergent in their rationale, origins, and details.

The remaining options go further beyond diagnosis and in the direction of either constructing a rational scheme or "starting from scratch" and relying upon the empirical patterns of coherence as they emerge from factor analysis of symptom data. Within the scope of the factorial approach, the investigator can either concentrate upon a single culture (emically) or on several cultures (etically). The former mode of operation is exemplified by Caudill and Schooler (1969), who obtained and named several culturally and clinically meaningful factors in the psychiatric symptom pools in Japan. Problems arose, however, when the same procedure was replicated in Taiwan (Rin, Schooler, & Caudill, 1972), yielding as it did a combination of factors, some of which were comparable across cultures and some unique to the site of investigation. Beiser (1975) identified four factors of neurotic experience in a large number of Senegalese respondents. The etic application of factor analysis is prominently represented in the work by Lorr and Klett (1968, 1969a, 1969b) and their international group of collaborators. These studies began with the application of the Inpatient Multidimensional Psychiatric Scale, an instrument developed in the United States, to samples of hospitalized patients in Japan and several European countries. This study brought forth a set of factors that was uniform in the various countries but showed a growing amount of residual variance as similarity decreased between the culture studied and the culture where the scale originated. The factorial approach, then, provides a useful expedient but is not the definitive solution in the search for universal units of psychopathological experience.

Units rationally derived, rather than empirically established, constitute the components of two proposed schemes. One of these schemes is presented within the framework of Phillips's (1968) organismic theory of adaptation and its failures. Phillips proposed two dimensions for organizing and comparing the expressions of psychopathology, differentiating such expressions according to *role*—or interpersonal mode of expression—and *sphere*—the organismic channel of manifestation. There are three *roles*: turning against self, turning against others, and avoidance of others. *Spheres* are classified in terms of action, affect, somatization, and thought. The advantage of Phillips's system is that it proceeds from the *symptom* as the basic building block, thus using an objective, public, mathematical method of establishing symptom dominance patterns rather than the highly complex, inferential, private process of traditional diagnostic attribution. Phillips's scheme has been applied in a number of cross-cultural studies (e.g., Draguns, Phillips, Broverman, Caudill, & Nishimae, 1971; Fundia, Draguns, & Phillips, 1971; Nachshon, Draguns, Broverman, & Phillips, 1972). It is not yet clear how complete and inclusive this categorization is for cross-cultural, worldwide use and what, if any, revisions and additions may emerge upon its further application. As yet, the problem of how symptom frequency and intensity interact has not been solved in establishing which sphere and role patterns are dominant in an individual. Does one intense symptom override several that are lower in their intensity? So far, only the number of symptoms and not their relative strengths are taken into account.

Of considerable potential, because of their flexibility and interpersonal character, are the various models of behavioral assessment (Hersen & Bellack, 1976; Kanfer & Saslow, 1965; Goldfried & Kent, 1972). While different in details, they aim at the systematic description of clinically relevant "target behaviors"—i.e., those responses that are considered worth changing by the individual directly affected, by the clinician, or by other persons in the individual's environment. Kanfer and Saslow (1965), in their elaborate scheme, classify observable responses into *symptoms* (dysfunctional behaviors to be learned, relearned, or extinguished), *deficits* (adaptive responses absent from the individual's repertoire), and *assets* (adaptive responses present in such a repertoire). In each case, it is essential to provide specification of the events in the environment that systematically precede and follow the onset of each response. To put it differently, the practitioner of behavioral assessment notes the situational and temporal variations in the occurrence and frequency of responses in any of these three categories. In addition to these data, modern exponents of behavioral assessment (Mahoney, 1974; Meichenbaum, 1977) urge the collection of information on mediational responses: the self-statements and internal dialogues that precede overtly observable behaviors. By these means data high in specificity, objectivity, and applicability across time and space are collected. The framework of behavioral assessment, moreover, provides a potent antidote to the excessive preoccupation with the symptoms and syndromes as self-contained and autonomous entities; maladaptive behavior is viewed as but a link in the chain of an ongoing interaction between the individual and his or her social milieu. For these reasons, the model of behavioral assessment would seem to be highly consonant with the needs and orientations of investigators of psychological disorder across cultures. It is therefore surprising and paradoxical that this model of collecting and classifying data on maladaptive behavior has not yet been systematically applied in cross-cultural research. Habits of thought, practice, and terminology do not change easily, and, as pointed out earlier, the cross-cultural investigation of abnormal behavior is heavily beholden to the medical model in conceptualization and to the Kraepelinian scheme in classification.

How is the study to be implemented?   Once the limits of the broad target population are established, and the lines of dividing it diagnostically are specified, sampling problems must be faced and solved. The bulk of the cross-cultural studies of psychopathology that have been published are based upon samples selected for availability or convenience, rather than their representativeness or randomness. This problem is not unique to the cross-cultural study of abnormal behavior (Brislin, Lonner, & Thorndike, 1973), but it is perhaps more serious than in other domains of cross-cultural psychology. Often, haphazardly selected "bunches" of subjects are used as substitutes for samples in the proper sense of the term (Brislin, 1974). Random or representative samples of the population have been used in some of the culturally oriented epidemiological studies (Cawte, 1972; Kidson & Jones, 1968; A. H. Leighton, et al., 1963) as well as in the comparisons of several subcultural groups sharing the same geographical habitat, e.g., Mexican Americans versus "Anglos" in Texas (e.g., Jaco, 1960) and French versus English Canadians in Montreal (Engelsmann, H. B. M. Murphy, Prince, Leduc, & Demers, 1972). In other situations, however, random or representative samples of psychologically disturbed individuals have rarely been available. A promising development for future investigations, worthy of emulation at other sites, has been the construction of a randomly stratified national sample of psychiatric patients in Japan (Kato, 1969). However, no cross-cultural studies with this sample have as yet been reported. Until these developments bear fruit, many of the findings in the culture and psychopathology literature remain suspect. To what extent their results are the function of the peculiarities of haphazard and nonrandom sample composition rather than genuine cultural parameters remains unknown.

In the absence of true samples in the statistical sense, investigators have turned to five provisional solutions in cross-cultural comparisons:

• Naturalistic studies
• Multidimensional matching
• Diagnostically unitary groups
• Multivariate research designs
• The inversion of dependent and control variables

The study by Saenger (1968) of pools of psychiatric clinic patients in the United States and the Netherlands provides an example of the *naturalistic research approach*. The patient aggregates were studied "as they were," without any attempts to partial out or otherwise control their inevitable sociological, demographic, and biographical disparities. What differences emerged across culture lines—and not surprisingly they were copious— were referred whenever possible to their most likely sources, which in many instances turned out to be other than cultural. The remainder of differences—for which the knowledge of the two settings provides no other plausible explanations—were provisionally traced to the differences between the two cultures in question. The adequacy of this approach is crucially dependent upon three considerations: a specific and detailed description of the subject characteristics, a thorough knowledge of the milieus in the broadly cultural as well as the narrowly institutional sense of the term, and the ability to disentangle on an informal nonstatistical basis the various and possibly interacting influences upon the results. The last condition, in particular, is notoriously difficult of fulfillment and, in any case, cannot be met in an objective and unambiguous manner. Thus, the naturalistic approach to cross-cultural comparison is useful at the beginning but is quite unsatisfactory at the end of the trail. It is very useful for identifying and exploring questions, but once raised, they must be answered by other means.

The *matching technique,* as exemplified in a number of studies (Draguns et al., 1971; Fundia, Draguns, & Phillips, 1971; Fabrega, Swartz, & Wallace, 1968), provides the appearance of rigorous control over potentially obtrusive social, although not cultural, disparities, such as educational, occupational, or marital status. It has, however, been subjected to severe criticism in the general methodological literature (Campbell & Stanley, 1966) as well as with specific reference to cross-cultural research (Boesch & Eckensberger, 1969; Brislin, Lonner, & Thorndike, 1973). Three pitfalls of matching have, in particular, been emphasized: the procedure wastes subjects, shrinking large subject pools to small samples; it produces regression effects when the matching criteria are related to independent variables; and it raises difficult, often intractable issues of generalization and inference since the "parent populations" corresponding to the matched groups of subjects do not exist in real life. To these three basic criticisms, two additional problems may be added: possible interactions between matching criteria and dependent variables go undetected and unrecognized (Draguns & Phillips, 1972) and genuine cultural differences in matching criteria, e.g., levels of education and literacy, are overlooked (Angelini, 1967). Acknowledging the merit of these criticisms, one may still consider matching to be an improvement over the naturalistic comparison of aggregates of subjects who differ demographically, biographically, as well as culturally. What must be emphasized is that the results of studies based upon matching must be interpreted conditionally, on the basis of the recognition of the limitations of this technique. Matching should be applied flexibly, in conjunction with other approaches. Fabrega, Swartz, and Wallace (1968), for example, performed both matched and unmatched comparisons in their studies of Mexican and Anglo patients in Texas, thereby contributing information on the effects of ethnicity on psychiatric symptomatology in its gross as well as its "pure" state. Study of the relationship of matching criteria to both dependent and independent variables in the gross subject samples should optimally precede, or at least accompany or follow, the implementation of comparisons based upon matching.

A multivariate research strategy is preferable, yet unfortunately not often applicable, for a host of practical, methodological, and conceptual reasons. The rather stringent requirements for the application of some of the classical research designs, such as the analysis of variance, are rarely met: control criteria may be interdependent, proportionality lacking, several of the cells hard to fill, and experimental manipulations absent. There are, however, a great many more innovative and flexible research designs available; a variety of such designs have been used in several modern bilateral and multilateral studies (Cooper, Kendell, Gurland, Sharpe, Copeland, & Simon, 1972; WHO, 1973).

In view of the complexities of this area of study, it is not surprising that a great many investigators have elected to restrict the scope of their studies to *diagnostically unitary groups.* This research strategy is least problematic in cases of low degrees of cultural contrast. In reference to a number of modern investigations of this type, few observers would question that depression as well as schizophrenia exist in both England and the United States (Cooper et al., 1972) or that depressive complaints are voiced by the members of the several ethnic groups in Hawaii (Marsella, Kinzie, & Gordon, 1973). The extension of this model to the entire range of cultural variation brings up more difficult and searching questions. Above all, it may be asked whether the category in question is meaningful at all the locations of the investigation and, if it is, whether it is diagnosed in a uniform and constant manner. As to the latter point, the area of psychiatric diagnosis has experienced in the seventies a number of important methodological improvements that permit diagnostic judgments to be made in a more public and explicit fashion than was hitherto possible. Principally, these innovations involve the development of explicit rules of diagnostic assignment proceeding from objectively observed symptoms and subjectively voiced complaints (e.g., Fischer, 1974; Spitzer & Endicott, 1969), and once these steps are taken, this operation can be readily computerized. These procedures have already been incorporated into some cross-cultural research (e.g., Cooper et al., 1972). Concerning the choice of diagnostic categories, it is intrinsically and intuitively more meaningful to devote a cross-cultural study to psychotic depression or schizophrenia than to passive-aggressive personality disturbance or hysteria.

There remains another expedient that is simple but has been as yet rarely applied in cross-cultural research on psychopathology: *the inversion of dependent and control variables.* Typically, the manifestations of abnormal behavior are studied as a function of cultural factors, with a variety of demographic, social, and biographic factors held constant. It is quite possible to invert the last two sets of variables, i.e., to study demographic and other characteristics of a psychiatric population that has identical symptom manifestations. In this way, groups within a population that are selectively susceptible to particular symptoms or disorders can be identified. An example of this approach is provided by Caudill (1963) and Rin (1969), who studied Japanese, American, and Taiwanese psychotics and found group differences in the representation of various sibling ranks. Comparisons of hospitalized psychiatric patients in New York and London revealed only negligible differences in symptomatology (Cooper et al., 1972), but they brought to light major disparities in the social composition of the samples (Fleiss, Gurland, Simon, & Sharpe, 1973), even though the authors attributed the age and sex differences between American and English depressives to psychiatrists' habits of diagnostic assignment. In a series of comparative studies, new ground was broken by comparing the social and personal characteristics of suicide victims in Los Angeles and two European capitals, Vienna (Farberow & Simon, 1969) and Stockholm (Rudestam, 1970, 1971, 1972), as well as among several ethnic groups in California (Reynolds, Kalish, & Farberow, 1975). With more extensive application, this procedure may shed light on the interplay of culture, social role, and stress in shaping psychological disorder, a topic of pivotal theoretical interest (Leighton & Hughes, 1961) on which most of the information extant continues to be qualitative and illustrative (Wittkower & Dubreuil, 1973).

All of these approaches provide only a partial solution to the problem of comparing psychological disturbance across cultures. It follows, then, that the best results may be achieved by concurrently embarking upon several research strategies in order to view the psychopathology of a culture from a variety of vantage points.

What measures are to be used?   The bulk of the available research reports pertain to gross symptomatic behaviors. Beyond the overt presentation of disturbance through observable actions and words, little progress has been made so far in investigating psychopathology and culture. Yet, most observers agree that there is more to psychopathology—in whatever cultural context it may be expressed—than the overt symptoms of the disturbance. The attitudes, thoughts, feelings, perceptions, motives, and conflicts of psychologically disturbed individuals remain to be cross-culturally explored. The role of projective techniques as a panculturally valid tool for the diagnosis of individuals and groups has been appropriately called into question (Lindzey, 1961; Spain, 1972; see also chapter by Holtzman in Volume 2 of this *Handbook*). Agreement with these criticisms, however, does not imply that projective tests, standard or tailor-made for a particular cross-cultural investigation, may not be useful as adjuncts to the collection of psychopathological data and as added avenues of communication that might reveal the interacting reflection of disturbance and culture within the individual's subjective world.

Appropriately flexible use of thematic tests is illustrated in the study of four East African cultures by Edgerton (1971), and such approaches can be profitably extended to the investigation of abnormal individuals. Al-Issa (1968) sought to integrate culturally oriented clinical observations with experimental laboratory data on schizophrenia. His approach implies that experimental comparisons of schizophrenics in the laboratory setting be undertaken across cultures. As far as is known, such comparisons have so far not been implemented, and there is no information on any interplay between culture and psychopathology in such domains of activity as perception, cognition, and learning. Zubin and Kietzman (1967) advocated the use of experimental procedures to separate culture-free from the culture-bound indicators of disorder. In their view, the first 1,000 milliseconds of a person's response to various intense and sudden sensory stimuli should be minimally contaminated by cultural influences; beyond this narrow limit, culture would increasingly shape the course and nature of the response. There are a few studies that have concerned themselves with attitudes of psychiatric patients across culture. Thus, Yamamoto (1972) was able to demonstrate differences between the Japanese and the American experience of "patienthood," with the Japanese responding in a more personal manner to the hospital setting and personnel. On a more global plane, formulations have been advanced on the hypothetical reflection of so broad a cluster of values as the Protestant ethic in psychiatric symptomatology (Draguns, 1974; Rotenberg, 1975). It might be of considerable interest to investigate the characteristics of the internalized set of social expectations and classifications known as subjective culture (Triandis, Malpass, & Davidson, 1972) in psychiatric patients and to compare their patterns of responses—across cultures—with similar psychopathological populations and—within cultures—with their normal counterparts.

What are to be the units of comparison? In answering this question the investigator is faced with four options: nosological categories, symptoms, empirically derived symptom groupings, or rationally derived symptom scores. The flowering of the culturally oriented study of psychopathology in the sixties and seventies has been characterized by the emphasis upon the symptom as the basic unit of observation and inquiry (Draguns, 1973). Two considerations have militated against the cross-cultural observation and comparison in terms of nosological categories. For one, these diagnostic assignments rest on complex cognitive judgments two or more steps removed from observable evidence; each of these steps may be productive of bias and error. For another, the identity, similarity, or usefulness of specific diagnostic categories or the entire set thereof is a matter of empirical inquiry and interpretation of findings. The cross-cultural literature (e.g., Kiev, 1972; Pfeiffer, 1970) is replete with statements asserting the worldwide occurrence of such conditions as schizophrenia or depression. These statements are plausible, but they have not been accompanied by actual empirical demonstrations of their validity in the cross-cultural literature. Several advances in the methodology of diagnosis, already mentioned in an earlier context, have permitted investigators (Fischer, 1974; Spitzer & Endicott, 1969) to operationalize the processes and results of diagnostic activity and thereby to assure that diagnosis at two culturally distinct and geographically removed points is made on the same basis and in the same manner. These innovations may stimulate a renewed spurt of cross-cultural research with diagnostic entities as dependent variables.

Bypassing diagnosis, yet avoiding the fragmentation of symptom-centered studies, are two groups of studies, based respectively on modalities of organismic or interpersonal response and on symptom groupings derived in multivariate studies. The advantages and disadvantages of these constructs as units of cross-cultural investigation have been already discussed earlier in the chapter.

How are the results of these studies to be interpreted?   It is not enough to demonstrate differences that are of psychopathological interest in a bicultural or multicultural comparison, a task that, so far in this field, has been relatively easy to accomplish (Draguns, 1973). Rather, these differences must be traced to some attributes of the cultures in question. In the case of complex, modern nation states that have served as the sites of many of the cross-cultural comparisons of abnormal behavior, this search becomes increasingly difficult and challenging. Which of the many different cultural dimensions are responsible for the contrasts obtained in psychopathological manifestation? Not surprisingly, the discussion sections of most of the research reports in question are more dependent upon the personal and artistic sensitivity of their authors to the shades and nuances of the cultures involved in the comparisons than upon an empirical and objective assessment of cultural characteristics.

To resolve this ambiguity, the investigators in this field have only now begun to turn to a very practical and concrete expedient: to have the normal behavior of the patients' peers serve as the substitute for a set of abstract culture characteristics (Katz & Sanborn, 1973; Katz, Sanborn, Lowery, & Ching, 1978; Stewart, 1976). Staewen and Schönberg (1970) went a step further and added a third perspective—that of native healers—in their exploration of anxiety in Nigeria. A thorny conceptual issue is at least potentially resolved on the empirical plane, provided that both normal and abnormal groups are equated in variables that might influence psychopathology within as well as across cultures and that the observations on them are carried out in an equivalent manner.

One last question remains. How and when do we know that a relationship between culture and psychopathology has been established? Surprisingly, this question has been rarely posed, and even less often tackled, in the interdisciplinary literature on culture and psychiatric disorders. By contrast, modern anthropology has rediscovered Galton's problem: the challenge of separating truly cultural relationships from artifactual associations due to the spread and diffusion of a cultural trait (Naroll & Cohen, 1970). Investigations of relationships between culture and psychopathology would need to depend upon a worldwide sampling of independent cultural units to resolve this issue. Bicultural investigations are of necessity inadequate to establish a true link between culture and psychological disturbance, although they may provide valuable information of interest to the students of the two cultures in question.

Conclusions.   The basic theme of the preceding sections is the complexity of the cross-cultural information-gathering enterprise on psychological disturbance and the multiplicity of choices that are available to researchers in this area. A part of this complexity is traceable to the difficulty of studying or comparing individuals in their different physical habitats and social milieus, a problem shared by all those who work in cross-cultural psychology. But another source of this difficulty is inherent in the ambiguous and controversial status of concepts, units, and assumptions in contemporary abnormal psychology. In the face of this ambiguity, there is no one single research strategy to be proposed. In general, the investigator should be aware of, and minimally burdened by, the assumptions concerning the nature of psychological disturbance that are unspokenly accepted within his or her culture. The investigator should also be maximally explicit about his or her methodological and conceptual choices and the reasons for them. More specifically, cross-cultural studies of abnormal behavior should investigate not only the characteristics of individual disturbance but also the contexts of its occurrence—in the family, community, and institution (Draguns, 1973, 1977c). These contexts should be systematically varied, and the contribution of local and extraneous observers should be separated in assessing disturbed behavior. Above all, the investigators should proceed flexibly and be prepared to switch or combine their perspectives in order to capture the culturally unique and humanly universal features of psychopathology. Finally, they should remember that while disturbed behavior is real, the constructions imposed upon it are man-made; as such, they are fit to be examined for their appropriateness, revised, or replaced.

The Relationship between Culture
and Psychopathology: Conceptual
Considerations

At the end of the preceding section our concern was with the formal requirements for the demonstration of a relationship between culture and
psychopathology. Now we turn to the substantive aspects of such a relationship: the nature of the bridge between the culture and the disturbance
in its midst. The formulation and confirmation of such relationships is the
raison d'être of cross-cultural psychology. As has been pointed out (Jahoda, 1975), comparative cross-cultural research acquires meaning only if
the results of data gathering generate the formulation of a universally applicable principle (see chapter by Lonner in Volume 1). The concern with
the culturally particular is at the service of the search for the human universal. In the case of culture and psychopathology, its investigators are
searching for the terms of the generic relationship between psychological
disturbance and its cultural setting. At this point, a comprehensive statement of such a relationship has not been attempted by anybody. Nonetheless, there are tentative indications of its possible nature which the
sections below will attempt to capture. To this end, we must concern our-
selves with the directions, locus, and scope of this relationship.

Direction of the Relationship: Exaggeration or Contrast?

If culture and psychopathology are related, the direction of this relation in
reference to statistically modal and normatively appropriate behavior
should be specifiable. In much of the accumulated research, this problem
only comes up on the plane of post hoc explanations of culturally characteristic patterns of abnormal behavior. To echo these explanations (Opler
& Singer, 1959; Draguns et al., 1971), three possibilities can be presented.

*Abnormal behavior represents an exaggeration of the typical adaptive behavior of its
given milieu.*   It is a reduction to absurdity of the sum total of culturally
shared social learning—a caricature of behavior patterns characteristic
within the culture. Within the limits of this formulation, the abnormal behavior is deviant only in a limited sense. To be sure, it represents a departure from the standards of appropriateness. This departure, however,
occurs in the direction of exaggeration of the typical, expected, and prevalent behavior patterns. In Devereux's (1956) view, the culture provides an
implicit command to its potentially disturbed members: "Don't do it—but
if you do, go about it in this manner" (p. 34). As Devereux further put it:

"Each society has rather clear-cut ideas of 'how the insane behave'." And these ideas, it might be added, are related to the ways in which its normal members behave. The behavior of psychologically disturbed individuals, then, is expected to exceed in frequency, duration, and intensity the characteristic and typical behavior patterns of their normally functioning peers within the same cultural milieu. Empirical results of several cross-cultural investigations (Draguns et al., 1971; Fundia et al., 1971; Nachshon et al., 1972) suggestively bolster this conception of psychopathology. Conversely, the research by Marsella, Kinzie, and Gordon (1973) and Marsella, Murray, and Golden (1974) on the experience of negative emotional states in subclinical and normal populations of different ethnicity in Hawaii bolsters the notion that the subjective experiences reported represent a diluted version of clinical symptomatology seen in these groups. Conclusive support for psychopathology as exaggeration of culturally modal characteristics is, so far, lacking. Such support can only be obtained if both normal and abnormal subjects from two or more cultures are included in the same study. Pending the realization of such plans, one can only note a parallel between the results of psychological studies with normals and anthropological descriptions of cultures on the one hand and the findings of investigations using psychiatric subjects on the other.

Abnormal behavior stands in a relationship of contrast to its culture.   As Schooler and Caudill (1964) put it, it constitutes the "path of greatest resistance," expressed through doing the unexpected, the culturally shocking, the socially unintelligible. Expressions of psychopathology across cultures are often impregnated with what Devereux (1956) called "social negativism." This formulation of a generic link between psychopathology and culture is less often invoked in the literature and may be considered as the polar opposite of the view of psychopathology as exaggeration or caricature. The two notions may be—but as yet have not been—differentially tested. The contrast view may also be construed as complementary to the caricature or exaggeration conception. The two formulations may be reconciled by positing different planes of expression, a possibility entertained by Devereux (1956), Draguns and Phillips (1972), and others. According to this hybrid position, the disturbed individual acts out what the normal counterpart of the same milieu dreams, wishes, and fears. He externalizes the subjective world shared by the members of his cultural group. This topic will be dealt with at greater length when the loci of the relationship between culture and psychopathology are presented.

Finally, a third and residual possibility has to be considered. *It is conceivable that abnormal behavior would vary across cultures but in a manner independent of variations in normal behavior.*   Possible reasons for such a presence of cross-cultural variations would include highly specific social learning of the behavior patterns corresponding to several clinical disorders, or an autonomous process of decompensation and regression unique to each disorder in question. Models for these kinds of relationships might be found in the findings of medical epidemiology. If this formulation holds, it would substantially strengthen the case for the concrete existence of various nosological entities as empirical givens rather than as conditional models and constructs. At the same time, such findings would strengthen the position of the advocates of the medical model in the area of cultural psychology in its most outspoken and traditional forms (e.g., Berne, 1959; Margetts, 1965). The varieties of psychological disturbance would need to be regarded as independent entities which, for a complex variety of reasons, might vary cross-culturally.

Loci of Cross-Cultural Relationships:
Some Leads and Possibilities

The available research points to a number of sites and planes on which the relationship between culture and psychopathology may be detected:

(1) Normal and abnormal behavior may be related on the same plane—that of overt behavior. It has, for example, been found (Fundia et al., 1971) that psychiatric patients in Argentina differ from their counterparts in the United States by their greater passivity in symptom expression, operationally defined—in this context—as diminution of activity level under stress. On a theoretical basis, an analogous contrast has been postulated between Latin American and Anglo American populations by the Mexican psychologist, Diaz-Guerrero (1967), and corroborated in an extensive series of studies (Holtzman, Diaz-Guerrero, & Swartz, 1975). Empirically, the results of comparisons of normal Argentine and United States subjects (Havighurst, DuBois, Csikszentmihalyi, & Doll, 1963) yielded the same axis of differentiation.

(2) Abnormal behavior may express the themes, concerns, wishes, and illusions of its time and place. Delusions and hallucinations, in particular, lend themselves to the reflection of the themes and ideas of their milieus (Al-Issa, 1977; H. B. M. Murphy, 1972a; Weinstein, 1962). Lenz (1964) painstakingly traced the origins of specific delusional contents through several decades of accumulated records in a psychiatric hospital in Austria. Electric current first appeared in delusions in 1902, robots in 1913, and radio waves in 1924. Studies of symptom content across time in several countries that have experienced dramatic and abrupt political upheavals over the last fifty years, such as Austria (Lenz, 1964), Czechoslovakia

(Bouchal, 1958), Germany (Müller, 1970), Indonesia (Pfeiffer, 1963), Italy (Agresti, 1959), Japan (Asai, 1964; Hasuzawa, 1963), and Taiwan (Rin, Wu, & Lin, 1962), demonstrate that the political events, symbols, and imagery of various periods leave their mark upon psychiatric symptoms, albeit in a transformed and distorted fashion. In the United States, Phillips (1968) reviewed a rich panorama of historical changes in psychiatric symptomatology over the twentieth century that have paralleled, at least in part, changes in values and attitudes in the population at large.

(3) In a more subtle manner, the symptomatology of psychiatric patients may express the implicit philosophy—or world view—of the culture at a specific time. Within the framework of contemporary European philosophical psychiatry, Tellenbach (1972) traced a number of culture variations in manifestations of psychopathology to the implicit culturally shared assumptions concerning the nature of reality, space, time, corporality, and activity. A patient living in a world in which myth and reality are intermingled, as exemplified by the Siriono of Bolivia (Pagés Larraya, 1977), would express his pathology very differently from one in which palpable reality and myth are sharply dichotomized. Tellenbach specifically linked the experience of mythical world to the alleged infrequency of depressions in a variety of preindustrial, traditional non-Western settings. From a different point of view, Bastide (1965, p. 274) asserted that the "world of madness . . . is nourished by the images and scenes of its environment." On the observational plane, Kimura (1965, 1967), in a series of phenomenological analyses of depression in Japan, traced its characteristic modes of expression to the implicit assumptions concerning social interaction and individuality in Japanese language and culture. For these sociolinguistic reasons, the Japanese rarely view themselves as separate from their social context. In ethnocentric Western terms, their sense of self is typically undeveloped. In depression, their referents of self-blame and guilt are therefore situational, social, and concrete. Their Western counterparts, by contrast, burden themselves with self-accusations of an abstract, intrapersonal, and general nature. In relation to more traditional clinical manifestations, both Al-Issa (1977) and H. B. M. Murphy (1967) stressed the relationship between hallucinations and delusions and their plausibility within the confines of a given cultural milieu. In particular, Murphy identified subtle patterns of facilitation of delusional activity in cultures where story telling is positively valued and where expressions of fantasy are cultivated. In the case of hallucinations, Al-Issa (1977) hypothesized that both their frequency and their psychiatric meaning would vary as a function of culturally shared acceptance of magical phenomena. The differential distribution of visual and auditory hallucinations would be dependent on the importance of these two senses in communication and information processing. These hypotheses remain to be systematically investigated.

(4) Abnormal behavior may act out the myths of its culture.   This possibility has, so far, seen little investigation. Among the Dogon of West Africa, Parin (1967) was able to detect some patterns of similarity between some of the social roles assumed by the psychologically disturbed members of the tribe and the behavior patterns encountered in well-known episodes of their mythology. Striking documentation has been provided by the Yugoslav psychiatrist, Jakovljević (1961), who discovered the features of an extinct folk ritual in the symptomatology of Macedonian hysterics. The better-known cultural syndrome of *wiitiko* of the Ojibwa Indians (Parker, 1960), with its enactment of cannibalism and destructiveness in conformity with a myth, represents another myth being transformed into psychopathology. In relation to other culture-bound syndromes, H. B. M. Murphy (1972a) traced the transformation of behavior expressed through *amok* and *latah* from culturally prescribed roles in specific historical contexts to deviant and pathological expressions in the modern period. The question is open to what extent myths—in the narrow or wide sense—shape the symptoms of individuals in contemporary technologically developed settings. Townsend (1975a) concluded on the basis of his comparisons in Germany and America that modern Western nation states are guided by general conceptions of mental disorder, grounded in cultural beliefs and attitudes, while more traditional settings prescribe a specific role and script of psychopathology, as exemplified by *latah, amok,* and *wiitiko.* It should be kept in mind, however, that even at the sites of their origin, culture-bound syndromes by no means represent the only disturbances of their respective settings (Yap, 1974).

(5) The behavior of psychiatric patients may show affinities to the stereotypes of their respective cultural groups.   Such a possibility, in particular, is worth investigating in various culturally pluralistic settings in which people often interact, and are perceived, in terms of ethnic stereotypes. Finney (1963) investigated the relationship of stereotypes to patterns of symptoms and test scores among the several ethnic groups in Hawaii. On the basis of these preliminary results, the mechanism by means of which the stereotype is transformed into a symptom is not quite clear. Do psychiatric patients simply exaggerate their premorbid behavior, in conformity with the "kernel of truth" theory of prejudice, or do they step into the role assigned to them by the majority group, as the scapegoat theory of prejudice would imply? More generally, one may ask whether the locus of the continuity between the symptom and stereotype is in the behavior of the patient or in the eye of the beholder?

(6) Psychopathological behavior may vary across cultures as a function of different conceptions of the patient role (Parsons, 1951).   This possibility was suggested by some of the early studies of the contrasting behavior patterns of Irish

and Italian schizophrenics in the United States (Opler & Singer, 1959). More recently, patient roles in psychiatric institutions across cultures were investigated by Yamamoto (1972) in Japan and the United States. The observations by Katz and Sanborn (1973), on the striking differences in patient behavior as a function of the setting in which it is observed, also bear upon this problem, especially since Katz and Sanborn found interactions between setting and ethnicity in their research on several ethnic groups in Hawaii. These findings converge in suggesting that the role of the psychiatric patient is a more specialized derivative of the role of being sick, at least in the settings where psychological disturbance is so structured. A blueprint for enacting such a role is widely shared and culturally patterned. The provocative thesis by K. Erikson (1966), that the existing institutions shape and structure their society's conceptions of deviance and influence its rates toward constancy and stability, is in keeping with this view and remains to be systematically applied in cross-cultural comparison.

(7) Various measures of psychological disturbance may serve as social indicators of the culture in which they occur. The idea of characterizing a culture by means of its characteristic parameters of disturbed behavior is a novel one and, so far, has been systematically used in only a few recent investigations. Its utilization, however, has a long prehistory in a specialized field of inquiry—the study of suicide rates in relation to social and cultural characteristics—going back to Durkheim (1897/1951) and continuing to our day (Farber, 1968; Farberow, 1975; Henry & Short, 1954; Hendin, 1964). Use of a broader range of social indicators, e.g., psychiatric hospitalization, alcohol usage, deaths from specific psychophysiological disorders, and homicide, has been pioneered by Lynn (1971) and Rudin (1968) in attempts to link these characteristics to prevailing cultural features and personality patterns. Both of these multicultural studies have led to alternative interpretation of their findings and to controversy (e.g., Barrett & Franke, 1970; H. B. M. Murphy, 1972c). Obviously, there are both hazards and opportunities inherent in the use of these data: Their interpretation is crucially dependent on the adequacy of various nationally tabulated social statistics, and a single statistic is often traceable to a complex set of social antecedents. Even though, at this early stage, this area of inquiry has yielded nothing definitive, the prospect of linking social statistics on psychopathology with their cultural sources would appear to be both reasonable and promising.

It is obvious that the evidence pertaining to the above seven links between culture and psychological disturbance is rather unevenly distributed. In quantitative terms, data are fragmentary on the relationship of cultural themes, myths, philosophical assumptions, and social stereotypes to patterns of disturbed behavior. More importantly, the mechanism of social influence, which transforms these subtle, abstract, and subjective phenomena into visible, socially inappropriate behavior is not conceptually specified nor is it empirically established. On the basis of evidence extant, it is only possible to catch glimpses of the source and product of this social process. Much would be gained by a careful, naturalistic analysis of the several phases or steps between the sharing or experiencing of a cultural phenomenon and its ultimate disordered expression. At this point, the seven possibilities advanced are presented primarily for their heuristic rather than substantive value. In any case, it is striking that the literature on psychopathology and culture is replete with references to their relationship, but its terms are rarely further articulated and specified. With full awareness of the gaps in conceptualization and evidence, the foregoing section has been written to fill the need for such specification.

Interaction Models: Sources of Cultural
Difference outside the Patient

The preceding sections have implicitly rested on the assumption that the patient is the sole or major source of any cross-cultural variation in psychopathology. It would be more reasonable, however, to accept such a view as a hypothesis rather than a premise. The alternative view is that all cross-cultural differences come about in a social transaction in which the patient, the psychiatrist, and the community participate (Edgerton, 1969; Newbrough, 1972). There is the realization, however, that many cross-cultural differences attributed to patient behavior may, to various degrees, be influenced by psychiatrists, treatment settings, and communities (Draguns, 1973). Waxler (1974) went so far as to suggest that societies differ in the labels that they impose on disordered behavior and in reaction to it, while behavior itself remains culturally invariant. These differences, however, are not necessarily artifactual and are themselves legitimate objects of cross-cultural investigation, for both substantive and methodological reasons. The acts of identifying, describing, labeling, and hospitalizing a psychiatric patient are irreducibly social and cultural; in any encounters between the potential patient on the one hand and family member, peer, community agent, and mental health professional on the other hand, culture is a silent participant. As these contacts are made across cultural or subcultural gulfs, such participation becomes explicit. Culture provides the standards and norms against which the potentially pathological behavior is judged and evaluated. Psychiatrists and psychologists, in particular, are thought by the public—and think of themselves—as primarily technical experts on behavioral disturbance. Critics of the medical model (e.g., Szasz, 1961; Scheff, 1966) have highlighted another aspect assumed as part of their professional role: that of judging the permissible limits of social deviance.

The social learning position (Ullmann & Krasner, 1975) also stresses the role of agents in the individual's environment in reinforcing and extinguishing his or her responses. A person's behavior is constantly shaped and maintained by models and agents of reinforcement. This view is consonant with the observations and phenomena on psychological disturbance in various cultures, and cross-cultural evidence has been liberally utilized in some of the prominent statements of the social learning position (Ullmann & Krasner, 1975). With the exception of Guthrie's (1972) and Higginbotham's (1976) attempts at interpreting cross-cultural data on maladaptation within a social learning frame of reference, there are few signs of influence or even awareness of this theoretical position in the technical literature on cross-cultural variations in psychological disturbance.

In this light, the activities of mental health professionals become a legitimate object of investigation, as does the study of critical incidents that transform a member of the community into a "psychiatric patient" or "crazy person." In analyzing the concept of disease in relation to society, Fabrega (1974) formulated a multistep process model of the social transactions that accompany the personal experience of bodily or psychological distress. Application of this model to the phenomena of psychological disturbance in relation to culture would presuppose its study over time and across locations. *Careers* of psychiatric patients would need to be emphasized, rather than the investigation of their symptomatology at a frozen moment. So far, few cross-cultural investigators have taken the time factor into account. The monocultural study of the progress of Brazilian psychiatric patients through their communities and mental health facilities by Brody (1973) is a notable exception.

The Substantive Evidence: What Is Known?

Pull in Two Opposite Directions:
The Worldwide and the Culture-bound

Two tendencies immediately become apparent upon a panoramic examination of the results of research on psychopathology and culture. One body of findings emphasizes the worldwide invariance of psychopathology and brings forth the universal common denominators of the behavioral expression and phenomenal experience of psychological disturbance. This trend has been in evidence from the early studies of hospitalized populations in Africa (Tooth, 1950), to the modern methodologically complex comparative investigations of psychotic modes of expression (Cooper et al., 1972; WHO, 1973).

The opposing point of view links the manifestations of disturbed behavior with the actions and reactions of people around the person who is designated as the primary object of psychiatric concern. This position is traceable to cultural relativism, compatible with community psychology and the social learning position, and has likewise been represented in research on culture and psychopathology for many decades. From this perspective, cross-cultural investigation of disturbed behavior can only be artificially confined to the actions and reactions of the labeled and identified psychiatric patient. So viewed, the conduct of cross-cultural investigation of psychopathology becomes a specialized area of social psychology in its concern with face-to-face interactions in dyads and larger groups of people. At the same time, the concerns of cross-cultural study of abnormal behavior blend in with the orientation and outlook of those theoreticians and practitioners who have emphasized the interpersonal and social, rather than an exclusively intrapsychic, character of psychological disturbance.

These two trends are, of course, not conceptually exclusive. Often they do not appear in pure form. Conceptually, they are not impossible to integrate. Nonetheless, at this time they are more often represented in the parallel and often divergent ways. The advocacy of one position or the other is at this time the more typical stance in textbooks and theoretical writings (e.g., Ellenberger, 1968; Kiev, 1972; Opler, 1967; Pfeiffer, 1970; Poggiali & Maffei, 1968) than is reconciliation and integration.

The Universal Aspects of Psychopathology

There is a multitude of observational and research reports in the literature pointing to the high degree of similarity and uniformity in psychopathological modes of expression in culturally diverse locales. Several more specific variants of this general assertion may be distinguished:

1. Abnormal and disturbed behavior occurs, and is recognized as such, in a wide variety of cultures in all parts of the world.
2. The principal categories of psychopathology, e.g., schizophrenia, affective psychosis, and neurosis, occur everywhere around the world.
3. The incidence and prevalence of these conditions in their several diagnostic categories and in toto is identical, or varies little, in several cultures.
4. The modes of manifestation of the various disorders are recognizably similar or even identical across cultures.
5. Even disorders that, at first glance, appear to be unique to the culture in question turn out on closer examination to be syndromes well known to Western psychiatry despite their culturally characteristic trappings.

On the first of these statements, the evidence strongly points to its validity. On the basis of the wide variety of cultures in which clinically recognizable psychological disturbance has been observed, it can be reasonably concluded that psychopathology is a worldwide phenomenon. It occurs in tribal, archaic, traditional groups as well as in complex modern civilizations. Kennedy (1973), Kiev (1972), and Pfeiffer (1970) have summarized the pertinent evidence in their recent surveys of the literature, which is impressive in the variety of cultures, observational perspectives, methodologies, and data obtained. Nonetheless, definitive conclusions are premature for two reasons. The pertinent findings are in the form of a mosaic of observations contributed by a variety of investigators. None has yet attempted a pancultural or representative sampling of psychopathology. The delimitation of what is psychopathology and what is not becomes difficult at points further removed, culturally and geographically, from the investigator's base of observation. The lines between psychological and physical disorder become blurred; several writers (Fabrega, 1974; Wallace, 1972) have commented that dichotomizing these disorders may be a differentiating characteristic of our cultural tradition that is absent in a great many other cultures. In Africa, for example, a number of disorders present a picture akin to schizophrenia in America or Western Europe; in reality, they are the behavioral consequences of widespread physical diseases (German, 1972; Jilek & Jilek-Aal, 1970). At this point it can be asserted that no culture has as yet been described in which, on careful examination, psychological disorders have been found absent. If psychopathology has not yet reliably or conclusively been demonstrated to be universal, it certainly is very widely represented in cultures that differ maximally among themselves on any conceivable axis of differentiation.

Somewhat more controversial is the assertion that the principal components of the traditional classificatory grid are represented panculturally. This indeed is the position of most of the authorities and reviewers in the field. The two current textbooks of transcultural psychiatry (Kiev, 1972; Pfeiffer, 1970) abide by it as do a number of modern surveys (e.g., Dunham, 1976; Guthrie, 1972; Kennedy, 1973; Wittkower, 1969; Wittkower & Dubreuil, 1973; Wittkower & Rin, 1965). Yet, it is extremely difficult to make a definitive judgment on this issue because of the complexities of intermingling observers' expectations and frames of reference with subjects' behavior. Until recently, the existing evidence has been in the form of psychiatric observers' clinical impressions brought back from highly contrasting cultures, which they were able to refer to traditional diagnostic constructs. More cautiously, one could say that schizophrenia, manic-depressive psychosis, hysteria, and so forth are diagnosed in widely different cultural contexts. Agreement with this assertion still leaves open the question whether the same disorder is diagnosed in the same way around the world. New developments in making the diagnostic process in psychiatry more objective and explicit make the resolution of this issue possible. Uniform diagnostic procedures have been applied in two recent research projects and have yielded results that point to a remarkable degree of cross-cultural constancy of such clinical entities as schizophrenia and psychotic depression. One of these projects is the so-called United States–United Kingdom study (Cooper et al., 1972), which endeavored to trace the gross differences in the diagnostic distribution of hospitalized psychiatric patients in these two English-speaking countries. The other is the World Health Organization (1973) project on schizophrenia, designed to standardize diagnostic practices and scrutinize symptom expression in nine countries: Colombia, Czechoslovakia, Denmark, India, Nigeria, Taiwan, the Soviet Union, the United Kingdom, and the United States.

The Anglo-American comparison centered upon the investigation of patient characteristics and diagnostic practices in public psychiatric hospitals in New York and London. Its specific purpose was to trace the source of major differences between Great Britain and the United States in the incidence of schizophrenia and affective psychosis, as reported in the national health statistics of these two countries (Kramer, 1969). The findings point to the psychiatrists and not the patients as the principal carriers of this cultural contrast. Once the diagnostic practices were standardized, the difference in the proportions of schizophrenics in the hospitals of the two countries vanished, and the discrepancy in the rates of affective psychosis was much reduced and only remained in a residual form as a function of the greater representation of drug addicts and alcoholics among the admitted psychiatric patients in New York, as compared with London.

The World Health Organization (1973) study pointed to the similarity of nonchronic psychiatric patients, free of organic pathology, seeking services at residential psychiatric facilities in nine countries. This conclusion was reached on the basis of similarity across the nine research centers in the rank ordering of predetermined symptoms associated with schizophrenia, the emergence of similar clusters of symptoms in all of the centers, and, finally, the identification of a concordant or core group of schizophrenics in all of the sites of investigation. These findings constitute an impressive demonstration of similarity of the major patterns of clinical psychopathology across countries different in ideological orientation, historical background, level of economic development, type of social organization, and many other features. Nonetheless, there are some hints of cross-cultural divergence and difference in the major store of findings accumulated by the WHO investigators. Reliability across centers proved to be difficult to establish for behavior, affect, and rapport, three areas of observation that are crucial for the diagnostic differentiation of subtypes of schizophrenia. This finding suggests that, in assessing these three parameters of patient behavior, diagnosticians proceeded from the standards of appropriateness for their respective cultures, which were nonidentical. Moreover, the patient profiles compared across countries by means of analysis of variance proved to be significantly different, with the United States groups of patients contributing a major share of contrast with the other patients. It remains unclear whether this finding is a function of the peculiarities of diagnostic practice of the United States psychiatrists or of the United States culture.

Despite these indications of cross-cultural difference, the thrust of this research highlights the parallels and similarities among the identically diagnosed hospitalized psychiatric patients in nine culturally very different milieus. Proceeding from this base, Carpenter, Strauss, and Bartko (1973) have further extended these results and made them practically useful for working clinicians by identifying nine positive and three negative signs that are equally valid in all the nine countries for the diagnosis of schizophrenia. In Taiwan and in Denmark, in Colombia as in Czechoslovakia, these signs produce correlations with diagnostic criteria of about equal order. Thus, schizophrenia is interculturally indicated by restricted affect, poor insight, thinking aloud, poor rapport, incoherent speech, unrealistic information, and widespread, bizarre, and/or nihilistic delusions. By contrast, the three cross-culturally constant counterindicators of schizophrenia include waking early, depressed facial features, and expression of elation. In another extension of the World Health Organization study, Fischer (1974) found a moderately high level of concordance between uniform computerized diagnosis based on symptoms and clinical diagnostic judgments at the various research centers. Apart from this corroboration of similarity in diagnostic categorization, Fischer (1974) confirmed the tendency toward the use of a broad concept of schizophrenia in Nigeria, the United States, and the Soviet Union and the reliance upon a narrow-band concept of the same disorder in the remaining six countries. These findings, however, must be evaluated while keeping in mind the limitations of the data base and procedures of the World Health Organization study. There was no attempt made in this research to deal with the indigenous conceptualizations of disorder or to relate the symptom patterns discovered to their meanings in their respective cultures. No data on the independent criterion validity of the basic data-gathering tool of the investigation, the Present Status Examination, were obtained, and the information collected in the study was limited to verbal productions during interviews. Ambitious as the project was, it was confined to settings that had experienced a great deal of pull toward the worldwide late-twentieth-century civilization, as anticipated by Lévi-Strauss (1974). What the project demonstrated was the ability of pretrained psychiatrists from several countries to describe and rate the disturbance of preselected patients in a similar manner. From the methodological point of view, this achieve-ment is not trivial, but it is different from the demonstration of actual uni-formity of symptoms and syndromes at their various distinct sites.

In substantive terms, the findings of the World Health Organization fit in with earlier work based on questionnaire responses of psychiatrists from all of the regions of the world (Murphy, Wittkower, & Chance, 1967; Murphy, Wittkower, Fried, & Ellenberger, 1963) which also pointed to a core of symptoms of schizophrenia and depression around the world. In the case of schizophrenia, social and emotional withdrawal, delusions, and flat affect were among its frequent symptoms at all sites. In the case of de-pressions, its prominent symptoms in all regions included despondency, fatigue, loss of weight, and loss of sexual interest.

Broadly similar conclusions were reached by J. M. Murphy (1976) upon the examination of the data on the prevalence and incidence of gross psychological disorder, its modes of expression, and the indigenous tech-niques of labeling and handling it in a number of traditional non-Western cultures, particularly the Eskimo of Alaska and the Yoruba of Nigeria. Murphy was impressed with the similarity between these settings and the West in both the actual occurrence of the most serious psychotic disor-ders, as well as in the several cultures' perception of—and response to—them. Her conclusions rest on retrospective and indirect data; nonetheless, she feels that these data are sufficiently strong and consistent to refute the central tenet of the social role theory in its most outspoken form (e.g., Scheff, 1966; Goffman, 1961) as interpreted by Murphy (1976), i.e., that each culture shapes the manifestations of psychological disorder indepen-dently. Murphy's (1976) argument, however, leaves ample room for roles and stereotypes of psychological disorder to contribute to their modes of expression in various cultures. Thus, support is accumulating for the no-tion that the two major varieties of psychosis present an identical core in different countries, that they can be uniformly diagnosed in widely differ-ent cultural contexts, and that some of the apparent differences in their prevalence are traceable to psychiatrists and not to patients.

Still, there are limits to generalization from these studies. None of the investigations reviewed is worldwide in the selection and representation of subjects. Indeed, truly pancultural data collection has not yet been at-tempted in cross-cultural psychology—normal or abnormal. In the ab-sence of such data, however, such questions as "Does schizophrenia exist throughout the world?" do not admit of a clear and definitive resolution. Torrey (1973) reopened this issue by examining the classical reports pur-porting to find schizophrenia in settings untouched by modern Western influence and tentatively concluded that the evidence for positing schizo-phrenia as a universal disorder of the human condition is, at this point, in-adequate, although there is no denying that the disorder is encountered in social and cultural settings that are highly dissimilar.

When it comes to the distribution of the major categories of psychopathology, the evidence is, in the case of psychoses, ambiguous and, in the case of nonpsychotic syndromes, fragmentary. Early clinical and anthropological reports repeatedly mentioned the low incidence of depression among the hospitalized patients in Africa (Aal-Jilek, 1964; Carothers, 1953; Jilek, 1970; Tooth, 1950). These impressions were paralleled by findings pertaining to the low rates of depression among American blacks (Prange & Vitols, 1962). Both of these conclusions have been called into question. In the case of Africans, Collomb (1967) and Prince (1968) emphasize that there are higher numbers of depressed individuals than has been suspected before. Prince (1968) has analyzed these disparities and has traced them to several factors. For one, depression in African cultures is more likely to be handled outside psychiatric institutions by traditional culture-specific means (Field, 1960). Another factor is the unexpressive and inconspicuous manifestation of depression among Africans. Its symptoms could well be overlooked, especially by an observer from a different culture. Finally, Prince does not exclude the possibility that depression has experienced an increase in incidence from the forties to the sixties. He relates this trend to the increasing prestige-value of depressive modes of expression that may have accompanied modernization. In the case of blacks in the United States, the evidence is similarly inconclusive and may, again, be in part traceable to the difficulties of observing and diagnosing depression across a social gulf (Schwab, Brown, Holzer, & Sokolof, 1968).

This illustrates the major difficulties in arriving at definitive conclusions concerning the distribution of major syndromes in various populations. Two prerequisites for arriving at these conclusions would be the application of the same operational definitions of the disorder at two or more culturally distinct sites and the epidemiological study of these sites by means of the same methods. This objective has as yet not been completely implemented, although the closest approximation of such a series of investigations by cultures as different as those of Nova Scotians in Canada (Leighton, 1959), Yoruba in Nigeria (A. H. Leighton et al., 1963), and Eskimos of Alaska (J. M. Murphy, 1972) yielded surprising degrees of similarity in the modes of symptom expressions. There are, however, reports on specific sites and regions characterized by unusually high rates of schizophrenia: in the West of Ireland (Walsh & Walsh, 1970; Kelleher & Copeland, 1974; Kelleher, Copeland, & Smith, 1974) and in the Karst mountains in the Croatian Republic of Yugoslavia (Crocetti, Lemkau, Kulcař, & Kesić, 1971). These reports are based on serious epidemiological research. In the case of Ireland, the high prevalence rates have survived the application of objective diagnostic procedures developed in the United States–United Kingdom study (Cooper et al., 1972). On closer analysis by H. B. M. Murphy (1975), these differences appear to be traceable to historically conditioned socialization factors. In general, the epidemiological approach has not, as yet, fulfilled its promise in the area of cross-cultural comparison. In two recent reviews Dohrenwend and Dohrenwend (1974) and Kennedy (1973) pointed to the imperfections and complexities of this source of evidence for comparative purposes at this time. Thus, the current state of evidence does not yet justify rejecting the null hypothesis of the same rates of the major varieties of psychological disorders, especially in relation to psychosis. At the same time, the existing findings do not justify the acceptance of uniformity of distribution of these syndromes as a substantiated fact.

What has been said about diagnostic categories applies a fortiori to the general problem of incidence and prevalence of psychopathology. Too little factual information has been amassed to reject the null hypothesis, yet from all kinds of indirect evidence, it would appear extremely unlikely that the rates of overall psychological disturbance would eventually be found to be constant around the world. The range of the rates of prevalence and incidence in the available methodological research (e.g., Dohrenwend & Dohrenwend, 1969, 1974) would appear to vary too widely to be traceable entirely to artifacts. The mosaic of observations and findings on the cultural distribution of stress and responsiveness to it (Wittkower & Dubreuil, 1973) also makes it unlikely that the same proportions of people in widely different settings would succumb to some kind of psychological disturbance or distress at identical rates.

In reference to the modes of manifestation of several disorders, there is, again, a tradition of statements on the alleged cultural uniformity of psychopathological manifestations in a wide variety of settings (Berne, 1959; Bolman, 1968; Margetts, 1965; Page, 1965). The argument between the proponents of this view and their opponents is to a large extent semantic. What is a difference and how much does it matter? Some observers, e.g., Berne, were impressed with the ease with which they could recognize familiar diagnostic syndromes in foreign settings and concluded that whatever differences were detected were trivial and subsidiary. In a more objective manner, Page (1965) demonstrated that the presenting symptoms of newly admitted patients in France, Spain, Italy, and Portugal differed little among themselves and from the same symptoms in the United States. These findings, again, leave room for subtler and less obtrusive manifestations of cultural variations. Moreover, in a more recent study by the same author (Page, 1975), groups of patients in six countries of the Far East and the Pacific region were found to differ in the frequencies of aggressive, irrational, and depressive symptom groupings. The last category was more frequent in Western settings, e.g., Australia and New Zealand, and the remaining two in Asian milieus, e.g., Singapore and Hong Kong. The great majority of actual comparative cross-cultural studies reviewed elsewhere (Draguns, 1973; Draguns & Phillips, 1972) document culturally influenced variations in symptomatology of psychiatric patients. This evidence will be discussed at greater length later in the chapter. At this point, it may be said that there are no factual grounds for accepting the statement that psychopathology is uniform in its modes of manifestation.

The time has come to consider the final aspect of universality, that of the alleged reducibility of culture-bound syndromes such as *amok, latah, windigo,* and others to familiar and universal categories. Yap (1974) is the principal modern proponent of the view that these disorders are but culturally colored instances of syndromes found everywhere. The issue here again is interpretive and not factual. On the observational plane, there is no denying that the manifestations of frenzied, self-destructive, yet culturally patterned, acting out, such as *amok,* or the automatic-like mimicry, in *latah,* are very different patterns of manifestation from those found in the case studies seen by Western mental health professionals. The question is, what is lost and what is gained by including these syndromes in the customary classificatory grid. To Yap, this question is answered by referring to the advantages of the etic, comparative approach to culturally colored phenomena in psychopathology. The proponents of the opposite view point to the ambiguity of the possible criteria of inclusion into diagnostic categories (Murphy, 1972a) and to the danger of neglecting culturally characteristic aspects of the history of these phenomena, their dynamics, and function (Murphy, 1972a; Weidman & Sussex, 1971).

The Culturally Differentiating Features
of Psychopathology

All of the considerations advanced in the preceding section lead one to suspect that there is "another side of the coin." This section will bring to the fore reports that emphasize the cultural heterogeneity of psychopathological functioning. Evidence for universality has come from a number of large-scale reports, such as the WHO study, that have tapped several highly different cultures. By contrast, evidence in favor of heterogeneity of psychopathology is found in studies that, for the most part, are relatively limited in their scope and often pertain to population groups of moderate or low degrees of cultural contrast. Typically, these studies involve the comparison of individuals matched in diagnostic and biographical variables, or restricted to a single diagnostic category, or equated through the partialing out of social but not cultural characteristics. All of these attempts to slant the comparisons of psychopathology across cultures in the direction of the null hypothesis have not succeeded in eliminating differences in modes of symptom expression. Often these cultural differences are documented in populations that share the same physical habitat, social setting, and political structure—French- and English-speaking residents of Montreal (Engelsmann, et al., 1972; Murphy, 1974), members of the several Asian, Polynesian, and Caucasian ethnic groups in Hawaii (Katz & Sanborn, 1973), Christians and Moslems of Lebanon (Katchadourian, 1974), patients of Middle Eastern and European descent within the Jewish population of Israel (Nachshon et al., 1972)—and patients sharing the same habitat, but differing in ethnicity, as in Sarawak (Chiu, Tong, & Schmidt, 1973) and Taiwan (Rin & Lin, 1962). There are, to be sure, studies extant that deal with a more obvious and marked extent of cultural difference. Two sets of cultural comparison have been particularly numerous: those between Japanese patients and their counterparts in the United States (Draguns et al., 1971; Kitano, 1970; Schooler & Caudill, 1964) or in Germany (Kimura, 1965, 1967) and between Latin Americans and North Americans. In the latter case, comparisons have been conducted both in the macrocosm of international studies (Fundia et al., 1971) and the microcosm of interethnic research, usually comparing Mexican Americans and Anglo-Americans in the Southwestern states (Fabrega et al., 1968; Jaco, 1960; Stoker, Zurcher, & Fox, 1968). The remarkable feature of this work is that these investigations have yielded differences that are considerable in both extent and number and that these differences are by and large consistent despite variations in technique, methodology, and instrumentation. Moreover, there appears to be a detectable pattern of consistency between the results of these studies and the fund of the available information on differences between normal members of the same cultural groupings. In the case of the Latin American versus Anglo-American comparisons, these differences have often been found on the axis of passivity-activity, a dimension that, according to Diaz-Guerrero (1967), differentiates the key sociocultural premises of the English- and Spanish-speaking cultures of the Western hemisphere. These trends were accompanied by a greater emphasis upon deficit than disturbance in the Latin American patients, and by their greater preoccupation with social relations as compared with their United States counterparts. The results of the Japan–United States comparisons are consonant with the same formulation; Japanese patients express their symptoms in a more direct, spontaneous, and diffuse manner than their American counterparts. Americans are given to cognitive elaboration; Japanese symptoms appear more in the form of an immediate expression of distress. These findings are paralleled in the extensive anthropological and cross-cultural psychological literature on the normal Japanese. A number of these writings (Caudill, 1973; Norbeck & DeVos, 1961; Hamaguchi, 1965) stress the more immediate, less intellectualized experience of self and others in Japan. All of these differences would appear to strengthen suggestively the notion that psychological disorder is the continuation of cultural modal patterns of behavior on the plane of caricature.

Similar conclusions can be derived from the cross-cultural studies of depression. In some countries, notably Nigeria (A. H. Leighton et al., 1963) and traditional China (Tseng & Hsu, 1969), the concept of depression is absent, although its symptomatic components are readily observed but not semantically integrated. Such settings as India (Teja, Narang, & Aggrawal, 1971), Indonesia (Pfeiffer, 1970), Japan (Kimura, 1965), Thailand (Tongyonk, 1971), and Nigeria (Binitie, 1975) are no strangers to depression of clinical severity. However, in all of these Far Eastern and African cultures, the experience of depression is much less explicitly tied to guilt and self-devaluation than it is in the West. The worldwide surveys of depressive symptomatology (H. B. M. Murphy, Wittkower, & Chance, 1967) further substantiate these differences in experiencing depression as do the studies of subclinical depressive symptomatology undertaken among several ethnic groups in Hawaii (Marsella, Kinzie, & Gordon, 1973). The concept of depression without guilt may appear paradoxical or even nonsensical from the Western culture-bound perspective. Nonetheless, data from around the world converge in suggesting that self-blame is neither an essential nor a necessary ingredient of depression. Vegetative components appear more basic, as do the experiences of hopelessness and helplessness in the sense of some of the current conceptions of depression (Beck, 1967; Seligman, 1973).

On schizophrenia, there are monocultural reports focusing on the less elaborate clinical picture of schizophrenia in Africa south of the Sahara (Carothers, 1953; Tooth, 1950). Some writers have described African schizophrenia as a pallid copy of the original, or so at least it appears to the Western observer (Carothers, 1953). Particularly noteworthy is the infrequency of paranoid ideation in traditional, nonmodernized African settings (Jilek & Jilek-Aal, 1970; German, 1972). The worldwide surveys of schizophrenia by the Transcultural Psychiatric Research Center team in Montreal (H. B. M. Murphy, Wittkower, Fried, & Ellenberger, 1963) confirm the impression that paranoid schizophrenia is rarely encountered in a wide variety of non-Western, traditional, rural milieus. In the United States, Opler and Singer (1959) were able to demonstrate a number of subtle yet consistent differences between the symptom pictures, fantasy expressions, projective test responses, and other indicators in socioeconomically equated samples of Irish and Italian schizophrenics. Analogous findings pointing to contrasts in aggressive versus ideational symptomatology were reported on Filippinos and Japanese among the hospitalized psychiatric patients in Hawaii (Enright & Jaeckle, 1963). There is also evidence from cross-cultural comparisons of English and Mauritian psychiatric patients (Murphy & Raman, 1971; Raman & Murphy, 1972) and from interethnic studies of Canadian communities (Murphy, 1978; Murphy & Lemieux, 1967) that culture influences the course of schizophrenia, predisposing its members toward remission or chronicity. Murphy (1972b) proposed an elaborate scheme of value orientations and integration levels of a community as determinants of the course of psychotic disorder. Supporting his view are the findings that cultures characterized by a nonantagonistic orientation to nature—as something to adjust to rather than to overcome—have lower proportions of chronic psychiatric patients and a lower rate of relapses.

Outside of these two major varieties of psychosis, numerous reports attest to the existence of a disturbance marked by excitement and confusion, both dramatic and culturally patterned in its modes of expression, and usually short in duration. Such disorders have been described in West Africa (Collomb, 1965), several Caribbean countries (Bustamente, 1965; Kiev, 1969), and New Guinea (Langness, 1969). These syndromes shade off from the culturally prescribed and normally reversible possession states, discussed in chapters by Tseng and Hsu and Prince in this volume, into highly visible disturbances of psychotic proportions. There is no convenient slot in the standard American psychiatric classification (American Psychiatric Association, 1968) for these conditions, although they are officially included in the French classification scheme (Collomb, 1965). Some American authors (e.g., Hollander & Hirsch, 1964) maintain that such a disorder occurs in the United States even though it is not separately categorized and labeled. In any case, it appears to be much more prominent in non-Western settings, an impression that is borne out by the comparison of its prevalence rates in West Africa and France (Collomb, 1965). Some observers (e.g., Bustamente, 1965) relate the occurrence of this disorder to the experience of abrupt social change, although no systematic comparisons of its incidence have been undertaken as yet. Moreover, it is moot whether the syndromes described under such names as acute confusional state (Pagés Larraya, 1978) or bouffée délirante aiguë (Collomb, 1965), wild-man behavior (Burton-Bradley, 1968; Koch, 1968), transient psychosis (Jilek & Jilek-Aal, 1970), and hysterical psychosis (Langness, 1965) are etiologically and symptomatically identical (Yap, 1974). On a more fundamental plane, the question has been raised whether these prepatterned constellations of behavior represent culturally prescribed reversible role playing or psychological disturbance. On this subject, a spirited controversy has developed between Langness (1965, 1967) and Salisbury (1966, 1967, 1969) concerning "wild-man behavior" in New Guinea, the former considering it a variant of hysterical psychosis and the latter viewing it as the local form of theater.

All of these results point to considerable degrees of cultural shaping in the two major varieties of psychosis. Information is considerably sparser on the role of culture in pathogenesis. Both rates of psychiatric hospitalization and the distribution of major diagnostic categories within the psychiatrically hospitalized segment of the population vary widely across countries (Kramer, 1969). In the light of the findings by Cooper et al. (1972) recapitulated earlier, these figures should be treated with considerable caution as they may reflect to a greater extent the cross-cultural differences among psychiatrists than among the patients. Conclusive cross-cultural studies on true rates of psychiatric disorder—and on the possible degree of their cultural causation—are extremely difficult to conduct. In the absence of such research, one can only point to the results of a number of epidemiological studies, e.g., the Midtown Manhattan project in the United States (Srole et al., 1962), that demonstrated ethnic or subcultural differences in major psychological disorders. The verdict on the relation of culture to the causation of major psychopathology remains, in light of this fragmentary evidence, open, although there are partisans of the two opposing views. Opler (1967) believes that the culture enters into all stages of development of all psychological disorders, including schizophrenia, while Osmond and Hoffer (1966) maintain that the prevalence rate of schizophrenia is constant across cultures and suggest that this constancy provides proof of its immunity from cultural processes in its etiology. A number of writers (Dunham, 1976; Kiev, 1972; Kline, 1966; Zubin & Kietzman, 1967) take a middle-of-the-road position by conceding the role of culture in shaping the expressions of disorder while insisting on acultural—probably biological—process in its basic causation. At this point, their view probably accords best with the available facts, but it should be borne in mind that the available data on the role of culture in the causation of the major varieties of psychological disorder are extremely limited.

Areas of Relative Neglect: Neurosis, Personality
Disturbance, Disorders of Children, and Organic Syndromes

Most of the information in this chapter is selectively concentrated upon the most serious manifestations of human disturbance, those in the psychotic range. At the same time, the bulk of the available research has been concerned with adults, to the near exclusion of children and adolescents. Finally, there has been little interest in the interplay of culture and pathology in the area of brain disorders.

In reference to the first of these gaps, there are only scattered reports on the ambulatory disorders of various cultures that, in Western countries, would be classified neurotic. One exception to this rule is the specialized literature on culture-bound syndromes, covered elsewhere in this chapter. Within the range of less exotic neurotic manifestations, Wittkower and Termansen (1969) noted, on the basis of the available, mostly monocultural reports, the low frequency of obsessive-compulsive symptoms in a variety of Asian and African cultures and the greater representation of hysterical behaviors in these settings. These trends were paralleled in a comparison of out-patients in India and the United States by Gaitonde (1958). Jakovljević (1959, 1962, 1963) conducted several clinical and epidemiological studies in the several culturally distinct republics of Yugoslavia, as well as in France and Guinea. He found both differences in the prevalence rates of various symptoms and syndromes, as well as a number of connections between neurotic modes of expression and the culturally patterned socialization experiences at his various sites of investigation. According to Jakovljević, neurotic symptoms often represent a maladaptive exaggeration of culturally patterned coping mechanisms. A similar relationship between neurosis and culture is illustrated by the characteristic syndrome of pathological shyness or anthropophobia that has been a prominent object of scrutiny by psychiatrists in Japan (Kasahara & Sakamoto, 1971; Sakamoto, 1970). The response to strangers in the form of mild degrees of inarticulate self-consciousness is widely observed in Japan, and this tendency is pushed to an extreme in large numbers of Japanese neurotics. This syndrome is by no means confined to the Japanese culture, but to judge from the available post hoc comparisons as well as its prominence in the Japanese psychiatric literature, it looms larger both in the actual symptomatology and the public's perception in Japan than it does elsewhere.

In reference to the other major category of ambulatory disorder, that of personality disturbance, there are only episodic and anecdotal accounts in the literature. Guthrie (1972) found characteristic behavior patterns in certain socioeconomic and age brackets of Filippino society that reminded him of antisocial personality in the United States. He concluded, however, that this similarity was more apparent than real; the antisocial behavior was situation-specific and time bound and did not show the inflexibility and repetitiveness that are among the hallmarks of personality disturbance. J. M. Murphy (1972) reported that the Eskimos label and recognize patterns of chronic social rule breaking, but do not group them with the manifestations of "mental illness," for which they also have a name. In West Africa, Parin (1967) observed patterns of behavior among the Dogon that would appear to be classifiable as personality disturbance.

In reference to the psychological disturbances of childhood, Stutte (1971) called for their systematic cross-cultural investigation in relation to their antecedents in the course of socialization. As yet, such systematic research has not been undertaken, but fragmentary observations and comparisons are available. In Senegal, a culturally patterned disturbance has been observed that may constitute the local equivalent of infantile autism (Zempleni & Rabain, 1965). Interethnic comparisons within pools of subjects from an Israeli child guidance clinic (Draguns, Nachshon, Broverman, & Phillips, 1967; Nachshon et al., 1972; Skea, Draguns, & Phillips, 1969) and an out-patient facility in the American Southwest (Stoker &

Meadow, 1974) produced a host of differences that appeared to be indicative of contrasts in socialization and values of the groups compared. Stewart (1976) included both normal and disturbed groups in her comparison of English and American children by means of the Story Participation Test, a new thematic projective technique. Apart from a wealth of specific differences, normal and disturbed samples were more sharply differentiated in England than in the United States, suggesting national differences in the "threshold" of recognizing emotional disorder in children. In reference to broad themes, disturbed English children inclined toward avoidance of expressing feeling, were more anxious, and voiced more negative affect. The results are broadly similar to the symptom differences observed in an Anglo-American comparison of a homogeneous and unique population: the offspring of military personnel from these two countries stationed in West Germany who were seen in psychiatric clinics (Britton & Cordes, 1970). Finally, the epidemiological study of several tribal groups of Australian aborigines (Cawte, 1972) is notable for including psychiatric census data on children, identifying several typical patterns of their disturbance, and relating them to antecedent factors in the form of external stress and intrafamilial socialization practices.

What all these shreds of evidence point to is culture's impact upon psychological disturbance of childhood. Questions remain open on how these influences interact with the type of disorder, age, sex, and other characteristics. At the current, early stages of development of this research area, there is a concentration of concern with the product rather than the process of the disturbance.

The disregard of cultural factors in the study of psychiatric disorders with an established organic etiology is, by comparison with the preceding two topics, more understandable and justifiable. Is it not reasonable to attribute functional disorders to psychological causes that admit cultural shaping and to trace organic disorders to biological causes, by definition culturally immutable? Fabrega (1974), Leighton and Hughes (1961) and Wallace (1972) remind us that cultural and biological factors are neither dichotomous nor mutually exclusive. Rather, these two influences interpenetrate the causation and expression of disturbed behavior. Wallace's (1972) description of the Artic hysteria of the Eskimo, or *pibloktoq*, illustrates how a calcium deficiency, rooted in culturally sanctioned dietary habits, causes, and cultural learning, shapes this culture-bound disorder. The fields of medical anthropology and of cultural epidemiology of physical diseases (Fabrega, 1974) amply demonstrate that physical distress and dysfunction can be both caused and patterned by culture. Cultural impact just does not stop at the threshold of physical illness. It stands to reason then that cultural factors might be explored in relation to diseases of the central nervous system and of their direct and indirect psychological effects. This, however, has been only sparingly and sporadically done. To be sure, some of the major culturally oriented epidemiological studies (e.g., A. H. Leighton et al., 1963; J. M. Murphy, 1972; Cawte, 1972) include tallies of organic symptoms and/or syndromes, but the information extant is too limited to arrive at any integrative statement concerning the role of culture in modeling the expression of these disorders. A report of the United States–United Kingdom project staff (Copeland, Kelleher, Kellett, Gourlay, Barron, Cowan, de Gruchy, Gurland, Sharpe, Simon, Kuriansky & Stiller, 1974), comparing senile patients in New York and London points to the importance of standardizing observations and excluding psychiatrists' judgment as a source of cultural variance: the symptom differences found were traceable to observers and not the patients.

Beyond the Patients: Psychiatrists, Community Agents,
and Families as Sources of Cultural Difference

If disturbed behaviors are linked to the culturally characteristic patterns of behavior, the same relationship should hold on the plane of community response to psychological disturbance. Yet, this source of cultural difference has so far seen much less investigation than the various parameters of the identified and labeled patients' behavior. The focus has been all too restrictedly placed upon the patient as the sole carrier of any cross-cultural difference in psychopathology. Only recently have the investigators come to focus upon the family transactions (Papajohn & Spiegel, 1974), community processes (Brody, 1973), and social negotiations (Edgerton, 1969) as sources of cross-cultural difference. Psychological disorder, to be properly understood, must be conceived and studied as social interaction, at all times involving several people and extending over time. At this point one can only register leads in this direction, without being able to present any integrated sets of findings.

In relation to public attitudes toward mental illness, a small body of cross-cultural literature has been growing over the years, and the results confront us with a paradox. On the one hand, within developing countries such as Costa Rica, tolerance and acceptance of the mentally ill is positively correlated with higher level of modernization (Adis Castro & Waisanen, 1967), and this finding is paralleled by reports of greater acceptance of the mentally ill by people higher in educational attainment (Zavalloni, 1965) in developed countries. On the other hand, the results available do not confirm the notion that economically and technologically advanced countries are necessarily the most tolerant toward the mentally ill. A variety of actual and post hoc comparisons between several Latin

American countries and the United States converge in reporting greater degrees of acceptance and tolerance for the mentally ill in Latin America (Bechtel & Gonzalez, 1971; Brody, 1973; Micklin & León, 1972). Interestingly, there are additional fragmentary data suggesting more tolerance of the mentally ill in Japan than in the United States (Terashima, 1969). One way of tentatively explaining these surprising differences is to refer them to Weber's (1930) concept of the Protestant ethic, extended to the area of culture and psychopathology by Rotenberg (1975), and applied to the examination of differences between the North American, Japanese, and Latin American experiences of psychopathology by Draguns (1974). According to these formulations one of the outgrowths of the Protestant ethic, more prevalent in North America than in South America or Japan, was the dichotomization of the "elect" and the "damned." Possibly, this dichotomous view results in a harsher and more rejecting attitude toward psychiatric patients even in the present-day secularized United States society. The data collected in Latin America and in Japan fit in with, although they do not provide conclusive proof for, this conceptualization. The only blemish at this time is the finding by Brody (1973) that in Rio de Janeiro, Protestant family members were even more prone than Catholics to accept the concept of mental illness.

Another global explanation of cross-cultural differences in attitudes was advanced by Levine (1972), who attempted to establish contrasts in conceptions and attitudes toward mental illness as a function of long-term experience with democratic or totalitarian systems of government. His data were consonant with the position that coerciveness toward deviants—characteristic of dictatorial authoritarian regimes—would generalize in the form of rejecting attitudes toward the mentally ill.

In a more direct manner, attitudes toward psychological disorder may reflect the dominant conceptions concerning the nature of such disturbance within the mental health professions of the respective countries. The importance of this source of differences was demonstrated in a series of comparisons between Germany and the United States in which mental hospital personnel, segments of the general public, and patients participated (Townsend, 1975a, 1975b). Germans tended to regard mental illness as a long-term state—to be cured, if at all, by expert intervention. By contrast, Americans emphasized environmental stress, malleability of behavior, and the importance of the patient's own efforts in overcoming the disorder. These differences, uncovered by means of interviews and attitude scales, parallel and perhaps exaggerate the prevailing views of psychopathology in the German and American professional literature. Along somewhat similar lines, Sechrest, Fay, Zaidi, and Flores (1973) found, upon comparing attitudes toward mental disorder among college students in the United States, the Philippines, and Pakistan, that the two Asian groups were less influenced by the modern mental health ideology—widely diffused by the media in the United States—but were not necessarily less realistic and informed concerning mental disorder as it is expressed in their own countries.

What remains to be done is to relate the prevailing attitudes toward psychological disturbance to observable symptom manifestations. Some links have been sketched by Draguns (1974), Sechrest et al. (1973), and Townsend (1975a, 1975b), but there is as yet no study extant in which these two bodies of data have been interrelated and compared.

Meanwhile, some complexities of this area of investigation remain to be faced. Zavalloni (1965), in an early cross-cultural study, took issue with the supposedly unitary nature of attitudes toward mental illness and brought to light their characteristic inconsistency and ambivalence. In particular, she was able to show that these attitudes varied independently in the occupational and social contexts. Of particular importance in relation to cross-cultural psychology, she demonstrated that the direction of cross-cultural differences may be distinct—and even opposite—in these two milieus. Thus, subjects in the continental United States exhibited greater tolerance toward mental illness in the work setting than did their counterparts in England and Hawaii. Conversely, a trend toward greater acceptance of social and residential proximity was in evidence in England, and cross-cultural differences in this respect were particularly marked at the lower rungs of the socioeconomic ladder. Nor is the object of such attitudes unitary. In the United States, England, Germany, Nigeria, and Colombia, "mental illness" is rather sharply differentiated in the public view from "emotional distress," "nervous breakdown," "nervous depression," and other euphemisms, all of which, by contrast with "mental illness," connote a benign, temporary, and reversible state of subjective distress and social inefficiency (Zavalloni, 1965; León & Micklin, 1971; Townsend, 1975a, 1975b; Awaritefe & Ebie, 1975).

These formulations, contestable at this time, might be heuristically useful in relating attitudes toward psychological disorder to sets of broadly comparable dimensions, useful both intraculturally and cross-culturally. Future work might undertake to relate attitudes toward mentally ill to the prevailing patterns of psychiatric symptomatology.

Culture not only formulates attitudes toward the mentally ill, but it also shapes the conceptions of the nature of the disorder and of the lines of division within it. Anthropologists, psychiatrists, and psychologists have long been sensitive to the existence of comprehensive systems of classificatory conceptions of psychological disturbance in cultures outside of the Western mainstream. A wealth of ethnopsychiatric information has been collected (e.g., Sal y Rosas, 1973; Seguin, 1972). Most of the research on ethnopsychiatric systems and on folklore psychiatry pertains to social groups at a rather high degree of cultural contrast from our own. What should not be overlooked, however, is that our own communities harbor their implicit conceptions on the nature of psychological disorder in general and on its units of classification. These informal and inarticulate ideas of what constitutes psychological disorder, and what its lines of division are, are important to identify for cross-cultural as well as for applied, practical reasons, e.g., in the planning of community service.

Finally, attention needs to be paid to the cultural roles of the psychiatrist—and the psychologist—as the guardians of the permissible and tolerable limits of social eccentricity (Carstairs, 1959). Recently, great progress has been made in objectifying and computerizing the diagnostic operations of psychiatrists and making them cross-culturally comparable. As mentioned, the work by Englesmann et al. (1971) and by Kendell, Pichot, and von Cranach (1974) now makes it possible to provide objective translations from the categories of one national diagnostic system into another, thereby removing one source of ambiguity in cross-cultural comparisons of psychopathological manifestation. Yet at the same time, no commensurate systematic attempt has been undertaken to study the contribution of the psychiatrist to the diagnostic process as the agent of his culture, charged with the comparison of a deviant individual's behavior with the baselines of social expectations for his cultural milieu and with the range of acceptable departure from these standards. By way of piecemeal information, national differences among psychiatrists have been reported in ratings of symptom severity (Fabrega & Wallace, 1967), use of symptom data in arriving at identical diagnoses (Seifert, Draguns, & Caudill, 1971), numbers of symptoms reported, and reliabilities of symptoms observed (Sandifer, Hordern, Timbury, & Green, 1968, 1969). In particular, there is an abundant harvest of reports on Anglo-American differences between diagnosticians, antedating or paralleling the United States–United Kingdom project (Cooper et al., 1972) and consonant with its conclusions (Edwards, 1973; Katz, Cole, & Lowery, 1969; Sandifer et al., 1968, 1969). Within that project, however, cultural variation in the use of diagnostic labels was treated as "error," to be reduced and eliminated through more objective diagnostic procedures, rather than to be investigated as a legitimate course of cultural variation. Yet there are good reasons to explore any cultural sources of the British psychiatrists' penchant for diagnosing depression and their American colleagues' generosity in applying the label of schizophrenia. As yet, it is impossible to spell out the details of a specific model of cultural influence upon psychopathology. However, its features should incorporate the recognition of the multilateral transaction between the patient, the community, and the psychiatrist, with each of the participants to this transaction contributing a share of cultural variance (Adis Castro, 1970; Draguns, 1973).

Pancultural Relationships:
Theoretical Models

So far, this chapter has been concerned with the existence and scope of cultural differences in the expressions of psychopathology. The time is now at hand to relate these variations to a number of global cultural parameters. The various cultures around the world could be construed as an arena for the investigation of those cultural dimensions that enhance, inhibit, or shape the expressions of psychological disturbance. Such a quest is usually undertaken in recognition of the culturally narrow, mostly Western, base on which our knowledge of social influences upon abnormal behavior rests.

A relatively modest form of this quest is provided by replications of studies, usually undertaken by Americans in their own country, in other cultural settings. There have been studies conducted that attempt to replicate findings originally obtained in the United States on the relationship between social competence and symptom manifestation in Japan (Draguns, Phillips, Broverman, & Caudill, 1970) and on the association between social class and mobility and psychiatric symptomatology in Argentina (Saks, Edelstein, Draguns, & Fundia, 1970). The results of these studies point to similarity, but not identity, of such relationships across cultural lines. The series of investigations by Lorr and Klett (1968, 1969a, 1969b) can be considered attempts to replicate the factorial composition of American symptomatology in eight different countries. The study by E. B. Foa and Chatterjee (1974) tested the consistency of the relationship between perceptions of interpersonal behavior and psychopathology in the United States, India, and Senegal. They found that in all three countries psychiatric patients were characterized by lower differentiation between self and others in comparison with normal controls, a result that is consonant with tenets of U. G. Foa and E. B. Foa's (1974) facet theory according to which the subjective representation of social relationships becomes more differentiated with ontogenesis and loses this differentiation in psychopathology.

More ambitious are the several attempts to relate social antecedents to psychopathological variables on the basis of multicultural investigations. Dohrenwend and Dohrenwend (1969, 1974) sought such a pattern of regularity in their retrospective analysis of a large number of epidemiological studies around the world. Heterogeneous as this source of data was, it enabled the Dohrenwends to conclude that the rates of psychopathology are somewhat higher in urban than in rural settings, that women show higher rates of neurosis than men, that men exceed women in rates of personality disorder, that psychopathology is disproportionately concentrated at the lower rungs of the socioeconomic ladder, and that personality disorder and schizophrenia are the two conditions overrepresented at the lower-class level. This cluster of findings is consistent with the explanation that the rates and severity of disorder vary directly with the degree of stress imposed, but they do not exclude the possibility of social selection, i.e., that vulnerable individuals drift into urban lower-class settings and bring their pathology with them. Work is now in progress to resolve this issue (see Dohrenwend & Dohrenwend, 1974).

Other multicultural research projects sought to identify the characteristics of the cultures that are propitious for the disproportionate occurrence of specific psychological disorders. In reference to depression, Chance (1964) concluded from the results of the worldwide inquiry into depression that this disorder thrived under conditions of high social cohesion and represented the pathology of social overintegration. Data are more complex and less interpretable as to whether schizophrenia is fostered by social disintegration, although this view has been advanced in the literature (Arieti, 1959).

More global and daring views have been introduced, but they have often been only sporadically and haphazardly tested. An early article by Arsenian and Arsenian (1948) formulated the dichotomy of tough and easy cultures, the former characterized by rigid prescribed roles and severe sanctions for transgressions against them, the latter marked by a variety of options open to individuals and by few penalties for deviation. Among many other consequences, the Arsenians predicted differences in the rates of psychological disorder between these two types of societies. But the "toughness" of a culture has never been operationalized, and the Arsenians' suggestive and plausible ideas have not been put to an empirical test.

A better-known view is that by Leighton (1959) who posited social disintegration as a major determinant of psychopathology. In this view, there is an upper limit to social and environmental instability that a person can tolerate without showing the effects of personal disintegration. The epidemiological research by Leighton and his collaborators in Canada (D. C. Leighton et al., 1963) and Nigeria (A. H. Leighton et al., 1963) was directly designed to test this theory. These projects contributed evidence on differences in rates of psychological disorders as a function of various degrees of disintegration within communities. More recent research extended the application of these concepts to the comparison in the rates of disorder among a number of aboriginal Australian groups at different levels of social integration, with positive results (Cawte, 1972). In all of these projects, however, tests were conducted cross-sectionally—in several communities at the same time. A longitudinal approach that would investigate the rates of disorder in the same community over time would appear to be more conclusive but also more difficult to undertake. Lin

(1953) and Lin et al. (1969) conducted two epidemiological studies in Taiwan fifteen years apart and found an increase in the rate of disorder in the second study, which had been completed after a period of dramatic social change that, presumably, brought about some social disorganization. Other findings, summarized by Guthrie and Tanco in this volume, raise the question, however, of the more specific features of social disorganization that produce psychopathology. Guthrie and Tanco's point is that rapid social transformation is not necessarily accompanied by an increase in psychological disturbance or other adverse social effects. What the specific factors are that facilitate or impede coping with a rapidly changing world is not quite clear. Other formulations (Marsella, Escudero & Gordon, 1972; Misra, 1975; Parker & Kleiner, 1966) have introduced concepts and developed measures to shed light on this issue. In particular, they attempt to translate social and cultural factors into personal psychological experiences related to the frustrations endured and gratifications enjoyed, discrepancies between ideal and actual conditions in the person's environment, and other specifiable, if subjective factors. These variables may serve as a bridge in transmuting objective social characteristics into individual pathological experience.

These considerations also apply to a related object of inquiry: the disorders of immigrants. Early global formulations took it for granted that rates of psychological disorder would be higher among immigrants, as compared with sedentary populations. Proceeding from this assumption, attempts were made to trace these putative differences to one of two factors: "self-selection" of psychologically vulnerable individuals for the experience of migration or the "general hazard" associated with being uprooted and having to readapt to a new and different culture (cf. Sanua, 1970). In its pure form, neither of these formulations has received empirical support (cf. Draguns & Phillips, 1972; Sanua, 1970). Moreover, the accumulation of empirical studies calls into question the generalization that immigrants as a group are necessarily more susceptible to psychological disorders than their more sedentary counterparts, either in the host country or in the country of origin (Draguns & Phillips, 1972; Lasry, 1977; Sanua, 1970). As with the experience of rapid and discontinuous social change, psychological distress and disturbance are prominently encountered in some, but not in all, migratory populations. Taft (1977) has identified six sources of stress that immigrants commonly encounter and that correspond to the several meanings of the concept of culture shock (Oberg, 1960). These are:

1. The strain involved in expanding effort on adaptation; speaking a new, and imperfectly known, language; abiding by unfamiliar customs; following a variety of novel rules of behavior.

2. The sense of loss attendant to being uprooted, particularly prevalent among involuntary or forced migrants such as refugees and expellees.
3. The rejection of the newcomer by the host population.
4. The confusion of one's roles, values, and feelings.
5. Rejection of the host culture by the newcomer, with attendant feelings of discomfort, anxiety, indignation, or disgust.
6. The feeling of helplessness and ineffectuality in dealing with the new culture.

These six sources of stress vary across the specific situations of culture contact that are involved in immigration and are traceable to the characteristics of the two cultures in question—the host and the immigrant community—and the personality characteristics and cognitive resources of the migrants, as well as a host of situational factors. All of these potential influences upon maladaptive and adaptive responses of immigrants have not yet been disentangled in the voluminous, but not quite conclusive, literature on immigrants' disorders. A reasonable expectation is that immigrants' adjustment would vary inversely with the severity of the six major sources of stress. There is empirical support for the pathogenic effect of high barriers against social acceptance of newcomers upon their behavior (Murphy, 1965); conversely, a positive, welcoming attitude of the host population appears to reduce the experience and manifestation of abnormal behavior (Weinberg, 1961). Isolated migrants find themselves at higher risk than larger groups of people from the same country (Alexander, Workneh, Klein, & Miller, 1976; Cade & Krupinski, 1962; Mintz & Schwartz, 1964). The degree of pressure to conform to the host country's cultural patterns, whether externally imposed or internally experienced, is negatively related to the adequacy of immigrants' adaptation (Murphy, 1961). In relation to personality resources, Pintér (1969), on the basis of a thorough study of both adequately functioning and psychiatrically impaired Hungarian refugees in Switzerland, identified a number of personal and demographic factors that protect an immigrant against decompensation. These include average or above average intelligence, with a practical orientation; a reasonably high aspiration level, especially in relation to cultural and linguistic relearning; extraversion; flexibility; active and emotionally responsive coping; high frustration tolerance; and age over forty or under twenty. This composite of characteristics was derived in a specific place and on a specific population. It remains to be seen to what extent these predictors will prove applicable across cultures, populations, and circumstances of migration.

On a commonsense as well as theoretical basis it is reasonable to expect that the sense of alienation or anomie is a major, although not the sole, mediator of psychopathology among migrants. As Guthrie and

Tanco point out in their chapter, there is as yet no demonstrated connection among migration, alienation, and psychopathology. The two literatures on the results of stresses of migration and the sources and consequences of alienation, respectively, continue to be parallel and independent.

As yet, the study of psychopathology in individuals who have experienced migration and/or rapid social change has not yielded conclusive findings on the limits of human cultural plasticity. What kind of cultural change under what kinds of circumstances must be endured in order to produce psychopathological effects? This question remains unanswered. Preliminary hints suggest that external social influences are insufficient to predict the nature and intensity of such a response. What is needed is information on how the person constructs the experience of cultural change or difference before the maladaptive effects of such experience can be predicted and understood.

Practical Implications:
Toward an Applied Cross-Cultural
Community Psychology

Information included in this chapter is potentially relevant to the development and delivery of mental health services outside of their customary cultural setting. Mental health professionals are seeking to meet the mental health needs in a variety of cultures around the world, but "the literature regarding such consultations in the cross-cultural context is sparse indeed" (Westermeyer & Housman, 1974, p. 34). What emerges from the rather scattered writings in this area (Argandoña & Kiev, 1974; Collomb, 1973a, 1973b; Boroffka, 1964, 1970; Higginbotham, 1976, 1979) is that importing, copying, and imitating culturally extraneous conceptions, institutions, and services is never sufficient. Moreover, no culture stands helplessly by in the face of psychological entanglements and distress of its members. The local conceptions, services, and practices can often be effectively integrated into comprehensive plans of treatment.

In confronting a new and different culture, the mental health professional faces a number of challenges and pitfalls. Wintrob (1976) has vividly described the personal reactions, confounded by culture shock and countertransference, that must be faced in the demanding task of coping with a set of new and different social ground rules and responding to human distress. Collomb (1973a) has identified three attitudes that mental health professionals often adopt. One of them is the view that mental health problems are the same everywhere and so are the solutions for them. Therefore, there is no need to take culture into account except, possibly, as an obstacle that stands in the way of implementing the universally applicable blueprint of institutions and services. Its opposite is the stance of radical cultural relativism, according to which each society is an independent and self-contained unit; one has to begin from scratch, nothing learned in one culture is of any value in another. Finally, there is the tendency to idealize the host culture and its concepts and services; indigenous notions are accepted with the same lack of critical judgment that accompanies the imposition of extraneous services at the hands of the proponents of traditional pancultural model of psychological disturbance. Optimal solutions are to be sought by avoiding these three extremes.

Higginbotham (1976) proposed a specific model for the assessment of a culture and for the incorporation of the results of this assessment into planning and delivery of mental health services. The implementation of this model involves four steps: (1) assessment of cultural perceptions of problem behavior, (2) specification of norms of individual adjustment, (3) description of the indigenous healing practices and of the network of their delivery, and (4) formulation of the expected community relationships with the system for delivering services. Once these four preliminary tasks are completed, the treatment program can be designed with maximal sensitivity to the needs and characteristics of the culture in question. Beyond the formulation of this proposal, Higginbotham (1979) designed, and reported some preliminary data on, The Ethnotherapy and Culture Assessment Scale, which provides information on the degree of congruity between the community's needs and the services actually provided. This information can be used in designing new programs or in revising existing ones. Finally, the instrument is useful in shedding light on cultural conceptions of psychological disturbance and of appropriate means of treatment and intervention. Higginbotham (1976) presented an explicit model for assessing the culture in question and then accommodating to the culture in planning and delivering mental health services.

What runs through as a common thread in the various cross-cultural endeavors in developing mental health services is the emphasis upon a cooperative rather than paternalistic attitude (Torrey, 1970), which involves taking seriously, and learning from, the culture in which services are being developed. The concept of a "culture broker," as a mediator between the milieu of the patient and the institutionalized culture-bound setting of the mental health professional, has been developed and applied in the multiethnic setting of Florida (Sussex & Weidman, 1975; Weidman, 1975).

A major concern of the practitioners of mental health across cultural frontiers is the entry problem, i.e., how to introduce and make meaningful the services that the professional is equipped to render. Argandoña and Kiev (1974), proceeding from the public health model, suggest that the borderline problems between psychiatry and physical medicine might serve the purpose of introducing and making acceptable the broader range of mental health services. Indeed, the role of a physician is much more widely known in many countries around the world than that of a psychiatrist or psychologist. Another potentially applicable model is the educational one—of starting with the teaching about psychological problems and their management preparatory to offering direct psychological services. Finally, the precedent of applying behavior modification in naturalistic settings, i.e., outside of the clinic or laboratory (Tharp & Wetzel, 1969) lends itself to extension across cultural lines.

The several programs of such services described share the feature of cooperation rather than confrontation with indigenous services, and a respect for the skill and observational experience of its practitioners. The goal is the integration of the existing services with newly developed ones (Collomb, 1973b), and a number of promising programs along these lines have been reported from Guyana (Singer et al., 1967), Senegal (Collomb, 1967), Nigeria (Lambo, 1965; Erinosho, 1976), and the Papago Indians of Arizona in the United States (Kahn & Delk, 1973). The World Health Organization has initiated a systematic study of strategies for extending mental health care on a comprehensive communitywide basis. This research is being simultaneously conducted in four developing countries: Senegal, Sudan, India, and Colombia (Diop, Collignon, & Gueye, 1976).

These various efforts have for the most part developed independently of the accumulation of information on cross-cultural psychopathology, yet these data are potentially useful to the practitioners as are the practitioners' observation and experience to cross-cultural researchers (Draguns, 1977c; Higginbotham, 1976). These facets of professional activity have not yet fused into an integrated whole.

Conclusions

What is the meaning of the aggregate of data so far collected in the course of the interdisciplinary quest for the relationship between culture and psychopathology? Potentially, these bits of information might contribute to the understanding of cultures in the light of psychopathology and of psychopathology in the light of culture. Our attempts to make sense out of the available array of findings is organized under these two headings.

Culture through the Prism of Psychopathology

While the extent of cultural shaping of psychopathological manifestations is, at this point, unclear, the very existence of a substantial amount of information in this area of inquiry suggests that culture is one of the influences upon psychopathological expression. Consequently, culture can be viewed through the prism of its psychopathology. At this point, some variant of the exaggeration or caricature notion has received more support than other possible explanations of the direction of this relationship. This tentative support opens possibilities of eventually linking psychopathology on a worldwide basis with some of the well-known dimensions and typologies of normal patterns of culturally characteristic behavior. Thus, the road would seem to be clear for exploring the psychopathology of achievement orientation (McClelland, 1961) and for continuing the forays aimed at linking psychopathology with the various socially oriented conceptions of activity-passivity (Diaz-Guerrero, 1967). Beyond these possibilities of global or multilateral comparisons, the study of psychopathology can substantially enrich our understanding of the ethos of a given culture. Sensitive mental health professionals (e.g., Lenz, 1964) have long recognized that the psychiatric wards are far from socially isolated; they echo and reflect the concerns of their place and time. The content and style of the prevailing symptomatology is relatively easy to record. Symptoms may provide valuable clues as to what the preoccupations of a culture are and in what manner they are expressed. Similarly, how a culture treats and conceives its "mentally ill" may be of interest in its own right. Beyond that, it sheds light on the culture's areas of threat and vulnerability and how they are handled. As at least a partial product of its culture, psychopathology may have some unique features that, for lack of cross-cultural perspective of most investigators and practitioners, have so far gone unrecognized. Potentially, however, the quest for the cultural uniqueness of psychopathology in style, content, and patterning of expression does not appear to be an unrealistic undertaking.

These possibilities come to mind even though the findings on psychopathology and culture are, at this time, limited in content, method, population, and substance. As indicated early in the chapter, the entire armamentarium for the exploration of overt behavior and subjective experience can be applied in the cross-cultural study of psychopathology, but it has only sparingly been so applied. Moreover, it has been pointed out that the research effort has been lopsidedly concentrated upon the most serious psychopathological disorders, to the neglect of milder ambulatory ones. Almost the entire field of culture and psychopathology is given over to the studies of adults, yet psychologically disturbed children, at different stages of their socialization, may be particularly valuable to study across cultures. Finally, the very acts of labeling, by professionals and community agents, should be investigated as a series of meaningful social operations that potentially shed light on cultural characteristics.

Psychopathology through the Prism of Culture

If the basic question—from a culture's point of view—is how it is reflected through psychopathology, the fundamental concern—from the perspective of psychopathology—is how much it varies with culture. At this point, this question cannot be given a specific, quantitative, and meaningful answer that would hold true across variations of psychopathology, culture, and their various possible interactions. What can be said is that, during the seventies, the case for a unitary pancultural core in at least the most serious categories of disturbance, the two major functional psychoses, has been strengthened. Schizophrenia and affective psychoses appear to be recognizable, and a few of their major symptoms are virtually uniform at various points around the world. This does not negate the statements on cultural shaping made in the preceding section, but it restricts their scope. It may be that the current state of evidence is temporary, occasioned by the availability of lavish support for investigations centered upon the immutability of psychopathology. Even if this is so, the notion of each culture completely creating psychopathology in its own image will hardly be resurrected. Some kind of interaction of the humanly universal, and the culturally particular, needs to be posited. What is the source of the humanly universal component in psychological disturbance? Is it genetic—or more generally biological—or traceable to early psychodynamics or to the irreducibility of basic human dilemmas? The answers to these questions go beyond the restricted inquiry into the interplay of culture and psychopathology. While cross-cultural research on psychopathology cannot answer these questions, it can contribute its findings toward the formulation of an answer.

In this ambiguous state of the evidence a number of tentative generalizations can be offered concerning the specifics of the culture's role in psychopathology. Of necessity, they represent the present author's highly tentative view on the basic trends in a complex and ambiguous array of evidence, and, therefore, they carry with them a high risk of refutation and disconfirmation. Nonetheless, they may be worth stating, perhaps for no better reason than to reduce the inevitable confusion that comes from attempting to summarize the details of this area of investigation.

By way of a general conclusion it can be said that there is a limited number of dimensions to which the essentials of abnormal behavior can be panculturally reduced. These include the axes from "low" to "high" in affective experience or mood, consensual to idiosyncratic in the perceptual-cognitive domain, tense to relaxed in organismic expression, and reliable and appropriate to their opposites in social behavior. On any and all of these axes there are limits to individual ("I suffer; I can't bear it") and social ("This cannot be allowed to go on; something must be done about it") tolerance. With the exception of high-low, all of these axes are unipolar. The extremes on these dimensions roughly correspond to affective psychosis, schizophrenia, neurosis, and personality disturbance, respectively. This correspondence is only approximate because these diagnostic categories were described at specific points in time and space and were then assumed to be universally valid syndromes. Consequently, they were overspecified. The problem of what is universally valid and culturally particular about these syndromes has been further complicated by three factors:

1. The application of the Kraepelinian nomenclature throughout the world,
2. The exportation of Western psychiatric institutions to other cultures,
3. The imitation of "Western" symptoms and complaints by patients in the process of modernization, e.g., as observed in relation to depression in Africa.

These three trends have strongly tipped the balance toward the etic end of the scale and may have resulted in an overemphasis on the culturally invariant features of psychopathology. These tendencies have however, been offset in part by the emic emphases on exotic syndromes and on cultural plasticity in symptom formation. Nonetheless, there are good indications that the four dimensions outlined above are universal in determining appraisal of fitness and appropriateness of individual behavior, even though they may to varying degrees be perceived as relevant to psychological disorder. Personality disturbance, for instance, may be more typically construed as a matter of personal "weakness" or "badness" than of illness or disorder. In any case, ample room remains for cultural variations in thresholds of tolerance by self and others for these various disturbances, the culture's preoccupation with—or sensitivity to—particular kinds of disorders, the social shaping of the specific manifestations of disturbance, their course, outcome, and other factors.
     In more specific terms, the following conclusions appear warranted:

• No disorder is entirely immune to cultural shaping.
• None of the disorders so far investigated are entirely traceable to cultural or social characteristics nor do they vary over their entire range in response to cultural variations.
• Psychoses are to a lesser degree influenced in their manifestations by culture than are nonpsychotic disorders.
• Among psychoses, affective disorders appear to be more susceptible to cultural shaping than are the schizophrenias, but at this time, this is only a tentative formulation.
• Variations in the manifestations of major psychoses appear to be meaningfully related to social, economic, technological, religious, and other features of their societies.

- Regardless of the nosological category, differences are more marked on the plane of symptom than syndrome.
- Among symptoms, those in the areas of cognition, perception, and affect are less influenced by culture than those pertaining to role and social behavior.
- Both psychotic depression and schizophrenia appear to be characterized by a few symptoms that are culturally immutable.
- While the cultural plasticity of patient characteristics has been overestimated by many, the cultural plasticity of the other, nonpsychopathological participants in the transactions involving the patient has been very widely, or perhaps even universally, underestimated.

These points give comfort to neither the extreme opponents of the medical model—who would hold that both the supraordinate entity of psychopathology as well as its component categories are illusory—nor do they bolster the position of the most outspoken defenders of the medical model—that the syndromes of psychological disorder and distress are illnesses like any other, such a malaria, tuberculosis, or typhoid fever. Rather, the truth would seem to lie somewhere in between: that there are recognizably similar disorders in widely different social settings that in a flexible and general sense are broadly similar to illness or dyscrasia (Yap, 1974), that they represent a disruption between the individual and his milieu requiring remedial and corrective action (Fabrega, 1974), and that they involve suffering (Cawte, 1977; Kendell, 1975; Sánchez, 1975). But the existing data also admit other possibilities: that social roles and socially imposed labels impinge upon the process of psychological disorder and that they are shaped in a continuous, albeit implicit, dialogue between the distressed individual and his community. The product of these interactions is the phenomenon of personal disturbance—the individual's own unique attempt to shoulder his or her burden of experience, from whatever source, and to come to terms with a specific social environment.

Notes

1. This chapter was discussed at the Conference of Contributors to the *Handbook of Cross-Cultural Psychology* in Honolulu, Hawaii, January 1976. The author would like to thank all of the participants at that meeting for their constructive and helpful comments. Special thanks are conveyed to the members of the evaluation committee on this chapter: Howard N. Higginbotham, Liwayway Angeles, and Michael O'Driscoll who contributed a thorough and sophisticated critique. Additional comments were received from Caroline Keating and Ihsan Al-Issa and are gratefully acknowledged. Howard N. Higginbotham went carefully over the prefinal version of the chapter and shared a number of thoughtful and realistic suggestions.

2. The scope of this chapter precludes the possibility of systematically considering issues, findings, and trends on psychological disturbance by geographical region or cultural area. In addition to texts on transcultural psychology (Kiev, 1972; Pfeiffer, 1970) and an annotated bibliography on culture and mental health (Favazza & Oman, 1977), the interested reader is referred to articles by Burton-Bradley (1970), Giordano (1973), Giordano and Giordano (1976), German (1972), León (1972), Neki (1973), Racy (1970), and Wittkower & Termansen (1969), the writings of several authors edited by Petrilowitsch (1967), the several overviews in *Transcultural Psychiatric Research Review* (Cawte, 1977; Hahn, 1978; Hippler, 1975; Kim & Rhi, 1976; Ogino, Kuba, & Suzuki, 1977; Rao, 1978; Tongyonk, 1977; Westermeyer, 1977), and, in a broader sense, the four volumes edited by Caudill and Lin (1969) and Lebra (1972, 1974, 1976).

References

AAL-JILEK, L. Geisteskrankheiten und Epilepsie im tropischen Afrika. *Fortschritte der Neurologie und Psychiatrie*, 1964, *32*, 213–259.

ADIS CASTRO, G. Salud mental, investigación y contexto sociocultural. In J. Mariategui & G. Adis Castro (Eds.), *Epidemiología psiquiátrica en América latina.* Buenos Aires: Fondo para la salud mental, 1970.

ADIS CASTRO, G., & WAISANEN, F. Modernidad y tolerancia: El caso de las actitudes hacia la enfermedad mental. *Acta Psiquiátrica y Psicológica de América Latina*, 1967, *13*, 149–157.

AGRESTI, E. Studio delle variante cliniche del temi i dei contenuti deliranti in epoche diversi. Confronti dei vari tipi di delirio a distanza del circa un seculo. *Rivista di patologia nervosa e mentale*, 1959, *80*, 845–865.

ALEXANDER, A. A., WORKNEH, F., KLEIN, M. H., & MILLER, M. H. Psychotherapy and the foreign student. In P. Pedersen, W. J. Lonner, & J. G. Draguns (Eds.), *Counseling across cultures.* Honolulu: University Press of Hawaii, 1976.

AL-ISSA, I. Problems in the cross-cultural study of schizophrenia. *Journal of Psychology*, 1968, *71*, 143–151.

———. Social and cultural aspects of hallucinations. *Psychological Bulletin*, 1977, *84*, 570–587.

AMERICAN PSYCHIATRIC ASSOCIATION. *Diagnostic and statistical manual of mental disorders.* (2nd Ed.) (DSM-II.) Washington, D.C.: The Association, 1968.

ANGELINI, A. Alguns problemas metodólogicos na pesquisa transcultural. In C. F. Hereford and L. Natalicio (Eds.), *Aportaciones de la psicología a la investigación transcultural.* Mexico City, Mexico: Trillas, 1967.

ARGANDOÑA, M., & KIEV, A. *Mental health in the developing world.* New York: Free Press, 1974.

ARIETI, S. Manic depressive psychosis. In S. Arieti (Ed.), *American handbook of psychiatry* (Vol. I). New York: Basic Books, 1959, pp. 419–454.

ARIETI, S., & METH, J. M. Rare, unclassifiable, collective, and exotic psychotic syndromes. In S. Arieti (Ed.), *American handbook of psychiatry.* New York: Basic Books, 1959.

ARSENIAN, J., & ARSENIAN, J. M. Tough and easy cultures: A conceptual analysis. *Psychiatry*, 1948, *11*, 377–385.

ASAI, T. The contents of delusions of schizophrenic patients in Japan: Comparison between periods 1941–1961. *Transcultural Psychiatric Research Review*, 1964, *1*, 27.

AWARITEFE, A., & EBIE, J. C. Contemporary attitude toward mental illness in Nigeria. *African Journal of Psychiatry*, 1975, *1*, 37–43.

BANDURA, A. A social learning interpretation of psychological dysfunctions. In P. London & D. Rosenhan (Eds.), *Foundations of abnormal psychology*. New York: Holt, Rinehart & Winston, 1968.

BARRETT, E., & FRANKE, R. Psychogenic death: A reappraisal. *Science*, 1970, *167*, 304–306.

BASH, K. W., & BASH-LIECHTI, J. Studies of the epidemiology of neuropsychiatric disorders among the rural population of the province of of Khuzestan, Iran. *Social Psychiatry*, 1969, *4*, 137–143.

BASTIDE, R. *La sociologie des maladies mentales*. Paris: Flammarion, 1965.

BECHTEL, R. B., & GONZALEZ, A. Comparison of treatment environments among some Peruvian and North American mental hospitals. *Archives of General Psychiatry*, 1971, *25*, 64–68.

BECK, A. T. *Depression: Clinical, experimental, and theoretical aspects*. New York: Harper, 1967.

BEISER, M. Epidémiologie psychiatrique dans un pays sous-développé. *Acta psychiatrica belgica*, 1975, *75*, 221–236.

BEISER, M., BENFARI, R. C., COLLOMB, H., & RAVEL, J. L. Measuring psychoneurotic behavior in cross-cultural surveys. *Journal of Nervous and Mental Disease*, 1976, *163*, 10–23.

BEISER, M., RAVEL, J. L., COLLOMB, H., & EGELHOFF, C. Assessing psychiatric disorder among the Serer of Senegal. *Journal of Nervous and Mental Disease*, 1972, *154*, 141–151.

BENEDICT, R. Culture and the abnormal. *Journal of Genetic Psychology*, 1934, *1*, 60–64.

BERNE, E. Comparative psychiatry and tropical psychiatry. *American Journal of Psychiatry*, 1956, *113*, 193–200.

————. Difficulties of comparative psychiatry. *American Journal of Psychiatry*, 1959, *116*, 104–109.

BINITIE, A. A factor-analytic study of depression (African and European). *British Journal of Psychiatry*, 1975, *127*, 559–563.

BOESCH, E. E., & ECKENSBERGER, L. H. Methodische Probleme des interkulturellen Vergleichs. In C. F. Graumann, L. Kruse, & B. Kroner (Eds.) *Sozialpsychologie: I. Halbband: Theorien und Methoden: Handbuch der Psychologie. Band 7/1*. Göttingen: Verlag für Psychologie, 1969.

BOLMAN, W. Cross-cultural psychotherapy. *American Journal of Psychiatry*, 1968, *124*, 1237–1244.

BOROFFKA, A. Psychiatrie in Nigeria. *Zentralblatt für Neurologie und Psychiatrie* 1964, *176*, 103–104.

————. Different ways of starting mental health care. *Psychopathologie Africaine*, 1970, *6*, 181–199.

BOUCHAL, M. Změny v obsahu priznaku schizofrenie a parafrenie pod vlivom společensko historického vývoje. *Československá Psychiatrie*, 1958, *54*, 149–153.

BRISLIN, R. W., LONNER, W. J., & THORNDIKE, R. M. *Cross-cultural research methods.* New York: Wiley, 1973.

BRITTON, R. S., & CORDES, C. K. A comparison of child psychiatric morbidity in American and British military families overseas. *Journal of the Royal Army Medical Corps*, 1970, *116*, 11–16 (*Transcultural Psychiatric Research Review*, 1973, *10*, 180–182).

BRODY, E. B. *The lost ones: Social forces and mental illness in Rio de Janeiro.* New York: International Universities Press, 1973.

BURTON-BRADLEY, B. G. The amok syndrome in Papua and New Guinea. *Medical Journal of Australia*, 1968, *55*, 252–256.

————. Transcultural psychiatry in Papua and New Guinea. *Journal of Cross-Cultural Psychology*, 1970, *1*, 177–183.

BUSTAMENTE, J. A. La réaction psychotique aiguë, la transculturation, le sous-développement et les changements sociaux. *Psychopathologie Africaine*, 1965, *5*, 223–233.

CADE, J. F., & KRUPINSKI, J. Incidence of psychiatric disorders in Victoria in relation to country of birth. *Medical Journal of Australia*, 1962, *49*, 400–404.

CAMPBELL, D., & STANLEY, J. *Experimental and quasi-experimental design for research.* Chicago: Rand McNally, 1966.

CAROTHERS, J. C. *The African mind in health and disease* (Monograph No. 17). Geneva: World Health Organization, 1953.

CARPENTER, W. T., STRAUSS, J. S., & BARTKO, J. J. Flexible system for the diagnosis of schizophrenia: Report from the WHO International Pilot Study of Schizophrenia. *Science*, 1973, *179*, 1275–1278.

CARSTAIRS, G. M. The social limits of eccentricity. In M. K. Opler (Ed.), *Culture and mental health.* New York: Macmillan, 1959.

CATTELL, R. B., & WARBURTON, F. W. A cross-cultural comparison of patterns of extraversion and anxiety. *British Journal of Psychology*, 1961, *52*, 375.

CAUDILL, W. Sibling rank and style of life among Japanese psychiatric patients. *Proceedings of the Joint Meeting of the Japanese Society of Psychiatry and Neurology and the American Psychiatric Association in Tokyo*, 1963, 35–40.

————. The influence of social structure and culture on human behavior in Japan. *Journal of Nervous and Mental Disease*, 1973, *157*, 249–258.

CAUDILL, W., & LIN, T. (Eds.). *Mental health research in Asia and the Pacific.* Honolulu: East-West Center Press, 1969.

CAUDILL, W., & SCHOOLER, C. Symptom patterns and background characteristics of Japanese psychiatric patients. In W. Caudill and T. Y. Lin (Eds.), *Mental health research in Asia and the Pacific.* Honolulu: East-West Center Press, 1969.

CAWTE, J. E. *Cruel, poor, and brutal nations: The assessment of mental health in an Australian Aboriginal community by short-stay psychiatric field team methods.* Honolulu: University Press of Hawaii, 1972.

————. Social and cultural influences on mental health in Aboriginal Australia: A summary of ten years' research. *Transcultural Psychiatric Research Review*, 1976, *13*, 23–38.

————. Multidisciplinary collaboration in fieldwork: Australian studies. *Transactions of the New York Academy of Sciences, 1977, 285, 664-675.*

CHANCE, J. A cross-cultural study of social cohesion and depression. *Transcultural Psychiatric Research Review,* 1964, *1,* 19-21.

CHIU, T. L., TONG, J. E., & SCHMIDT, K. E. A clinical and survey study of latah in Sarawak, Malaysia. *Psychological Medicine,* 1972, *2,* 155-165.

COLLOMB, H. Bouffées délirantes en psychiatrie africaine. *Psychopathologie Africaine,* 1965, *1,* 167-239.

————. Aspectes de la psychiatrie dans l'Ouest Africain. *Aktuelle Fragen der Psychiatrie und Neurologie,* 1967, *5,* 229-253.

————. L'avenir de la psychiatrie en Afrique. *Psychopathologie Africaine,* 1973a, *9,* 343-370.

————. Rencontre de deux systèmes des soins. A propos de thérapeutiques des malades mentales en Afrique. *Social Science and Medicine,* 1973b, *7,* 623-633.

COOPER, J. E., KENDELL, R. E., GURLAND, B. J., SHARPE, L., COPELAND, J. R. M., & SIMON, R. *Psychiatric diagnosis in New York and London.* London: Oxford University Press, 1972.

COPELAND, J. R. M., KELLEHER, M. J., KELLETT, J. M., GOURLAY, A. J., BARRON, M. A., COWAN, D. W., DE GRUCHY, J., GIERLAND, B. J., SHARPE, L., SIMON, R., KURIANSKY, J., & STILLER, P. Diagnostic differences in psychogeriatric patients in London and New York: United Kingdom–United States diagnostic project. *Canadian Psychiatric Association Journal,* 1974, *19,* 267-271.

CROCETTI, C. M., LEMKAU, P. V., KULČAR, Z., & KESIĆ, B. Selected aspects of the epidemiology of psychoses in Croatia, Yugoslavia. III. The cluster sample and the results of the pilot survey. *American Journal of Epidemiology,* 1971, *94,* 126-134.

DAWSON, J. Urbanization and mental health in a West African community. In A. Kiev (Ed.), *Magic, faith and healing: Studies in primitive psychiatry today.* New York: Free Press, 1964.

DENKO, J. D. The role of culture in mental illness of non-Western peoples. *Journal of American Women's Medical Association,* 1964, *19,* 1029-1044.

————. How preliterate peoples explain disturbed behavior. *Archives of General Psychiatry,* 1966, *15,* 398-409.

DEVEREUX, G. Normal and abnormal. In Anthropological Society of Washington, *Some uses of anthropology: Theoretical and applied.* Washington, D.C.: The Society, 1956.

————. *Mohave ethnopsychiatry and suicide: The psychiatric knowledge and the psychic disturbances of an Indian tribe.* Washington, D.C.: Smithsonian Institution, 1961.

DEVOS, G. A. Transcultural diagnosis of mental health by means of psychological tests. In A. V. S. DeReuck & R. Porter (Eds.), *Transcultural psychiatry.* Boston: Little, Brown, 1965.

————. The relationship of social and psychological structures in transcultural psychiatry. In W. P. Lebra (Ed.), *Culture-bound syndromes, ethnopsychiatry, and alternate therapies.* Honolulu: University Press of Hawaii, 1976.

DIAZ-GUERRERO, R. Sociocultural premises, attitudes, and cross-cultural research. *International Journal of Psychology,* 1967, *2,* 79-88.

DIOP, B., COLLIGNON, R., & GUEYE, M. Présentation de l'étude concertée de l'O.M.S. sur les stratégies pour l'extension des soins de santé mentale. *Psychopathologie Africaine*, 1976, *12*, 173–188.

DOHRENWEND, B. P., & DOHRENWEND, B. S. *Social status and psychological disorder.* New York: Wiley, 1969.

———. Social and cultural influences on psychopathology. *Annual Review of Psychology*, 1974, *25*, 419–452.

DRAGUNS, J. G. Comparisons of psychopathology across cultures: Issues, findings, directions. *Journal of Cross-Cultural Psychology*, 1973, *4*, 9–47.

———. Values reflected in psychopathology: The case of the Protestant ethic. *Ethos*, 1974, *2*, 115–136.

———. Studying abnormal behavior cross-culturally. In J. W. Berry and W. J. Lonner (Eds.), *Applied Cross-Cultural Psychology. Papers from the Second International Conference of IACCP.* Amsterdam: Swets and Zeitlinger, 1975.

———. Mental health and culture. In D. S. Hoopes, P. B. Pedersen, & G. W. Renwick (Eds.), *Overview of intercultural education, training and research. I. Theory.* Washington, D.C.: Society for Intercultural Education, Training, and Research, 1977a.

———. Problems of defining and comparing abnormal behaviors across cultures. *Annals of the New York Academy of Sciences*, 1977b, *285*, 664–675.

———. Advances in methodology of cross-cultural psychiatric assessment. *Transcultural Psychiatric Research Review*, 1977c, *14*, 125–143.

DRAGUNS, J. G., NACHSHON, I., BROVERMAN, I. K., & PHILLIPS, L. Ethnic differences in psychiatric symptomatology: A study of an Israeli child guidance clinic population. Paper at the Eastern Psychological Association, Boston, April 1967.

DRAGUNS, J. G., & PHILLIPS, L. *Psychiatric classification and diagnosis: An overview and critique.* Morristown, N.J.: General Learning Press, 1971.

———. *Culture and psychopathology: The quest for a relationship.* Morristown, N.J.: General Learning Press, 1972.

DRAGUNS, J. G., PHILLIPS, L., BROVERMAN, I. K., & CAUDILL, W. Social competence and psychiatric symptomatology in Japan: A cross-cultural extension of earlier American findings. *Journal of Abnormal Psychology*, 1970, *75*, 68–74.

DRAGUNS, J. G., PHILLIPS, L., BROVERMAN, I. K., CAUDILL, W., & NISHIMAE, S. The symptomatology of hospitalized psychiatric patients in Japan and in the United States: A study of cultural differences. *Journal of Nervous and Mental Diseases*, 1971, *152*, 3–16.

DuBOIS, C. *The people of Alor.* Cambridge, Mass.: Harvard University Press, 1944.

DUNHAM, H. W. Society, culture, and mental disorder. *Archives of General Psychiatry*, 1976, *33*, 147–156.

DURKHEIM, E. *Suicide* (J. A. Spaulding & G. Simpson, trans.). Glencoe, Ill.: Free Press, 1951. (Originally published, 1897.)

EDGERTON, R. B. Conceptions of psychosis in four East African societies. *American Anthropologist*, 1966, *68*, 408–425.

———. On the "recognition" of mental illness. In S. Plog & R. B. Edgerton (Eds.), *Changing perspectives in mental health.* New York: Holt, Rinehart & Winston, 1969.

———. *The individual in cultural adaptation.* Berkeley: University of California Press, 1971.

EDWARDS, G. Diagnosis of schizophrenia: An Anglo-American comparison. *International Journal of Psychiatry,* 1973, *11,* 442–452.

ELLENBERGER, H. Intérêt et domaines d'application de l'ethno-psychiatrie. *Proceedings of the Fourth World Congress of Psychiatry.* Amsterdam: Excerpta Medica, 1968.

ENGELSMANN, F., MURPHY, H. B. M., PRINCE, R., LEDUC, M., & DEMERS, H. Variations in responses to a symptom check-list by age, sex, income, residence, and ethnicity. *Social Psychiatry,* 1972, *7,* 150–156.

ENGELSMANN, F., VINAŘ, P., PICHOT, P., HIPPIUS, H., GIBERTI, F., ROSSI, L., & OVERALL, J. E. International comparison of diagnostic patterns. *Transcultural Psychiatric Research Review,* 1971, *7,* 130–137.

ENRIGHT, J. B., & JAECKLE, W. R. Psychiatric symptoms and diagnosis in two subcultures. *International Journal of Social Psychiatry,* 1963, *9,* 12–17.

ERIKSON, K. T. *Wayward Puritans: A study in the sociology of deviance.* New York: Wiley, 1966.

ERINOSHO, O. A. Lambo's model of psychiatric care. *Psychopathologie Africaine,* 1976, *12,* 35–44.

FABREGA, H. J. *Disease and social behavior: An interdisciplinary perspective.* Cambridge, Mass.: MIT Press, 1974.

FABREGA, H. J., SWARTZ, J. D., & WALLACE, C. A. Ethnic differences in psychopathology: Clinical correlates under varying conditions. *Archives of General Psychiatry,* 1968, *19,* 218–226.

FABREGA, H., & WALLACE, C. A. How physicians judge symptoms: A cross-cultural study. *Journal of Nervous and Mental Disease,* 1967, *142,* 486–491.

FARBER, M. L. *Theory of suicide.* New York: Funk & Wagnalls, 1968.

FARBEROW, N. L. *Suicide in different cultures.* Baltimore, Md.: University Park Press, 1975.

FARBEROW, N. L., & SIMON, M. D. Suicide in Los Angeles and Vienna. *Public Health Reports,* 1969, *84,* 389–403.

FAVAZZA, A. R., & OMAN, M. *Anthropological and cross-cultural themes in mental health: An annotated bibliography, 1925–1974.* Columbia, Mo.: University of Missouri Press, 1977.

————. Overview: Foundations of cultural psychiatry. *American Journal of Psychiatry,* 1978, *135,* 293–303.

FIELD, M. J. *Search for security: An ethnopsychiatric study of rural Ghana.* Evanston, Ill.: Northwestern University Press, 1960.

FINNEY, J. C. Psychiatry and multiculturality in Hawaii. *International Journal of Social Psychiatry,* 1963, *9,* 5–11.

FISCHER, M. Development and validity of a computerized method for diagnosis of functional psychosis. *Acta Psychiatrica Scandinavica,* 1974, *50,* 243–288.

FLEISS, J. L., GURLAND, B. J., SIMON, R., & SHARPE, L. Cross-national study of diagnosis of the mental disorders: Some demographic correlates of hospital diagnosis in New York and London. *International Journal of Social Psychiatry,* 1973, *19,* 180–186.

FOA, E. B., & CHATTERJEE, E. Self-other differentiation: A cross-culturally invariant characteristic of mental patients. *Social Psychiatry,* 1974, *9,* 119–122.

FOA, U. G., & FOA, E. B. *Social structures of the mind.* Springfield, Ill.: Thomas, 1974.

FROMM, E. *The sane society.* New York: Holt, Rinehart & Winston, 1955.

FUNDIA, J. A., DRAGUNS, J. G., & PHILLIPS, L. Culture and psychiatric symptomatology: A comparison of Argentine and United States patients. *Social Psychiatry,* 1971, *6,* 11–20.

GAITONDE, M. R. Cross-cultural study of psychiatric syndromes in out-patient clinics in Bombay, India, and Topeka, Kansas. *International Journal of Social Psychiatry,* 1958, *4,* 98–108.

GERMAN, G. A. Aspects of clinical psychiatry in sub-Saharan Africa. *British Journal of Psychiatry,* 1972, *121,* 461–479.

GIORDANO, J. *Ethnicity and mental health: Research and recommendations.* New York: American Jewish Committee, 1973.

GIORDANO, J., & GIORDANO, G. P. Ethnicity and community mental health. *Community Mental Health Review,* 1976, *1,* No. 3, 1, 4–14, 15.

GOFFMAN, E. *Asylums: Essays on the social situation of patients and other inmates.* New York: Doubleday, 1961.

GOLDFRIED, M. R., & KENT, R. N. Traditional versus behavioral personality assessment: A comparison of methodological and theoretical assumptions. *Psychological Bulletin,* 1972, *77,* 409–420.

GOVE, W. (Ed.). *The labeling of deviance: Evaluating a perspective.* New York: Wiley, 1975.

GUTHRIE, G. M. *Culture and mental disorder.* Reading, Mass.: Addison-Wesley, 1972.

HAHN, R. A. Aboriginal American psychiatric theories. *Transcultural Psychiatric Research Review,* 1978, *15,* 29–58.

HAMAGUCHI, E. A bibliographic overview of the postwar studies of Japanese culture. *Psychologia,* 1965, *8,* 50–62.

HASUZAWA, T. Chronological observations of delusions in schizophrenics. *Proceedings of the Joint Meeting of the Japanese Society of Psychiatry and Neurology and the American Psychiatric Association, Tokyo,* 1963. (Suppl. no. 7, *Folia Psychiatrica et Neurologica Japanica.*)

HAVIGHURST, R. J., DuBOIS, M. E., CSIKSZENTMIHALYI, M., & DOLL, R. *Las actitudes personales y sociales de adolescentes de Buenos Aires y de Chicago.* Washington, D.C.: Panamerican Union, 1963.

HELGASON, T. Epidemiology of mental disorders in Iceland. *Acta Psychiatrica Scandinavica,* 1964, Suppl. 173, 1–258.

HENDIN, H. *Suicide and Scandinavia.* New York: Grune & Stratton, 1964.

HENRY, J. P., & SHORT, T. J. *Suicide and homicide.* Glencoe, Ill.: Free Press, 1954.

HERSEN, M., & BELLACK, A. S. *Behavioral assessment: A practical handbook.* New York: Pergamon, 1976.

HIGGINBOTHAM, H. N. A conceptual model for the delivery of services in non-Western settings. *Topics in Culture Learning,* 1976, *4,* 44–52.

———. Culture and mental health services in developing countries. In A. J. Marsella, T. Ciborowski, & R. Tharp (Eds.), *Current perspectives on cross-cultural psychology.* New York: Academic Press, 1979.

HIPPLER, A. E. Transcultural and psychiatric and related research in the North American Arctic and Subarctic. *Transcultural Psychiatric Research Review,* 1975, *12,* 103–115.

HOLLANDER, M. H., & HIRSCH, S. J. Hysterical psychoses. *American Journal of Psychiatry, 1964, 120, 1066–1074.*

HOLTZMAN, W. H., DIAZ-GUERRERO, R., & SWARTZ, J. D. *Personality development in two cultures.* Austin: University of Texas Press, 1975.

HONIGMANN, J. J. Toward a distinction between psychiatric and social abnormality. *Social Forces, 1953, 31, 274–277.*

———. *Culture and personality.* New York: Harper, 1954.

JACO, E. G. *The social epidemiology of mental disorders.* New York: Russell Sage, 1960.

JACOBY, J. The construct of abnormality: Some cross-cultural considerations. *Journal of Experimental Research in Personality, 1967, 2, 1–15.*

JAHODA, G. Presidential address. In J. W. Berry & W. J. Lonner (Eds.), Applied cross–cultural psychology: Selected papers from the Second International Conference of IAACP. Amsterdam: Swets & Zeitlinger, 1975.

JAKOVLJEVIĆ, V. Doprinos proučavanju uloge psiholoških uticaja sociokulturne sredine u patogenezi neuroza. *Neuropsihijatrija, 1959, 7, 39–55.*

———. La survivance d'un rite culturel archaïque—fête des Roussales—sous la forme des maniféstations hystériques. *Comptes Rendus, VI Congres International des Sciences Ethnologiques—Anthropologiques,* Paris, 1961.

———. Milieu culturel et nevroses. *Annales médico-psychologiques, 1962, 120(1),* 470–481.

———. Transkulturno-psihijatricka proučavanja u Gvineji. *Neuropsihijatrija, 1963, 11, 21–38.*

JILEK, W. G., & JILEK-AAL, L. Transient psychoses in Africans. *Psychiatria Clinica, 1970, 3, 337–364.*

JONES, I. H. Psychiatric disorders among aborigines of the Australian western desert. *Social Science and Medicine, 1972, 6, 263–267.*

KAHN, M. W., & DELK, J. L. Developing a community mental health clinic on the Papago Indian reservation. *International Journal of Social Psychiatry, 1973, 19,* 299–306.

KANFER, F. H., & SASLOW, G. Behavioral analysis: An alternative to diagnostic classification. *Archives of General Psychiatry, 1965, 12, 529–538.*

KASAHARA, Y., & SAKAMOTO, K. Eureuthrophobia and allied conditions: A contribution toward the psychopathological and cross-cultural study of a borderline state. In S. Arieti (Ed.), *The World Biennial of Psychiatry and Psychology* (Vol. 1), New York: Basic Books, pp. 292–310.

KATCHADOURIAN, H. A comparative study of mental illness among the Christians and Moslems of Lebanon. *International Journal of Social Psychiatry, 1974, 20,* 56–67.

KATO, M. Psychiatric epidemiological surveys in Japan: The problem of case finding. In W. Caudill & T. Lin (Eds.), *Mental health research in Asia and the Pacific.* Honolulu: East-West Center Press, 1969.

KATZ, M. M., COLE, O. J., & LOWERY, H. A. Studies of the diagnostic process: The influence of symptom perception, past experience, and ethnic background on diagnostic decisions. *American Journal of Psychiatry, 1969, 125, 937–947.*

KATZ, M. M., & SANBORN, K. O. Multi-ethnic studies of psychopathology and normality in Hawaii. In B. S. Brown & E. F. Torrey (Eds.), *International Collaboration in Mental Health.* Washington, D.C.: U.S. Government Printing Office, 1973.

KATZ, M. M., SANBORN, K. O., LOWERY, H. A., & CHING, J. Ethnic studies in Hawaii: On psychopathology and social deviance. In L. C. Wynne (Ed.), *The nature of schizophrenia.* New York: Wiley, 1978.

KELLEHER, M. J., & COPELAND, J. R. M. Psychiatric diagnosis in Ireland: A videotape study. *Journal of the Irish Medical Association,* 1974, *67,* 87–92.

KELLEHER, M. J., COPELAND, J. R. M., & SMITH, A. J. High first admission rates for schizophrenia in the west of Ireland. *Psychological Medicine,* 1974, *4,* 460–462.

KENDELL, R. E. The concept of disease and its implications for psychiatry. *British Journal of Psychiatry,* 1975, *127,* 305–315.

KENDELL, R. E., PICHOT, P., & VON CRANACH, M. Diagnostic criteria of English, French, and German psychiatrists. *Psychological Medicine,* 1974, *4,* 187–195.

KENNEDY, J. G. Cultural psychiatry. In J. H. Honigmann (Ed.), *Handbook of social and cultural anthropology.* Chicago: Rand McNally, 1973.

KIDSON, M. A., & JONES, I. H. Psychiatric disorders among Aborigines of the Australian Western desert. *Archives of General Psychiatry,* 1968, *19,* 413–423.

KIEV, A. Transcultural psychiatry: Research problems and perspectives. In S. C. Plog & R. B. Edgerton (Eds.), *Changing perspectives in mental illness.* New York: Holt, Rinehart & Winston, 1969.

———. *Transcultural psychiatry.* New York: Free Press, 1972.

KIM, K. I., & RHI, B. Y. A review of Korean cultural psychiatry. *Transcultural Psychiatric Research Review,* 1976, *13,* 101–114.

KIMURA, B. Vergleichende Untersuchungen über depressive Erkrankungen in Japan und Deutschland. *Fortschritte der Psychiatrie und Neurologie,* 1965, *33,* 202–215.

———. Phänomenologie des Schulderlebnisses in einer vergleichenden psychiatrischen Sicht. *Aktuelle Fragen der Psychiatrie und Neurologie,* 1967, *6,* 54–65.

———. Mitmenschlichkeit in der Psychiatrie. *Zeitschrift für klinische Psychologie,* 1972, *20,* 3–13.

KITANO, H. L. Mental illness in four cultures. *Journal of Social Psychology, 1970, 80,* 121–134.

KLINE, N. S. A theoretical framework for transcultural psychiatry. *American Journal of Psychiatry,* 1966, *123,* 85–87.

KLUCKHOHN, C. *Navajo witchcraft.* Boston: Beacon, 1962.

KOCH, K. F. On possession behavior in New Guinea. *Journal of the Polynesian Society,* 1968, *77,* 135–146.

KRAEPELIN, E. Vergleichende Psychiatrie. *Zentralblatt für Nervenheilkunde und Psychiatrie,* 1904, *15,* 433–437.

KRAMER, M. *Applications of mental health statistics.* Geneva: World Health Organization, 1969.

KUHN, T. S. *The structure of scientific revolutions.* Chicago: University of Chicago Press, 1962.

LAMBO, T. A. Psychiatry in the tropics. *Lancet,* 1965, *2,* 1119–1121.

LANGNESS, L. L. Hysterical psychosis in the New Guinea Highlands: A Bena-Bena example. *Psychiatry,* 1965, *28,* 258–277.

———. Rejoinder to R. Salisbury. *Transcultural Psychiatric Research Review,* 1967, *4,* 125–130.

―――. Hysterical psychosis: The cross-cultural evidence. *American Journal of Psychiatry*, 1969, *6*, 95–100.

LASRY, J.-C. Cross-cultural perspective on mental health and immigrant adaptation. *Social Psychiatry*, 1977, *12*, 49–55.

LEBRA, W. (Ed.). *Transcultural research in mental health. Mental health research in Asia and the Pacific* (Vol. II). Honolulu: University Press of Hawaii, 1972.

―――. *Youth, socialization, and mental health.* Mental health research in Asia and the Pacific (Vol. III). Honolulu: University Press of Hawaii, 1974.

―――. *Culture-bound syndromes, ethnopsychiatry, and alternate therapies. Mental health research in Asia and the Pacific* (Vol. IV). Honolulu: University Press of Hawaii, 1976.

LEIGHTON, A. H. *My name is legion.* New York: Basic Books, 1959.

LEIGHTON, A. H., & HUGHES, J. M. Cultures as causative of mental disorder. *Millbank Memorial Fund Bulletin*, 1961, *39*, 441–472.

LEIGHTON, A. H., LAMBO, T. A., HUGHES, C. C., LEIGHTON, D. C., MURPHY, J. M., & MACKLIN, D. B. *Psychiatric disorders among the Yoruba.* Ithaca, N.Y.: Cornell University Press, 1963.

LEIGHTON, D. C., HARDING, J. S., MACKLIN, D. B., MACMILLAN, A. M., & LEIGHTON, A. H. *The character of danger: Psychiatric symptoms in selected communities.* New York: Basic Books, 1963.

LENZ, H. *Vergleichende Psychiatrie.* Vienna: Maudrich, 1964.

LEÓN, C. A. Psychiatry in Latin America. *British Journal of Psychiatry*, 1972, *121*, 121–136.

LEÓN, C. A., & MICKLIN, M. Opiniones comunitarias sobre la enfermedad mental y su tratamiento en Cali, Colombia. *Acta Psiquiátrica y Psicológica de América Latina*, 1971, *17*, 385–395.

LEVINE, D. A cross-cultural study of attitudes toward mental illness. *Journal of Abnormal Psychology*, 1972, *80*, 111–114.

LÉVI-STRAUSS, C. *Tristes tropiques* (J. Weightman & D. Weightman, trans.). New York: Atheneum, 1974.

LIN, T. A study of the incidence of mental disorder in Chinese and other cultures. *Psychiatry*, 1953, *16*, 313–336.

―――. The epidemiological study of mental disorders. *WHO Chronicle*, 1959, *21*, 509–516.

―――. The epidemiological study of mental disorders by WHO. *Social Psychiatry*, 1967, *1*, 204–205.

―――. Reducing variability in international research. *Social Psychiatry*, 1969, *3*, 47.

LIN, T., RIN, H., YEH, E. K., HSU, C., & CHU, H. Mental disorders in Taiwan fifteen years later: A preliminary report. In W. Caudill & T. Lin (Eds.), *Mental health research in Asia and the Pacific.* Honolulu: East-West Center Press, 1969.

LINDZEY, G. *Projective techniques and cross-cultural research.* New York: Appleton-Century-Crofts, 1961.

LINTON, R. *Culture and mental disease.* Springfield, Ill.: Thomas, 1956.

LORR, M., & KLETT, C. J. Major psychiatric disorders: A cross-cultural study. *Archives of General Psychiatry*, 1968, *19*, 652–658.

―――. Cross-cultural comparison of psychotic syndromes. *Journal of Abnormal Psychology*, 1969a, *74*, 531–545.

————. Psychotic behavior types: A cross-cultural comparison. *Archives of General Psychiatry*, 1969b, *20*, 592–598.

LYNN, R. *Personality and national character.* New York: Pergamon, 1971.

MAHONEY, M. J. *Cognition and behavior modification.* Cambridge, Mass.: Ballinger, 1974.

MARETZKI, T., & NELSON, L. D. Psychopathology among Hawaii's Japanese: A comparative study. In W. Caudill & T. Lin (Eds.), *Mental health research in Asia and the Pacific.* Honolulu: East-West Center Press, 1969.

MARGETTS, E. L. Methods of psychiatric research in Africa. In A. V. S. DeReuck & R. Porter (Eds.), *CIBA Symposium on Transcultural Psychiatry.* London: Churchill, 1965.

MARSELLA, A. J., ESCUDERO, M., & GORDON, P. Stresses, resources, and symptom patterns in urban Filipino men. In W. P. Lebra (Ed.), *Transcultural research in mental health.* Mental health research in Asia and the Pacific (Vol. II). Honolulu: University Press of Hawaii, 1972.

MARSELLA, A. J., KINZIE, D., & GORDON, P. Ethnic variations in the expression of depression. *Journal of Cross-Cultural Psychology*, 1973, *4*, 435–458.

MARSELLA, A. J., MURRAY, M. D., & GOLDEN, C. Ethnic variations in the phenomenology of emotions: I. Shame. *Journal of Cross-Cultural Psychology*, 1974, *5*, 312–328.

MARSELLA, A. J., WALKER, E., & JOHNSON, F. Personality correlates of depressive disorders of female college students of different ethnic groups. *International Journal of Social Psychiatry*, 1973, *19*, 77–81.

McCLELLAND, D. C. *The achieving society.* Princeton, N.J.: Van Nostrand, 1961.

MEICHENBAUM, D. *Cognitive behavior modification: An integrative framework.* New York: Plenum, 1977.

MICKLIN, M., & LEÓN, C. A. Rechazo al enfermo mental en una ciudad sudamericana: Un análisis comparativo. *Acta Psiquiátrica y Psicológica de América Latina*, 1972, *18*, 321–329.

MINTZ, N. L., & SCHWARTZ, D. T. Urban ecology and psychosis: Community factors in the incidence of schizophrenia and manic depression among Italians in Greater Boston. *International Journal of Social Psychiatry*, 1964, *10*, 101–118.

MISRA, R. K. Mental health: A cross-cultural approach. In J. W. Berry and W. J. Lonner (Eds.), *Applied cross-cultural psychology: Papers from the Second International Conference of IACCP.* Amsterdam: Swetz and Zeitlinger, 1975.

MONTAGUE, A. Culture and mental illness. *American Journal of Psychiatry*, 1961, *118*, 15–23.

MÜLLER, H. Das Dritte Reich im Wahn Anstaltskranker (Heil- und Pflegeanstalt Lübeck-Stecknitz). *Psychiatria Clinica*, 1970, *3*, 20–30.

MUÑOZ, L., MARCONI, J., HORWITZ, J., & NEVEILLAN, P. Cross-cultural definitions applied to the study of the functional psychoses of Chilean Mapuches. *British Journal of Psychiatry*, 1966, *112*, 1205–1215.

MURPHY, H. B. M. Social change and mental health. In Milbank Memorial Fund, *Courses of mental disorder: Review of epidemiological knowledge.* New York: Milbank Memorial Fund, 1961.

————. Migration and the major mental diseases. In M. B. Kantor (Ed.), *Mobility and mental health.* Springfield, Ill.: Thomas, 1965.

————. Cultural aspects of the delusion. *Studium Generale*, 1967, *20*, 684–692.

————. History and the evolution of syndromes: The striking case of latah and amok. In M. Hammer, K. Salzinger, & S. Sutton (Eds.), *Psychopathology*. New York: Wiley, 1972a.

————. Chronicity, community, and culture. Paper at Colloques sur traitements au long cours des états psychotiques, Paris, February, 1972b.

————. Review of "Personality and National Character" by Richard Lynn. *Transcultural Psychiatric Research Review*, 1972c, *9*, 101–104.

————. Differences between the mental disorders of French Canadians and British Canadians. *Canadian Psychiatric Association Journal*, 1974, *19*, 247–258.

————. Alcoholism and schizophrenia in the Irish: A review. *Transcultural Psychiatric Research Review*, 1975, *12*, 116–139.

————. European cultural offshoots in the New World: Differences in their mental hospitalization patterns. Part I: British, French, and Italian influences. *Social Psychiatry*, 1978, *13*, 1–19.

MURPHY, H. B. M., & LEMIEUX, M. Quelques considérations sur le taux élevé de schizophrenie dans un type de communauté canadienne-française. *Canadian Psychiatric Association Journal*, 1967, *12*, Special Issue, S71–S81.

MURPHY, H. B. M., & RAMAN, A. C. The chronicity of schizophrenia in indigenous tropical peoples: Results of a twelve-year follow-up in Mauritius. *British Journal of Psychiatry*, 1971, *118*, 489–497.

MURPHY, H. B. M., WITTKOWER, E. W., & CHANCE, N. A. Cross-cultural inquiry into the symptomatology of depression: A preliminary report. *International Journal of Psychiatry*, 1967, *3*, 6–15.

MURPHY, H. B. M., WITTKOWER, E. W., FRIED, J., & ELLENBERGER, H. A cross-cultural survey of schizophrenic symptomatology. *International Journal of Social Psychiatry*, 1963, *9*, 237–249.

MURPHY, J. M. A cross-cultural comparison of psychiatric disorder: Eskimos of Alaska, Yorubas of Nigeria, and Nova Scotians of Canada. In W. P. Lebra (Ed.), *Transcultural research in mental health* (Vol. II). Honolulu: University Press of Hawaii, 1972.

————. Psychiatric labeling in cross-cultural perspective. *Science*, 1976, *191*, 1019–1028.

MURPHY, J. M., & LEIGHTON, A. H. Native conceptions of psychiatric disorder. In J. M. Murphy & A. H. Leighton (Eds.), *Approaches to cross-cultural psychiatry*. Ithaca, N.Y.: Cornell University Press, 1965.

NACHSHON, I., DRAGUNS, J. G., BROVERMAN, I. K., & PHILLIPS, L. Acculturation and psychiatric symptomatology: A study of an Israeli child guidance clinic population. *Social Psychiatry*, 1972, *7*, 109–118.

NAROLL, R. Cultural determinants and the sick society. In S. C. Plog & R. B. Edgerton (Eds.), *Changing perspectives of mental illness*. New York: Holt, Rinehart & Winston, 1969.

NAROLL, R., & COHEN, R. (Eds.). *A handbook of method in cultural anthropology*. New York: Museum of Natural History Press, 1970.

NEKI, J. S. Psychiatry in South-East Asia. *British Journal of Psychiatry*, 1973, *123*, 257–269.

NEWBROUGH, J. R. Concepts of behavior disorder. In S. E. Golann & C. Eisdorfer

(Eds.), *Handbook of Community Psychology*. New York: Appleton-Century-Crofts, 1972.

NORBECK, E., & DeVos, G. Japan. In F. L. K. Hsu (Ed.), *Psychological anthropology* (1st Ed.). Homewood, Ill.: Dorsey, 1961.

OBERG, K. Culture shock: Adjustment to new cultural environments. *Practical Anthropology*, 1960, *7*, 177–182.

OGINO, K., KUBA, M., & SUZUKI, J. A review of transcultural psychiatric research in Japan. *Transcultural Psychiatric Research Review*, 1977, *14*, 7–22.

OPLER, M. K. *Culture and social psychiatry*. New York: Atherton, 1967.

OPLER, M. K., & SINGER, J. L. Ethnic differences in behavior and psychopathology: Italian and Irish. *International Journal of Social Psychiatry*, 1959, *2*, 11–23.

ORLEY, J. H. *Culture and mental illness: A study from Uganda*. Nairobi, Kenya: East African Publishing House, 1970.

OSMOND, H., & HOFFER, A. A comprehensive theory of schizophrenia. *International Journal of Neuropsychiatry*, 1966, *2*, 302–309.

PAGE, J. D. Cultural-national differences in symptomatology in hospitalized psychotic patients. *Yearbook of the American Philosophical Society*, 1965, 343–344.

―――. *Psychopathology: The science of understanding deviance* (2nd ed.). Chicago: Aldine, 1975.

PAGÉS LARRAYA, F. El complejo cultural de la locura en los moro-ayoreos. *Acta Psiquiátrica y Psicológica de América Latina*, 1973, *19*, 253–264.

―――. La psicopatología entre los sirionó. *Acta Psiquiátrica y Psicológica de América Latina*, 1977, *23*, 247–266.

PAPAJOHN, J., & SPIEGEL, J. *Transactions in families: A modern approach to resolving cultural and generational conflicts*. San Francisco: Jossey-Bass, 1974.

PARIN, P. Zur Bedeutung von Mythus, Ritual und Brauch für die vergleichende Psychiatrie. *Aktuelle Fragen der Psychiatrie and Neurologie*, 1967, *6*, 179–196.

PARKER, S. The Wiitiko psychosis in the context of Ojibwa personality and culture. *American Anthropologist*, 1960, *62*, 603–623.

PARKER, S., & KLEINER, R. J. *Mental illness in the urban Negro community*. New York: Free Press, 1966.

PARSONS, T. *The social system*. Glencoe, Ill.: Free Press, 1951.

PAUL, G. L. Chronic mental patient: Current status-future directions. *Psychological Bulletin*, 1969, *71*, 81–94.

PÉLICIER, Y. La psychologie des peuples et la psychiatrie. *Revue de Psychologie des Peuples*, 1968, *23*, 288–302.

PETRILOWITSCH, N. (Ed.). Beiträge zur vergleichenden Psychiatrie. *Aktuelle Fragen der Psychiatrie und Neurologie*, 1967, *6*.

PFEIFFER, W. M. Vergleichende psychiatrische Untersuchungen bei verschiedenen Bevölkerungsgruppen in Westjava. *Archiv für Psychiatrie und Nervenkrankheiten*, 1963, *204*, 494–414.

―――. *Transkulturelle Psychiatrie: Ergebnisse und Probleme*. Stuttgart: Thieme, 1970.

PHILLIPS, L. *Human adaptation and its failures*. New York: Academic Press, 1968.

PHILLIPS, L., & DRAGUNS, J. G. Classification of the behavior disorders. *Annual Review of Psychology*, 1971, *22*, 447–482.

PICHOT, P. Le diagnostique par ordinateur et la nosologie psychuiatrique. *Presse Medicale*, 1967, 75, 1269–1274.

PINTÉR, E. Wohlstandsflüchtlinge. Eine sozialpsychiatrische Studie an ungarischen Flüchtlingen in der Schweiz. *Bibliotheca Psychiatrica et Neurologica*, 1969, No. 138.

POGGIALI, B., & MAFFEI, G. Cultural patterns and related psychiatric nosography. *Proceedings of the Fourth World Congress in Psychiatry*. Amsterdam: Excerpta Medica, 1968.

PRANGE, A. J., & VITOLS, M. M. Cultural aspects of the relatively low incidence of depression in Southern Negros. *International Journal of Social Psychiatry*, 1962, 8, 104–112.

PRINCE, R. The changing picture of depressive syndromes: Is it fact or diagnostic fiction? *Canadian Journal of African Studies*, 1968, 1, 117–192.

RACY, J. W. Psychiatry in the Arab East. *Acta Psychiatrica Scandinavica*, 1970, Suppl. 211.

RAMAN, A. C., & MURPHY, H. B. M. Failure of traditional prognostic indicators in Afro-Asian psychotics: Results of a long-term follow-up survey. *Journal of Nervous and Mental Disease*, 1972, 154, 238–247.

RAO, A. V. Some aspects of psychiatry in India. *Transcultural Psychiatric Research Review*, 1978, 15, 7–28.

RESNER, G., & HARTOG, J. Concepts and terminology of mental disorders among the Malays. *Journal of Cross-Cultural Psychology*, 1970, 1, 369–381.

REYNOLDS, D. K., KALISH, R. A., & FARBEROW, N. L. A cross-ethnic study of suicide attitudes and expectations in the United States. In N. L. Farberow (Ed.), *Suicide in different cultures*. Baltimore, Md.: University Park Press, 1975.

RIN, H. Sibling rank, culture, and mental disorders. In W. Caudill & T. Lin (Eds.), *Mental health research in Asia and the Pacific*. Honolulu: East-West Center Press, 1969.

RIN, H., & LIN, T. Mental illness among Formosan aborigines as compared with the Chinese in Taiwan. *Journal of Mental Science*, 1962, 108, 134–146.

RIN, H., SCHOOLER, C., & CAUDILL, W. A. Culture, social structure and psychopathology in Japan and Taiwan. *Journal of Nervous and Mental Disease*, 1972, 157, 296–312.

RIN, H., WU, K.-C., & LIN, C.-L. A study of the content of delusions and hallucinations manifested by the Chinese paranoid psychotics. *Journal of the Formosan Medical Association*, 1962, 61, 47–57.

ROTENBERG, M. The Protestant ethic against the spirit of psychiatry: The other side of Weber's thesis. *British Journal of Sociology*, 1975, 26, 52–65.

ROTH, M. Neurosis, psychosis, and the concept of disease in psychiatry. *Acta Psychiatrica Scandinavica*, 1963, 39, 128–145.

RUDESTAM, K. E. Some cultural determinants of suicide in Sweden. *Journal of Social Psychology*, 1970, 80, 225–227.

———. Stockholm and Los Angeles: A cross-cultural study of the communication of suicidal intent. *Journal of Consulting and Clinical Psychology*, 1971, 36, 82–90.

———. Demographic factors in Sweden and the United States, *International Journal of Social Psychiatry*, 1972, 18, 79–90.

RUDIN, S. Psychogenic death. *Science*, 1968, 160, 901.

SAENGER, G. Psychiatric patients in America and the Netherlands: a transcultural comparison. *Social Psychiatry*, 1968, *3*, 149–164.

SAKAMOTO, Y. Some topics of Japanese psychiatry in relation to Western psychiatry. *Osaka City Medical Journal*, 1970, *16*, 71–78.

SAKS, M. J., EDELSTEIN, J., DRAGUNS, J. G., & FUNDIA, T. A. Social class and social mobility in relation to psychiatric symptomatology in Argentina. *Revista Interamericana de Psicología*, 1970, *4*, 105–121.

SAL Y ROSAS, F. Algunas observaciones sobre el folklore psiquiátrico del Perú. *Acta Psiquiátrica y Psicológica de América Latina*, 1973, *19*, 56–65.

SALISBURY, R. Possession in the New Guinea Highlands: Review of literature. *Transcultural Psychiatric Research Review*, 1966, *3*, 103–108.

———. Salisbury replies. *Transcultural Psychiatric Research Review*, 1967, *4*, 130–134.

———. Possession on the New Guinea Highlands. *Transcultural Psychiatric Research Review*, 1969, *6*, 100–102.

SÁNCHEZ, L. J. ¿Se justifica una anti-nosología psiquiátrica? (Ofensa y defensa de la clinica medica). *Revista de Neuro-Psiquiátria*, 1975, *38*, 1–30.

SANDIFER, M. G., HORDEN, A., TIMBURY, G. C., & GREEN, L. M. Psychiatric diagnosis: A comparative study of North Carolina, London and Glasgow. *British Journal of Psychiatry*, 1968, *114*, 1–9.

———. Similarities and differences in patient evaluation by U.S. and U.K. patients. *American Journal of Psychiatry*, 1969, *126*, 206–212.

SANUA, V. D. Immigration, migration and mental illness. In E. B. Brody (Ed.), *Behavior in new environments*. Beverly Hills, Calif.: Sage, 1970.

SAVAGE, C., LEIGHTON, A. H., & LEIGHTON, D. C. The problem of cross-cultural identification of psychiatric disorders. In J. M. Murphy & A. H. Leighton (Eds.), *Approaches to Cross-Cultural Psychiatry*. Ithaca, N.Y.: Cornell University Press, 1965.

SCHEFF, T. J. *Being mentally ill: A sociological theory*. Chicago: Aldine, 1966.

SCHOOLER, C., & CAUDILL, W. Symptomatology in Japanese and American schizophrenics. *Ethnology*, 1964, *3*, 172–178.

SCHWAB, J. J., BROWN, J. M., HOLZER, C. E., & SOKOLOF, M. Current concepts of depression: The sociocultural. *International Journal of Social Psychiatry*, 1968, *14*, 226–234.

SECHREST, L., FAY, T., ZAIDI, H., & FLORES, L. Attitudes toward mental disorder among college students in the United States, Pakistan, and the Philippines. *Journal of Cross-Cultural Psychology*, 1973, *4*, 342–360.

SEGUIN, C. A. Ethno-psychiatry and folklore psychiatry. *Revista Interamericana de Psicología*, 1972, *6*, 75–80.

SEGUIN, C. A., CASTRO, R., VALDIVIA, O., & ZAPATA, S. Cuadros clinicos y cultura, sobre un nuevo methodo de agrupacíon nosografica en psiquiátria. In *Third World Congress of Psychiatry Proceedings* (Vol. II). Montreal: Toronto University Press and McGill University Press, 1961.

SEIFERT, J. A., DRAGUNS, J. G., & CAUDILL, W. Role orientation, sphere dominance, and social competence as bases of psychiatric diagnosis in Japan: A replication and extension of American findings. *Journal of Abnormal Psychology*, 1971, *78*, 101–106.

SELIGMAN, M. E. P. Depression and learned helplessness. In R. J. Friedman & M.

M. Katz (Eds.), *The psychology of depression: Contemporary theory and research.* New York: Grune & Stratton, 1973.

SINGER, P., AARONS, L., & ARONETTA, E. Integration of indigenous practices of the Kali cult and Western psychiatric modalities in British Guiana. *Revista Interamericana de Psicología,* 1967, *1,* 103–114.

SKEA, S., DRAGUNS, J. G., & PHILLIPS, L. Ethnic characteristics of psychiatric symptomatology within and across regional groupings: A study of an Israeli child guidance clinic population. *Israel Annals of Psychiatry and Related Disciplines,* 1969, *7,* 31–42.

SPAIN, D. H. On the use of projective techniques in psychological anthropology. In F. L. K. Hsu (Ed.), *Psychological anthropology* (2nd ed.). Cambridge, Mass.: Schenkman, 1972.

SPITZER, R., & ENDICOTT, J. Diagno II: Further developments in a computer program for psychiatric diagnosis. *American Journal of Psychiatry,* 1969, *125,* 12–20.

SROLE, L., LANGNER, R. S., MICHAEL, S. T., OPLER, M. K., & RENNIE, T. A. C. *Mental health in the metropolis.* New York: McGraw-Hill, 1962.

STAEWEN, C., & SCHÖNBERG, F. *Kulturwandel und Angstentwicklung bei den Yoruba Westafrikas.* Munich: Weltforum-Verlag, 1970.

STEWART, P. *Children in distress.* Beverly Hills, Calif.: Sage, 1976.

STOKER, D. H., & MEADOW, A. Cultural differences in child guidance clinic patients. *International Journal of Social Psychiatry,* 1974, *20,* 186–202.

STOKER, D., ZURCHER, L. A., & FOX, W. Women in psychotherapy: A cross-cultural comparison. *International Journal of Social Psychiatry,* 1968, *15,* 5–22.

STUTTE, H. Über transkulturelle Kinderpsychiatrie. *Acta Paedopsychiatrica,* 1971, *38,* 229–231.

SUSSEX, J. N., & WEIDMAN, H. H. Toward responsiveness in mental health care. *Psychiatric Annals,* 1975, *5,* 306–311.

SZASZ, T. S. *The myth of mental illness.* New York: Harper-Hoeber, 1961

————. Psychiatric classification as a strategy of social constraint. In T. S. Szasz (Ed.), *Ideology and insanity.* New York: Doubleday, 1969.

TAFT, R. Coping with unfamiliar environments. In N. Warren (Ed.), *Studies in cross-cultural psychology* (Vol. 1). London: Academic Press, 1977.

TEJA, J. S., NARANG, R. L., & AGGARWAL, A. K. Depression across cultures. *British Journal of Psychiatry,* 1971, *119,* 253–260.

TELLENBACH, H. Das Problem des Massstabs in der transkulturellen Psychiatrie. *Nervenarzt,* 1972, *43,* 424–426.

TERASHIMA, S. The structure of rejecting attitudes toward the mentally ill in Japan. In W. Caudill & T. Lin (Eds.), *Mental health research in Asia and the Pacific.* Honolulu: East-West Center Press, 1969.

THARP, R. G., & WETZEL, R. J. *Behavior modification in the natural environment.* New York: Academic Press, 1969.

TONGYONK, J. Depressions in Thailand in the perspective of comparative-transcultural psychiatry. *Journal of Psychiatric Association of Thailand,* 1971, *16,* 337–354; 1972, *17,* 44–65.

————. Transcultural psychiatry in Thailand: A review of last two decades. *Transcultural Psychiatric Research Review,* 1977, *14,* 145–162.

TOOTH, G. C. *Studies in mental illness in the Gold Coast.* London: HMSO, 1950.

TORREY, E. F. Mental health services for American Indians and Eskimos. *Community Mental Health Journal*, 1970, *6*, 447–463.

————. Is schizophrenia universal? An open question. *Schizophrenia Bulletin*, 1973, 7, 53–59.

TOWNSEND, J. M. Cultural conceptions, mental disorders, and social roles: A comparison of Germany and America. *American Sociological Review*, 1975a, *40*, 739–752.

————. Cultural conceptions and mental illness: A controlled comparison of Germany and America. *Journal of Nervous and Mental Disease*, 1975b, *160*, 409–421.

TRIANDIS, H. C., MALPASS, R. S., & DAVIDSON, A. H. Cross-cultural psychology. *Biennial Review of Anthropology*, 1972, 1–84.

————. Psychology and culture. *Annual Review of Psychology*, 1973, *24*, 355–378.

TRIANDIS, H. C., VASSILLIOU, V., VASSILIOU, G., TANAKA, Y., & SHUNMUGAM, A. V. *The analysis of subjective culture*. New York: Wiley, 1972.

TSENG, W.-S., & HSU, J. Chinese culture, personality formation, and mental illness. *International Journal of Social Psychiatry*, 1969, *16*, 5–14.

ULLMANN, L. P., & KRASNER, L. *A psychological approach to abnormal behavior* (2nd ed.). Englewood Cliffs, N.J.: Prentice-Hall, 1975.

WALLACE, A. F. C. *Culture and personality*. New York: Random House, 1961.

————. Mental illness, biology, and culture. In F. L. K. Hsu (Ed.), *Psychological anthropology* (2nd ed.). Cambridge, Mass.: Schenkman, 1972.

WALSH, D., & WALSH, B. Mental illness in the Republic of Ireland—first admissions. *Journal of the Irish Medical Association*, 1970, *63*, 365–370.

WAXLER, N. E. Culture and mental illness: A social labeling perspective. *Journal of Nervous and Mental Disease*, 1974, *159*, 379–395.

WEBER, M. *The Protestant ethic and the spirit of capitalism* (T. Parsons, trans.). London: Unwin University Books, 1930.

WEIDMAN, H. H. Concepts as strategies for change. *Psychiatric Annals*, 1975, *5*, 312–314.

WEIDMAN, H. H., & SUSSEX, J. H. Culture values and ego functioning in relation to the atypical culture-bound reactive syndromes. *International Journal of Social Psychiatry*, 1971, *17*, 83–100.

WEINBERG, A. A. *Migration and belonging*. The Hague: Nijhoff, 1961.

WEINSTEIN, E. A. *Cultural aspects of delusion*. New York: Free Press, 1962.

WESTERMEYER, J. Psychiatry in Indochina: Cultural issues during the period 1965–1975. *Transcultural Psychiatric Research Review*, 1977, *14*, 23–38.

WESTERMEYER, J., & HOUSMAN, W. Cross-cultural consultation for mental health planning. *International Journal of Social Psychiatry*, 1974, *20*, 34–38.

WINTROB, R. M. Psychotherapy in interpersonal perspective: Some personal reflections. In P. Pedersen, W. J. Lonner, & J. G. Draguns (Eds.), *Counseling across cultures*. Honolulu: University Press of Hawaii, 1976.

WISHNER, J. Convergent trends in psychopathology. *Proceedings of the Seventeenth International Congress of Applied Psychology*. Brussels: Editest, 1972.

WITTKOWER, E. D. Perspectives of transcultural psychiatry. *International Journal of Psychiatry*, 1969, *8*, 811–824.

WITTKOWER, E. D., & DUBREUIL, G. Psychocultural stress in relation to mental illness. *Social Science and Medicine*, 1973, 7, 691–704.

WITTKOWER, E. D., & RIN, H. Transcultural psychiatry. *Archives of General Psychiatry*, 1965, 13, 387–394.

WITTKOWER, E. D., & TERMANSEN, P. E. Cultural psychiatric research in Asia. In W. Caudill & T. Lin (Eds.), *Mental Health Research in Asia and the Pacific.* Honolulu: East-West Center Press, 1969.

WORLD HEALTH ORGANIZATION. *Report of the international pilot study of schizophrenia.* Geneva: World Health Organization, 1973.

YAMAMOTO, K. A comparative study of "patienthood" in the Japanese and American mental hospital. In W. P. Lebra (Ed.), *Transcultural research in mental health* (Vol. II). Honolulu: University Press of Hawaii, 1972.

YAP, P. M. *Comparative psychiatry: A theoretical framework.* Toronto: University of Toronto Press, 1974.

ZAVALLONI, M. Ambivalence sociale et attitudes a l'égard de la maladie mentale. *Bulletin du CERP*, 1965, 14, 203–216.

ZEMPLENI, A., & RABAIN, J. L'enfant Nit Ku Bon. Un tableau psychopathologique chez les wolof et lebou du Sénégal. *Psychopathologie Africaine*, 1965, 1, 329–441.

ZUBIN, J., & KIETZMAN, M. L. A cross-cultural approach to classification of schizophrenia and other mental disorders. In J. H. Hoch & J. Zubin (Eds.), *Psychopathology of schizophrenia.* New York: Grune & Stratton, 1967.

ZUNG, W. W. K. A cross-cultural survey of symptom depression. *Archives of General Psychiatry*, 1969, 126, 116–121.

ZUTT, J. Transkulturelle Psychiatrie. Grundsätzliche Erwägungen über ihre Möglichkeiten. *Nervenarzt*, 1967, 38, 6–9.

5

Familial and Sociocultural Antecedents of Psychopathology[1]

Victor D. Sanua

Contents

Abstract

Various theories have been proposed to explain the development of psychological deviances. One area that has been found to be the least well documented is the sociocultural influence on pathology.

This chapter reviews research that has emphasized the possible contributions of sociocultural variables to the development of pathology. It suggests that in order to avoid erroneous conclusions, it is necessary to study normal behavior before recognizing pathology in specific groups.

References will be made to research pertaining to autistic children and childhood schizophrenia, studies of family therapy, and studies of different nationalities, ethnoreligious, and minority groups in the United States and abroad. The chapter points toward the advances that could be made in understanding deviant behavior, provided the research on the causes of mental illness is interdisciplinary.

Introduction

The relationship of the individual to his parents in their capacity as transmitters of the sociocultural values of their society and its role in the development of psychological disorders constitute a complex problem. Psychodynamic formulations have emphasized the impact of the family on the behavior of patients. Both social and cultural factors, however, unquestionably exercise an influence upon the family. Thus the culture molds the family, and the family molds the individual. Moreover, a variety of social forces outside the family affect the individual, particularly in the more complex societies.

To identify specific historical determinants of patterns of current deviance is a difficult task. Roff (1972) points out that in investigating antecedent conditions for a variety of adult maladjustments, "it becomes inescapably apparent that the most careful possible specification of early life history factors does not yield anything approaching a one-to-one correspondence between early conditions and later outcome" (p. 28). This chapter adds to this complexity by considering the often neglected sociocultural variables and reviewing the literature on familial antecedents of psychopathology from this perspective. It is well known that the various hypotheses concerning the effects of a pathogenic family are contested in the professional literature of the technologically developed countries. These formulations become even more controversial when applied to the world at large.

Kraepelin (1904/1974), well known for his work on the classification of schizophrenia, visited several mental institutions around the world and pioneered in reporting the effects of culture on mental illness. He concluded, "Just as an understanding of mental disorders has provided us with a profound insight into mental process, so might an exploration of the psychiatric features of a nation be expected to foster an understanding of the total national character. From this viewpoint, comparative psychiatry might be expected to become an important auxiliary science to the psychological study of nations" (p. 112). However, his observations were never systematically recorded. According to Lauter (1965), Kraepelin embarked upon the study of foreign cultures after becoming aware of the relationship between the increase in the incidence of mental disease and the development of industrialization. His interest in comparative psychopathology was also strengthened by his belief that European Jews manifested patterns of mental illness different from those of other Europeans.

Since the late 1950s and early 1960s, there has been a greater interest in the sociocultural aspects of mental illness, as evidenced by the large-scale epidemiological and etiological studies including the Midtown Manhattan study in New York (Srole, Langner, Michael, Opler, & Rennie, 1962; Langner & Michael, 1963), the New Haven study (Hollingshead & Redlich, 1958; Myers & Roberts, 1959; Myers & Bean, 1968), and the Stirling County study in Canada (D. C. Leighton, 1959; Hughes, Tremblay, Rapoport, & A. H. Leighton, 1960; D. C. Leighton, Harding, Macklin, Macmillan, & A. H. Leighton, 1963). A. H. Leighton (1959, 1974) and others believe that social variables such as community disintegration can cause psychological disturbance. Murphy (1975), after reviewing the literature on alcoholism and schizophrenia among the Irish, and Cawte (1976), upon investigating the social and cultural influences on mental health in aboriginal Australians, expressed similar views. However, the full impact of this trend towards epidemiological studies, based on sociocultural factors, has not made itself felt. An issue of the *Schizophrenia Bulletin* (1975) devoted to the contribution of the family in the etiology of schizophrenia does not include any consideration of the sociocultural differences among the families with respect to the development of psychopathology.

In an outspoken formulation on the cultural shaping of pathology, Slotkin (1955) pointed out that most human responses are learned, for individuals inherit only a limited repertory of responses. Therefore, a person's responses, whether normal or not, are greatly influenced by the cultural milieu. Slotkin emphasized the need for close collaboration among psychiatrists, clinical psychologists, and anthropologists in disentangling the threads of this influence. However, unresolved problems in achieving proficiency in both clinical and cultural fields remain; efforts toward integrating the instruction in several social sciences in universities are few (Sanua, 1977a).

On the other hand, Berne (1959, 1960) believes that mental illness is essentially independent of culture and that the "reservoir of endogenous psychoses (true prevalence) maintains a constant ratio regardless of racial, cultural, geographic and socio-economic conditions" (1960, p. 46). Berne claims that mental disorders were even more frequent in the preindustrial Fiji Islands than in recent times. In a survey of psychiatrists around the world regarding their views on the diagnosis, treatment and etiology of schizophrenia, Rogan, Dunham, and Sullivan (1973) found a clear schism between the proponents of biological and social etiologies. Most psychiatrists in Europe and Africa gave priority to biological factors, while their colleagues in Asia and the Americas emphasized social influences.

It is difficult to summarize studies of the antecedents of mental illness from the sociocultural and familial perspectives, for the objectives, strategies, measures, and populations in the studies have varied. Investigations carried out in cultures other than the United States are particularly hard to evaluate. Sanua (1961), at the conclusion of a review article on the sociocultural factors in families of schizophrenics, wrote:

> Although the evidence of the importance of family factors in the background of schizophrenics is quite compelling, the patterns of the home environment need to be more clearly defined and isolated from home patterns which lead to other types of psychoses, neuroses, and antisocial behavior. (p. 265)

One of the major limitations of the studies reviewed in the above paper was that the controls used in many cases were inadequate or nonexistent. Moreover, the sociocultural background of the subjects was not incorporated into the research design. Spiegel and Bell (1959), in an analysis of studies surveyed since 1930, found that only 80 percent of such studies had controls of any kind.

Three studies in particular illustrate the difficulty of comparing studies of the etiology of schizophrenia. Gerard and Siegel (1950) found that in 91.4 percent of the schizophrenic cases they studied there was exclusive attachment to the mother with extreme overprotectiveness, babying, and spoiling. In 57 percent of the cases the schizophrenic child was considered to be the favorite of his mother. Tietze (1949) in interviews with twenty-five mothers of male schizophrenics found that ten mothers overtly rejected their children, while fifteen were more subtle in their rejection. Thomas (1955) limited her study to the mother-daughter relationships of eighteen schizophrenics—mostly catatonic—admitted to St. Elizabeth Hospital in Washington, D.C. The mothers could not tolerate any verbal expression of hostility and were excessively restrictive and punitive after the patients had reached puberty. The majority of the fathers were dead, had deserted their families, or had been committed to mental institutions.

While all of these studies tried to describe the parent-child relationships in families with schizophrenic members, their samples and findings have little in common. The samples in the studies belonged respectively to (1) the lower and middle classes, (2) the middle and upper classes, and (3) the lower class. In the first study, informants were mostly Jews and Italians; in the second, mostly Protestants; and in the third, blacks. Values of class and culture could have influenced the patterns of parent-child relationships in these three groups.

A similar issue arises in regard to the relationship between psychopathology and birth order. Schooler (1961) indicated that studies done in the United States reveal little or no evidence of the effect of birth order upon mental illness among men, while research conducted outside of

North America provides such evidence. The ethnic heterogeneity of the American population may have obscured any clear findings, and contradictory findings may have resulted from the neglect of cultural factors. Hartog (1974) emphasized the fact that a transcultural view of the problem might clarify discrepant East-West observations. He presented a hypothesis based on sibling position that proposes increased vulnerability to mental illness for the oldest and youngest siblings in large families. Small families tend to minimize or obscure differences among siblings. He tried to reconcile universal family psychodynamics with cultural variables. Variables that may affect the frequency of different mental disorders among siblings are (1) the composition of the family (extended or nuclear), (2) the kind of communal child rearing best exemplified in the Israeli collective agricultural settlements, the *kibbutzim* (Beit-Hallahmi & Rabin, 1977), (3) the sex of the sibling, (4) the birth interval, (5) the social class, and (6) male dominance in the culture.

Cultural variables also affect the suicide rate. Farber (1968) pointed out that the characteristics of a culture are related to the frequency of suicide. In cultures with a high suicide rate one might expect also a large number of unsuccessful suicide attempts, perhaps more depression, and some susceptibility to depression even in normal personalities. Unusual stresses in particular cultures, according to Farber, may increase the number of persons susceptible to suicide. In short, suicide rates are an expression of the cultures in which they occur.

Hendin (1964) reached the conclusion that in the Scandinavian countries parent-child relationships, as the primary matrix for social learning and behavior, may be linked directly to the psychodynamics of suicide. The suicide rate of Norway is almost one-third that of Denmark and Sweden. Hendin attributed the differences in the suicide rates primarily to basic differences in Swedish and Danish versus Norwegian parents. Using psychoanalytic data from patients of the three countries, he posed a number of hypotheses to explain the differences and confirmed that the Norwegian mother, while encouraging the independence of her child, is very much emotionally involved with her offspring and allows more physical freedom. Also, Norwegian parents do not emphasize competition and success. The Swedish mother is more controlling and has more authority than the father. Danish mothers tend to punish the child by arousing guilt. Block and Christiansen (1966), using a Child-rearing Practices Report with university students in Scandinavia, supported Hendin's formulations developed in the course of clinical work with patients in psychotherapy.

For a number of years Dohrenwend (1975), and Dohrenwend and Dohrenwend (1969, 1974a, 1974b) have been trying to relate sociocultural and sociopsychological factors to the genesis of mental illness with particular emphasis on differences in social class. They believe that an analysis of rates of psychopathology in different sets of favored and disadvantaged ethnic groups under diverse situations of assimilation may provide a powerful cumulative test for assessing the antecedents of psychopathology. In a number of studies the antecedent conditions leading to mental disturbance are clearly attributed to the sociocultural values within the family, while in others the emphasis is on the more generally held societal values. However, the implication is that it is the family that impresses the social values upon its members. The Sixth International Congress of Social Psychiatry held in Yugoslavia in 1976 highlighted the general interest in the influence of the family upon psychopathology by selecting as the main theme of the convention the future of the family in a changing world.

Many investigators have tried to correlate parental characteristics with child behavior. Clarke and Clarke (1976) challenged the belief that the experiences of early childhood exert a disproportionate effect on the later development of the child. The contributors to the Clarkes' volume have weakened the concept of "formative years." Hess (1970) tried to relate both socioeconomic and ethnic influences to types of socialization. However, he was frustrated in this task by the narrow sociocultural base of studies of socialization, conducted, for the most part, with Caucasians in the United States. LeVine (1970), reviewing research on children across countries and cultures, concluded that studies of antecedent-consequent relations along a meaningful gradient of modernization should assume high priority in future research. A familiarity with this literature and its methodological problems would exercise a sobering influence on cross-cultural investigators of the socialization of deviant children. The studies that follow provide some evidence that sociocultural family characteristics affect child-rearing practices and child-parent relationships.

Some socially oriented studies of psychopathology emphasize culture, nationality, or ethnicity while other investigations emphasize social class. It is believed that in most instances one cannot deal with culture without considering social class and vice versa. Examples will be presented in this chapter to illustrate errors of interpretation arising from the neglect of one of these two variables. Murphy (1969) stated that culture in psychiatric research is either a complication that has to be controlled or a prime variable that should be studied. The mixing of subjects of different cultural backgrounds, as often practiced in research, makes no sense. Murphy's recommendation is expressed in a single word—diversification. It is safer and potentially much more informative to keep cultures distinct and to make separate comparisons within each. The same principle would apply to the variable of social class. While a number of studies control social class rather strictly, they do not control for culture; other studies control for culture but do not control for social class; and most studies, particularly those exploring the interaction of family members, neglect both social class and culture.

The Need to Study Normal Populations

The difficulties of comparing the family backgrounds of patients in various countries or even within the same country are complicated by differences in child-rearing methods. Psychiatrists and psychologists interested in the etiology of mental illness should familiarize themselves with subcultural and cross-cultural studies of normal families.

In 1946 Davis and Havighurst found that middle-class parents were stricter and more demanding in their child-rearing practices than lower-class parents. Approximately ten years later Sears, Maccoby, and Levin (1957) reported that middle-class mothers were more permissive than lower-class mothers. Bronfenbrenner's (1958) analysis of the literature on social class led him to conclude that American parents had become more flexible with regard to child-rearing practices, and this could explain the changes that might have taken place between 1946 and 1957. It is to be noted that some of the permissiveness that Davis and Havighurst (1946) found in their lower-class subjects possibly could be attributed to the fact that one-third of the mothers were Italian-born. McClelland, DeCharms, and Rindlisbacher (1955) controlled for ethnicity and found that Italian and Irish parents expect their children to become independent at an older age than Jewish and Protestant parents do. There were, however, differences between the Italian and Irish groups. Another complication is the mother's age and experience. Duvall (1946), in a well-controlled study of the social class of mothers who had raised children at different periods in time, reported that the mothers of older children, whom she characterized as "experienced mothers," tended to respond consistently in a more traditional manner and exercised greater discipline than mothers whose first children were five years of age or younger at the time of the study.

Even between such culturally similar countries as the USA and England, differences in child-rearing practices were found. Research conducted in England by Devereux, Bronfenbrenner, and Rodgers (1969) showed more role differentiation between mothers and fathers than was found in America. Also, differences between boys and girls were somewhat more marked in England than in the United States. More generally, it appears that parent-child relationships in America are "richer," "stronger," "more salient," and "more binding" than in England, where they seem somewhat "attenuated and strained." The difference in the process of socialization of British and American children, as it affects the development of pathological behavior, was confirmed by a study of the morbidity of children of British and American military families. Britton and Cordes (1970) supported the stereotype of the British child as being timid, frightened, excessively polite, uncreative, and the victim of the harsh regimentation of feelings, while the American child was found to be rowdy, undisciplined, defiant, and little concerned about his impact on others. Hetherington and Martin (1972) reviewed the research on the relationship between family members' interactions and psychopathology in children. Variations and deficiencies in methodologies stand in the way of deriving broad generalizations from this evidence. Moreover, a variety of social factors can affect the developmental process. None of the studies reviewed by Hetherington and Martin dealt with culture as a variable. The following early studies provide examples of the importance of this variable in understanding psychopathology.

Studies with Deviant Children
Considering Sociocultural Variables

In an early review Adler (1945) wrote that she was unaware of any comprehensive study examining the influence of different economic levels upon the development and the prognosis of neurosis and behavior problems among children. In her discussion of eating difficulties among children she stated that this symptom tends to arise in families placing an overemphasis on the consumption of food. Adler maintained that in hardly any family "where hungry eyes watch the child with the hope that he may leave some portion of its serving" do difficulties develop (p. 38). Adler hypothesized that when a child experienced difficulty in obtaining adequate food and was competing with a younger brother for his mother's attention, symptoms other than feeding problems would appear, such as fainting spells, bed-wetting, and others. Jewish children in the United States tend to have feeding difficulties and also suffer from enuresis. Adler suggested that lower-class children with behavior problems would tend to become delinquents and, later in life, criminals. On the other hand, upper-class children with behavior problems would tend to become social parasites—"playboys who remain socially acceptable" in view of the fact that they are protected by their economic backgrounds.

Meyers and Cushing (1936) controlled for religion in a study of children. These investigators examined the types and the incidence of behavior problems in relation to the cultural background of 150 children who were referred to consultation service from the elementary school system in Rochester, New York. The sample consisted of fifty children of southern Italian immigrants, fifty of Jewish parents—the majority of whom immigrated from Russia—and fifty children of Anglo-American background. While the groups of girls of British and Italian descent exceeded boys in the number of personality difficulties, differences between the

Jewish boys and girls were negligible. Among Italian children the incidence of overt, aggressive behavior difficulties, untidiness, and enuresis was rather high. Neglect and harsh treatment by parents was also significant among this group. On the other hand, both Italian and Jewish groups exceeded the group of British descent with regard to parental indulgence. Feeding difficulties, which were not reported for the other groups, were common among Jewish groups. Also distinctive for the Jewish group were the seclusiveness of the children, maternal overprotection, immaturity, and nagging mothers. The children of British descent had an excessive number of nervous habits and tended to come from broken homes and to be unwanted.

Rosengreen (1962) studied the case records of ten lower-class and ten middle-class disturbed children. Psychiatrists tended to use psychodynamic terminology and to suggest intrapsychic problems for middle-class patients, while comments for the lower-class patients were usually negative and rejecting, focusing upon the pathological aspects of the case and suggesting poor prognosis. Middle-class parents were found to be overly moralistic, imposing a strict ethical code and standard of achievement upon their children. The middle-class father was found to be weak and ineffective, the mother hostile and domineering. While the fathers showed a lack of interest in the family because of the demands of their careers, the mothers tended to be busy with community affairs.

A number of studies on children have dealt with the relationship of social class to mental illness and psychotherapy. Harrison, McDermott, Wilson, & Schrager (1965) found that the child of a professional has twice the chance of getting insight therapy compared to a child of a blue-collar worker. They stated, "The possibilities that the mental health professionals discriminate among children because of their class as we do among adults is distressing, but apparently true" (p. 417). The same statement could be made about the subjects of psychodynamically oriented research. Such investigators by and large concentrate their efforts on the deviancy of the middle- or upper-class white subjects. Less is known about the specific stresses of the lower-class children, particularly those belonging to minority groups.

A study of a deviant group without an equivalent study of a normal control is likely to lead to errors in interpreting the findings. What is required is information on a large sample of normal children belonging to different social and cultural backgrounds. Such a sample would be used as a basis of comparison with a deviant group. A report by Prall, Schulman, and Surer (1968) discussed the rationale and methodology of a study designed to determine age-appropriate characteristics of normal children. They have obtained 3,500 questionnaires covering children's attitudinal, behavioral, and physical characteristics. These findings remain to be compared and integrated with the results of maximally similar studies with disturbed children.

Classical Studies of Autism and Childhood Schizophrenia

A topic that continues to be controversial is whether childhood schizophrenia and infantile autism can be attributed to organic causes or to noxious environmental conditions. Sanua (1967) argued that if the sociocultural factors had been taken into account, there would be less controversy surrounding the etiology and character of the psychoses of childhood.

Kanner (1944), in his experiences with autistic children at Johns Hopkins University in Baltimore, found that these children had "cold, refrigerated parents." Bender (1956) in New York attributed childhood schizophrenia to organic causes.

To compound the problem, Mahler (1952), in New York with a large Jewish population, added another group in her reports on "symbiotic children," a category that Despert and Sherwin (1958) do not find very helpful clinically or effectively applicable in diagnosis. In Boston, Rank (1949) introduced the concept of the "atypical child." Bergman and Escalona (1949) postulated the "presence of primitive constitutional pre-ego factors" that make these patients very sensitive to sensory stimulation. Robinson and Vitale (1954) made their own contribution with "children with circumscribed interest patterns." All of these proposed categories presumably overlap with infantile autism.

Robinson (1961), in a review of the literature on childhood schizophrenia, wrote that early infantile autism is the earliest form of psychotic disturbance in children, and he assumed that the symbiotic child emerged after a period of more or less adequate ego development. In spite of this conclusion, he stated:

> Neither have we, as yet, been able to observe children whose behavioral patterns differ sufficiently from that described by Kanner to be listed under another diagnosis. We have concluded that children conforming to Mahler's description are rare. (p. 544)

It should be noted, however, that Robinson was Director of the Children's Center of Wyoming Valley in Wilkes-Barre, Pennsylvania, where the ethnic composition of the population is quite different from that of New York City. Caplan (1954), in a report on his experiences with children raised on kibbutzim in Israel, pointed out that in almost every case, autistic children had been raised by their own parents. Kibbutz children are generally reared by warm and demonstrative trained personnel in an atmosphere of affection. Boatman and Szurek (1960), following fifteen years of experience, concluded that the etiology of the psychotic disorders of childhood is entirely psychogenic. In contrast to this extreme, Goldfarb (1974) maintained that the type of patients seen at the Ittleson Clinic in New York conformed to the description given by Bender; several children fell in the category of "autism" while some others were "symbiotic." It is assumed that the Ittleson Clinic, as a research-oriented institution, serves a patient population that is more varied in cultural background than a private clinic. Goldfarb separated his schizophrenic children into two groups, one with a suspicion of organicity and another characterized by psychological dysfunctions caused by parental functioning and unclear maternal communication.

Kaufman, Frank, Heims, Herrick, and Wilner (1959) were able to delineate four types of mothers and fathers of schizophrenic children. They were diagnosed as pseudoneurotic, somatic, pseudodelinquent, and psychotic, with the classification depending upon their manifest defense structure. This classification was based on a study of forty parents of schizophrenic children in an outpatient clinic and on forty such parents in a state mental hospital. The investigators found that the parents ranged occupationally from college professor to unskilled laborer. Proportionately, more pseudoneurotic and somatic types of parents had their children in the outpatient clinic, while the pseudodelinquent and psychotic parents tended to have more children as inpatients. The article gives little indication of an awareness on the part of the authors of the posssible effects of the sociocultural variables on the parents' symptomatology. While all the children were diagnosed as schizophrenics, it would appear that parents of children in the outpatient clinic revealed different symptomatologies than parents of the children who were inpatients. Such differences between the two types of parents could be attributed to their social class. If social class had not been a factor, the four types of parents found by these authors would have been evenly distributed in both settings, inpatient and outpatient.

Hamilton (1959) suggested that the increase in the rate of childhood schizophrenia might be due to the pressures of modern culture. During the 1920s parents were seriously admonished by authoritative books to be unresponsive to their infants' needs for affection and comfort, particularly if they were boys. A rigid and emotionally sterile schedule was outlined for the parents, providing good techniques for the child's physical needs while ignoring his emotional needs. Hamilton states, "To saddle your son with an Oedipus complex became so frightening that some parents became frozen and reacted to their children with less warmth and display of affection than they gave their family pet" (p. 298). This statement is some-what exaggerated; otherwise, there might have been many more schizo-phrenic children. It would appear that only parents with a potential for "frigidity" might have used the prevailing strictures to justify their atti-tudes toward their children. It is difficult to estimate whether a more per-missive atmosphere, such as is prevailing at present, would tend to reduce the incidence of childhood schizophrenia.

Rose (1961) attributed two general causes, physiological and psycho-social, to the increase in the rate of childhood schizophrenia. Marriages are undertaken at a younger age, and there is a great increase in geo-graphical mobility. He indicated that between 16 and 33 percent of fami-lies in the child-rearing age with young children are reported to be constantly on the move. It would seem also that striving for social and eco-nomic improvement results in both marital partners entering the labor market, and, consequently, children are referred to day-care programs. From our own reading of the literature it is possible to speculate that mothers from cultural backgrounds or social classes that—according to the prevailing mores for rearing—encourage strict and rigid parental atti-tudes and frown on the expression of warmth would tend to have more autistic children. In cultural or social groups where the prevailing mores encourage overprotection and infantilizing, symbiotic children would be more prevalent.

Of potential cross-cultural relevance are the observations by Clerk (1961) on the role of the mother in influencing the verbal behavior of schizophrenic children. Some of these mothers preferred to use language rather than physical contact and gestures, even with children unrespon-sive to verbal communication. Consequently, such children become in-creasingly withdrawn and uncommunicative, even at a nonverbal level. Another group of mothers appeared to withdraw from active life after the birth of their child and to live through him or her. They favored prolonged physical contact and prevented the child from forming attachments to other adults. Such a child would develop language ability, but the use of language would remain individualized and distorted. It is impossible to integrate such a child into the community at large, and, as a result, he or she becomes the symbiotic child described by Mahler (1952). The normal mother, on the other hand, makes the shift from nonverbal to verbal com-munication at the appropriate time and according to the needs and ability of the child. It is tempting to relate these intracultural observations with the cross-cultural studies by Caudill and Weinstein (1969) in which the predominance of physical contact versus verbal communication emerged as a differentiator of maternal behavior in Japan and in the United States. These cross-cultural findings have not been extended to groups of dis-turbed children, however.

Later Studies in Infantile Autism and
Childhood Schizophrenia

In a study of black and Puerto Rican children, Korn (1964) found neither autism nor symbiosis. The predominant symptomatology was aggressiveness with bizarre behavior. Shodell (1967) compared the psychological adjustment of verbal and nonverbal children who had been diagnosed as schizophrenics. While the sample was small, twenty in each group, it is interesting to note that the variation in verbalizing ability was related to religion and nationality. The ratio of verbal to nonverbal ability among Jewish children was 1 to 1; Protestant children, 1 to 2.3; Italian children 4 to 1; and Irish, 1.7 to 1. All these children were from middle- and upper-class homes in Nassau County, New York. Nonverbal children appear to come least frequently from Italian families and most frequently from the Protestant families.

Sanua (1967) analyzed the case records of thirty-two schizophrenic children who had been admitted to the Psychiatric Institute of New York. The sample consisted of predominantly Jewish patients (sixteen) but also included Protestants (nine) and Catholics (nine). Of the sixteen Jewish children, one had been clearly identified as autistic, while all others had acquired speech. The single case of the autistic child, incidentally, came from a family in which the father had a Ph.D. in biology and was well known in his profession. He conformed, moreover, to the characteristics of the "refrigerated parent" as described by Kanner (1944).

Of nine Protestant patients, four autistic children came from upper-class homes in which the fathers were engaged in professional occupations. The five schizophrenic but nonautistic children in this group came from lower-class homes. Among the nine Catholics, only one child was identified as autistic, the father in this case being an accountant. The children with a schizophrenic diagnosis in this group came from lower-class families, and the fathers were all laborers.

Of course, these findings may be paralleled in normal groups of the same ethnic descent. As Draguns points out in this volume, one of the current needs of cross-cultural research on abnormal behavior is for normal control groups with culture as a constant. In the absence of such a provision the complex interactions between the effects of psychopathological syndromes and sociocultural influences cannot be disentangled.

It will be recalled that Kanner (1943) found that parents of autistic children tended to come from the high socioeconomic and professional classes. Two reviews have taken the opposite stand in this matter. Keith, Gunderson, Reifman, Bucksbaum, and Mosher (1976) argued that the high intelligence of parents of autistic children is a myth. In support of this contention they referred to Florsheim and Peterfreund's (1974) findings on the wide range of parental IQs in such populations. However, Florsheim and Peterfreund's results pertained to the general category of psychotic, rather than to specifically autistic, children. Ornitz and Ritvo (1976) concluded that the results of previous studies indicating a clustering of autistic children in the upper part of the socioeconomic distribution was not confirmed by three more recent investigations in the United States. In their words,

> The first of these (McDermott et al., 1967) compared the distribution of autistics and "non-autistic psychotics" among five social classes. Ritvo and associates (1971) compared families of autistics with those of matched (non-autistic) patients and the expected distribution based on population data. A third study (Allen et al., 1971) compared families of autistic patients with those of matched normal groups. (p. 615)

An examination of the samples in these three studies reveals that they may not have consisted exclusively of autistic children, as Ornitz and Ritvo (1976) had claimed. Kanner's (1943) criteria for the diagnosis of autism, it should be recalled, were threefold: (1) the inability to relate to people, (2) extreme autistic aloneness, and (3) an obsessive desire for the maintenance of sameness.

In the first of the three studies, McDermott, Harrison, Schrager, Lindy, and Killins (1967) found no significant difference in the distribution of *childhood schizophrenia* (italics mine) among five social classes in Ann Arbor, Michigan. Moreover, their sample of seventy-six included fifty-three borderline psychotic children. They explicitly stated that the low number of typically autistic or symbiotic children precluded any conclusions concerning these categories of pathology and socioeconomic class. "Do upper groups tend to isolate feelings more than others? It is felt that a characteristic of this group is to value the introspective and abstract style of thinking (versus the motoric style of the lower group) in their child-rearing practices" (p. 556). In light of this statement, it would be inaccurate to conclude that an absence of relationship between socioeconomic status and infantile autism was established in this study.

Similarly, the second study, by Ritvo, Cantwell, Johnson, Clements, Benbrook, Slagle, Kolly, and Ritz (1971), was not based upon *bona fide* cases of infantile autism, since "the presence of other symptoms (seizures) or diseases did not preclude the diagnosis of autism" (p. 301). King (1975) pointed out that (1) "pseudoretardates, children with atypical development, symbiotic children, and cases of childhood schizophrenia" were included in the sample of Ritvo et al. (1971). In his own study of autistic children King (1975) found that their parents were generally of above-average educational and socioeconomic level.

The last study Ornitz and Ritvo mentioned in support of the absence of a relationship between socioeconomic status and autism was by Allen, DeMyer, Norton, Pontius, and Yang (1971). However, these authors undertook to study the intellectuality of the parents of psychotics, subnormals, and normal children and not their socioeconomic class. They stated specifically that their study "confirms the findings by Lotter (1967) that parents of autistic children come from higher socioeconomic classes than those of brain-damaged children" (Allen et al., 1971, p. 324). Their population was composed of "33 *autistic and schizophrenic children* (italics mine), 33 matched normals, and 30 subnormals" (Allen et al., 1971, p. 311). The first two groups were matched for social class. A series of descriptive rating scales measured the parents' intellectuality—their preference for abstract, as opposed to practical, activities. The authors acknowledged that their interviews were at best a crude measure. All groups were found to be alike in intellectuality except for one significant difference between the parents of normal and autistic children, with the latter placing a lower value on academic success in their offspring. In more objective evaluation of the parents with the aid of the vocabulary subtest of the Wechsler Adult Intelligence Scale, the fathers—but not the mothers—of autistic children tended to score higher in intelligence than those of subnormal children. Kikuchi, Morimoto, Machida, Yamazaki, Yogashi, Shtara, Saido, Ito, & Hamada (1970) in Japan reported a similar trend: the IQs of the autistic children's fathers were higher than those of the controls; those of the mothers were indistinguishable from the general population.

In this writer's view, the three studies cited by Ornitz and Ritvo (1976) do not support the claim of the lack of a relationship between autism and parental socioeconomic status. Moreover, the first and the third study appear to be consonant with the hypothesis that the parents of autistic children gravitate toward the upper class socioeconomically and toward high intelligence cognitively. Cantwell, Baker, and Rutter (1978), in a review of the literature on the relationship between autism and social class, maintained that the evidence clearly indicated a tendency to higher IQs and superior social status among the parents of autistic children. However, such differences were found to be moderate. It is evident that Cantwell et al. (1978) interpreted the literature quite differently from Ornitz and Ritvo (1976) and Keith et al. (1976). Cantwell et al. (1978) further pointed out that the link between social class and autism did not appear to fit with a purely biological causation of autism. They felt that it remained an awkward finding that still demands an explanation.

There is a paucity of cross-cultural data on childhood schizophrenia and autism. An Argentine psychiatrist who had completed a three-year residency in a United States child psychiatric clinic and had returned to Argentina to become an experienced and prominent practitioner, stated in response to an inquiry on whether there were autistic children in Argentina:

In our present research with Leslie Phillips we are, for the time being, con-
firming his hypothesis that the less developed the individual—or the culture—the more the tendency to overt, active, physical characteristics of the
behavioral disturbance. The typical withdrawn child as described by Kanner
is a rarity among the patients I saw. Usually here they show, as I said, a very
disorganized type of behavior sometimes making the differential diagnosis
between feeblemindedness and schizophrenia difficult.*

A number of references, some representing extensive research efforts
in various countries, including Australia, Africa, Israel, Mexico, and Canada, support the effect of cultural variables on early infantile autism.

An intensive study in Australia conducted over twenty years involved
case search in the entire population of the state of New South Wales.
Harper and Williams (1976a) found autistic children of Greek and German immigrant parents significantly overrepresented. By contrast, no autistic children of Italian and Yugoslav parents were found, even though
these two ethnic groups were among the most numerous. They commented that the nonoccurrence of autism in the children of Italian parents
was "remarkable" (Harper & Williams, 1976b).

Lotter (1978a) is the first researcher who extended his interest in
studying autistic children of the indigenous populations of developing
countries. He feels that the psychological environment for children in developing countries is different from that in the technologically developed
countries, where childhood autism has been well described. Cross-cultural
research would tend to clarify the question of primary and secondary
psychogenic influences, which is a problem in the West. Some believe that
etiologically the symptoms of autism are secondary to more basic impairment in language and cognition (Rutter and Bartak, 1971).

Lotter visited nine major cities in six countries in Africa and compiled
a list of 1,312 disturbed children. He was able to identify nine children
who could be called "autistic" and thirteen "nonautistic." Looking at the
background of this small group of children, he noted that, while intergroup differences according to social class were not significant, they all
went in the same direction. If the five cases of children of mixed race are
included in his sample, 78 percent of the autistic children and 30 percent
of the nonautistic children belong to the elite. The small number of autistic children in Africa led Lotter to state, "A possibility therefore is that
autistic symptoms generally are less common in the African countries we
visited than in Britain" (p. 239). Furthermore, he indicated that a behavioral comparison with a British sample seemed to show that some prominent features of the syndrome were found to be very uncommon in Africa,
particularly rocking and head banging.

* From a letter received from Dr. Mauricio Knobel.

Another study that has cultural implications is the one conducted by Kaffman (1972), Medical Director of the Kibbutz Child and Family Clinic in Tel Aviv, Israel. He pointed out that it would be very hard to find any other place in the world where children would be subject to more intensive psychiatric observation. While he considered his sample small, he indicated it was worth mentioning that out of a patient load of 3,000 children during a period of fifteen years, he was able to identify only eight children who seemed to suffer from early psychosis with autistic features. However, all of them displayed "soft" signs of neurological impairment. Epileptic fits, complications during pregnancy, and premature births were implicated.

In the course of these years Kaffman failed to find a single "pure" case of psychogenic psychosis prior to the age of twelve. Kaffman offers two hypotheses to explain this complete lack of childhood psychosis. The first is that child-rearing practices in the kibbutz may prevent psychotic illness in children—incidentally, a theory subscribed to by Bettelheim (1967). The second is that early detection of deviation from normal standards, with immediate intervention, could be responsible for this nonexistence of psychogenic psychosis. Kaffman is more inclined to support this second hypothesis. Since the article was written in 1972, Dr. Kaffman has identified seven other cases of psychosis in children that, likewise, he considered organically determined.*

A Spanish psychiatrist (Romero Lara, 1975), reviewing the history of infantile psychoses, stated that "no data were found concerning such psychoses in Mexico and South America." This confirms the findings expressed previously by the Argentine correspondent.

It would seem, therefore, that the frequency of psychoses in early childhood appears to be less in Latin countries. The great enigma is whether this almost nonexistence of such illness in early childhood can be attributed to the ethos of family life in these countries or is due to the fact that the disease does not receive the recognition it gets in Anglo-Saxon countries.

Ney (1978), a psychiatrist from Canada, writes the following in connection with the rarity of early infantile autism among the Chinese:

> In the long debate on the nature and cause of infantile autism, it is surprising that there are no reports of Chinese autistic children. A Medlars II search of the literature found a number of studies on Japanese autistic and schizophrenic children and one alluding to Orientals, but no description of autism among Chinese. Reports of psychopathology among Chinese do not mention autism. Autistic children have not been diagnosed at the Peking Children's Hospital.

* Personal communication, 1979.

Since so many published studies do not present any information on the patient's sociocultural-religious background, this writer sent letters to a selected group of five psychiatrists who had published articles on childhood schizophrenia and requested this information. It is sufficient to say that one respondent acknowledged that the background of the patient was not taken into consideration in his studies but that this would be done in the future. Another respondent pointed out that since a large percentage of his patients were Jewish, it would not be possible to get a valid impression of childhood schizophrenia from this group and, therefore, it would be advisable to study a less selective group, such as could be found in a general clinic or hospital.

It is worth noting that the 1970s brought an increase in the number of papers on the organic etiology of childhood schizophrenia and infantile autism. According to Rutter and Bartak (1971), "Circumstantial evidence suggests (but does not prove) that the language and cognitive deficit contribute the primary handicap in autism, the social and behavioral abnormalities arising as secondary evidence" (p. 29). Werry (1972), however, found weaknesses in the retrospective nature of Rutter's work, his use of case records, questionable control groups, and unreliable symptoms. Ritvo (1976) indicated that "autism is a physical disease of the brain." However, he also pointed out that no information exists on its neuroanatomical or neurobiochemical causes and no specific etiologically based therapy is available. In a later review of the literature on the biochemical studies of autistic children and other groups, Ritvo (1977) concluded with the following remarks:

> In this brief annotation, we have surveyed the biochemical studies of patients with autism, childhood schizophrenia and related developmental disabilities. These studies have raised more questions than they have answered—a sure sign that our science is young. (p. 378)

Rimland (1964, 1974) is perhaps the most outspoken proponent of the organic approach, with a specific view on etiology centered in the reticular activating system. In Rimland's words (1974, p. 137), "Actually the disagreement as to the cause of psychosis in children is beginning to be dispelled, since, as I noted a decade ago (1964), so much evidence is accumulating against the psychogenic viewpoint that the ranks of this viewpoint are thinning rapidly." Anthony (1958), Bender (1956), and Klebanoff (1959) argued that disturbance in parent-child communication and relationship may be largely reactive to having a psychotic child. Guthrie and Wyatt (1975) concluded, upon reviewing biochemical studies, that "there is currently no evidence for a biochemical cause or correlation with the etiology of childhood schizophrenia." Hanson and Gottesman (1976) also reported no correlation between these two variables, nor did they find support for the genetic transmission of infantile autism and childhood schizophrenia in cases in which the onset occurred before the age of five. Kanner (1972) commented on this issue as follows:

> Even from a purely statistical point of view, the correlation of childhood schizophrenia with parental attitudes is far higher and more consistent than its correlation with heredity, configurations of the body, metabolic disorders, or any other factor. Even these few examples suffice to show how regardless of the problems of heredity and constitution, life experiences have confused these children, made normal relationship impossible and driven them to withdrawal and schizophrenic behavior. (p. 707)

An editorial in *The Lancet* (1976) concluded that even though clinical features of these disorders suggested organic disorders, biological investigations have been largely unrewarding. Thus the polemic concerning the relative merits of the biogenic and psychogenic hypotheses on the sources of childhood psychoses continues unabated.

A novel formulation on societal influences upon autism was provided by Tinbergen and Tinbergen (1972) and Tinbergen (1974). In their view, "childhood autism is actually on the increase in a number of *Western and Westernized societies*" (Tinbergen, 1974, p. 20, italics mine). They bemoan the fact that too little attention is paid to normal children who could serve as bases for comparison. Tinbergen is skeptical of hypotheses of genetic abnormality and brain damage in autism. At the same time he maintains that the incidence of autism is not random. Autistic children tend to be first-born, and their parents, in general, appear to be under strain. According to Tinbergen, such children, who are predisposed toward timidity, fail to develop "social bonding" either temporarily or permanently as a result of the modern urbanized, crowded, and stressful environment. Tinbergen sums up:

> There are strong indications that many autists suffer primarily from an emotional disturbance, from a form of anxiety neurosis, which prevents or retards normal affiliation and subsequent socialization, and this in its turn hampers or suppresses the development of overt speech, of reading, of exploration, and other learning processes, based on these three behaviors. (Tinbergen, 1974, p. 23)

Tinbergen found that "this corner of psychiatry is in a state of disarray." Wing and Ricks (1976) criticized his strong environmental stand and this criticism was followed by a rejoinder by Tinbergen. Wing (1974, p. 246) stated: "There are many different theories as to the nature of early childhood autism. None has, as yet, any solid foundation in facts derived from experiments and from criticism." This criticism is applicable to the proponents of biogenic and psychogenic views alike. Sanua (1961) deplored the neglect of cultural variables in psychogenically oriented research. Jacob (1975) bemoaned the disregard of socioeconomic differences in research on the family etiology of disturbance. Upon reviewing the available research, he found both age and socioeconomic status to be related to degrees of intrafamily conflict and parental dominance. Results, Jacob concluded, were in any case difficult to compare because of disparities among studies in diagnosis, techniques of measurement, demographic variables, and types of data analysis.

The importance of cultural factors in child psychiatry, as well as the lack of solid data on this topic, was emphasized by the West German psychiatrist Stutte (1972). He argued that more attention should be paid to ethnic influences in the prevalence and phenomenology of mental disturbance in children. Transcultural studies should make it possible to have more solidly based ideas on such variables as children's tolerance to stress, the typical   reaction of their development stage, and the ethnic stamp on their psychoses. Thus, it would seem that if one is to understand the antecedents of psychological disorders, the researcher should focus some of his attention upon sociocultural variables and their relationship to psychopathology.

Familial Antecedents of Mental Illness and Their Sociocultural Implications

A voluminous, complex, and controversial literature has come into being on the familial antecedents of psychopathology in general and schizophrenia in particular. It is neither possible nor necessary to review these findings and formulations in this chapter. The interested reader is referred to the reviews and other writings by Spiegel and Bell (1959), Foudraine (1961), Pollack and Gittelman (1964), Fontana (1966), Baxter (1966), Frank (1965), Rabkin (1965), Mednick and McNeil (1968), Offord & Cross (1969), Ward (1970), Hingtgen and Bryson (1972), Howells (1971), Heilbrun (1973), and Garmezy (1974, Part I; 1974, Part II). The preceding list of articles deals with the effects of socialization. In addition to this literature, there is a smaller but still extensive amount of writing on the process of intrafamily communication and interaction. Initiated by Bateson, Jackson, Haley, and Weakland (1956), this research has been surveyed and integrated by Mishler and Waxler (1966), Riskin and Faunce (1972), Olson (1972), and Hoekstra (1971). Varying in approach, rationale, methodology, instrumentation, and population, these two areas of research share a number of features. For one, they are disproportionately—although not exclusively—based upon United States samples. Within the United States, the investigators have either been noncultural in orientation, i.e., have not incorporated ethnic and other subcultural factors into their research designs, or they have, in the interest of homogeneity, limited their samples to the white, middle-class majority. Thus, apart from the well-known ambiguities and complexities in this store of evidence, it pertains largely to the majority in the United States, yet is often presented as though it referred to antecedents of psychological disturbance, or schizophrenia, on a worldwide basis. A smaller number of empirical and theoretical writings, which take sociocultural factors directly into account, will be reviewed in the next section.

Survey of Reviews with an Emphasis on the Sociocultural Aspects of Mental Disorders

The reviews to be considered below do not exclusively, or even prominently, deal with familial antecedents of psychological disorders. Instead, their emphasis is upon differences in epidemiology, demography, and symptomatology. Reviews on the *epidemiology* of mental illness from the sociocultural point of view have been written by Hunt (1959, 1960), Fried and Lindemann (1961), Montagu (1961), Mishler and Scotch (1963), and Sanua (1969a, 1970). The following authors discuss particularly *symptomatology*: Murphy, Wittkower, Fried, & Ellenberger (1963), Murphy, Wittkower, & Chance (1967), Al-Issa (1970), Rogan, Dunham and Sullivan (1973). Al-Issa (1977) discusses *hallucinations*.

Of more direct relevance to the theme of the present chapter are the conclusions by Saucier (1962), a French Canadian psychiatrist, that not only "isolation," but "social disorganization" or too punitive an experience in socialization may result in psychopathology. He encouraged the study of sociocultural aspects as a worthwhile extension of traditional psychiatry. A. H. Leighton and Hughes (1961) also believe in the importance of sociocultural factors influencing the origin, course, and outcome of psychiatric disorders. According to them, culture may be producing impairment through certain child-rearing practices. Other factors such as social disorganization might also be contributing to the problem. However, they caution that there is a gap between observations made and their assumed actual effect, i.e., mental disorders in the case of family interaction studies.

Kohn (1959, 1963, 1969, 1972, 1973) has periodically reviewed work on the relationship between social class and schizophrenia. In one of his articles, Kohn (1972) introduced the family as a mediating variable between social class and schizophrenia:

> The family, I suggest, is important principally because of its strategic role in transmitting to its offspring conceptions of social reality that parents have

learned from their own experience. In particular, many lower-class families transmit to their offspring an orientational system too limited and too rigid for dealing effectively with complex, changing, or stressful situations. This point of view, I believe, is consonant with recent psychiatric thinking about the family and schizophrenia, which emphasizes those communicational and cognitive processes in schizophrenia-producing families that contribute to the schizophrenic's difficulties in interpreting social reality. What is new is the assertion that these conceptions of reality, far from being unique to families whose offspring become schizophrenic, are widely held in the lower social classes, in fact arise out of the very conditions of life experienced by people in these segments of society. (p. 300)

However, Kohn (1973) was not entirely pleased with the foregoing formulations, since he introduced two other variables. He felt that while there is an impairment of ability to deal resourcefully with the problems of life, both genetic vulnerability and considerable stress must be considered antecedents of schizophrenia.

Brown, NiBhrolchain, and Harris (1975) present evidence that seems to challenge Kohn's conclusion regarding the lower efficiency of the working classes in dealing with their problems. In a survey of a sample of women living in South London, they found that the differences in the prevalence of psychiatric symptoms could be attributed to the fact that the problems of the lower-class woman take much longer to be solved and do not reflect any personal inability to cope effectively with them. Many difficulties of the middle-class women also seem quite intractable, but there is more hope of ameliorative action. Brown et al. have been able to identify four factors that increase the chances of developing psychiatric symptoms: loss of mother in childhood, three or more children aged below fourteen living at home, a lack of a confiding relationship with a husband or boyfriend, and a lack of full-time or part-time employment.

Sanua (1961) reviewed the literature on the relationship between sociocultural variables and schizophrenia with specific reference to the family as an intervening variable. He elaborated on the fact that many findings, both positive and negative, could be explained on the basis of methodological deficiencies, and particularly by their neglect of cultural variables. This review was updated and extended, both in relation to the entire gamut of schizophrenic conditions (Sanua, 1969a) and in relation to the more specific condition of childhood schizophrenia (Sanua, 1964). Sanua (1962a, 1963, 1964, 1965, 1967) also undertook a series of studies of schizophrenics belonging to different religious and ethnic backgrounds— Protestants, Italians, Irish, and Jews.

If the socialization process is considered as a preparation to face the complexities of life in adulthood, then psychopathology may be considered as a consequence of problems and complications in this process. The problem could be viewed from two perspectives: (1) early familial pathology may make it impossible for the individual to acquire the resources and strengths to face life's complexities, and (2) even in the absence of pathology in the process of socialization, the individual may be raised with certain incapacities that are manifested when he has to face major stress as an adult. This may explain differences in the process-reactive development of mental illness. Organic factors, in general, are added to the formula, but they may be conjectural. Even if these factors are empirically identified, it is still possible that what was surmised to be the cause is later found to be the effect of the disorder.

Studies of Mental Disorders with Specific Reference to Sociocultural Variables

Early reports in the literature purported to demonstrate that certain cultures have been devoid of mental illness. However, later contributions have shown that there is no culture that has been successful in eliminating stress during the process of socialization. Some cultures have developed mechanisms to reduce the impact of their coercive demands. Demands range from great severity to permissiveness. Arsenian and Arsenian (1948) have provided a conceptual analysis of "easy" and "tough" cultures.

Practically every country, furthermore, develops its own brand of psychiatry. As pointed out by Galdston (1957):

> There is an international surgery, but only a national psychiatry.... In all departments of medicine, the physician intercedes between man and nature, and, of course, nature is the same the world over. In psychiatry, however, the physician intercedes between not only man and nature, but often and mainly between man and society, that is the social organism, its structure, operations, exaction, etc., quite unlike nature's, is not the same the world over. Society frequently changes in the most astonishing ways "at the national border." (p. 105)

This probably explains the impossibility of having psychiatrists the world over agree to adopt a universal classification of mental disorders.

Wittkower and Prince (1974) have identified three categories of psychocultural stress leading to mental strain: (1) *cultural content*, (2) *social organization*, and (3) *sociocultural changes*.

1. The relationship between *cultural content* and mental disease is that some cultural elements may create tensions. Under cultural content Wittkower and Prince (1974) include (a) taboos, (b) value saturation, (c) value polymorphism, (d) role deprivation, and (e) sentiments. Taboos frustrate essential human needs. Excessive frustrations may arise from taboos related to food, aggression, sex, and others. However, taboos predispose to

mental illness only in conjunction with other cultural elements. No two persons adapt the values of their society in an identical manner. While cultural values reasonably guide some individuals' thoughts and behavior, others may not accept them, and still others come to be driven by them. Wittkower and Prince (1974) called the latter effect value saturation. The example they gave is the emphasis on success in the United States and the disability of many who vainly pursue it. From this basic frustration Merton (1957) developed his concept of anomie. Another example that Wittkower and Prince (1974) provided is Nazi Germany's obsession with racial purity, which culminated in extermination camps—a major manifestation of social pathology. Value polymorphism refers to the coexistence of antagonistic values within the same cultural system or within the same individual. For example, a person may be confronted with different ideologies in a complex society or may have to move from one socioeconomic class to another without the cultural provisions of proper strategies for making the transition. The result is the discontinuity of values and roles, as originally proposed by Benedict (1938). A business executive may have so much responsibility that it interferes with the gratifications derived from his other roles as father, husband, friend, and so on. A fourth source of stress is role deprivation, that is, the withdrawal of culturally and psychologically significant statuses and roles from some individuals. Here Wittkower and Prince (1974) included forced retirement and discrimination against minority groups. Fifth, they feel that the more intense the culture-bound sentiments, such as jealousy, fear of spirits, people, and so forth, the more widespread will be the disorder.

2. The second major category of psychocultural stress is *social organization*. Two concepts have relevance to it: (a) anomie and (b) rigidity. Anomie results from the lack of integration of social organization and is sometimes used synonymously with social disorganization such as unemployment, poverty, migration to urban areas, lack of education, and ethnic differences, all of which are sources of tensions that may have a significant effect on the rate of mental illness. Guthrie covers the role of the related concept "alienation" in psychopathology in the present volume. The opposite of anomie is social rigidity. Here, the values of the society are such that the individual is dominated and forced to conform. For example, small communities dominated by traditional values may impose status and roles on individuals unwilling to knuckle down to passive conformity. Some may leave the group but encounter later difficulties.

3. The third source of stress is *sociocultural change* associated with problems in acculturation that, particularly when combined with low social status and poverty, are bound to cause serious problems because of cultural shock. However, sociocultural changes do not always produce

emotional reactions but may be deleterious to mental health when combined with other stresses, such as anomie, value polymorphism, and role deprivation. Sanua (1970) reviewed the findings on migration and immigration and the complexities in deriving a general theory on the consequences of cultural change for mental health.

A number of studies illustrate areas of sociocultural stress as formulated by Wittkower and Prince (1974). It is obvious that some studies may overlap, and, in some cases, it is difficult to indicate clearly to which category they belong. While psychiatric problems emanating from *cultural content*, except for role deprivation, focus on familial influences, the other two sources of stress, *social organization* and *sociocultural change*, seem to be external.

Two further sections of studies that do not fit the Wittkower and Prince (1974) classification review research with particular reference to the symptomatology of various cultural groups studied, which could be related to the familial background of the patients.

Another section will provide a few illustrations of the family and the community counteracting psychological disorder.

Stress Caused by Cultural Content

Cultural elements create tension between individuals or generate anxieties within them. Following are studies pertaining to white ethnic groups in the United States, American blacks, and ethnic groups in Canada, as well as studies on Mexico, India, Japan, and Taiwan. Two reviews concern the effects of the woman's social role on the frequency of mental illness. The section also includes a few examples of studies conducted by European psychiatrists who, as indicated earlier in the chapter, tend to believe that psychoses are biologically determined.

Spiegel, Papajohn, Sweder, and Davidson (1966), using the transactional theoretical model and comparing a psychotic group with a nonpsychotic group, analyzed the stresses incurred by Greek families in the United States. In the sample of families with patients, there was a high degree of discord between the generations on the question of cultural values: the children had moved away toward American values while their immigrant parents had not. Stein (1973), using a Slovak-American family with a schizophrenic member, suggested also that the basic intrapsychic conflict within the family because of cultural conflicts will be manifested in mental illness. As in the case of the Greek families, the American experiences of the Slovak-American family had encouraged a negative identity. It served to exacerbate traditional conflicts within the Slovak community. It would seem that a rigid maintenance of old-world cultural values by the first-generation immigrants, which the new generation rejected, becomes a source of great stress and frustration for both children and parents.

Sanua (1962b) reviewed the literature on the relationship between minority status and psychological adjustment with particular reference to Jews. Brody's (1967) studies of black schizophrenics showed that the blacks have suffered from two family-mediated conflicts. While the black mother overtly urges her son to achieve any possible goal, she covertly communicates to him that he cannot achieve anything because he is black. This is similar to Bateson, Jackson, Haley, and Weakland's (1956) "double-bind" communication. The second source of conflict is the boy's desire to identify himself with blacks. He is at the same time in conflict over the unconscious wish of his parents, who sometimes desire to abandon the devalued identity associated with the subordinated role of black men in white society. Brody has found that disturbed blacks have a greater degree of hostility towards white men than normal blacks. This hypothesis may be reinforced by what Parker and Kleiner (1966) found among higher educated blacks in Philadelphia: those formerly living in northern cities suffered from more mental illness than black migrants from the South. Parker and Kleiner (1966) assumed that the larger discrepancy between aspiration and actual accomplishment found among northern blacks, as compared to southern blacks, was likely to cause problems in the former group. The two studies seemed to complement each other. Brody (1967) dealt with familial dynamics, while Parker and Kleiner (1966) concentrated on sociocultural values.

Kardiner and Ovesey (1951) have documented through the psychoanalysis of twenty-five black men the difficulties black mothers experience in providing economic and emotional stability for their families. It would appear that continuous frustration in childhood created a personality that had little confidence in human relations.

Abraham (1964), discussing the matrifocal familial structure among American blacks, demonstrated that economic difficulties led to acts of desertion by fathers and reinforced the woman-dominated family pattern resulting in their sons' facing psychological problems concerning their male identity. In view of the recent movement for change in social identity of the blacks, one wonders whether such conflicts, which Frazier (1940) and Kardiner and Ovesey (1951) originally described, still exist today. It certainly would be of interest to study the implications of the civil rights movement and racial integration on the self-image and mental health of the blacks in the United States.

In view of the strong belief in Europe that schizophrenia is organically and genetically determined, few European studies have taken into account the parental background of the patients. After being somewhat critical of the psychodynamic emphasis in the United States, Langfeldt (1961), a well-known Scandinavian psychiatrist, wrote:

However, after a sufficiently long acquaintanceship with American psychiatric institutions, one cannot help but be discouraged by the ignorance of many American psychiatrists with regard to the results of research in heredity, constitution, and biology, and in particular, with their almost complete disregard of ordinary diagnosis and prognosis. (p. 221)

While Langfeldt may be correct as far as interest in heredity is concerned, American psychiatrists, nevertheless, are interested in diagnosis and prognosis. Moreover, not all Nordic investigators seem to be organically oriented. Bjornsson (1974), using psychological tests and interviews with 1,100 children in Iceland, found that their parents' educational level, the occupational status of the father, maternal warmth and emotional involvement, and the child's IQ and his achievement in school were clearly related to mental health. If these relationships exist in a society that is quite homogeneous culturally, it can be inferred that in their more extreme forms—as found in different cultures—these variables may affect pathological behavior.

A series of reports by the Finnish psychiatrist, Alanen (1956, 1958, 1966, 1968) and his coworkers (Alanen, Arajärvi, and Vitamäki, 1964) emphasizes the disturbed personality characteristics of both the fathers and the mothers of schizophrenics. Although cultural variables are not stressed in these writings, Alanen's research is valuable for providing systematic evidence of parental personality disturbance and disruption of the parent-child interaction in families of schizophrenics at a site outside of the United States.

Sisek and Ljubin (1971), in a study of three groups of schizophrenic peasants, workers, and urbanized families in different regions of Yugoslavia, found marked contrast in superstitious beliefs, religious beliefs, and modes of living. All the patients were affected by their environment and felt rejected. Sisek and Ljubin stressed the importance of sociocultural factors in identifying precipitating events of schizophrenia. A study of the fathers of schizophrenics in West Germany by Erichsen (1973) revealed that they tended to be predominantly narcissistic and dominating. The feelings of the schizophrenics included varying degrees of idealization of the father and overt ambivalence towards him or rejection of his role in their lives.

Murphy and Lemieux (1967), studying fourteen rural communities in Quebec and Ontario, found that the rate of schizophrenia was much higher in three traditional French-Canadian communities than in any other. The highest incidence was among females, and the disorder struck especially at young, unmarried, and middle-aged women. The explanation given by these authors is that there is a discrepancy between the *actual* and *nominal* roles occupied by women in the traditional communities. A young French-Canadian woman who is given more education tends to be more vocal and active in associations and may take outside employment. However, she must maintain her social role as a woman—which is inferior—since society still regards the man as the head of the household in spite of any educational limitation he may have. She thus must not be critical of her husband in front of her children. The women in these traditional communities faced frustration and dilemmas much greater than those met with by women from Anglo-Saxon communities.

Gilbert (1959), beginning with the premise that the greater incidence of behavioral problems among male children in the United States might possibly be caused by the more difficult demands made on them, decided to investigate sex differences in mental health in a Mexican village. Administering the Rorschach Test to 106 inhabitants of a small Mexican village, he found that females were better adjusted than males. He suggested that the exaggerated sex differences in role expectations among the Mexicans were more anxiety-provoking for males than for females. Gilbert thought it necessary to consider social conflict in its full historical perspective, along with the social mores of a culture, to understand group differences in mental health. Diaz-Guerrero (1955), in a study of neurosis and the Mexican family structure, suggested after administering a test to measure the degree of psychological problems of urban Mexicans that many of their neurosis-provoking conflicts were "inner conflicts" triggered by clashes of values rather than by clashes of the individual with reality.

Bhaskaran (1955) found among upper-class Indian female psychotics a preponderance of dullness and apathy, which he attributed to the extremely strict upbringing to which these women were subjected. For the women, precipitating factors of psychosis were childbirth, abortion, and desertion, or nonacceptance, by the husband—a serious cultural stigma. In a study of paranoid schizophrenic patients of the upper-class Indians, male and female, Bhaskaran (1963) found that 54 percent of them had been indulged by their parents or surrogates and 18 percent had been rejected. Thus, the contradictions that have been found in the family background of schizophrenics in the United States are also encountered in some other countries. Sukthankar and Vahia (1963) studied 320 Indian patients diagnosed as schizophrenics and hysterics in a mental institution. The most common precipitating factors were familial and/or marital disharmony. There were no significant differences in the predisposing and precipitating factors in schizophrenia and hysteria. Among the various causes of familial disharmony, one stood out. The Indian female not only marries the husband but becomes part and parcel of the husband's family. Marriages are arranged without mutual consent. Women are not allowed to mix with members of the opposite sex. Males are also conflicted in their vocation, since this is generally a parental decision.

The importance of the role of the family was recently emphasized by the Japanese psychiatrist, Doi (1973). In describing the Japanese character, he developed the concept of *amae*, which he derived from early parent-child relationships during the socialization of the Japanese child. The term initially referred to the attitude of all normal children toward their mother, such as dependence, the desire to be loved passively, and the unwillingness to be separated from the warm mother-child relationship—feelings that are carried over into adult Japanese life. While this tendency may be common to mankind as a whole, Japanese social values seem to foster the expression of these feelings. Doi reported on his cultural shock in the United States:

> The "Please help yourself" that Americans use so often had a rather unpleasant ring in my ears before I became used to English conversation. The meaning, of course, is simply, "Please take what you want without hesitation," but literally translated, it somehow has the flavor of "nobody else will help you," and I could not see how it came to be an expression of good will. The Japanese sensibility would demand that, in entertaining, a host should show his sensitivity in detecting what was required, and he should himself "help" his guests. To leave a guest unfamiliar with the house to "help himself" would seem excessively lacking in consideration. (p. 13)

Doi undertook to explain the difference between Japanese and American personalities through the need for passive love implied in the concept of *amae* and concluded that the former, because of early cultural conditioning, develop *amae*. These feelings are prolonged into, and diffused throughout, their adult lives. The frustration of this need causes a great deal of disturbance among the Japanese. Contrary to previous studies cited—with the old cultural values imposing restrictions—in the Japanese case culturally derived needs that are not satisfied cause the disturbance.

Tseng and Hsu (1969) compared Chinese and American mental patients and provided some detailed information about the process of socialization in Chinese culture. The close relationship between child and mother, the extended family structure, the ritual mourning practices, and the inhibitions against expressing depressive moods verbally in Chinese families make for less frequent manifestations of depression among this group. On the other hand, there is a higher proportion of neurasthenics and complaints of somatic symptoms amongst traditional Chinese. Chinese culture tends to eliminate bisexual tendencies that may favor the development of homosexuality. While alcohol is readily available, alcoholism presents no serious problem. The family and society frown upon solitary drinking. When in conflict the Chinese appear to seek "satisfaction" by eating, by personal contact, and by gambling rather than by imbibing alcohol.

A more recent paper (Tseng, 1975) provides some case histories illustrating the Chinese tendency toward somatization in the absence of culturally sanctioned outlets for the spontaneous expression of emotion. Complaining about feelings of depression or loneliness would get little sympathy, while complaints of headaches, stomach pains, or palpitations are rewarded with attention.

Nathanson (1975) reviewed the literature on the higher rates of psychological disorder in women than men in Great Britain and the United States, in spite of their lower mortality rate and their greater resistance to degenerative disease. She suggested that the difficulties of a mentally sick woman's maintaining her household in the Western nuclear family account for the higher incidence of psychiatric disorder. The other two possible explanations, according to Nathanson—that women are more inclined to report distress and that their higher morbidity is related to the strain of the woman's social role—appear less plausible.

Subject to the methodological limitations discussed earlier, familial variables are associated with the offspring's psychological problems, presumably mediated by social stress. In the case of Doi's (1973) study, parental failure to satisfy culturally derived needs caused the disturbance.

Stress Caused by Social Organization:
Disorganization and Rigidity

The major contributor in developing hypotheses regarding the relationship between sociocultural disorganization and mental illness is A. H. Leighton (1974), who directed the Stirling County research study in Canada and later assumed the directorship of the Midtown Manhattan study. Instead of using the term "deviant behavior," Leighton preferred "behavior of psychiatric interest." The phrase implies a continuum from normal to impaired behavior. He felt that there would be more agreement among clinicians on the level of impairment of an individual than on his diagnosis. Also, he introduced the variable "social system." According to Leighton, the notion of good and poor functioning at the societal level is basic to the understanding of the concept of sociocultural disintegration. Communities can be assessed on this continuum of integration to disintegration. The relationship between psychiatric disorders and sociocultural disintegration is made possible by the following three developments: (1) breakdown in the functioning of the medical institutions (hospital, outpatient care, public health services) which can lead to organic disease because of the increase in unsanitary conditions and poor food resources; (2) the failure of child-nurturing and child-rearing patterns because of the economic breakdown in the social system, which results in a higher frequency of maternal deprivation, absent fathers, and poor peer relationships; and (3) stress derived from experiencing the world as a series of frustrations and disappointments. The system theory has influenced Leighton. In this view, individuals who may have the potential to reverse the trend may themselves be affected by the despair and, thus, by their withdrawal from participation in the activities of the community may speed up the process of disintegration. By introducing societal stress in his work, Leighton does not eliminate, however, the importance of psychodynamic theories.

The greater the disintegration, the greater the stress, and the larger the proportion of people in the population who would manifest mental disorders. Leighton studied ninety-six small communities in Canada and found a correlation between the amount of psychiatric impairment and the extent of social disintegration. In order to prevent further societal disintegration, Leighton suggested the development of a new kind of profession whose competence should be in three areas—mental health, the social systems, and the applied behavioral sciences.

A. H. Leighton, Lambo, Hughes, D. C. Leighton, Murphy, and Macklin (1963) demonstrated that his approach, which was devised for a developed, Western society, could successfully be modified and applied in a traditional African culture. He carried out a study among the Yorubas, a major tribe in Nigeria, and there also he found that social disintegration was correlated with psychological problems. It should be noted, however, that while in the United States higher education is related to lower admission rates to mental hospitals, D. C. Leighton, Hagnell, Kellert, A. H. Leighton, Harding, and Danley (1971), in a study in Lundby, Sweden, replicating the Stirling County Canadian research, found that the lowest occupational level had—contrary to expectation—the lowest prevalence of psychiatric disorders.

The following two studies link rigidity with psychological problems. Clark (1968), in comparing the aged in a community with a group of the aged in a mental institution, showed that cultural rigidity caused stress and concluded that in America the aged experience dramatic cultural discontinuity. Previously expected to be competitive, the aged require marked shifts in value orientation. It would appear that only those who adapt to such reordering of their behavior are likely to be accepted. In other words, there seems to be a "proper" manner of growing old.

Schwartzman (1973), who was interested in explaining some aspects of American culture, American families, and their relationship to mental illness, studied the problems caused by parental rigidity. He found that forty families who were out-patients in a mental health clinic and suffered from many kinds of symptoms tended to be rigid. The parents in these families could not tolerate change. The psychological distance between the children and the parents was not allowed to change in spite of the fact that the children had become more competent. According to Schwartzman (1973), the family must be able to adapt and to fit the changing needs of a changing society. At the same time, by adapting, it prepares the child to deal with change. On the basis of this finding, one can speculate that in an evolving society, when families maintain old traditions, whether they are of the old or of the new world, strife between the generations is bound to result in personality problems. On the other hand, in societies that tend to be static and are not exposed to change, conflicts may be minimized, and, as a result, the incidence of mental illness may be lower.

Stress Caused by Sociocultural Change

In general, such variables as immigration, mobility, acculturation, and de-tribalization have been found to be related to psychiatric problems. A few examples from the research literature will show how cultural change can effect individuals psychologically. The studies concern American Jews, Mexican Americans, Puerto Ricans, Greeks in the United States, and groups that were relocated from one part of a city to another, as well as Indians, Israelis, Arabs, and South Africans.

Sanua (1959a, 1959b) found that the longer the ancestry of Jewish families in the United States, the better the adjustment of the adolescents as measured by a personality inventory. By contrast, results on the Rorschach Multiple Choice Ink Blot Test showed an opposite trend. The third-generation Jewish adolescents, while showing good adjustment on the personality inventory, gave evidence of a greater degree of anxiety and insecurity on the Rorschach Multiple Choice Test than first and second generation Jewish adolescents. The assumption was that the higher the degree of acculturation of Jews without total acceptance by the dominant group, the greater the likelihood of problems of adjustment. Stonequist (1937) proposed that the Jewish adolescent of the third-generation group, without strong identification in either the dominant or the minority culture, experienced the greatest adverse stress resulting from individual marginality. Thus, it would appear that a selective adoption of the values of two competing cultures may augur poorly for psychological health.

Fernando (1975), who compared Jewish and Protestant depressed patients with normal controls in England strengthened the marginality hypothesis. Depression was more likely to occur among married than single individuals, except in the case of Jewish men. Paternal inadequacy and the weakening of ethnic ties and religious influence were related to depression among Jews but not among Protestants.

In a review of the literature on the psychological adjustment of Jews and non-Jews measured by objective scales of personality, Sanua (1962b) found contradictory and inconsistent results. However, with a chronological arrangement of the studies a general trend emerged. In studies carried out in the 1930s, Jews tended to have a higher maladjustment score than non-Jews, while in the ensuing decades these differences disappeared. A few of the studies showed that Jewish subjects enjoyed better psychological adjustment than non-Jewish subjects. One may assume that there was a greater degree of acculturation to the American ethos by the generation that had had greater exposure to the dominant values of American society which are inextricably reflected in the objective scales of personality.

Bart (1968) found the rate of depression to be unusually high among middle-aged Jewish women in comparison to their black and white non-Jewish counterparts. She traced this disproportion to the unusually strong emotional tie between mother and children, especially sons, in the Jewish family. Depression occurs following the loss of this maternal role. Non-Jewish women exhibiting this "typical Jewish pattern" in relating to their children were found to be equally vulnerable to depression.

Freed (1965) found no difference in ethnic identification between psychotic and nonpsychotic Jews. Jewish subjects enjoyed a high degree of security derived from parental affection. However, he believes that if there should be an economic collapse or an ascendance of anti-Semitism, neuroses would decrease and psychoses increase. Armstrong (1965) does not believe that ethnic and religious background has any effect on the incidence or type of mental disturbance among Jews. It is the degree of acculturation to American norms that seems to have the greatest influence on the overall incidence of mental illness. Rinder (1963), found that while psychosis is low for Jews, neurosis is high.

According to Srole, Langner, Michael, Opler, and Rennie (1962), the very low percentage of serious mental impairment among Jews may be explained as follows:

> Mobilization of anxiety about the instability of the Jewish exilic environment may historically have been established as a conditioning pattern of the Jewish family structure. In one direction, such anxiety, subsequently magnified in the adult by extrafamily life conditions, may be reflected in our finding of an unusually large concentration of Midtown Jews in the subclinical mild category of symptom formation. On the other hand, this large component of historically realistic anxiety, as generated in the Jewish family, may function prophylactically to immunize its children against the potentially disabling sequelae of the more severe pressures and traumas of existence. (p. 308)

A series of studies by Fabrega (1970) with Mexican Americans in Texas showed that nonpatient Mexican Americans who are socially productive are overrepresented at both ends of a value scale measuring traditionalism. Three-quarters of the patients were found to be in the central part of the scale. Thus, an exclusive reliance on Mexican or Anglo-American values provided psychological consistency that enabled the individual to be productive.

Maldonado-Sierra, Trent, and Fernandez-Marina (1960) in a series of studies found that Puerto Rican nonneurotics were more accepting of traditional values of the Latin-American family than were neurotics and suggested that there were subtle differences between the Mexican Americans and the Puerto Ricans. They also felt that Puerto Rican "Americanization" is causing greater emphasis on personal achievement, energy, a shift from family to personal orientations, and a shift from fatalism and acceptance to optimism and initiative than is true for Mexican Americans. Rates of admission to hospitals for Puerto Ricans in New York were found to be quite high compared to those of other ethnic groups (Malzberg, 1956).

Meadow, Stoker, and Zurcher (1967) conducted a study of the relationship between sex roles and schizophrenia among Mexican Americans in Texas. They found that the women of Mexican cultural background were able to maintain a relatively stable personal adjustment by virtue of their supporting role in the family. On the other hand, male Mexicans, because of a transition in their role, were constantly frustrated by their marginality. Not only was their *machismo* (a culturally conditioned emphasis upon masculinity) devalued, but they found themselves the objects of ethnic discrimination. According to the authors, this accounted for the high rate of schizophrenia among Mexican-American males.

Another problem is the adjustment to a different culture and environment by those who try to become independent of their parents by leaving home. Dunkas and Nikelly (1972), studying the "Persephone Syndrome" (so-called after the Greek goddess) in sixty Greek women who separated from their parents and married in the United States, hypothesized that the typical cohesiveness of the Greek family encouraged mother-daughter loyalty. However, when daughters are separated from their mothers through marriage in the United States, the stress resulting from guilt feelings following the abandonment of the mother may bring about depression. Thus, according to Dunkas and Nikelly, while the mother-daughter attachment in the country of origin may not be recognized as a problem, it becomes one upon exposure to a different culture and causes a serious problem.

Fried (1965) illustrated a similar problem in adjustment. He found that forced relocation in urban areas in Boston had disrupted working-class communities and that this disruption resulted in very real grief. However, the higher the status was, the better the adaptation to relocation. In most of the examples given so far, cultural change has caused problems of adaptation. However, as Wittkower and Prince (1974) indicated, there must be other elements such as age, personality type, socioeconomic status, social expectation, and so forth connected with cultural change to make it deleterious to mental health.

Rao (1964), finding the male-female ratio in hospitals in India to be three to one, indicated that these figures probably reflected unfavorable attitudes toward institutionalizing women. Rao (1966) later pointed out that the Indians of higher caste were more represented in admissions to public hospitals, as such persons tended to be more subject to the pressures of cultural change, and tensions might be higher because of the need to meet the demands of the sophisticated world. In Pakistan, Rahman (1971) likewise found that the majority of patients were literate (70.4 percent) and the admission rate was higher for the more educated patients contrary to what is usually the case in the United States, where the lower-class patients tend to be overrepresented in mental institutions (Hollingshead & Redlich, 1958). It should be noted that Rose (1964) found that in Italy, with a rise in social status as evaluated by education and migration to the nation's capitol, the rate of paranoid schizophrenia went up. Ramon (1972) in Israel conducted some rather sophisticated, exploratory research on the antecedents of schizophrenia. While the dominant culture in the country is Western oriented, about half of the population is of Middle-Eastern ancestry. Ramon (1972) believes that cultural change can influence a family involved in this social process to the extent that one of its offspring can exhibit schizophrenic behavior. The merit of the study is that she took into consideration communication within the family and its cultural background. Ramon hypothesized that families experiencing serious problems of acculturation would show fewer psychological disturbances as a whole, although one of the members might manifest schizophrenia. In the absence of abrupt cultural change Ramon predicted the development of schizophrenia on the basis of disturbed communication within the family. Four types of families were included in the study: two triads of twenty Polish and Yemenite families with a schizophrenic child and two control groups consisting of Polish and Yemenite families with a child who had suffered from polio, i.e., a total of forty families. Ramon administered the Thematic Apperception Test cards to each individual and analyzed stories for defects in communication according to the Singer and Wynne (1966) method. Stories were also scored for Kluckhohn's and Strodtbeck's (1961) types of value orientation. Ramon's work confirmed the hypothesis that the families of schizophrenics expected to score higher on the cultural deviance scale (the Yemenites) would be lower in defects in communication than the comparable group (the Poles). Ramon concluded that on an individual basis the treatment of a Yemenite family should be directed at clarifying conflicts in values rather than the intrapsychic conflicts of the schizophrenic family member. Their chances of recovery would be better than that of the schizophrenics of the Polish sample, since the latter showed a higher degree of psychopathology in communication than the Yemenite sample.

The following four studies were undertaken in Arab countries that are presently undergoing rapid social change. Ammar and Ledjri (1972) carried out an extensive study of Arab schizophrenics in Tunisia. The report of this investigation appears in their book reviewing familial conditions in the development of schizophrenia. The bibliography, which included approximately 1,000 references, is quite comprehensive and very important, since it contains numerous contributions from non-English sources. In their sample of approximately 300 patients in Tunisia, Ammar and Ledjri (1972) found that 32.5 percent of the schizophrenics had lost their fathers before the age of fifteen. Of the cases whose parents were still living, 40 percent had weak mothers and hard, authoritarian fathers. Fifteen percent had authoritarian fathers who were covertly opposed by the mother. In 25 percent of the cases the mothers of the subjects were found to be authoritarian and the fathers weak. In 8 percent of the cases both parents exhibited explosive characteristics, and in 16 percent the parents bickered constantly. The findings are suggestive; the question that remains concerns the prevalence of paternal authoritarianism in normal Tunisian families.

Essedik (1972), another Tunisian psychiatrist, who studied psychiatric morbidity among Arab workers transplanted to France, stated in the conclusion of his research that the concept of the "schizophrenogenic mother" or "schizophrenogenic familial milieu" should be complemented by the concept of the "psychotogenic social milieu." Arab workers in France have to cope with the usual "social rejection," which their children interiorize. El-Islam (1974) used the expression "culture-bound neurosis" to account for four neurotic symptoms found in sixty female patients in Qatar, one of the Arab sheikdoms on the Arabian Peninsula. The symptoms were giddiness, palpitation, nausea, and general fatigue, which other patients did not exhibit. There was a high percentage of women who were husbandless or childless or had experienced the threat of the loss of their husband—predicaments that cause a great deal of stress among traditional Arab women. While these problems may be found in the West, they probably do not have the same impact, particularly since Western women have a wider range of options besides marriage and motherhood. The choices of Qatari women are, by contrast, circumscribed, and their status is crucially tied to their roles as wives and mothers.

In the Sudan, contrary to the general findings in the West where education generally is correlated with mental health, Hamad (1974) found that the higher the father's level of education, the more mental disorder the students attending Khartoum University experienced. This finding is reminiscent of the results of the Indian and Pakistani studies recapitulated earlier.

The last two studies stand in contrast. In the former (El-Islam) stress has been experienced as a result of traditional role expectation while in the latter (Hamad), educated fathers stand in contrast to the general lack of education of the earlier generation of Sudanese.

Because of the Arabs' social values, which have traditionally restricted women's sexual expression, their culture provides an outlet through the zar cult. A healing ceremony directed by a zar leader and his assistants, it allows women during trance a spontaneous, if vicarious, expression of their repressed sexuality. Devils that provide excitement and releases not otherwise available are consciously and unconsciously invented. Kennedy (1967) feels that the zar is a viable and functional adjustment under conditions of more or less perpetual stress. Recently Sanua (1977b) reviewed this ritual in the Arab world. The general attitude towards women in the Arab world is not really a function of religion but primarily a function of cultural values. Dodd (1974), for example, found that the difference between educated Christians and Moslems with regard to the woman's role in Middle-Eastern society is small and inconsistent. Thus, both contacts with relatives and treatment within the community may prevent chronicity in the schizophrenic and result in relief from stress. Furthermore, closeness with persons of one's own background may have some positive effect on the rate of admissions to hospitals.

Another example of the consequences of cultural change in a traditional society is an epidemiological study conducted in an Indian village by Carstairs and Kapur (1976). The village had three castes. The Brahmins are the most educated, richest, and are mainly landowners. The Bants are more educated than the Mogers but have a comparatively higher proportion living below subsistence level. The Bants mainly are tenant cultivators and the Mogers are mainly fishermen. The latter two groups share the Aliya-Santana tradition. The Brahmins, though more modern than the Bants and Mogers, show the least willingness to mix with the lower castes. Women have been found to have a higher prevalence of somatic symptoms than men. Bants have more somatic symptoms than Brahmins or Mogers. Moger women have the highest possession rate. Brahmin males have the highest proportion of those with psychotic symptoms. Psychosis, epilepsy, and mental retardation are commonest in those below twenty years old. Somatic symptoms appear to be more commonly reported by literates.

It would seem that both a strict adherence to the traditional social values and the experience of rapid social change might lead to stress. However, the latter effect could also occur in developed countries. For example, Gunten (1974) conducted a longitudinal study of a village in the Swiss Alps that had long been isolated before it became a world-renowned mecca for tourists. Economic changes resulted in general stress and inadequate adaptation, which gave rise to all kinds of psychiatric problems and behavioral disorders among its inhabitants.

Abramson (1961) contended that social change increased youth-parent conflicts. He found that ill health among Indian families in South Africa was associated with a discrepancy in traditionalism between the mother and the daughter. When the mother was more traditional compared to other mothers, there was more evidence of ill health among daughters who were relatively "modern" than among those who were relatively "traditional." This finding is similar to those of Spiegel et al. (1966) and Stein (1973) in samples of minority groups undergoing acculturation in the United States (discussed earlier in this chapter).

There are a number of contradictions in the studies reviewed in this section. It would appear, for example, that in certain areas advanced education may be related to psychiatric disturbance, while, by contrast, most of the findings in the United States would indicate that a higher level of education is conducive to mental health. Thus, a search for a single social cause for serious mental illness would certainly fail. On the other hand, what seems to be rather consistent in these studies is that cultural change, in general, results in stress, maladaptation, and various psychological problems. The implications of this finding for the type of treatment necessary to counteract the noxious effect of these social changes are far-reaching.[2]

Studies in the Symptomatology of Mental Illness

The next few studies to be reviewed focus primarily on the overt behavior of the deviant person and the relationship of his symptoms to the patient's familial background. The groups surveyed in this section include various ethnoreligious groups in the United States, American blacks, Jews living in countries outside the United States, and psychotics in Burma, Japan, Hawaii, and the Arab world.

Singer and Opler's (1956) comparison of the symptomatology of Irish and Italian male schizophrenics constituted some of the first systematic studies on the cultural background of schizophrenics in the United States. On the basis of the researchers' knowledge of familial interaction in the traditional Italian culture, they pointed out the freedom with which feeling is expressed in this setting, frequently in the context of a conflict between a powerful father and his oldest son. They hypothesized and demonstrated that this conflict is magnified when the son is schizophrenic. Stein (1971), studying Italian and Irish young males both normal and disturbed, found that the Irish youths expressed passive aggression in contrast to the active aggressive manifestations of the young Italians. Fantl and Shiro (1959) conducted a similar study with females and most of their results paralleled those with the male subjects. One of the general findings was that Italians exhibited more pronounced behavioral difficulties with authority figures than did the Irish. Like Singer and Opler (1956), Piedmont (1966) studied the literature on the German and Polish communities in the United States. He then selected a number of parameters that he hypothesized would differentiate the behavior of schizophrenics from these two groups. He felt that since emotional outlets are permitted or proscribed with the appropriate sanction of both the community and the family, schizophrenic patients would reflect such influences. In other words, prior cultural experiences affect the emotional expression of the schizophrenic. Subjects of German background were found to be more hostile and to have a greater delusional system with paranoid features. They would tend to be passive-aggressive and show sadomasochistic traits. Few were alcoholic. Subjects of Polish background were more anxious, dependent-passive, alcoholic, and showed somatic and hypochondriacal symptoms with catatonic features.

Stoker (1966) and Stoker and Meadow (1974) investigated the nature of the symptoms of Mexican and Anglo-American children attending child guidance clinics in Arizona. In the 1966 study, Stoker attempted to find the roots of psychopathology and to obtain more direct information about families that might be producing future hospital patients. They found that the Mexican-American children experienced problems concerned with the expression of hostility, whereas the Anglo-American children had difficulties with anxiety. While the Mexican-American children tended to act out hostile and unacceptable impulses, the Anglo-American children typically directed the hostility towards themselves. The most important general difference between those two cultural groups was the lack of disturbance of interpersonal relationships in the Mexican-American children as compared to the Anglo-American children. Stoker and Meadow (1974) provided a detailed symptomatic differentiation of the two groups and attributed the differences to culturally determined aspects of family structure, family interaction, and role conflicts.

It is worthwhile to note a discrepancy between the study of Anglo-American children in Texas, who directed hostility toward themselves as compared to Mexican-American children, and the children of American servicemen living abroad (Britton & Cordes, 1970), who tended to be rowdy, undisciplined, and defiant as compared to their more timid and frightened British counterparts.

Is it possible that such differences could be attributed in part to the selection of cases by the agencies involved or to the origin of the referral? There is some evidence for this latter effect. Andrulis (1974) attempted to ascertain the paths by which clients of different ethnic affiliation moved through a comprehensive mental health center. He found that young Mexican-Americans were referred to the center most frequently by nonmedical professionals, while young Anglo patients tended to be referred by their families. The diagnoses of the Anglo cases tended to be deferred pending the collection of additional information, while the Mexican-American group was typically diagnosed as suffering from more transient situational disorders, and many were diagnosed as mentally retarded. Furthermore, the families of the Mexican-American children tended to terminate their treatment earlier. Thus, the Mexican-American families were less inclined to refer their children for psychiatric help, and they also tended to withdraw them from treatment sooner. These two factors certainly complicated the interpretation of studies of psychiatric illness within the United States.

Breen (1968) found that there was a higher incidence of paranoid schizophrenia among blacks while Jewish schizophrenics tended to be hebephrenic, catatonic, or simple. He suggested that the basic cultural values between the two groups would account for these differences. Children in black families tend to receive harsh treatment; there is a free expression of aggression; and they continue to fear assault as they grow older. On the other hand, in Jewish families the emphasis is on strong family ties, the withholding of aggressive expression, and the development of dependency. When carried to an extreme, this results in the different types of schizophrenia mentioned above. Figelman (1968), following Breen's study of the withholding of aggression, hypothesized that the internalization of anger among Jews would increase the incidence of affective disorders. He confirmed his hypothesis by studying two groups of acutely schizophrenic, hospitalized blacks and Jews in the same state mental institution. There was a high incidence of depression among Jews and a high incidence of paranoid schizophrenia among blacks.

While Figelman (1968) realized that the Jewish patients tended to belong to a higher socioeconomic class, he felt that a Jewish patient in a state hospital would be of lower socioeconomic status than the Jewish population in general.

Keeler and Vitols (1963) noted that lower-class blacks had more auditory and visual hallucinations than middle-class whites. It is possible that these differences could be attributed to differences in social class rather than to sociocultural factors.

Sanua (1960) formulated the hypothesis that there are sociocultural components in the patients' reactions of Jewish patients to stressful situations and disabilities. He compared the reactions of Jewish, "Old American," Irish-American, and black amputees to the loss of a limb. A major difference was that the Jewish patient was more likely to cry and express deep mourning at the loss of a limb than a non-Jewish patient because Jewish families permit overt expression of affect. In the case of mental illness, Jewish and Irish relatives seem to react differently to the symptoms of the patient in their family, a finding that seems to support partially the previous study. According to Wyland and Mintz (1976), the Irish are more likely to complain about symptoms pertaining to emotional expression, while the Jewish families are more likely to complain about symptoms pertaining to deviant thought processes and language.

The following studies were carried out earlier by American researchers abroad or psychiatrists in the respective countries. In some studies comparisons were made between the samples of patients in two different countries.

Grewel (1967) found differences in symptomatology between Ashkenazi Jews of German-Polish origin and Sephardi Jews of Spanish-Portuguese origin in Holland. Ashkenazi Jews tended to be vivacious, extroverted, and versatile, while Sephardic Jews were described as quiet, restrained, and often dignified in behavior. Dutch Ashkenazi Jews in particular exhibited a high percentage of manic-depressive psychoses, and it was twice as high among the women (21 percent) as among the men (9 percent). On the average, 11 percent of the Sephardi patients were depressed. In Israel, Goldman (1971) likewise found differences between the Ashkenazim and the Sephardim. The former showed a broader grouping of symptoms indicating mood disorders, while the latter tended to show more limited groupings of more acute symptoms indicating schizophrenic disorders.

Hitson and Funkenstein (1959) have tried to relate familial patterns to the type of mental illness exhibited in the United States and Burma. They compared the families of ten *depressed* patients (three Jewish, three Italian, one Russian, one black, and two of mixed background) with the families of six *paranoid* patients (two black, two of Irish, one of Swiss, and one of Canadian descent) in Boston. The authors found that in the depressed group the dominant parent placed responsibility with the children, who could anticipate the expectations of authority figures. In families with paranoid patients the picture was found to be different. The dominant parent expected the children to carry out the orders as given, irrespective of past orders and regardless of contradiction. Hitson and Funkenstein (1959) suggested that the family pattern of paranoid schizophrenics in Boston is similar to the pattern in Burma—complete domination by the parents resulting in aggression being directed against the outside world. In support of their argument they cited the homicide rate in Burma, one of the highest in the world.

Caudill (1964), researching the effect of sibling position on the incidence of psychosis in Japan, found that in families in which a traditional occupation was pursued (but not in other families) the oldest son and the youngest daughter had more responsibility towards the family and therefore a higher frequency of psychosis. The youngest daughter usually takes care of aging parents. Sofue (1964) presented findings that at first glance seem to contradict Caudill's result. Sofue reported that in a survey of the incidence of neurotic symptoms among students at a Japanese university the symptomatology of the youngest sons appeared to be worse than that of the eldest sons. One explanation is that the youngest sons, being permitted more dependence, might be more willing to admit neurotic difficulties. Their greater ability to communicate their troubles and rely on others might spare them psychosis as Caudill's results suggested.

The manifestations of schizophrenia in Japan and in the United States in citizens of Japanese ancestry appear to be different (Enright & Jaeckle,

1963). There is the possibility that the Japanese in Hawaii, having discarded the values of the old country and having acculturated to American values, manifest the same symptomatology that is usually found among Americans in general. Takatomi, Suzuki, and Dendo (1972, 1973), studying schizophrenic patients in Japan, found that differences between Japanese and Western practices of child rearing had implications for psychoanalytic theory. They suggested that the concepts of the Oedipus complex and separation anxiety are not relevant to the Japanese family. Since the child is regarded as the center of the family, his conflicts are not with his parents but with his siblings, who are his rivals for attention. Japanese children remain close to their mothers throughout their lives. The Western idea of independence, self-reliance, and the process of socialization are counter to the very structured Japanese social system, which emphasizes age, hierarchy, and self-control. Sakamoto (1969) found that the closer a Japanese is to an ill member of the family, the slower is the former's recognition of mental illness in his relative. In general, a mother is the last to accept that her son is seriously ill, while outsiders are the first to recognize that a problem exists. In Japanese society, members of the family are more oriented toward the family and society than toward individuals. Cultural differences may be manifested even in the kinds of crimes committed. Kumasaka, Smith, and Aiba (1975) compared types of major crimes in New York and Tokyo. Among the authors' findings were that the frequency of infanticide is higher in Tokyo and that intruders in New York sought confrontation with their victims more actively than their Japanese counterparts, and they discussed the underlying social and cultural factors contributing to this difference.

In a study of mental patients in Kuwait, Parhad (1963) found that 70 percent of the male patients were considered to be passively dependent and feminine in character and 90 percent of the women had aggressive personalities. This is contrary to the usual expected behavior of males and females, as the tendency is for men to be extremely dominant and females quite compliant and passive. As homosexuality is quite widespread in the Arab world and many patients complained of pain in the legs and back pain that was attributed to nonexistent "piles," Parhad interpreted these symptoms as the result of somatization of homosexual conflicts. It is to be noted that in homes in which one parent, generally the father, had died during the patient's childhood, he tended to be better educated than the general population. Both of these findings tend to be contrary to the usual expectations in the United States. Another common symptom in the Arab world is sexual impotence, which is usually connected with back pain. The Arab's belief that the back is the source of sperm and manhood is a connection found in the Koran (Okasha & Demerdash, 1975). According to Elsarrag (1968), since potency is highly valued, considerable anguish is engendered in people who feel incapable of adequate performance.

The generalization to be drawn from all such studies is that the symptomatology of the mentally ill is strongly influenced by the culture and background of the patients. Elsewhere (Draguns, 1973; Draguns & Phillips, 1972), it has been pointed out that in some cultures, for example, in Japan and Puerto Rico, the behavior of the psychotic seems to stand in contrast to norms and standards of appropriateness in these cultures, especially with respect to sex roles. Further intensive studies would be required to understand why in some cultures the symptoms are a caricature of the culture, while in others the symptoms appear contrary to the values of the culture. This is a topic that Draguns also discusses in this volume.

Cultural Values That Reduce the
Impact of Mental Illness

A number of studies illustrate how the support of the family and the social system can be mobilized to reduce the effect of psychological disorders and even eliminate them.

Rin and Lin (1962) found that among the Formosan aborigines and the Chinese living in Taiwan, psychotic cases tended to follow a relatively favorable clinical course and prognosis. One reason may be that the community itself is therapeutic, since there is an absence of any stigma attached to mental illness, and the interest of the community in the patient's illness tends to reduce the deterioration. In Africa, likewise, parents take care of the patients in special villages while they are still hospitalized (Lambo, 1961). This would certainly tend to reduce the isolation that patients in the United States suffer after being committed to a mental institution. In a later study Rin (1967), found that patients who lost their parents in childhood showed a better prognosis than those who had lived with severely pathological patients. He assumed that among the Chinese it is easier to have substitute parents and that they act in some ways to counteract the trend towards more serious mental illness found in patients with pathological parents. The lack of a father substitute during childhood tended to lead the female child in Chinese families to a higher risk of severe psychotic disturbance. In general, he found that the fathers of schizophrenics tended to be rejecting and domineering, while the mothers were found to be overprotective and domineering.

Kaplan and Johnson (1964) found that while drunk, the Navaho can express behavior that otherwise would be unconscionable to him. The Navaho community has an elaborate purification ceremony that convinces the patient the "bad stuff" that has overtaken him is vanquished and can no longer cause trouble. The concern and goodwill of the group are focused on the individual to give him a good moral boost, which motivates him to feel better.

Parsons (1961) found that Italian psychiatric patients, in general, do not follow the general course of deterioration that is usually found in the United States. She suggested that the presence of strong family ties served to buffer the stresses of social isolation and economic deprivation and thus might alter the course of the schizophrenic process. Sunshine (1971) found both black and Irish patients to have a larger proportion of heavy drinkers. Another similarity between these two groups was that they seldom engaged in disruptive behavior on the wards. Italians and Puerto Ricans, on the other hand, exhibited similar symptomatology, as they share many aspects of the Latin culture, including philosophy of life and design for living. Blacks and Irish have no such common heritage, but they have independently evolved similar family roles and values and the same characteristic means of coping with stress. This convergence has helped generate symptoms that have differentiated them from Puerto Ricans and Italians.

Mintz and Schwartz (1964) showed in a study in Boston that the closeness and in-group feeling of the Italian family could serve to counterbalance the consequences of poverty. They found that the incidence of schizophrenia was inversely related to the density of Italians in the communities in which they lived. Thus, among Italian Americans, unlike other groups, poverty is not a major factor in mental illness. Instead, it appears that closeness of contacts with friends and relatives is a salient determinant in maintaining good mental health. Murphy (1968) reported that the Chinese had the lowest rate of hospital admissions of all ethnic groups in British Columbia, Canada, where they are represented in large numbers. In Ontario, however, where they are few and scattered, they have the highest admission rates of any ethnic group.

It is possible that institutionalization tends to produce chronicity in patients. Sommer and Hall (1958) do not agree that when the mental patient enters the hospital, he has already rejected the values of society. Using a special scale of alienation, they found that acute cases in the admission wards were less alienated than were hospital physicians and psychiatrists. On the basis of their research, Sommer and Hall (1958) concluded that large mental institutions produced more alienation than they treated. Discussion about alienated patients, therefore, should be focused on the "disculturating effect" of the hospital rather than on the relationship between alienation and psychopathology.

Conclusion

This chapter has been a survey of some of the literature on the antecedents of psychopathology with specific reference to the sociocultural background of the family of the mentally ill and indications of new pathways in research that have developed recently.

In general, it was found that the studies after 1970 were more sophisticated and showed more ingenuity than those conducted prior to 1960. While the sociocultural variables were scarcely mentioned in early studies, investigators in recent years have become more and more aware of the possible effects of cultural variables on mental illness. Except in certain specific studies, however, there does not appear to be a concerted effort to include the familial background of patients as a major variable. Goldfarb (1970), who has conducted extensive research in child psychosis, indicated that there *"has not been sufficient or adequate investigation of the correlation between socio-economic factors and cultural factors"* (page 774, italics mine) and the specific clinical attributes of children diagnosed as suffering from psychosis, schizophrenia, autism, symbiotic psychosis, or any of the other designations employed for these overlapping groups of children. He pointed out that Sanua (1961, 1964, 1967, 1969a) has "properly stressed the persistent need for assaying the linkage between socio-cultural conditions in the background of diagnosed schizophrenic children and their symptomatic manifestations" (Goldfarb, 1970, p. 774).

One problem is that psychiatrists and psychologists have not been exposed during their training years to social scientists in other disciplines, who could have provided them with a wider scope of concepts and techniques for assessing psychopathology. This probably explains why psychodynamic considerations have consumed most of their attention. As far as is known, there appears to be only one center that was founded to prepare formally investigators in interdisciplinary research, i.e., the Center of Transcultural Psychiatric Studies at McGill University, headed by E. D. Wittkower and H. B. M. Murphy. Lesse (1968) called attention to an urgent need for trained psychosociologists who would comprehend the interrelationship between broad sociodynamic and psychodynamic forces.

Another major development has been the establishment of the National Project of Ethnic America by the American Jewish Committee. Giordano (1973, 1976a, 1976b) and Giordano and Giordano (1977) summarized the research and provided recommendations for the development of mental health programs with effective group settings and guidance facilities to deal with the daily anxieties and social and familial backgrounds of the various ethnic groups in the United States, particularly the "white ethnic" groups.

A systematic summary of the findings in the field poses difficulties. Because of the diverse populations studied by psychiatrists of different orientations, the data are not cumulative. Turner, Zabe, Raymond, and Diamond (1969) have pointed out the importance of the selection of the sample in regard to consistency in epidemiological research. They have shown that variations in sampling sources from different combinations of in-patient and out-patient facilities can produce divergent findings with schizophrenics.

A number of transnational efforts have been made since 1970. Their purpose is to study symptomatology and problems of diagnosis. One is the Anglo-American Comparative Research Study (Cooper, Kendell, Gurland, Sharpe, Copeland, & Simon, 1972); the other, the International Pilot Study of Schizophrenia by the World Health Organization (WHO, 1971). These efforts have shown that it is possible for investigators of different nationalities to carry out collaborative research.

Research conducted in recent years by Indian, Japanese, Korean (Suk Whan Oh, Chung, Park, & Bae, 1963; Suk Whan Oh, 1963), and Chinese (Taiwan) psychiatrists (Rin & Lin, 1962; Rin, 1967) certainly has enriched the literature. The Chinese (Taiwan) have dwelt more on the family background of patients and, in general, have found that the father, contrary to the findings in the West, seems to play a more important role in pathology than the mother. In general, research in the West has neglected the father as a pathogenic agent. It is presumably for this reason that the concept of the "schizophrenogenic" parent is applied mostly to mothers. On the other hand, the closer association between mother and children and the facility for obtaining surrogate parents have reduced or attenuated the seriousness of mental illness in the Orient. Because of the tightness of family life and the maintenance of contacts with the community and relatives, it appears that chronicity is not as frequent as in the West, where large, impersonal mental hospitals tend to increase alienation in parents separated from their relatives and restrained from active participation in the community. There has been some recognition of this problem through the construction of smaller hospital units and in recent years the development of community mental health centers to provide primary and secondary prevention.

The paucity of research on the lower social class and on blacks in particular stands out. However, with normal controls Miller, Challas, and Gee (1972) conducted one study as a follow-up on another of children of schizophrenic, welfare, and convict mothers. In general, all groups displayed many behavioral problems in school psychiatric referrals, antisocial behavior, arrests, high residential mobility, school drop-outs, failures on draft tests, and so forth. Miller et al. came to the surprising conclusion that the life experiences of these subjects seem to reflect the effects of growing up poor in an urban world; the children of schizophrenic mothers do not differ markedly from other children of the poor.

This chapter endeavored to demonstrate that an understanding of psychological disorders is not possible unless researchers and therapists take into consideration that familial, social, and cultural background of their subjects or patients. In the last two decades the establishment of a number of new journals, usually with "social psychiatry" in the title, as well as the convening of conferences on the subject, augurs well for the field of mental health. An integration of the sociocultural factors with the deviancy of the individual could be extremely useful in his or her treatment. As Giordano (1973) pointed out, the emphasis for the future would be not only to use the adaptive capabilities of the individual but to seek support from his family and his social and ethnic group.

After reviewing psychiatry in the Japanese culture, Naka and Kawakita (1964) reached the following conclusions, which express the main thrust of this chapter:

> It is our thought that it would be the best plan for the social psychiatrist to make comparative studies of the social background of each country or community. Then the meaning of the several cultural forces might be brought into relation with each country's psychiatric disorders, for the promotion of mental health in the world. For this ultimate purpose, the special habits and customs of a people require close study and relating to psychiatry on a world-wide scale. Some basic principles helpful for furthering humane international personal relationships could be drawn from intensive effort in this cooperative work. (p. 303)

It is hoped that an integration of data from research conducted along these suggested lines with comparable samples in different subcultural environments and in different countries will lead to more valid and universal findings.

Note

1. The author acknowledges with gratitude the constructive critique of an earlier version of this chapter by Angela Ginorio and Michael O'Driscoll at the Conference of Contributors to this *Handbook* at the Culture Learning Institute, East-West Center, Honolulu, Hawaii, in January 1976.

2. Higginbotham (1976) has documented the problems involved in providing psychiatric services in areas with non-Western cultural values.

References

ABRAHAM, R. D. *Deep down in the jungle: Negro narrative folklore from the streets of Philadelphia.* Atboro, Pa.: Folklore Association, 1964.

ABRAMSON, J. H. Observations on the health of adolescent girls in relation to culture change. *Psychosomatic Medicine,* 1961, 23, 156–165.

ADLER, A. Influence of the social level on psychiatric symptomatology of childhood difficulties. In *Sociological foundations of the psychiatric disorders of childhood: Proceedings of the Twelfth Institute of the Child Research Clinic, of the Woods School with the collaboration of the School of Medicine of Duke University, Durham, N.C.,* 1945.

ALANEN, Y. O. On the personality of the mother and the early mother-child relationship of 100 schizophrenic patients. *Acta Psychiatrica Neurologica Scandinavica,* 1956, Suppl. 80, 227–233.

————. The mothers of schizophrenic patients. *Acta Psychiatrica Neurologica Scandinavica*, 1958, Suppl. 124, 5–361.

————. The family in the pathogenesis of schizophrenic and neurotic disorders. *Acta Psychiatrica Scandinavica*, 1966, Suppl. 189, 9–654.

————. From the mothers of schizophrenic patients to interactional family dynamics. In D. Rosenthal & S. S. Kety (Eds.), *The transmissions of schizophrenia.* Oxford: Pergamon, 1968.

ALANEN, Y. O., ARAJÄRVI, I., & VITAMÄKI, O. Psychoses in childhood. *Acta Psychiatrica Scandinavica*, 1964, Suppl. 174, 1–93.

AL-ISSA, I. Cross-cultural studies of symptomatology in schizophrenia. In I. Al-Issa & W. Dennis (Eds.), *Cross-cultural studies of behavior.* New York: Holt, Rinehart & Winston, 1970.

————. Social and cultural aspects of hallucinations. *Psychological Bulletin*, 1977, *84*, 570–587.

ALLEN, J., DeMYER, M. K., NORTON, J. A., PONTIUS, W., & YANG, E. Intellectuality in parents of psychotic, subnormal and normal children. *Journal of Autism and Childhood Schizophrenia*, 1971, *1*, 311–326.

AMMAR, S., & LEDJRI, H. *Les conditions familiales de développement de la schizophrénie.* Paris: Masson, 1972.

ANDERSON, C., & MEISEL, S. An assessment of family reaction to the stress of psychotic illness. *Hospital and Community Psychiatry*, 1976, *27*, 868–971.

ANDRULIS, D. P. Ethnicity as a variable in the utilization and referral patterns of a comprehensive mental health center (Doctoral dissertation, University of Texas, Austin, 1973). *Dissertation Abstracts International*, 1974, *34*(11-A), 7034.

ANTHONY, J. An experimental approach to the psychopathology of childhood: Autism. *British Journal of Medical Psychology*, 1958, *31*, 211–225.

ARMSTRONG, G. Mental illness among American Jews. *Jewish Social Studies*, 1965, *27*, 103–111.

ARSENIAN, J., & ARSENIAN, J. M. Tough and easy cultures: A conceptual analysis. *Psychiatry*, 1948, *11*, 337–385.

BART, P. B. Depression in middle-aged women: Some sociocultural factors (Doctoral dissertation, University of California, Los Angeles). *Dissertation Abstracts*, 1968, *28*(11-B), 4752.

BATESON, G., JACKSON, D. D., HALEY, J., & WEAKLAND, K. Toward a theory of schizophrenia. *Behavioral Science*, 1956, *1*, 251–264.

BAXTER, J. C. Family relationships variables in schizophrenia. *Acta Psychiatrica Scandinavica*, 1966, *42*, 362–391.

BEIT-HALLAHMI, B., & RABIN, A. I. The kibbutz as a social experiment and as a child-rearing laboratory. *American Psychologist*, 1977, *32*, 532–541.

BENDER, L. Schizophrenia in childhood: Its recognition, description, and treatment. *American Journal of Orthopsychiatry*, 1956, *26*, 499–506.

BENEDICT, R. Continuities and discontinuities in cultural conditioning. *Psychiatry*, 1938, *1*, 161–167.

BERGMAN, P., & ESCALONA, S. K. Unusual sensitivities in very young children. *The Psychoanalytic Study of the Child*, 1949, *3–4*, 333–352.

BERNE, E. Difficulties of comparative psychiatry. *American Journal of Psychiatry*, 1959, *116*, 104–109.

————. A psychiatric census of the South Pacific. *American Journal of Psychiatry,* 1960, *117,* 44–47.

BETTELHEIM, B. *The empty fortress—infantile autism and the birth of the self.* New York: Free Press, Collier-Macmillan, 1967.

BHASKARAN, K. A psychiatric study of schizophrenic patterns in an Indian mental hospital. *International Journal of Social Psychiatry,* 1959, *5,* 41–46.

————. A psychiatric study of paranoid schizophrenics in a mental hospital in India. *Psychiatric Quarterly,* 1963, *37,* 734–751.

BJORNSSON, S. Epidemiological investigation of mental disorders of children in Reykjavik, Iceland. *Scandinavian Journal of Psychology,* 1974, *15,* 244–254.

BLOCK, J., & CHRISTIANSEN, B. A test of Hendin's hypothesis relating suicide in Scandinavia to child-rearing orientation. *Scandinavian Journal of Psychology,* 1966, *7,* 267–288.

BOATMAN, M. J., & SZUREK, S. A. A clinical study of childhood schizophrenia. In D. D. Jackson (Ed.). *The etiology of schizophrenia.* New York: Basic Books, 1960, pp. 389–440.

BREEN, B. Culture and schizophrenia: A study of Negro and Jewish schizophrenics. *International Journal of Social Psychiatry,* 1968, *14,* 282–289.

BRITTON, R. S., & CORDES, C. K. A comparison of child psychiatric morbidity in American and British military families overseas. *Journal of the Royal Army Medical Corps,* 1970, *116,* 11–16.

BRODY, E. B. Sociocultural influences in vulnerability to schizophrenic behavior. In J. Romano (Ed.), *The origins of schizophrenia.* Amsterdam: Excerpta Medica, 1967.

BRODY, E. B. (Ed.). *Behavior in new environments: Adaptation of migrant populations.* Beverly Hills, Calif.: Sage, 1970.

BRONFENBRENNER, U. Socialization and social class through time and space. In E. Maccoby, T. M. Newcomb, & E. L. Hartley (Eds.), *Readings in social psychology* (3rd ed.). New York: Holt, Rinehart & Winston, 1958.

BROWN, G. W., NIBHROLCHAIN, M., & HARRIS, T. Social class and psychiatric disturbance and women in an urban population. *Sociology,* 1975, *9,* 223–254.

CANTWELL, D. P., BAKER, L., & RUTTER, M. Family factors. In M. Rutter & E. Schopler (Eds.), *Autism: A reappraisal of concepts and treatment.* New York: Plenum, 1978.

CAPLAN, G. Clinical observations on the emotional life of children in the communal settlements in Israel. In M. J. E. Senn (Ed.), *Problems of infancy in childhood.* New York: Josiah Macy Jr. Foundation, 1954

CARSTAIRS, G. M., & KAPUR, R. L. *The great universe of Kota: Stress, change and mental disorders in an Indian village.* Berkeley: University of California Press, 1976.

CAUDILL, W. Sibling rank and style of life among Japanese psychiatric patients. *Proceedings of the Joint Meeting of the Japanese Society of Psychiatry and Neurology and the American Psychiatric Association.* Tokyo: Japanese Society of Psychiatry and Neurology, 1964, 35–40.

CAUDILL, W., & WEINSTEIN, H. Maternal care and infant behavior in Japan and America. *Psychiatry,* 1969, *32,* 12–43.

CAWTE, J. E. Social and cultural influences on mental health in aboriginal Australia: A summary of ten years research. *Transcultural Psychiatric Research Review,* 1976, *13,* 23–38.

CLARK, M. The anthropology of aging: A new area for studies of culture and personality. in L. Neugarten (Ed.), *Middle age and aging.* Chicago: University of Chicago Press, 1968.

CLARKE, A. M., & CLARKE, A. D. B. *Early experience: Myth and evidence.* New York: Free Press, 1976.

CLERK, G. A reflection on the role of the mother in the development of language in the schizophrenic child. *Canadian Psychiatric Association Journal,* 1961, *6,* 252–256.

COLEMAN, M. *The autistic syndrome.* Amsterdam: North-Holland Publishing Company, 1976.

COOPER, J. E., KENDELL, R. E., GURLAND, B. J., SHARPE, L., COPELAND, J. R. M., & SIMON, R. *Psychiatric diagnosis in New York and London: A comparative study of mental hospital admissions.* London: Oxford University Press, 1972.

DAVIS, A., & HAVIGHURST, R. J. Social class and color differences in child-rearing. *American Sociological Review,* 1946, *11,* 698–710.

DESPERT, J. J., & SHERWIN, A. C. Further examination of diagnostic criteria in schizophrenic illness and psychoses of infancy and early childhood. *American Journal of Psychiatry,* 1958, *114,* 784–790.

DEVEREUX, E. C., BRONFENBRENNER, U., & RODGERS, R. R. Child rearing in England and the United States: A cross-cultural comparison. *Journal of Marriage and the Family,* 1969, *31,* 257–270.

DIAZ-GUERRERO, R. Neurosis and the Mexican family structure. *American Journal of Psychiatry,* 1955, *112,* 411–417.

DODD, P. C. The effect of religious affiliation on woman's role in Middle Eastern Arab society. *Journal of Comparative Family Studies,* 1974, *5,* 117–129.

DOHRENWEND, B. P. Sociocultural and social psychological factors in the genesis of mental illness. *Journal of Health and Social Behavior,* 1975, *16,* 365–392.

DOHRENWEND, B. P., & DOHRENWEND, B. S. *Social status and psychological disorder,* New York: Wiley, 1969.

―――. *Stressful life events: Their nature and effects.* New York: Wiley, 1974a.

―――. Social and cultural influences on psychopathology. *Annual Review of Psychology,* 1974b, *25,* 419–452.

DOI, T. *The anatomy of dependence.* Tokyo: Kodansha International, 1973.

DRAGUNS, J. G. Comparisons of psychopathology across cultures: Issues, findings, directions. *Journal of Cross-Cultural Psychology,* 1973, *4,* 9–47.

DRAGUNS, J. G., & PHILLIPS, L. *Culture and psychopathology: The quest for a relationship.* Morristown, N.J.: General Learning Corporation, 1972.

DUNKAS, N., & NIKELLY, G. The Persephone Syndrome: A study of conflict in the adaptive process of married Greek female immigrants in the U.S.A. *Social Psychiatry,* 1972, *7,* 211–216.

DUVALL, E. M. Conceptions of parenthood. *American Journal of Sociology,* 1946, *52,* 193–203.

EL-ISLAM, F. M. Culture bound neurosis in Qatari Women. *Transcultural Psychiatric Research Review,* 1974, *11,* 167–168.

EL SARRAG, M. E. Psychiatry in the Northern Sudan: A study in comparative psychiatry. *British Journal of Psychiatry,* 1968, *114,* 945–948.

ENRIGHT, J. B., & JAECKLE, W. R. Psychiatric symptoms and diagnosis in two sub-cultures. *International Journal of Social Psychiatry*, 1963, 9, 12–17.

ERICHSEN, F. Der Vater der Schizophrenen: I and II. *Zeitschrift für Psychotherapie und Medizinische Psychologie*, 1973, 23, 130–140, 169–185.

ESSEDIK, J. Aspect sociogène de la morbidité psychiatrique chez l'ouvrier Arabe transplanté en France. *Comptes Rendus. Congrès des Psychiatres et Neurologues de Langue Française*, Tunis, 1972, 1407–1420.

FABREGA, H., JR. Mexican-American of Texas: Some social psychiatric features. In E. Brody (Ed.), *Behavior in new environments: Adaptation of migrant populations.* Beverly Hills, Calif.: Sage, 1970.

FANTL, B., & SCHIRO, J. Cross-cultural variables in the behavior patterns and symptom formation of 15 Irish and 15 Italian female schizophrenics. *International Journal of Social Psychiatry*, 1959, 4, 245–253.

FARBER, M. L. *Theory of suicide.* New York: Funk & Wagnalls, 1968.

FERNANDO, S. J. M. A cross-cultural study of some familial and social factors in de-pressive illness. *British Journal of Psychiatry*, 1975, 127, 46–53.

FIGELMAN, M. A comparison of affective and paranoid disorders in Negroes and Jews. *International Journal of Social Psychiatry*, 1968, 14, 277–281.

FLORSHEIM, J., & PETERFREUND, O. The intelligence of parents of psychotic children. *Journal of Autism and Childhood Schizophrenia*, 1974, 4, 61–70.

FONTANA, A. E. Familial etiology of schizophrenia: Is the scientific methodology possible? *Psychological Bulletin*, 1966, 66, 214–227.

FOUDRAINE, J. Schizophrenia and the family: A survey of the literature 1956–1960 on the etiology of schizophrenia. *Acta Psychotherapeutica*, 1961, 9, 82–110.

FRANK, G. H. The role of the family in the development of psychopathology. *Psychological Bulletin*, 1965, 64, 191–205.

FRANKNOI, J., & RUTTENBERG, B. A. Formulation of the dynamic economic factors underlying infantile autism. *Journal of the American Academy of Child Psychiatry*, 1971, 10, 713–738.

FRAZIER, R. F. *Negro youth at the cross-ways.* Washington, D.C.: American Council of Education, 1940.

FREED, E. X. Ethnic identification of hospitalized Jewish psychiatric patients: An exploratory study. *International Journal of Social Psychiatry*, 1965, 11, 110–115.

FRIED, M. Transitional functions of working class communities: Implications for forced relocation. In M. B. Kantor (Ed.), *Mobility and mental health.* Springfield, Ill.: Thomas, 1965.

FRIED, M., & LINDEMANN, E. Sociocultural factors in mental health and illness. *American Journal of Orthopsychiatry*, 1961, 31, 87–101.

GALDSTON, I. International psychiatry. *American Journal of Psychiatry*, 1957, 114, 103–108.

GARMEZY, N. Children at risk: The search for the antecedents of schizophrenia. Part II. Ongoing research programs, issues and intervention. *Schizophrenia Bulletin*, 1974, 9, 55–125.

————, with the collaboration of SANDRA STREITMAN. Children at risk: The search for the antecedents of schizophrenia. Part I. Conceptual models and research methods. *Schizophrenia Bulletin*, 1974, 8, 14–90.

GERARD, D. L., & SIEGEL, L. J. The family background of schizophrenia. *Psychiatric Quarterly*, 1950, 24, 47–73.

GILBERT, G. M. Sex differences in the mental health in a Mexican village. *International Journal of Social Psychiatry*, 1959, 5, 208–213.

GIORDANO, J. *Ethnicity and mental health: Research and recommendations.* New York: Institute of Human Relations, American Jewish Committee, 1973.

————. Community mental health in a pluralistic society. *International Journal of Mental Health*, 1976a, 5, 5–15.

————. Ethnicity and community mental health: A review of the literature. *Community Mental Health Review*, 1976b, 1, 1–5.

GIORDANO, J., & GIORDANO, G. *Ethnocultural factors in mental health: Literature review and bibliography.* New York: American Jewish Committee, 1977.

GOLDFARB, W. Childhood psychosis. In P. S. Mussen (Ed.), *Carmichael's manual of child psychology* (Vol. II). New York: Wiley, 1970.

————. Distinguishing and classifying the individual schizophrenic child. In S. Arieti & G. Caplan (Eds.), *American Handbook of Psychiatry* (Vol. II). (2nd ed.). New York: Basic Books, 1974.

GOLDMAN, I. M. Psychopathology of European and Afro-Asian Jews (Doctoral dissertation, Rutgers University). *Dissertation Abstracts*, 1971, 32(6-B), 3634–3635.

GREWEL, F. Psychiatric differences in Ashkenazim and Sephardim. *Psychiatria, Neurologia, Neurochirurgia*, 1967, 70, 339–347.

GUNTEN, G. [Social change and mental health.] *Psychiatria Clinica*, 1974, 7, 287–313.

GUTHRIE, R., & WYATT, R. J. Biochemistry and schizophrenia III. A review of childhood psychosis. *Schizophrenia Bulletin*, 1975, 12, 19–30.

HAMAD, B. Some factors in relation to mental health in Khartoum University students. *Journal of the American College of Health Association*, 1974, 23, 127–133.

HAMILTON, D. M. The changing picture of dementia praecox. *Journal of the Kentucky State Medical Association*, 1959, 57, 297–301.

HANSON, D. R., & GOTTESMAN, I. I. The genetics, if any, of infantile autism and childhood schizophrenia. *Journal of Autism and Childhood Schizophrenia*, 1976, 6, 209–233.

HARPER, J., & WILLIAMS, S. Early environmental stress and infantile autism. *Medical Journal of Australia*, 1974, 61, 341–346.

————. Infantile autism: The incidence of national groups in a New South Wales survey. *Medical Journal of Australia*, 1976a, March 6th, 299–301.

————. Infantile autism—national groups. Letter to the Editor. *Medical Journal of Australia*, 1976b, May 8th, 721–722.

HARRISON, S. I., McDERMOTT, J. F., WILSON, P. T., & SCHRAGER, J. Social class and mental illness in children: Choice of treatment. *Archives of General Psychiatry*, 1965, 13, 411–417.

HARTOG, J. A. Transcultural view of sibling rank and mental disorder. *Acta Psychiatrica Scandinavica*, 1974, 50, 33–49.

HEILBRUN, A. B. *Aversive maternal control: A theory of schizophrenic development.* New York: Wiley, 1973.

HENDIN, H. *Suicide and Scandinavia.* New York: Grune & Stratton, 1964.

HESS, R. D. Social class and ethnic influences on socialization. In P. H. Mussen (Ed.), *Carmichael's manual of child psychology* (3rd ed). New York: Wiley, 1970.

HETHERINGTON, E. M., & MARTIN, B. Family interaction and psychopathology in children. In H. C. Quay & J. S. Werry (Eds.), *Psychopathological disorders of childhood.* New York: Wiley, 1972, pp. 30–82.

HIGGINBOTHAM, H. N. A conceptual model for the delivery of psychological services in non-Western settings. *Topics in Culture Learning,* 1976, 4, 44–52 (East-West Center, Honolulu, Hawaii).

HINGTGEN, J. N. & BRYSON, C. Q. Recent developments in the study of early childhood psychoses: Infantile autism, childhood schizophrenia and related disorders. *Schizophrenia Bulletin,* 1972, 5, 5–54.

HITSON, H. M., & FUNKENSTEIN, D. H. Family patterns and paranoidal structure in Boston and Burma. *International Journal of Social Psychiatry,* 1959, 5, 182–190.

HOEKSTRA, R. C. The "double-bind," that is to say, the psychic stranglehold. *Psychiatria, Neurologia, Neurochirurgia,* 1971, 74, 391–400.

HOLLINGSHEAD, A. B., & REDLICH, F. C. *Social class and mental illness.* New York: Wiley, 1958.

HOWELLS, J. G. Family psychopathology and schizophrenia. In J. G. Howells (Ed.), *Modern perspectives in world psychiatry,* Chapter 14, 391–424. New York: Brunner/Mazel, 1971.

HUGHES, C. C., TREMBLAY, M. A., RAPOPORT, R. N., & LEIGHTON, A. H. *People of Cove and Woodlot Communities from the viewpoint of social psychiatry. II. The Stirling County study of psychiatric disorder and sociocultural environment.* New York: Basic Books, 1960.

HUNT, R. G. Sociocultural factors in mental disorder. *Behavioral Science,* 1959, 4, 96–106.

————. Social class and mental illness: Some implications for clinical theory and practice. *American Journal of Psychiatry,* 1960, 116, 1065–1069.

JACOB, T. Family interaction in disturbed and normal families: A methodological and substantive review. *Psychological Bulletin,* 1975, 82, 33–65.

KAFFMAN, M. Characteristics of the emotional pathology of the kibbutz child. *American Journal of Orthopsychiatry,* 1972, 42, 692–709.

KANNER, L. Autistic disturbances of affective contact. *Nervous Child,* 1943, 2, 217–250.

————. Early infantile autism. *Journal of Pediatrics,* 1944, 25, 211–217.

————. *Child psychiatry* (4th ed.). Springfield, Ill.: Thomas, 1972.

KAPLAN, B., & JOHNSON, D. The social meaning of Navaho psychopathology and psychotherapy. In A. Kiev (Ed.), *Magic, faith and healing.* New York: Free Press, 1964.

KARDINER, A., & OVESEY, L. *The mark of oppression: A psychosocial study of the American Negro.* New York: Norton, 1951.

KAUFMAN, I., FRANK, T., HEIMS, L., HERRICK, J., & WILNER, L. Parents of schizophrenic children: III. Four types of defense in mothers and fathers of schizophrenic children. *American Journal of Orthopsychiatry,* 1959, 29, 460–472.

KEELER, M. H., & VITOLS, M. M. Migration and schizophrenia in North Carolina Negroes. *American Journal of Orthopsychiatry,* 1963, 33, 554–557.

KEITH, S. J., GUNDERSON, J. G., REIFMAN, A., BUCKSBAUM, S., & MOSHER, L. R. Special report: Schizophrenia 1976. *Schizophrenia Bulletin*, 1976, 2, 509–565.

KENNEDY, J. G. Nubian zar ceremonies as psychotherapy. *Human Organization*, 1967, 26, 185–194.

KIKUCHI, M., MORIMOTO, Y., MACHIDA, S., YAMAZAKI, A., YOGASHI, Y., SHTARA, M., SAIDO, Y., ITO, N., & HAMADA, M. [Family dynamics of autistic children: Report on parental intelligence.] *Psychiatria et Neurologica Japonica*, 1970, 72, 639.

KING, P. Early infantile autism: Relationship to schizophrenia. *Journal of the American Academy of Child Psychiatry*, 1975, 14, 666–682.

KLEBANOFF, L. Parental attitudes of mothers of schizophrenic, brain-injured and retarded and normal children. *American Journal of Orthopsychiatry*, 1959, 29, 445–454.

KLUCKHOHN, F., & STRODTBECK, F. *Variations in value orientations.* New York: Row, Peterson, 1961.

KOHN, M. L. Social class and parental values. *American Journal of Sociology*, 1959, 64, 337–351.

————. Social class and parent-child relationships: An interpretation. *American Journal of Sociology*, 1963, 68, 471–480.

————. *Class and conformity: A study in values.* Homewood, Ill.: Dorsey, 1969.

————. Class, family and schizophrenia: A reformulation. *Social Forces*, 1972, 50, 295–304.

————. Social class and schizophrenia: A critical review and a reformulation. *Schizophrenia Bulletin*, 1973, 7, 60–79.

KORN, S. Family dynamics and childhood schizophrenia: A comparison of the family background of two low socioeconomic minority groups, one with schizophrenic children, the other with rheumatic fever children (Doctoral dissertation, Yeshiva University, New York). *Dissertation Abstracts*, 1964, 25 (B), 2049.

KRAEPELIN, E. Vergleichende Psychiatrie. *Zentralblatt für Nervenheilkunde und Psychiatrie*, 1904, 15, 433–437. (Also in English in *Transcultural Psychiatric Research Review*, 1974, 11, 108–112.)

KUMASAKA, Y., SMITH, R. J., & AIBA, H. Crimes in New York and Tokyo: Sociocultural perspectives. *Community Mental Health Journal*, 1975, 11, 19–26.

LAMBO, T. A. A plan for the treatment of the mentally ill in Nigeria: The village system at Aro. In L. Linn (Ed.), *Frontiers in general hospital psychiatry*. New York: International Universities Press, 1961.

Lancet, What is childhood autism? *Lancet* 2 No. 7988, 2 October 1976, 723–724.

LANGFELDT, G. Scandinavia. In L. Bellak (Ed.), *Contemporary European psychiatry*. New York: Grove, 1961.

LANGNER, T. S., & MICHAEL, S. *Life stress and mental health.* New York: Free Press, 1963.

LAUTER, H. Kraepelin's Bedeutung für die Kulturpsychiatrie [Kraepelin's importance for cultural psychiatry]. *Transcultural Psychiatric Research Review and Newsletter*, 1965, 11, 9–12.

LEIGHTON, A. H. *My name is legion.* New York: Basic Books, 1959.

————. Social disintegration and mental disorder. In S. Arieti & G. Caplan (Eds.), *American handbook of psychiatry* (2nd ed.). New York: Basic Books, 1974.

LEIGHTON, A. H., & HUGHES, J. M. Cultures as causative of mental disorders. In *Causes of mental disorders: A review of epidemiological knowledge.* New York: Milbank Memorial Fund, 1961.

LEIGHTON, A. H., LAMBO, T. A., HUGHES, C. C., LEIGHTON, D. C., MURPHY, J. M., & MACKLIN, D. B. *Psychiatric disorder among the Yoruba.* Ithaca, N.Y.: Cornell University Press, 1963.

LEIGHTON, D. C., HAGNELL, O., KELLERT, S. R., LEIGHTON, A. H., HARDING, J. S., & DANLEY, R. A. Psychiatric disorder in a Swedish and a Canadian community: An exploratory study. *Social Science and Medicine,* 1971, 5, 189–209.

LEIGHTON, D. C., HARDING, J. S., MACKLIN, D. B., MACMILLAN, A. M., & LEIGHTON, A. H. *The character of danger: Psychiatric symptoms in selected communities* (Vol. 3). New York: Basic Books, 1963.

LESSE, S. The influence of socioeconomic and sociotechnologic systems on emotional illness. *American Journal of Psychotherapy,* 1968, 22, 569–576.

LEVINE, R. A. Cross-cultural study in child psychology. In P. H. Mussen (Ed.), *Carmichael's manual of child psychology* (3rd ed.). New York: Wiley, 1970.

LORION, R. Patient and therapist variables in the treatment of low-income patients. *Psychological Bulletin,* 1974, 81, 344–354.

LOTTER, V. Epidemiology of autistic conditions in young children: II. Some characteristics of the parents and children. *Social Psychiatry,* 1967, 1, 163–173.

————. Childhood autism in Africa. *Journal of Child Psychology and Psychiatry,* 1978a, 19, 231–244.

————. Follow-up studies. In M. Rutter and E. Schopler, (Eds.), *Autism: A reappraisal of concepts and treatment.* New York: Plenum, 1978b, Chapter 32, pp. 475–496.

MAHLER, M. Child psychosis and schizophrenia: Autistic and symbiotic infantile psychosis. *Psychoanalytic Study of the Child,* 1952, 7, 286–305.

MALDONADO-SIERRA, E. D., TRENT, R. D., & FERNANDEZ-MARINA, R. Neurosis and traditional family beliefs in Puerto Rico. *International Journal of Social Psychiatry,* 1960, 6, 237–246.

MALZBERG, B. Mental disease among Puerto Ricans in New York City. *Journal of Nervous and Mental Disease,* 1956, 123, 262–269.

McCLELLAND, D. C., DeCHARMS, R., & RINDLISBACHER, A. Religious and other sources of parental attitudes towards independence training. In D. C. McClelland (Ed.), *Studies in motivation,* New York: Appleton-Century-Crofts, 1955.

McDERMOTT, J. F., HARRISON, S. I., SCHRAGER, J., LINDY, J., & KILLINS, E. Social class and mental illness in children: The question of childhood psychosis. *American Journal of Orthopsychiatry,* 1967, 37, 548–557.

MEADOW, A., STOKER, D. H., & ZURCHER, L. A. Sex role and schizophrenia: A cross-cultural study. *International Journal of Social Psychiatry,* 1967, 1, 250–259.

MEDNICK, S., & McNEIL, T. F. Current methodology in research on the etiology of schizophrenia: Serious difficulties which suggest the use of the high-risk group method. *Psychological Bulletin,* 1968, 70, 681–693.

MERTON, R. K. *Social theory and social structure.* Glencoe, Ill.: Free Press, 1957.

MEYERS, M. R., & CUSHING, H. H. Types and incidence of behavior problems in relation to cultural background. *American Journal of Orthopsychiatry,* 1936, *6,* 110–116.

MILLER, D., CHALLAS, G., & GEE, S. Children of deviants: A fifteen-year follow-up study of children of schizophrenic mothers, welfare mothers, match controls and random urban families. Unpublished report, 1972.

MINTZ, N. L., & SCHWARTZ, D. T. Urban ecology and psychosis: Community factors in the incidence of schizophrenia and manic depression among Italians of Greater Boston. *International Journal of Social Psychiatry,* 1964, *10,* 101–118.

MISHLER, E. G., & SCOTCH, N. A. Sociocultural factors on the epidemiology of schizophrenia: A review. *Psychiatry,* 1963, *26,* 315–351.

MISHLER, E. G., & WAXLER, N. E. Family interaction processes and schizophrenia: A review of current theories. *International Journal of Psychiatry,* 1966, *2,* 375–428.

MONTAGU, A. Culture and mental illness. *American Journal of Psychiatry,* 1961, *118,* 15–23.

MURPHY, H. B. M. *Mental hospitalization patterns in twelve Canadian subcultures.* Montreal: Department of Psychiatry, McGill University, 1968.

———. Handling the cultural dimension in psychiatric research. *Social Psychiatry,* 1969, *4,* 11–18.

———. Alcoholism and schizophrenia in the Irish: A review. *Transcultural Psychiatric Research Review,* 1975, *12,* 116–139.

MURPHY, H. B. M., & LEMIEUX, M. Quelques considérations sur le taux élevé de schizophrénie dans un type de communauté canadienne-française. *Canadian Psychiatric Association Journal,* 1967, *12,* Special Issue, S72–S81.

MURPHY, H. B. M., WITTKOWER, E. W., & CHANCE, N. A. Cross-cultural inquiry into the symptomatology of depression: A preliminary report. *International Journal of Social Psychiatry,* 1967, *3,* 6–15.

MURPHY, H. B. M., WITTKOWER, E. W., FRIED, H., & ELLENBERGER, H. A cross-cultural survey of schizophrenic symptomatology. *International Journal of Social Psychiatry,* 1963, *9,* 237–249.

MURPHY, J. M., & LEIGHTON, A. H. (Eds.). *Approaches to cross-cultural psychiatry.* Ithaca, N.Y.: Cornell University Press, 1965.

MYERS, J. K., and BEAN, L. L. *A decade later: A follow-up of social class and mental illness.* New York: Wiley, 1968.

MYERS, J. K., & ROBERTS, B. H. *Family and class dynamics in mental illness.* New York: Wiley, 1959.

NAKA, S., & KAWAKITA, Y. Psychiatry in Japanese culture. *Diseases of the Nervous System,* 1964, *25,* 298–303.

NATHANSON, C. A. Illness and the feminine role: A theoretical review. *Social Science and Medicine,* 1975, *9,* 57–62.

NEY, P. Are there Chinese autistic children? Paper presented at the Symposium of the Pacific Association for Autistic Children at the University of British Columbia, Vancouver, B. C., Canada, 1978.

OFFORD, D. R., & CROSS, L. A. Behavioral antecendents of adult schizophrenia: A review. *Archives of General Psychiatry,* 1969, *21,* 267–283.

OKASHA, A., & DEMERDASH, A. Arabic study of cases of functional sexual inadequacy. *British Journal of Psychiatry*, 1975, *126*, 446–448.

OLSON, D. Empirically unbinding the double-bind: A review of research and conceptual reformulation. *Family Process*, 1972, *11*, 69–94.

OPLER, M. K. *Culture and mental health: Cross-cultural studies.* New York: Macmillan, 1959.

————. Cultural determinants of mental disorders. In B. Wolman (Ed.), *Handbook of child psychology.* New York: McGraw-Hill, 1965.

————. *Culture and social psychiatry.* New York: Atherton, 1967.

ORNITZ, E. M., & RITVO, E. R. The syndrome of autism: A critical review. *American Journal of Psychiatry*, 1976, *133*, 609–621.

PARHAD, L. Some cultural factors affecting treatment in a psychiatric out-patient department in Kuwait. *Transcultural Psychiatric Research Review*, 1963, *14*, 22–26.

PARKER, S., & KLEINER, R. J. *Mental illness in the urban Negro community.* New York: Macmillan, 1966.

PARSONS, A. A schizophrenic episode in a Neapolitan slum. *Psychiatry*, 1961, *24*, 109–121.

————. *Belief, magic and anomie: Essays in psychological anthropology.* New York: Free Press, 1969.

PIEDMONT, E. B. Ethnicity and schizophrenia: A pilot study. *Mental Hygiene*, 1966, *50*, 374–379.

POLLACK, M., & GITTELMAN, R. K. The siblings of childhood schizophrenics: A review. *American Journal of Orthopsychiatry*, 1964, *34*, 868–874.

PRALL, R. C., SHULMAN, J., & SURER, L. A study of normal child behavior. *Pennsylvania Psychiatric Quarterly*, 1968, *8*, 5–14.

RABKIN, L. Y. The patient's family: Research methods. *Family Process*, 1965, *4*, 105–132.

RAHMAN, R. Schizophrenia and social class in Pakistan. In M. Stojanorie (Ed.), *Proceedings of the Third International Congress of Social Psychiatry.* Zagreb, Yugoslavia, 1971, *10*, 269–276.

RAMON, S. The impact of culture change on schizophrenia in Israel. *Journal of Cross-Cultural Psychology*, 1972, *3*, 373–382.

RANK, B. Adaptation of the psychoanalytic technique for the treatment of young children with atypical development. *American Journal of Orthopsychiatry*, 1949, *19*, 130–139.

RAO, S. Birth order and schizophrenia. *Journal of Nervous and Mental Disease*, 1964, *138*, 87–89.

————. Socioeconomic groups and mental disorders. *Psychiatric Quarterly*, 1966, *40*, 667–691.

RIMLAND, B. *Infantile autism.* New York: Appleton-Century-Crofts, 1964.

————. Infantile autism: Status and research. In A. Davids (Ed.), *Child personality and psychopathology: Current topics* (Vol. 1.). New York: Wiley, 1974.

RIN, H. A family study of Chinese schizophrenic patients: Loss of parents, sibling rank, parental attitude, and short-term prognosis. *Journal of the Formosan Medical Association*, 1967, *66*, 461–469.

RIN, H., & LIN, T. Mental illness among Formosan aborigines as compared with the Chinese in Taiwan. *Journal of Mental Science,* 1962, *108,* 134–146.

RINDER, I. D. Mental health of American Jewish urbanites: A review of the literature and predictions. *International Journal of Social Psychiatry,* 1963, *9,* 104–109.

RISKIN, J., & FAUNCE, E. E. An evaluative review of family interaction research. *Family Process,* 1972, *11,* 365–455.

RITVO, E. R. Autism: From adjective to noun. In E. R. Ritvo (Ed.), *Autism: Diagnosis, current research and management.* New York: Spectrum, 1976.

———. Biochemical studies of children with the syndrome of autism, childhood schizophrenia and related developmental disabilities: A review. *Journal of Child Psychology and Psychiatry,* 1977, *18,* 373–379.

RITVO, E. R., CANTWELL, D., JOHNSON, E., CLEMENTS, M., BENBROOK, F., SLAGLE, S., KOLLY, P., & RITZ, M. Social class factors in autism. *Journal of Autism and Childhood Schizophrenia,* 1971, *1,* 297–310.

ROBINSON, J. F. The psychoses of early childhood. *American Journal of Orthopsychiatry,* 1961, *31,* 536–550.

ROBINSON, J. F., & VITALE, L. J. Children with circumscribed interest patterns. *American Journal of Orthopsychiatry,* 1954, *24,* 755–766.

ROFF, M. Some problems in life history research. In M. Roff & D. F. Ricks (Eds.), *Life history research in psychopathology* (Vol. 1). Minneapolis: University of Minnesota Press, 1972.

ROGAN, E. N., DUNHAM, H. W., & SULLIVAN, T. M. A worldwide transcultural survey of diagnostic treatment and etiological approaches in schizophrenia. *Transcultural Psychiatric Research Review,* 1973, *10,* 107–110.

ROMERO LARA, F. History of infantile psychoses: Incidence and epidemiology, definition and general concepts. *Neurología, Neurocirugía, Psiquiatría* (Mexico), 1975, *16,* 147–152.

ROSE, A. The prevalence of mental disorders in Italy. *International Journal of Social Psychiatry,* 1964, *10,* 87–100.

ROSE, J. A. Stress outcome: Schizophrenia or creativity. *Pediatrics,* 1961, *28,* 472–479.

ROSENGREEN, W. R. The hospital careers of lower and middle child psychiatric patients. *Psychiatry,* 1962, *25,* 16–22.

RUTTENBERG, B. A. A psychoanalytic understanding of infantile autism and its treatment. In D. W. Churchill, G. D. Alpern, & M. K. DeMyer (Eds.), *Infantile autism.* Springfield, Ill.: Thomas, 1971.

RUTTER, M. Diagnosis and definition. In Michael Rutter and Eric Schopler (Eds.), *Autism: A reappraisal of concepts and treatment.* New York: Plenum, 1978.

RUTTER, M., & BARTAK, L. Causes of infantile autism: Some considerations from recent research. *Journal of Autism and Childhood Schizophrenia,* 1971, *1,* 20–32.

RUTTER, M., & SCHOPLER, E. *Autism: A reappraisal of concepts and treatment.* New York: Plenum, 1978.

SAKAMOTO, Y. A study of the attitude of Japanese families of schizophrenics towards their ill members. *Psychotherapy and Psychosomatics,* 1969, *17,* 365–374.

SANUA, V. D. Differences in personality adjustment among different generations of American Jews and non-Jews (Doctoral dissertation, Michigan State University, 1956). *Dissertation Abstracts,* 1959a, *19,* 3358–3359.

————. Differences in personality adjustment among different generations of American Jews and non-Jews. In M. K. Opler (Ed.), *Culture and mental health.* New York: Macmillan, 1959b.

————. Sociocultural factors in response to stressful life situations: Aged amputees as an example. *Journal of Health and Human Behavior,* 1960, *1,* 1–24.

————. The sociocultural factors of families of schizophrenics: A review of the literature. *Psychiatry,* 1961, *24,* 246–265.

————. Comparison of Jewish and Protestant paranoid and catatonic patients. *Diseases of the Nervous System,* 1962a, *23,* 320–325.

————. Minority status and psychological adjustment. *Jewish Journal of Sociology* (London), 1962b, *4,* 242–252.

————. The sociocultural aspects of schizophrenia: A comparison of Protestant and Jewish schizophrenics. *International Journal of Social Psychiatry,* 1963a, *9,* 27–36.

————. The etiology and epidemiology of mental illness and problems of methodology. *Mental Hygiene,* 1963b, *47,* 607–621.

————. The sociocultural aspects of childhood schizophrenia: A review of the literature with special emphasis on methodology. Presented at the Second Annual Institute of Research Methodology in Childhood Schizophrenia, American Orthopsychiatric Association, Chicago, March, 1964.

————. Social disorganization in families of schizophrenics belonging to various ethno-religious groups—Protestant, Jewish, Italian, and Irish. *Psychiatry Digest,* 1965, *26,* 45–59.

————. Sociocultural aspect of therapy and treatment of mental illness: A review of the literature. In L. E. Abt & B. F. Riess (Eds.), *Progress in clinical psychology.* New York: Grune & Stratton, 1966.

————. The sociocultural aspects of childhood schizophrenia: A discussion with special emphasis on methodology. In G. H. Zuk & I. Boszormenyi-Nagy, (Eds.), *Family therapy and disturbed families.* Palo Alto, Calif.: Science and Behavior Books, 1967.

————. The sociocultural aspects of schizophrenia: A review of the literature. In L. Bellak & L. Loeb (Eds.), *The schizophrenic syndrome.* New York: Grune & Stratton, 1969a.

————. Religion, mental health and personality: A review of empirical studies. *American Journal of Psychiatry,* 1969b,*125,* 1203–1213.

————. Immigration, migration and mental illness: A review of the literature with special emphasis on schizophrenia. In E. Brody (Ed.), *Behavior in new environments: Adaptation of migrant populations.* Beverly Hills, Calif.: Sage, 1970.

————. Diagnostics and psychotherapy and minority groups: The importance of sociocultural factors in the training of clinical psychologists. Presented at the Fortieth Annual Convention of the New York State Psychological Association, New York, May 13–15, 1977a.

————. Psychological intervention in the Arab World: A review of folk treatment. Presented at the Eighty-fifth Convention of the American Psychological Association, San Francisco, August, 1977b.

————. Cross-cultural study of paranoid schizophrenia. In J. B. Calhoun (Ed.), *Perspectives on adaptation, environment and population.* Bethesda, Md.: National Institute of Mental Health (in press).

SAUCIER, J. F. Essay on the sociocultural aspects of mental disease. *Union Medicale du Canada,* 1962, *91,* 627–637.

Schizophrenia Bulletin 14, Fall 1975.

SCHOOLER, C. Birth order and schizophrenia. *Archives of General Psychiatry,* 1961, *4,* 91–97.

SCHWARTZMAN, J. The American family and mental illness: An ethnography of family dysfunction (Doctoral dissertation, Northwestern University). *Dissertation Abstracts International,* 1973, *34*(6-B), 2435.

SEARS, R. R., MACCOBY, E. E., & LEVIN, H. *Patterns of child rearing.* Evanston, Ill.: Row, Peterson, 1957.

SHODELL, M. J. Personalities of mothers of nonverbal and verbal schizophrenic children (Doctoral dissertation, Yeshiva University). *Dissertation Abstracts,* 1967, *28*(3-B), 1175.

SINGER, J. L., & OPLER, M. K. Contrasting patterns of fantasy and mobility in Irish and Italian schizophrenics. *Journal of Abnormal and Social Psychology,* 1956, *53,* 43–47.

SINGER, M., & WYNNE, L. C. Principles of scoring communication defects and deviances in parents and schizophrenics: Rorschach and T.A.T. scoring manuals. *Psychiatry,* 1966, *29,* 260–288.

SISEK, I., & LJUBIN, N. Sociocultural factors related to a schizophrenic patient. In M. Stojanovic (Ed.), *Proceedings of the Third International Congress of Social Psychiatry* (Vol. 4). Zagreb, Yugoslavia, 1971, *10,* 282–285.

SLOTKIN, J. S. Culture and psychopathology. *Journal of Abnormal and Social psychology,* 1955, *51,* 259–275.

SOFUE, T. Tokyo modaiga kusei mi okeru tekio katei no ichi bunseki [An analysis of the degree of judgment in Tokyo college students]. *Japanese Annals of Social Psychology,* 1964, *5,* 133–160.

SOMMER, R., & HALL, R. Alienation and mental illness. *American Sociological Review,* 1958, *23,* 418–420.

SPIEGEL, J. P., & BELL, N. W. The family of the psychiatric patient. In S. Arieti (Ed.), *American Handbook of Psychiatry.* New York: Basic Books, 1959.

SPIEGEL, J. P., PAPAJOHN, J. C., SEDER, D. L., & DAVIDSON, W. D. The effect of acculturation stress on the mental health of an American ethnic group. Unpublished paper, May, 1966.

SROLE, L., LANGNER, T. S., MICHAEL, S. T., OPLER, M. K., & RENNIE, T. A. C. *Mental health in the metropolis: The midtown Manhattan study* (Vol. 1). New York: McGraw-Hill, 1962.

STEIN, H. F. Cultural specificity in patterns of mental illness and health: A Slovak-American study. *Family Process,* 1973, *12,* 69–82.

STEIN, R. F. *Disturbed youth and ethnic family patterns.* Albany: State University of New York Press, 1971.

STOKER, D. H. Personality, psychopathology, and culture: Mexicans in the USA. *Pennsylvania Psychiatric Quarterly,* 1966, *6,* 30–37.

STOKER, D. H., & MEADOW, A. Cultural differences in the child guidance clinic patients. *International Journal of Social Psychiatry,* 1974, *20,* 186–202.

STONEQUIST, E. *The marginal man.* New York: Scribner, 1937.

STUTTE, H. Über Transkulturelle Kinderpsychiatrie. *Acta Paedopsychiatrica,* 1971, *38,* 229–231.

SUK WHAN OH, KIU HAN CHUNG, CHO YUL PARK, & DAE KIOON BAE. Family backgrounds of schizophrenics. *Journal of Pusan Medical College*, 1963, *3*, 183–189.

SUK WHAN OH. The etiological significance of interpersonal environment of Korean mental patients. *Journal of Pusan Medical College*, 1963, *3*, 349–384.

SUKTHANKAR, H. K., & VAHIA, N. S. Influence of social and cultural factors in schizophrenia and hysteria. Presented at the First International Congress of Social Psychiatry, London, 1963.

SUNSHINE, N. G. Cultural differences in schizophrenia (Doctoral dissertation, City University of New York). *Dissertation Abstracts International*, 1971, *32*, 1197–1198.

TAKATOMI, T., SUZUKI, K., & DENDO, H. [A study of families of schizophrenic patients: II. Differences between the characteristic features found in the parent of male patients and those of female patients. *Journal of Mental Health*], 1972, *20*, 41–76.

TAKATOMI, T., SUZUKI, K., & DENDO, H., [A study of families of schizophrenic patients. III. Child discipline in our country and family dynamics of schizophrenics. *Journal of Mental Health*], 1973, *21*, 137–158.

THOMAS, R. C. *Mother-daughter relationships and social behavior.* Washington, D.C.: Catholic University of America Press, 1955.

TIETZE, T. A study of mothers of schizophrenic patients. *Psychiatry*, 1949, *12*, 55–65.

TINBERGEN, N. A development of a modern concept. In C. H. Schiller (Ed.), *Instinctive behavior.* New York: International Universities Press, 1957.

———. Ethology and stress diseases. *Science*, 1974, *185*, 20–27.

TINBERGEN, E. A., & TINBERGEN, N. Early childhood autism: An ethological approach. *Advances in Ethology*, 1972, *10*, 1–52. (Supplement to *Journal of Comparative Ethology*)

———. The etiology of childhood autism. A criticism of the Tinbergen's theory. A rejoinder. *Psychological Medicine*, 1976, *6*, 545–549.

TSENG, W.-S. The nature of somatic complaints among psychiatric patients: The Chinese case. *Comprehensive Psychiatry*, 1975, *16*, 237–245.

TSENG, W.-S., & HSU, J. Chinese culture, personality and mental illness. *International Journal of Social Psychiatry*, 1969, *16*, 5–14.

TURNER, R. J., ZABE, L., RAYMOND, J., & DIAMOND, J. Field survey methods in psychiatry: The effects of sampling strategy upon findings on research in schizophrenia. *Journal of Health and Social Behavior*, 1969, *10*, 289–297.

WARD, A. J. Early infantile autism. *Psychological Bulletin*, 1970, *73*, 350–362.

WERRY, J. S. Childhood psychosis. In H. C. Quay & J. S. Werry (Eds.), *Psychopathological disorders of childhood.* New York: Wiley, 1972.

WING, L. Concept of autism: A review. *Australian Paediatry Journal*, 1974, *9*, 246–247.

WING, L., & RICKS, D. A criticism of the Tinbergen's etiological theory. The etiology of childhood autism. *Psychological Medicine*, 1976, *6*, 533–543.

WITTKOWER, E. D., & PRINCE, R. A review of transcultural psychiatry. In S. Arieti & G. Caplan (Eds.), *American handbook of psychiatry.* New York: Basic Books, 1974.

WOLFENSTEIN, M. Two types of Jewish mothers. In M. Mead & M. Wolfenstein (Eds.), *Childhood in contemporary cultures*. Chicago: University of Chicago Press, 1955.

WORLD HEALTH ORGANIZATION. *Report of the International Pilot Study of Schizophrenia. I. Results of the initial evaluation phase*. Geneva: WHO, 1973.

WYLAN, L., & MINTZ, N. Ethnic differences in family attitudes toward psychotic manifestations, with implications for treatment programmes. *International Journal of Social Psychiatry*, 1976, 22, 86–95.

6

Depressive Experience and Disorder across Cultures[1]

Anthony J. Marsella

Contents

Abstract

Although depression is considered to be one of mankind's oldest known disorders, it continues to remain a source of great confusion and debate to lay people and professionals alike. Cross-cultural studies of depression hold much promise for increasing our knowledge of depression because they offer us an opportunity to validate our notions about the conception, distribution, manifestation, measurement, personality correlates, and sociocultural causes of depressive experience and disorder. Based on an extensive review of the cross-cultural literature on these topics, the following conclusions were reached: (1) Depressive experience and disorder vary considerably as a function of sociocultural factors. (2) The epidemiology of depression is not known because of limitations in research methods, but there is reason to believe that the frequency of depression is higher in Western societies. (3) The experience and manifestation of depression differ as a function of Westernization. Those cultures evidencing subjective epistemological orientations tend to avoid the psychologizing of experience and thus do not manifest psychological and existential symptomatology in depression. (4) Depression assessment methods are highly ethnocentric and need to emphasize greater attention to somatic and interpersonal processes in the diagnosis of depression in non-Western cultural settings. (5) Personality correlates of depression vary across cultures with respect to the presence or absence of guilt, self-concept discrepancy, and body image dissatisfaction. (6) Existing sociocultural theories of depression are lacking in explanatory and predictive power and require more comprehensive views of the mechanisms by which sociocultural factors influence the various parameters of depression.

Introduction

The purpose of the present chapter is to provide a review of the literature on cross-cultural studies of depression. The review is divided into seven major sections, each of which includes several subsections that detail the major research findings. The major sections are addressed to (1) existing literature review articles on cross-cultural studies of depression, (2) conceptions of depression across cultures, (3) the epidemiology of depression across cultures, (4) the manifestation of depression across cultures, (5) the assessment of depression across cultures, (6) the personality correlates of depression across cultures, and (7) the sociocultural theories of depression. Following each content section, there is a discussion regarding the current status of the topic and the research needs for the future.

Depression is considered to be one of mankind's oldest known psychological disorders. References to depression and its variants appear in the writings of ancient India (Rao, 1975) and ancient Greece and Rome (Zilboorg, 1939; Rosen, 1968). Yet, in spite of the antiquity of our interest and concern, depression still remains a source of great mystery to clinician and researcher alike. As a psychiatric concept, depression lacks clarity. It is used to denote a mood, a symptom, and a syndrome. This lack of clarity in definition and meaning has greatly impeded research efforts.

Although there are reasons for optimism, there are also reasons for caution. The future may well demand a complete reconceptualization of existing notions regarding depression. One research strategy, which holds much promise for increasing our knowledge on depression, is the cross-cultural approach, offering as it does an opportunity to examine the nature of Western assumptions about mental disorders against a background of alternative viewpoints. In doing so, ethnocentric biases can be more thoroughly examined, and new insights about the nature of the phenomena can be attained. This is especially true for depression since it constitutes a major portion of psychiatric research efforts and yet continues to elude our understanding.

Literature Reviews of Cross-Cultural Studies of Depression

There have been a number of literature reviews of cross-cultural studies of depression. Essentially, these can be divided into two distinct groups. One consists of those publications covering the research on depression as part of larger literature review regarding cross-cultural psychiatry. The other group consists of those publications specifically covering cross-cultural depression research. They will be discussed in that order.

General Reviews

The growth of interest in the study of mental disorders among different ethnocultural groups has stimulated the publication of a number of books and journal articles aimed at summarizing the existing state of affairs in the field. One of the first reviews was published by Benedict and Jacks (1954). Based on a coverage of the meager information available at that date, Benedict and Jacks concluded that "depressive states, in any form, . . . are relatively rare in the native populations studied" (p. 384). Most of the studies cited by Benedict and Jacks in their comments on depression were conducted in Africa during the colonial period. Al-Issa (1970) included a brief section on cross-cultural studies of depression in his review of the literature on "culture and symptoms." Al-Issa's paper comments on both the expression and the prevalence of depression in different cultures; it also offers some interpretations of reported differences. Kiev (1972) presents a small section on cross-cultural depressive studies in his book on transcultural psychiatry. However, the section is more noteworthy for Kiev's observations and interpretations about the "rarity of depressive disorders" in certain cultures than it is for literature review purposes.

Nevertheless, some coverage of cross-cultural depression in the literature is available. One of the best general reports was published by German (1972a), who focused his discussion on psychiatry in sub-Saharan Africa. In the process, he provided an excellent overview of depression research among Africans. German offers a detailed analysis of some of the classic psychiatric investigations conducted in Africa.

With the exception of German's paper, the value of the other publications is largely limited to their listing of cross-cultural depression studies. In most instances, the number of references cited is too limited to be of value for review purposes. German's paper stands out among this group by virtue of its perceptive analysis of the African depression studies and their implication for understanding the phenomena of depression.

Specific Reviews of the Cross-Cultural Depression Literature

Based on the current author's search of the literature, nine articles were identified that could qualify as literature reviews regarding cross-cultural studies of depression. These include the following: Prince (1968), Pfeiffer (1968), Silverman (1968), Bagley (1973), Sartorius (1973), Fabrega (1974, 1975), and Singer (1975).

Prince's (1968) article is particularly important because it summarizes the research literature on depression in Africa in both the colonial and postcolonial eras. The paper is exhaustive in coverage, and it also provides excellent evaluative comments regarding the different findings. Prince's comments will be discussed in a subsequent section on the manifestation of depression across cultures. Silverman's (1968) publication provides information on epidemiological studies of depression across cultures. Many of the articles covered in Silverman's review are pre-1960 and thus offer a valuable historical perspective. Pfeiffer's (1968) paper reviews forty cross-cultural studies of depression, of which twenty-two are from non-Western cultures. Pfeiffer's conclusions will be discussed at length in a later section of this chapter. Bagley (1973) summarizes the literature on occupational class and depression. Essentially, Bagley's paper is not a cross-cultural review but rather a within-culture review. Nevertheless, it is of considerable value in highlighting possible cultural influences on depression.

Sartorius (1973) reviewed a small number of studies in his report on the epidemiology of depression. However, he offered several important observations, many of which stem from his experience as the coordinator for international collaborative research projects conducted via the World Health Organization. Sartorius's report represents one of the first efforts to systematize the depression literature. Fabrega's (1974, 1975) papers are less a review of the literature and more an analysis of the potential influence of culture and social factors on depression. However, a number of cross-cultural studies on the rates and expression of depression are cited as references for his comments. Fabrega (1975) concluded that cultural factors are quite important in depression.

Singer's (1975) paper provides the most comprehensive coverage of cross-cultural depression studies of all the papers discussed. A valuable aspect of his paper is his coverage of the different sociocultural theories of depression. Unfortunately, most of the references included in the review are only briefly discussed. Although Singer is critical of the methodological limitations of much of the research, he concludes that the concept of depression is "universally valid." Kleinman (1977) is extremely critical of Singer's conclusions and accuses him of a number of conceptual and methodological errors, including "category fallacies" (imposing culturally biased categories on deviant behaviors in non-Western cultures) and a "disease preoccupation" (disease is an entity that is independent of a cultural context). From the viewpoint of references, Singer's paper is the most extensive, but, from the viewpoint of rigorous evaluation of the issues and findings in cross-cultural studies of depression, the most important papers are those of Prince (1968) and Fabrega (1974, 1975).

Conceptions of Depression
across Cultures

A small number of papers have commented on the conception of depression across cultures. These papers have raised some important questions regarding the nature of depression among different cultural groups by calling attention to the absence of conceptually equivalent words or concepts for depression in several diverse cultural groups including Nigerians (Leighton, Lambo, Hughes, Leighton, Murphy, & Macklin, 1963), Canadian-American Indians (Terminsen & Ryan, 1970), and Chinese (Tseng & Hsu, 1969).

Of special interest is a study conducted by Benoist, Roussin, Fredette, and Rousseau (1965). In contrast to previous reports involving ethnocultural groups with diverse cultural backgrounds from Western populations, Benoist et al. studied a group of French Canadians. They found only 5 percent of their sample labeled a case involving "sadness, insomnia, fatigue, and loss of interest" as depressed. The authors observed that the French Canadians in their sample regarded "depression" as largely a "nervous condition" similar to what may be called a "nervous breakdown." They concluded that it would be wrong to use a dictionary translation of depression for the French Canadian because of the lack of conceptual equivalence.

Several investigators have conducted empirical studies regarding the conceptualization of depression across cultures. Leff (1973) reported that

Chinese and Nigerian subjects evidenced a strong correlation between different emotional states (depression and anxiety) measured by the Present State Examination. He concluded that certain non-Western ethnocultural groups may not differentiate between emotional states in a manner analogous to Western people. Rather, emotional states are experienced as more undifferentiated conditions. These ideas are elaborated upon in Leff (1977), which provides an excellent review of cross-cultural studies of emotion.

Tanaka-Matsumi and Marsella (1976) investigated the subjective experience of depression among Japanese nationals, Japanese Americans, and Caucasian Americans through the use of word associations to the terms "depression" and "yuutsu." The latter word was derived as the Japanese word most equivalent to depression on the basis of extensive back translation and conceptual equivalence procedures. The authors found the word association patterns to the two words differed considerably for the Japanese nationals and the two American subsamples. The former associated largely external referent words such as "rain," "cloudy," "dark," while the latter associated largely internal referent words such as "sadness," "despair," and "loneliness." The authors suggest the differences may be mediated by contrasting self-structures in the two groups which influence the subjective experience of depression.

Tanaka-Matsumi and Marsella (1977) also conducted a study requiring the same sample of Japanese nationals, Japanese Americans, and Caucasian Americans to evaluate the words "depression" and "yuutsu" on a twenty-five-scale semantic differential questionnaire. A factor analysis of the questionnaire yielded completely different factorial structures for each of the ethnic groups. These findings suggest that depression has a different connotative meaning for each of the groups. This was not a surprising finding since previous research (Marsella, Murray, & Golden, 1974) also reported ethnocultural variations in the connotative meaning of a variety of emotional states.

Yet another approach to understanding the conceptualization of depression across cultures has been the study of indigenous categories of mental disorder. This approach was used by Resner and Hartog (1970) in Malaysia; Schmidt (1964) in Borneo; Prince (1964), Edgerton (1966), and Orley (1970) in Africa; and Boyer (1964) among American Indians. In all instances, there were *no* concepts that represented depression as either a disease symptom or syndrome. This fact should not be taken lightly since it points to a possible bias among many Western-oriented investigations that pay little heed to indigenous conceptions of disorder in arriving at conclusions regarding the distribution and expression of depression.

One thing that becomes apparent in the various reports regarding the conceptions of depression is that the term is not well represented among the lexicon of non-Western people. This does not mean that depression, as it is defined in the West, is absent in cultures that do not have conceptually equivalent terms but, rather, that it is conceptualized differently and may be experienced differently. It is quite obvious that even though individuals from different cultural groups may have similar physiological changes, the recognition, interpretation, and behavioral representation of the problem may vary across cultures. Further, the social response to the behavioral representation may also differ. Thus, "depression" would be embedded in an entirely different context and assume an entirely different meaning across cultures.

Epidemiology of Depression across Cultures

Epidemiology is that branch of medical public health that is concerned with the distribution or rates of disorder in the natural environment. Psychiatric epidemiology is concerned with the distribution of mental disorders. In determining the distribution, researchers use a number of indices, which yield different types of information about the parameters of the disorder under study. One of the most popular epidemiological indices is the prevalence rate, or the number of cases active at a given time or for a given time period. To determine the prevalence rate, researchers study both "treated" and "untreated" cases. "Treated" cases include all those individuals receiving treatment in various institutions or clinical service facilities. "Untreated" cases include all those individuals not receiving formal care. Typically, the "untreated" cases are identified through community surveys. The present paper will discuss epidemiological studies of depression based on both the "treated" and "untreated" case approaches (see Marsella, 1978).

Prevalence Rates Based on "Treated" Case Approaches

Table 6-1 contains a summary of point prevalence epidemiological studies of depression based on "treated" cases. The results suggest dramatic variations in the rates of depression across cultures. Clearly, from the viewpoint of research approach, some cultures have high rates of depression and others have low rates. However, there are so many limitations with this research approach that it would probably be much safer to conclude that we know relatively little about depression rates across cultures. For example, rates of depression based on "treated" cases assume that all individuals have the same access to treatment facilities and the

Table 6-1 Clinic and Hospital Admission (Treated) Prevalence Rates for Depressive Disorders[1,2,3,4]

Investigator	Country	Population	Affective Psychoses	Neurotic Depression
Carothers (1953)	Kenya	160 Blacks	1.5%	
		222 Whites	22.0%	
Earle & Earle (1956)	British Guiana	259 Mixed ethnic groups	7.0% Depression	
			4.0% Mania	
Hes (1960)	Israel	2684 Israelis	3.7%	
			(83% European Jews)	
			(12% Israel-born Jews)	
			(3% African Jews)	
Collomb & Zwingelstein (1961)[a]	Senegal	1600 Senegalese	6.3%	
Rose (1964)	Italy	4965 Italians	31.0%	
Sathyavathy & Sundararaj (1964)[b]	India	445 Indians (Outpt.)	4.9%	
Surya et al. (1964)[b]	India	2731 Indians	0.0%	
Malzberg (1965)	USA	6427 Blacks	.5%	
		40221 Whites	2.7%	
Hadlik & Bojanovsky (1967)	Czechoslovakia	6722 Czechs	12.3% Primary depressions	
Vitols (1967)	USA	? Blacks	2.3% Psychotic depression	
Elsarrag (1968)	Northern Sudan	2160 Sudanese (Arab & black African)	9.0% Mania	
			6.0% Depression	
Okasha, Kamel, & Hassan (1968)	Egypt	1000 Egyptians	13.2%	10.7%
Saenger (1968)	Netherlands & USA	300 Dutch (Outpt.)		24.0%
		534 American (Outpt.)		53.0%
Cooper et al. (1969)	England & USA	145 Englishmen	16.6%	
		145 Americans	46.2%	
Kato (1969)	Japan	9066 Japanese	3.7%	
Hellon (1970)	Canada	168 Indians	4.8%	

Study	Country	Sample		
Kelly et al. (1970)	Canada	119 Métis	2.3%	
		25 Eskimos	12.0%	
		337 English	6.0%	
		314 French	4.7%	
Teja & Narang (1970)	India	1180 Indians	17.4%	
Terminsen & Ryan (1970)	Canada	320 American Indians	3.0%	4.0%
Lapuz (1972)	Philippines	419 Filipinos		13.1%
Sethi & Gupta (1972b)	India	1120 Indians (Private)	34.2% Depression	
		1000 Indians (Hospital)	18.1% Depression	
Singer (1975)	Hong Kong	? Chinese	7.0%	
Bagadia et al. (1973)	India	2678 Indians	8.7%	
Schoenfeld & Miller (1973)	USA (Southwest)	348 Indians	.6%	23.0%
Shinfuku et al. (1973)	Japan	801 Japanese (1971)	18.5% Depression	
		(1969)	13.4% Depression	
		(1966)	8.2% Depression	
		(1964)	7.1% Depression	
Taipale & Taipale (1973)[c]	People's Republic of China	? Chinese	2.0%	
Sainsbury (1974)[c]	People's Republic of China	? Chinese	5.0%	

[a] From German (1972)   [b] From Rao (1966)   [c] From Singer (1975)

[1] Prevalence rates include both point and period data.

[2] Percentages are expressed as a proportion of total disorders with the exception of Kelly et al. (1970), which excluded OBS and mental retardation.

[3] Studies cited are only for post-1950 era; see Silverman (1968) for pre-1950 studies.

[4] Other studies not included here because of difficulties determining the specific percentages of affective disturbances, include Sedivec (1968) and Yap (1965).

same motivation to seek treatment. Obviously, this is not the case. Further, there are serious problems regarding diagnostic reliability. These problems are compounded across cultures, especially with depression.

For example, in several studies examining diagnostic tendencies among psychiatrists from different countries (e.g., Cooper, Kendell, Gurland, Sartorius, & Farkas, 1969; Cooper, Kendell, Gurland, Sharpe, Copeland & Simon, 1972; Gurland, Fliess, Sharpe, Simon, Barrett, Copeland, Cooper & Kendell, 1972; Rawnsley, 1968), profound differences were found in the tendencies of psychiatrists from different countries to diagnose people as depressed. The Cooper et al. (1969) study found that hospital staff in the USA diagnosed 16.6 percent of 145 consecutive admissions as depressed while English hospital staff diagnosed 46.2 percent of a comparable sample of admissions depressed. In a broader study, Gurland et al. (1972) reported that American psychiatrists diagnosed only 12.9 percent of new admissions as depressed while English psychiatrists diagnosed 30.9 percent. Rawnsley (1968) found a tendency among American psychiatrists to use neurotic and involutional melancholic diagnostic categories while English and Danish psychiatrists tended to use psychotic depression as a diagnosis. Clearly, penchants for certain diagnostic categories exist among psychiatrists from different countries when it comes to depression and these penchants make it extremely difficult to arrive at substantive conclusions.

Based on the most current and thorough analysis of psychiatric epidemiology studies available, Dohrenwend and Dohrenwend (1974) concluded, "Our own analysis of the evidence bearing on this problem has led us to dismiss from consideration for the most part studies dealing solely with treated rates" (p. 419). At best, studies based on "treated" cases can offer us a source of hypotheses, especially with regard to cultural influences on various subtypes of psychiatric disorder. Why is it, for example, that the percentage of affective disorders receiving treatment varies so greatly across cultures? Does this tell us something about the perceived status of depressed people within a given culture? Or, does it offer us a clue into the patterning of depression across cultures? Or, does it point out the possibility that existing conceptions of depression are ethnocentric? These questions deserve study.

Prevalence Rates Based on "Untreated" Case Approaches

Tables 6-2 and 6-3 contain a summary of point and period prevalence epidemiological studies of depression based on "untreated" cases. With the exception of the Eaton and Weil (1955) study of Hutterites, the remainder of the studies are based on non-Western populations. The rates

Table 6-2 Community Survey (Untreated) Point Prevalence Rates for Depressive Disorders (Post-1950)

Investigator	Country	Population	Affective Psychoses	Neurotic Depression
Böök (1953)[a]	Sweden	8981 Swedes	.2/1000	
Essen-Möller (1956)[a]	Sweden	2550 Swedes	2.0/1000	
Helgason (1961)[a]	Iceland	3843 Icelanders	10.4/1000	25.5/1000
Sørensen & Strömgren (1961)[a]	Denmark	6447 Danes	7.8/1000	26.5/1000
Ivanys et al. (1964)[a]	Czechoslovakia	66165 Czechs	1.5/1000	

[a] From Silverman (1968)

Table 6-3 Community Survey (Untreated) Period Prevalence Rates for Depressive Disorders (Post-1950)

Investigator	Country	Population	Affective Psychoses	Neurotic Depression
Lin (1953)	Republic of China (Taiwan)	19931 Chinese & Taiwanese	.7/1000	
Eaton & Weil (1955)[a]	Canada & USA	8542 Hutterites	.9/1000	
Fallers & Fallers (1960)[b]	Uganda			
Yoo (1961)	Korea	11974 Koreans	.9/1000	
Rin & Lin (1962)	Republic of China (Taiwan)	11442 Taiwanese aboriginals	.3/1000	
Dube (1964)[c]	India		2.7/1000	
Sethi & Gupta (1967)	India	300 Indian families	6.9/1000 urban	
Sethi & Gupta (1972a)	India	500 Indian families	1.5/1000 rural	
Kato (1969)	Japan	23993 Japanese	.2/1000 (1954 study)	
		44092 Japanese	.2/1000 (1963 study)	
Lin et al. (1969)	Republic of China (Taiwan)	29184 Chinese & Taiwanese	.5/1000	
Jones & Horne (1973)	Australia	2360 aboriginals	1 case	1 case

[a] From Silverman (1968)   [b] From German (1972)   [c] From Rao (1966)

NOTE: Other community survey studies, not included because of difficulties determining the specific distribution of depression, include Watts (1956), Srole et al. (1962), Leighton, D., et al. (1963), Gillis, Lewis, & Slabbert (1968), Hallstrom (1970), Weeke et al. (1970).

are uniformly low and one is inclined to conclude that depression is not a serious psychiatric problem among the populations studied. However, once again, limitations in the research approach raise doubts about the accuracy of the conclusions.

Dohrenwend and Dohrenwend (1965, 1969, 1974), in their reviews of psychiatric epidemiology studies based on field research methods pointed out a number of serious problems. For example, definitions of disorder vary across the studies. Further, there are differences in the degree of contact with the case. In some instances, case identification is made by relatively untrained interviewers while, in other instances, psychiatrists do the case identification in the field. Also, if key informants are used to identify cases, the criteria they use may be biased. If Western notions of mental disorder are used as guidelines for case identification, are there empirical reasons for this? Dohrenwend and Dohrenwend (1974) stated,

> We are in a situation then where different concepts and methods of assessment in the epidemiological studies have led to vastly different assessments of rates of psychopathology. Moreover, there is no way to choose, on the basis of the evidence, a subtest of these studies in which more valid procedures have been employed. (p. 427)

The research findings do offer some valuable hypotheses, and it is stimulating to reflect on the possibility of an international collaborative research project using similar research methods but emically relevant categories of disorder. Indeed, both indigenous and professional criteria could be used for case identification purposes. The variations and similarities in the cases identified by the different sets of criteria could then be compared.

In summary, although a considerable number of epidemiological studies of depression have been conducted, it is extremely difficult to reach any substantive conclusions about the rates of depression across cultures. Limitations in the basic research approaches used obviate many interpretations of the findings and especially a comparison of the findings. Unfortunately, the current status of our knowledge forces the present author to conclude that we still know very little about cultural differences in the rates of depression.

Manifestation of Depression across Cultures

There have been numerous reports regarding the manifestation of depression across cultures. However, these reports are difficult to evaluate as a group because of the variability in the research strategies used to examine the manifestation of depression across cultures. Among the research strategies that have been used are the following: clinical observations, culture-specific disorders, matched diagnosis, matched samples, international surveys, and factor analysis. The research will be discussed according to these strategies. This will be followed by a discussion of the findings.

Clinical Observations: Review Papers

Several publications summarize the literature on the manifestation of depression across cultures: Prince (1968), Racy (1970), German (1972a), and Pfeiffer (1968). Prince's paper compares the many psychiatric studies conducted among black Africans in the colonial and postcolonial periods. According to Prince, of the fourteen reports published prior to 1957, only one—Field, 1960—reported instances of depression among black African people. The others concluded that psychotic depression is extremely rare and does not assume forms similar to Western depressions (i.e., self-blame is absent; suicidal ruminations are absent). However, Prince observed that in twenty-one reports published after 1957, the rate of depression is claimed to be quite frequent, though the forms it assumes still vary from the Western patterns. Prince offers a number of explanations for the variability in the results.

Racy (1970) published one of the most extensive reports available on psychiatric problems among Arabs. According to Racy, depression is evidenced by a number of somatic complaints including gastrointestinal difficulties, loss of appetite, and weight loss. Guilt and feelings of self-depreciation are virtually absent and suicide is very rare. Of interest is the fact that depression among the Westernized and affluent Arabs assumes forms more similar to depression in the West.

German (1972a) summarized the psychiatric research among the people of sub-Saharan Africa. In the section on affective psychoses, German noted that mania often predominates over classical depression patterns among Africans. Further, guilt feelings, depressive affect, and suicidal ruminations are generally absent. Quoting Collomb and Zwingelstein (1961), German (1972a) claimed that depressed patients in Senegal "do not appear to be deeply unhappy or miserable; ideas of self-accusation and guilt are absent, and suicide is rare; the disorder is characterized rather by ideas of persecution, anxiety, hypochondriasis, and somatic complaints" (p. 470).

Pfeiffer (1968) summarized forty reports of depression from twenty-two non-European countries. According to Pfeiffer, there is a core of depressive symptomatology that does exist across cultures. This core involves sleep, libido, and appetite dysfunctions and abnormal body sensations

Mood changes are not always found because of cultural variations in self-descriptions. Motor agitation or retardation and apathy are also found in some instances. Guilt, as it is conceptualized in the West is not found; however, there is a variant of Western guilt that Pfeiffer feels is present, and this involves a loss of relationship to a social group. Persecutory feelings may also arise if the environment assumes a threatening role. Pfeiffer concludes that the presence of somatic dysfunctioning or complaints, in the absence of any psychological report of depression or mood variation, is sufficient to warrant a diagnosis of depression. This is questionable! Should we attach a Western label to a group of symptoms found among non-Western people without the similar symptoms of guilt, mood depression, motor retardation, and so forth? What may be needed are diagnostic categories relevant to specific cultures. These categories should be emically derived!

Clinical Observation: Empirical Studies

Reports based on clinical observation are by far the most frequent research strategy used in examining the manifestation of depression across cultures. Unfortunately, this approach is also subject to the greatest error because of the subjectivity of the observers and the failure to report problem behavior within the framework of the patient's culture. That is to say, the observer is typically viewing the patient in professional categories that may have questionable validity, especially as groups increasingly differ from Western lifestyles.

Afghanistan.   Waziri (1973) reported numerous similarities between urban Afghan depressed patients and traditional psychiatric manifestations of depression (e.g., depressed mood, loss of appetite, sleep disturbance, libidinal deficits, and so on). Suicidal intents or thoughts were absent, but wishes for death were present. Unfortunately, Waziri's comments are based on limited clinical experience and do not apply to a full population sample. To the extent that patients are Westernized, similarities in depression are not unusual, but there is an absence of data on rural non-Westernized populations.

Iraq.   Bazzoui (1970) reported on the features of depression among ninety-eight Iraqi patients suffering from affective disorders. In contrast to Waziri's findings among Afghans, Iraqi patients do not seem to evidence very many ideas of unworthiness and self-depreciation. However, the two reports do agree that suicidal ideation and attempts are quite infrequent. Basically, among the people of Iraq depression manifests itself by "physical symptomatology and hysterical behavior." In addition, paranoid ideation and projection are quite common. Mania among Iraqi patients lacks the joyous mood of Western cases and also tends to be far more antisocial and aggressive.

India.   There have been many important studies on the manifestation of depression in India. Rao (1973) examined thirty South Indian patients. According to Rao, all thirty of the cases had sleep difficulties (e.g., insomnia, early waking, sleeplessness) and suicidal tendencies. Twenty-five reported depressive affect and diurnal variation, twenty-four reported anxiety, twenty-two loss of libido, twenty-one agitation, and nineteen loss of energy. This pattern is, of course, similar to Western patients labeled as depressed, but, this is not unusual since the patients were Westernized and did not represent Indians who maintain traditional lifestyles. Even with this, guilt feelings and motor retardation were found among only eight patients.

The findings of Teja and Narang (1970) and Teja, Narang, and Aggarwal (1971) regarding Northern Indians disagree with those of Rao. These authors examined the depression patterns of 100 patients seen at the psychiatric clinics of two medical education centers. Both depressed mood and work difficulty were found among 100 percent of the patients. Late insomnia and somatic anxiety were found among 92 percent, psychic anxiety and suicidal idea among 80 percent, motor retardation and loss of insight among 77 percent, and middle insomnia among 76 percent of the patients. Guilt was present in 48 percent of the cases. According to Teja and his coworkers, somatic complaints are a basic source of differences between Indian and Western depressed patients with the former manifesting a much higher proportion. Teja et al. (1971) observed, "The Indian patient . . . uses the medium of the body more often for expressing inner tension" (p. 258). It was also noted that agitation and anxiety are much more common among Indian patients: "Indian depressives are significantly more often agitated and anxious than the Western cases. . . . They [the Indians] make any endeavor to constrain the outflow of inner tensions into the external channels of emotional expression" (p. 258). When present, guilt among Indians was considered to be of a more "impersonal" nature than guilt among Western patients, since the latter are likely to assume more personal responsibility for failure. The manifestation of many somatic symptoms among Indian patients was also reported by Bagadia, Jeste, Dave, Doshi, and Shah (1973), who found 78 percent of Indian patients in Western India reported somatic symptoms while guilt feelings were reported by only 5.3 percent of the patients.

Davis (1973) reported the findings of several studies of depression among Indians. He noted that it is difficult to distinguish between types of depression (e.g., endogenous versus neurotic) because of the rarity of many indices including guilt feeling, diurnal mood variation, delayed insomnia, and so forth. However, he does feel the diagnosis of involutional melancholia is well defined among Indians.

Indonesia.   In a review of psychiatric disorders among the people of Indonesia, Pfeiffer (1967) concluded that loss of vitality and sleep disturbances are common among Indonesian depressed patients but feelings of sadness are often absent. Pfeiffer noted that these depressions may more accurately be called "vital depressions" or "somatic depressions." Guilt feelings are absent or rare, as are feelings of inadequacy. Pfeiffer wrote, "In Indonesia . . . the worth or value of a person is not determined by their achievement and it is perfectly acceptable that one can do nothing for months. Thus a deterioration in achievement does not need to cause guilt and feelings of inadequacy" (p. 111).

Japan.   A number of investigators have concluded that somatic features appear to dominate the depression picture among Japanese people (e.g., Shinfuku, Karasawa, Yamada, Tuasaki, Kanai, & Kawashima, 1973; Yoshimita, Kawano, & Takayama, 1971; Ohara, 1973). Both Shinfuku et al. and Ohara found a decline in the frequency of guilt feelings and suicidal ideation among Japanese over the course of the past two decades. Ohara also found a 33 percent increase in bipolar depressions and a 54 percent decrease in unipolar depressions.

Philippines.   Lapuz (1972) discussed depression among 419 Filipinos seen by her in private practice. Her target group ranged in age from thirteen to sixty years of age and included both males and females. The largest numbers were students and housewives. Although little information is provided on social class, the patients seem to be overwhelmingly from the middle and higher social classes. According to Lapuz, depression was part of the problem presented by most patients (fifty-five had specific diagnosis of reactive depression). However, it should be noted the patients themselves did not report depression. Other reports of Filipinos suggest that depression is very seldom found.

For example, in describing depression among samples of in-patient, out-patient, and community Filipinos, Sechrest (1963) stated:

> A third problem not occurring as frequently as one would expect is depression and guilt. Patients frequently are described as "sad" or "depressed" (more often as *looking* sad or depressed) but there is scarcely ever any elaboration on the description that would lead one to suppose that the patient really fits the psychiatric category of depression. For example, no instances were found of patients complaining of feelings of worthlessness, of hopelessness, of impending doom, and only two instances were found of complaints of being or feeling guilty. . . . The investigator would conclude, then, that depression is quite infrequent among Filipinos. (p. 199)

Sechrest's research will be discussed further in the matched-groups research strategy section.

Taiwan.   Kleinman (1977) examined twenty-five cases of depression at a university psychiatric clinic in Taiwan. Twenty-two cases initially complained only of somatic symptoms. Even in subsequent treatment, ten cases never admitted to psychological affect problems. High degrees of somatization among Chinese were also reported by Tseng (1975) and Gaw (1976).

Culture-specific Depressive Disorders

One of the most popular research strategies in the field of cross-cultural psychiatry has been the study of culture-specific disorders. This approach investigates mental disorders that appear to be "unique" to specific ethnocultural groups. Included in this category are such disorders as *koro*, *latah*, *amok*, *susto*, *windigo*, and *pibloktoq*. For many researchers, these disorders are not, in fact, unique; rather, they are simply variants of mental disorders found across the world. In contrast, other researchers believe that the disorders do represent relatively specific forms of dysfunction whose causes and patterns are intimately linked to cultural factors. This issue is still hotly debated and will not be pursued here. However, the author will discuss culture-specific disorders that have been considered depressive equivalents, though still unique in pattern and form to distinct cultural settings.

Tawatl ye sni.   Johnson and Johnson (1965) reported a pattern of disorder found among Sioux Indians in North America. It is called *tawatl ye sni* or "totally discouraged." They claim that the disorder is also found among other Plains Indians. Johnson and Johnson report that the Sioux categories of disorder are not parallel with those of Western psychiatric classification systems. However, the "totally discouraged" pattern was noticeable to the authors as a recurrent phenomenon warranting their identification of it as a syndrome. Essentially, the "totally discouraged" syndrome involves feelings of helplessness, thoughts of death, and a preoccupation with ideas of ghosts and spirits.

Because of various cultural traditions among the Sioux, an emphasis on spirit world is a part of normal functioning. The reality bounds are not as firmly established as is the case in certain Western societies. Thus, individuals move in and out of mystical experiences far more readily. Further, the belief that "there's no way out . . . there's nothing he can do" is not very different from many fatalistic beliefs found in other parts of the world, and fatalism can actually serve a positive function. For example, in the Philippines, the phrase "Bahala na!," which loosely translates as "It's up to God" or "It is not in my hands" actually serves a useful function in alleviating the stresses of life (Marsella, Escudero, & Gordon, 1972). Within this context, one wonders if it is legitimate for an outsider to term this behavior a depressive disorder much like other Western psychiatric diagnostic entities. One must ask whether the "disorder" is largely a function of modern-day reservation life, which limits the alternatives for living among the Sioux and thus stimulates increased preoccupation with death as a return to the happy days. If life itself were happier, it is conceivable that the preoccupation with death would not be a viable alternative for coping.

Hiwa:Itck. Yet another type of depressive equivalent that has been discussed within the context of culture-specific disorders is termed "*Hiwa:Itck*" or the "heartbreak" syndrome. Devereux (1961), an anthropologist, reported this pattern among elderly Mohave (American Indian) men. Essentially, it is manifested by loss of appetite, sleep difficulties, mourning behavior, and threats of killing others. It is said to occur only among married people who lose their spouses. The men love their wives very greatly and when they lose them their "hearts break."

In many respects, the behavior pattern appears quite similar to those in Western societies when loss occurs, especially loss of a loved one. There is the combination of remorse and anger and even confusion. Perhaps *Hiwa:Itck* should not be labeled a "culture-specific" syndrome but rather a form of grief reaction to the loss of a loved one.

Susto. The only other culture-specific syndrome known to the current author that might qualify as a depressive equivalent is *susto* (Gobeil, 1973; Kiev, 1968; Rubel, 1964). *Susto* is found mainly among Central and South American populations of Latino ancestry. *Susto* refers to "soul loss" and is characterized by weakness, loss of appetite, sleep difficulties, fear, motor retardation, reduced sexual drive, and a number of anxiety indicators (sweating, diarrhea, rapid heart beat). In many respects it is similar to what is called "agitated depression" in Western psychiatric parlance. There are a number of different causes for the disorder, including sudden fright, witchcraft (e.g., curses), breaking taboos, and so on. The dysfunction appears to have a sudden onset that can be traced to a distinct event or occurrence.

Comment on culture-specific disorders. All of these disorders raise questions regarding the universality of depression. The latter two (*Hiwa:Itck* and *susto*) are, in many respects, similar in appearance to depressive dysfunctions found among Western people. The first disorder, "totally discouraged," provides a good example of normative behavior that may appear "pathogenic" to Western psychiatric professionals, especially those who lack a full understanding of the cultural milieu in which the behavior is embedded. Yet the disorder may not be considered as deviancy or "disease" by culture members. Further, it does not assume a form that is similar to depression among Western people such as the motor retardation, guilt feelings, loss of purpose, and the various physiological complaints.

In the current author's opinion, it is extremely difficult to speak of "culture-specific" and "non-culture-specific" disorders. All forms of disorder are necessarily a function of culture, since it is impossible to separate an individual from a cultural context. In this respect all disorders are "culture-specific." Even a physiological reaction must be interpreted and responded to by an "evaluative" person, and the evaluative framework will obviously be learned in a culture context. More research needs to be done using the emic or indigenous framework. Far too often, Western-trained researchers have simply imposed their own orientation.

Matched Diagnosis

The matched diagnosis strategy for studying the manifestation of depression across cultures provides a good opportunity to compare the symptoms manifested by different ethnocultural groups sharing similar diagnoses. This strategy has been particularly popular in the United States in studies comparing American blacks (Negroes) and American whites. Tonks, Paykel, and Klerman (1970) and Hanson, Klerman, and Tanner (1973) both concluded that the differences between black and white depressed patients were minimal and that the similarities between the two groups were far more prominent than differences. But Simon, Fliess, Gurland, Stiller, and Sharpe (1973) found several important differences, leading them to conclude that blacks "have a quality to their depression different from whites" (p. 509). Helzer (1975) conducted a study of bipolar depression among male American blacks and whites hospitalized in the Saint Louis area. The groups differed only with respect to a higher incidence of initial insomnia among the blacks. There were no differences in levels of euphoria, irritability, hyperactivity, flight of ideas, grandiosity, and so forth. The study is the only one concerned with mania across cultures and does appear to be deserving of further study, especially since many blacks evidencing manic-type behaviors may be mistakenly diagnosed as schizophrenic.

Kimura (1965) compared depression among samples of endogenous depressives admitted to university psychiatric clinics in Japan (Kyoto) and Germany (Munich). Kimura suggests that there is a greater tendency to "tolerate" depressive phenomena in Japan where the word *kanashi* (sad) also connotes beautiful and affectionate. This may be why depressive disorders are not diagnosed as frequently in Japan according to Kimura. Guilt feelings occur in both groups; however, guilt among the Japanese is directed toward ancestors and even fellow workers. Suicide was more prevalent among German patients, but suicidal acts were more common among the Japanese patients. Thus, Kimura contends that depression appears less frequently in Japan and when it does, some of the components observed among Germans differ. More than an empirical account of variations, Kimura's paper offers a valuable analysis of why the variations may occur. His observations regarding the Japanese mind are excellent.

The matched diagnosis strategy is limited by the fact that patients from different ethnocultural groups receiving the same diagnosis should possess at least some similarities in the manifestation of disorder or one should question why they are diagnosed the same. Yet, since diagnosis is often based on a small number of highly visible symptoms that are keyed to particular diagnostic categories, it is conceivable that a comparison across a broader number of symptoms would reveal interesting variations that might reflect cultural factors. All of the studies discussed in the present section are limited by virtue of their failure to compare systematically the subjects across a broad array of symptoms. Even with this constraint, Tonks et al. (1970) and Simon et al. (1973) still found variations in depression, especially across the psychological and behavioral components. This is consistent with the findings of other research strategies.

Matched Sample

The matched sample research strategy compares the symptom profiles of individuals from different cultural groups who are matched for such demographic characteristics as age, gender, and social class. Essentially, the premise of this strategy is that with constant sampling characteristics, differences and similarities can be identified without confounding of diagnostic preferences. A number of studies have been conducted using this research approach.

Stoker, Zurcher, and Fox (1968) compared the symptom profiles of twenty-five female Mexican-American patients and twenty-five female Anglo-American outpatient patients. The Mexican-American patients manifested significantly higher frequencies of symptoms in the sphere of affective functioning. According to Stoker et al. (1968), the basic Mexican-American pattern appeared to be agitated depression with greater hostility, hyperactivity, crying spells, sleeplessness, somatic complaints, suicidal attempts, and withdrawal. In contrast, the depressive states in the Anglo-Americans were characterized by guilt feelings and psychological and physical retardation. The Mexican-American group also had especially high percentages of gastrointestinal somatic complaints. The authors related the findings to Mexican-American cultural traditions and lifestyles in which the affective sphere of functioning is important. It should be noted that Meadow and Stoker (1965) found similar results in an earlier study of hospitalized psychotic patients from the two cultural groups.

Sechrest (1969) compared male and female chronic patients from the Chicago State Hospital (USA) and the National Mental Hospital of the Philippines. Sechrest used a quasi-random sampling procedure for the selection of cases in the two locations and then analyzed the records for the complaints present on admission. He found that only 3 percent of the Filipino cases were described as sad or depressed. Guilt feelings and suicidal attempts and threats were also quite low in comparison to the American sample.

Phillips and Draguns have been among the foremost proponents of the matched sample research strategy. In combination with a number of colleagues in several countries, Phillips and Draguns have extensively studied the manifestation of psychiatric disturbances across cultures. They reported results of studies comparing American samples with Japanese patients (Seifert, Draguns, & Caudill, 1971; Draguns, Phillips, Broverman, Caudill, & Nishimae, 1971), Argentinian patients (Fundia, Draguns, & Phillips, 1971), and Israeli patients (Skea, Draguns, & Phillips, 1969).

This research has been carried out within the framework of the social competence conceptualization of psychopathology and thus makes use of a different approach from traditional symptom comparison. Essentially, groups are compared in terms of differences in *role orientation* (turning against others, turning against self, and avoidance of others) and *sphere dominance* (thought, affect, somatization, and action). In all studies, cultural differences were found in the affective sphere of functioning.

International Survey

One of the earliest approaches used to study depression across cultures was initiated by H. B. M. Murphy and Eric Wittkower from the McGill University Transcultural Psychiatric Research Program. These investigators (Murphy, Wittkower, & Chance, 1964, 1967) requested psychiatrists in thirty countries to provide a description of depression symptomatology on a four-point scale basis ("usually found" to "rarely found"). As a first step, the psychiatrists from the different countries were asked to report only on patients showing four "classic" signs of depression: depressed mood, diurnal mood variation, insomnia with early morning awakening, loss of interest in the environment. The cooperating researchers were then asked to evaluate these patients on twenty-three other symptoms.

Murphy et al. (1964, 1967) reported that twenty-one countries indicated that depression as manifested by the four classic signs was frequent. However, nine countries indicated this type of depression was infrequent or rare. In the areas where depression was reported to be frequent, the primary symptoms included fatigue, loss of sexual interest, anorexia, weight loss, and self-accusatory ideas. Variations in the expression of depression were also present among the groups who reported frequent patterns of depression as evidenced by the classical signs. The infrequent depression group, which was largely non-Western, noted that excitement, ideas of influence, and semimutism were quite characteristic of depressed individuals.

While the international survey strategy offers a valuable approach for the study of the expression of depression, it can only be valuable to the extent that the investigators do not begin with a priori notions about the nature of depression. If they do, this will channel their observations into preset categories and limit the true value of the international survey approach, which offers a comparison of a spectrum of symptoms generated by each distinct culture under study. The international survey approach holds promise if conducted properly. Indeed, it will probably be through international surveys that the understanding we are seeking will develop. The Murphy et al. (1964, 1967) studies are a good start.

Factor Analysis

The use of factor analysis and other multivariate data analysis procedures is a relatively recent strategy for studying the manifestation of depression across cultures. The value of factor analysis is that it offers researchers an objective method for examining the patterns of depression-related symptoms. With factor analysis, symptoms are grouped on the basis of quantified information rather than subjective impression. Thus, the limitations inherent in having a biased clinical observer are attenuated. Nevertheless, factor analysis can only generate patterns based on the input material. It is, therefore, imperative that efforts made to identify the manifestation of disorders, such as depression, include a broad spectrum of symptoms.

Caudill and Schooler (1969) factor-analyzed a group of twenty-four symptoms for a sample of male and female Japanese patients. They found that depression among the males was characterized by sadness, irritation, loss of appetite, suicidal attempts, and sleep disturbances. Among females it was characterized by sadness, self-depreciation, suicidal attempts, loss of appetite, withdrawal, and apathy. Thus, the factor analysis revealed some interesting differences in the manifestation of depression for the two sexes.

Marsella et al. (1972) used factor analysis to identify patterns of disorder among normal Filipino men living in Manila. Using a sixty-symptom checklist, they found a pattern of depression that was characterized by "agitated" dimensions. For example, the depression pattern included the following symptoms: feeling tense and irritable, sleeping poorly at night, feeling sad and depressed, feeling afraid, crying, headaches, excessive energy, rumination about the past, and remaining in bed. Based on their research, Marsella et al. (1972) suggested that this approach could reduce ethnocentricity in psychiatric classification by permitting the identification of the patterns of disorder for each unique cultural group.

Subsequently, Marsella, Kinzie, and Gordon (1973) reported a study on the expression of depression among depressed Japanese-American, Chinese-American, and Caucasian-American male and female college students. Marsella et al. (1973) first identified depressed individuals on the basis of scores on the Zung Depression Scale (Zung, 1969) and then administered a sixty-item symptom checklist composed of a broad spectrum of problems covering cognitive, somatic, affective, and interpersonal domains of functioning. The symptom checklist was then submitted to a factor analysis for each of the ethnocultural groups. The results indicated that Japanese Americans evidence a strong interpersonal component in the expression of depression (e.g., dislike being around others, doesn't want to talk to others, doesn't care for appearance). Chinese Americans show a strong somatic component (e.g., stomach pains, sleep difficulty, weakness), and Caucasian Americans manifest the more traditional existential patterns (e.g., despair, loss of purpose, hollow and empty feeling). The authors suggested that the symptom dimensions manifested by the different ethnocultural groups were a function of differences in the "self" structure conditioned by the various cultural traditions.

More recently, Binitie (1975) compared the factorial structure of the Hamilton Rating Scale for a group of depressed Westernized Nigerian and a group of English patients. Unfortunately, there is no information in the article regarding the demographic characteristics of the samples; thus, one does not know about age, social class, or educational levels. Nevertheless, Binitie reported that the Nigerian sample showed no evidence of guilt, but, depressed mood, motor retardation, and somatic symptoms were present. Suicidal rumination was also absent from the Nigerian sample. In contrast, the British sample showed all the signs of classic depression. Without more information regarding the characteristics of the Nigerian sample, it is impossible to ascertain whether the results can be generalized beyond those Nigerians who are Westernized. For example, German (1972b) and Diop (1967) found that acculturated African depressed patients presented similar pictures to Western people while unacculturated Africans did not.

Comments on Cross-Cultural Studies on the
Manifestation of Depression

The current review of the manifestation of depression across cultures reveals that depression does not assume a universal form. Of special importance is the fact that the psychological representation of depression occurring in the Western world is often absent in non-Western societies. However, somatic aspects do appear quite frequently regardless of culture. Oftentimes, it is only when individuals in non-Western societies become more Westernized that we find similarities in the patterns of depression found in the Western world. This psychological representation involves reports of depressed mood, guilt, and feelings of self-depreciation. The fact that this is absent in many cultures suggests that the epistemic framework of a culture must be considered in evaluating psychiatric disorders. "Depression" apparently assumes completely different meanings and consequences as a function of the culture in which it occurs.

The variations in the manifestation of depression across cultures are among the major findings to emerge from cross-cultural psychiatric research. In the author's opinion, this finding suggests that depression as it is currently construed by professionals is questionable. Depressed somatic functioning does not have to have psychological implications! If a culture tends to label experience in psychological terms, then the picture of depression known in the West may emerge. Once this occurs (i.e., feelings of despair, guilt, unworthiness, lack of purpose), suicide may be an inevitable consequence because the perception of the world becomes dramatically altered. In many non-Western cultures this does not occur and suicide is rare.

Without psychological representation, it is conceivable that somatic problems may pass more quickly and be more amenable to direct treatment approaches sanctioned by the culture. It is when the psychological representation occurs that the somatic experience of depression assumes completely different consequences and implications. The dysfunction is now exacerbated and expanded to new levels of experience. The new dimension will obviously channel perceptions of the individual in a direction that we associate with the "terrible gloom and despair" found in the most severe Western cases. Suicide is then more probable.

Another important byproduct of the cross-cultural research on the manifestation of depression appears to be a reconceptualization of the Western notion of "guilt." Researchers have suggested that the experience of "guilt" can be extended beyond traditional notions regarding violations of individual conscience to failure to meet social expectations and norms. Further, it has been suggested that projective mechanisms found in non-Western people who are depressed may actually mask self-punitive dynamics. Thus, the research points out the possibility of expanding current notions of guilt.

These conclusions raise some interesting research possibilities for both laboratory and field studies of depression. For example, suppose a group of individuals experiencing only somatic signs of depression was compared with a group experiencing both somatic and psychological signs of depression across such orthogonal indices of functioning as reaction time, cortical arousal, sensory thresholds, and so forth. Would it be possible to identify differences between the two groups? Or, does the psychological representation of the problem influence patterns of functioning? It is important that more research be conducted on the emic categories of psychiatric dysfunction across cultures through the use of methodological approaches capable of eliciting indigenous organizational structures (e.g., componential analysis). It would then be possible to know in what categories different cultures include somatic depressions or whether somatic depressions are even considered disorders. These are some of the questions that deserve careful inquiry.

Assessment of Depression across Cultures

Inpatient Multidimensional Psychiatric Scale (IMPS)

There have been many cross-cultural studies on the assessment of depression. Lorr and Klett (1968) compared the symptom profiles of 100 men and 100 women in each of six countries (England, France, Germany, Italy, Japan, and Sweden) on the Inpatient Multidimensional Psychiatric Scale (IMPS), an interview form that yields a profile of scores across thirteen-factor analytically derived syndromes. All subjects were newly hospitalized psychotic patients and were either not receiving drugs or were on minimal drug dosages. The patients ranged in age from eighteen to fifty-six.

For all the samples, the traditional diagnosis of anxious depression was highly correlated with the "anxious intropunitiveness," "depressive mood," and "somatic complaints" subscales of the IMPS. However, interesting ethnocultural differences did appear. For example, among the Japanese males (Japanese were the only non-Western group), the correlation between the diagnosis and the "anxious intropunitiveness" subscale was less than among the European samples; further, the "somatic complaints" subscale correlation with the diagnosis was higher. It is also noteworthy that the anxious depression diagnosis correlated positively with the "paranoid projection" and "motor retardation" subscales for the Japanese males but not for the European males.

Among females, the anxious depression diagnosis for the Japanese showed a smaller correlation with the "anxious intropunitiveness" subscale and a higher correlation with the "somatic complaints" subscale than was the case for the European groups. The "motor retardation" subscale also showed a higher correlation among the Japanese than was the case for the European groups. Although the findings concerning the ethnocultural

groups' differences were not discussed by Lorr and Klett, they are important because they point out variations in the expression of anxious depression through the use of a systematic assessment instrument.

One of the limitations of the IMPS is that the items making up the
various subscales were generated on Western samples. It is conceivable
that many of the subscales would contain different items if they were developed for non-Western groups. That is to say, a subscale like "anxious
intropunitiveness" might well be measured by a different set of items in
Japanese culture. One way to approach this problem is to factor analyze
the items in the *IMPS* for each of the different cultural groups assessed.
Nevertheless, within these constraints, the results so far suggest that the
study of depression via structured interview formats is a valuable strategy.
In the Lorr and Klett (1968) study, the findings indicate that anxious depression does have a different profile for Japanese than for European
groups.

Depression Adjective Check List

Levitt and Lubin (1975) conducted a national survey of depression in the
USA with use of the Depression Adjective Check List (DACL). They
scored the DACL for both 2,617 white and 315 black males and females.
The DACL consists of a series of self-report affect descriptors (i.e., sad,
happy, blue). The blacks scored significantly higher than the whites on the
DACL. However, both groups were well within the normal limits of functioning and the group difference was only .70. The significance was largely
a function of the large sample size. The authors did not include an item
analysis of the group differences, so it was not possible to look at ethnic
patterns of affect descriptors. In the current author's opinion, the assessment of depression by affect descriptors has limited cross-cultural validity, since many ethnocultural groups do not verbally label their affective
states. It is simply not part of their epistemological orientation.

The Zung Depression Scale

William Zung has developed a popular self-rating scale for depression
that has been used in a number of different countries. In the first cross-
cultural study of the Zung Scale (Self-Rating Depression Scale, or SDS),
Zung (1969) found that his twenty-item symptom frequency checklist
correlated highly with physicians' ratings of depression in England (.65),
Australia (.52), Germany (.51), Czechoslovakia (.50), Switzerland (.45), and
Japan (.43). It is noteworthy that the lowest correlation occurred in Japan,
which was the only non-Western country included in the sample. The
total number of depressed subjects for all the countries was 343 (this number was not broken down for the different countries). The Zung Scale

contains items that tap affective, biological, and psychological functioning. No breakdown was given on the culture groups' scores for the different symptom groups. However, the fact that the Japanese evidenced the lowest correlation once again points out the possibility that the depression patterns in Japan do not present the same picture as in the Western world or that the criteria for diagnosing someone as depressed in Japan are different. More recently, Zung and his colleagues have validated his scale in India (Zung & Master, 1975), the Netherlands (Zung, van Praag, Dijkstra, & Van Winzum, 1975), and Spain (Conde-Lopez & Sánchez de Vega, 1969; Conde-Lopez, Escriba, & Izquierdo, 1970).

Zung (1972) also examined depression among 1,981 normal adult subjects in Czechoslovakia, England, Germany, Spain, Sweden and the United States. There were a majority of females in the Swedish, English, and American samples and a majority of males in the Czech sample. The gender distribution was equal for the other two samples. The age distribution was also unbalanced across the six countries. Zung found that the Czechs had the highest overall depression score. Indeed, the Czech mean exceeded the depressed level for American norms. The next highest group was the Swedes and then the Germans. According to Zung, these findings suggest much higher levels of depression among normal populations for these groups. A subsequent factor analysis of the Zung Scale for each of the samples yielded different loading patterns for the twenty items. This suggests that Zung may not be measuring the same thing for the different samples. These findings point out the need to establish emic norms, since the use of American norms indicates that many normal Czechs, Swedes, and Germans are "clinically" depressed. This could best be done by beginning with emic definitions of depression followed by the generation of local norms for each symptom.

In general, there is reason to believe that the Zung Scale offers a valuable research instrument for cross-cultural studies of depression, but it is probably most effective as a screening tool rather than a refined research scale since it covers only a small number of symptoms. Further, it is probably most valid in sociocultural milieus that share similarities in levels of Westernization. In non-Western countries, there is reason to believe it can be useful among more educated sections of the population who do not maintain traditional lifestyles.

Cross-Validation Studies of Depression Scales

Marsella, Sanborn, Kameoka, Shizuru, and Brennan (1975) compared five depression scales (Beck Depression Scale, Katz-Hogarty Depression Scale, Multiple Affect Adjective Check List, MMPI Depression Scale, and Zung Depression Scale) on samples of normal male and female Caucasian

Americans, Chinese Americans, and Japanese Americans. They cross-validated the measures against one another for each of the six subgroups. The measures correlated highly for the Caucasian males and females, the Japanese males and females, and the Chinese females; however, the correlations dropped considerably for the Chinese males. Most of the correlations were around .60 for the previous groups. Obviously, a perfect relationship does not exist among the scales.

Variations in the correlations were attributed to differences in scale formats and contents. For example, the Beck utilizes symptom severity, the Zung utilizes symptom frequency, and the MMPI utilizes simple yes or no responses to indicator items that have no face validity for depression. The MAACL is based on an adjective checklist format for mood state descriptors. Thus, with all of this variability in content and format, it is conceivable that an individual in a given culture could be labeled as depressed on one scale but normal on another. Clearly, content and scale format are critical in identifying depression among different cultural groups. Unfortunately, Marsella et al. (1975) examined only normal populations. Thus, it is difficult to extend their findings to clinical groups. It is possible that clinical patients from different cultures would show greater cross-validation correlations among the different measures.

The Comprehensive Symptom Checklist

Marsella and Tanaka-Matsumi (1976) compared normal male and female Japanese nationals, Japanese Americans, and Caucasian Americans on the sixty-item Comprehensive Depression Symptom Checklist (Marsella and Sanborn, 1973). This instrument provides an assessment of sixty symptoms associated with depression in terms of their frequency, intensity, and duration. Thus, it offers a more thorough view of depression patterns than other instruments currently in use. Marsella and Tanaka-Matsumi attempted to compare baselines in the frequency, intensity, and duration of various symptoms for the different groups studied so that normal limits for symptom patterns could be emically established. The results of the study proved quite interesting because they highlighted the fact that different ethnocultural groups can have similar frequencies of a problem but different intensities or durations. Or, different groups can have the same intensity but different frequencies or durations and so on. This technique offers researchers a more detailed picture of profiles for different ethnocultural groups.

For example, Marsella and Tanaka-Matsumi found that Japanese Americans reported higher frequencies of ruminations than Japanese nationals or Caucasian Americans, but durations for the problem were similar. The Japanese Americans also reported greater frequencies of worrying than the other two groups, but the intensity of the worries were less than for the Japanese nationals. Caucasian Americans reported greater frequencies of feeling anxious and tense but were similar to the other groups in terms of the intensity and duration of the problem. Japanese nationals and Caucasian Americans showed similar frequencies and durations for the problem of wanting to avoid people but differed with respect to the intensity of the problem. These variations across the dimensions of frequency, intensity, and duration suggest that greater care must be given to the total shape of symptomatology across cultures. The mere listing of the presence or absence of a symptom can be misleading. Marsella and Tanaka-Matsumi plan to study depressed samples in each of the cultures in the future to compare the baseline differences between clinical and normal samples within cultures and across cultures. Further, they intend to factor analyze the checklist to obtain objective patterns.

The Hamilton Rating Scale

Yet another instrument used in cross-cultural studies of depression is the Hamilton Rating Scale. This scale requires professionals to rate patients across a spectrum of depressive symptomatology. Fernando (1966, 1969) used this instrument in studies of different cultural groups in London, England. He found no differences among Jews, Protestants, and Catholics on the Hamilton in terms of level of depression. He did not conduct an item analysis across the different groups. Binitie (1975) also used the Hamilton Scale in a study of depression among Nigerian and English patients. Although no group difference results were provided, a factor analysis of the Hamilton Scale for each of the ethnic groups revealed differences in symptom patterns suggesting a different structure for unique cultural groups. The Hamilton Rating Scale has also been used in India (Teja & Narang, 1970; Teja, Narang, & Aggarwal, 1971).

The MMPI

The greatest amount of research on the measurement of depression across cultures has been conducted with the MMPI (Minnesota Multiphasic Personality Inventory). This research will not be reviewed here because of its scope, and the reader is referred to Butcher and Pancheri (1975) who provide a survey of cross-cultural MMPI studies. Virtually all of the MMPI research has utilized the entire MMPI Scale without focusing on depression. However, some studies have concentrated on depressed populations. For example, Pancheri (1975) compared male and female neurotic depressives between the ages of twenty and thirty who resided in Rome, Italy, and Berne, Switzerland. The Italian neurotic depressives scored significantly higher on four subscales of the MMPI: hysteria, depression, hypochondriasis, and paranoia. These findings suggest a greater quality of affective arousal among the Italians and point out, once again, the importance of content and format in the measurement of depression across cultures.

Research on the cross-cultural assessment of depression points to the importance of defining the concept of depression in terms that are relevant to the culture under study and to the importance of using formats that are culturally unbiased. Clearly, formats emphasizing the measurement of depression through the endorsement of mood descriptors may be inappropriate for cultures that do not label inner mood states. Similarly, the use of formats (e.g., MMPI) based on indicator items that are validated on specific cultural samples is also inappropriate, since there is no basis for determining whether the indicator items (e.g., "I cry easily") are relevant to the culture under study. In the author's opinion, the most useful approach may be to develop symptom norms for both depressed and normal populations in every culture in terms of frequency, intensity, and duration symptom parameters along the lines of the Marsella-Sanborn (1973) Comprehensive Depressive Symptom Checklist. The items included in such a checklist should be generated emically and etically. Only in this way can we move toward more valid measures of depression in diverse culture groups.

Personality Correlates of Depression across Cultures

Hostility

Several reports of the personality correlates of depression across cultures have been published. These reports have generally focused on four personality characteristics: hostility, guilt, self-concept, and body image. Fernando (1969) compared forty-nine Jewish depressed patients (both reactive and endogenous) and fifty Christian depressed patients (both reactive and endogenous) living in London. There were no differences in social class between the groups and ages ranged from eighteen to sixty-one. Fernando found that Roman Catholic women in the Christian sample were more hostile than the other two groups of women (Jewish and Protestant). He also found that Protestant women were more intropunitive and Jewish women more extropunitive. There were no differences among the male groups. Fernando related the differences to child-rearing patterns regarding independence and discipline. Kendell (1970) reviewed the research on aggression and depression from an epidemiological viewpoint and concluded that there appears to be a relationship between the inhibition of aggressive responses and depression. Kendell contends that both the mood and syndrome of depression are related to inhibition of aggression arising from frustration. Certain cultures encourage the inhibition of aggression more strongly than others, and this may lead to increased rates of depression.

Guilt

The overwhelming majority of cross-cultural studies of depression in non-Western societies have reported that guilt is not a part of the depression syndrome. Further, when guilt does occur, it assumes a different form than it does in the West. Two reports have specifically focused on guilt and depression across cultures. El-Islam (1969) examined 197 depressed Egyptian outpatients from different religious backgrounds. He found no differences in the frequency of guilt between Christians (Coptics) and Moslems. However, literate patients exhibited greater guilt than illiterate patients. El-Islam suggests that guilt occurs with greater frequency than is recognized in the non-Western world but is often missed diagnostically because of patient tendencies to project blame onto others. He claims if researchers probe more deeply, they will find that projected blame masks true guilt.

Wintrob (1968) suggests that certain delusional systems among tribal Liberians in Africa may serve to ameliorate the guilt and worthlessness associated with depression. The delusional systems present a different picture of depression and may account for the variations in depression that are found. Guilt is considered to arise from violations of sexual mores held by tribal societies.

Rao (1973), based on clinical observations of forty-two consecutive male and female admissions—with the diagnosis of endogenous depression—to a psychiatric service in India, found that approximately forty percent of the patients expressed feelings of guilt. Of special interest is the fact that almost half of the thirty-one Hindus in the study expressed ideas of guilt. In most of these cases the guilt was related to lack of care for children and failure in duty toward family including spouse and parents. Rao contends that guilt is not an important part of depression among Indians, in spite of its occurrence in many cases. Although guilt was identified, there is a question in the current author's mind about the meaning of the guilt and its conceptual equivalence to guilt in the Western world. In a study of the semantic meaning of the term "guilt" among Japanese, Chinese, and Caucasian Americans, Marsella, Murray, and Golden (1974) found different connotative meanings in the term for the different ethnic groups. Rao's paper requires a greater explanation of the concept of guilt in India if it is to be valuable in understanding the personality correlates of depression across cultures.

Self-Concept

Marsella, Walker, and Johnson (1973) examined the correlation between real versus ideal self-concept discrepancy and depression among normal Caucasian-American, Chinese-American, and Japanese-American females. They found that self-concept discrepancy and expression correlated .58 for the Caucasians and .72 for the Chinese but only .19 for the Japanese. They suggested that the low correlation among the Japanese group was because of the ritualistic tendency among the latter to engage in self-abasing behaviors all of the time. Thus, depression states do not assume any special status with respect to self-abasement. However, the fact that the self-concept descriptions were based on Caucasian relevant descriptors raised a serious question about the applicability of the terms for the Japanese group. A subsequent study of Marsella, Sanborn, Shizuru, Brennan, and Kameoka (1974) utilizing self-concept descriptors generated by Japanese Americans revealed that the previous finding may have been spurious, since the correlation between self-concept discrepancy and depression among Japanese Americans increased to .39. Yanagida and Marsella (1978) found the relationship varied for different generations of Japanese Americans. The *Nisei* (first) generation did not manifest a relationship.

Body Image Satisfaction

Marsella, Brennan, Kameoka, and Shizuru (1974) investigated the relationship between satisfaction with one's body image and depression among normal and depressed male and female Caucasian Americans, Chinese Americans, and Japanese Americans. They found that dissatisfaction with body image correlated highly with depression among all three ethnocultural groups. The findings suggest that body image dissatisfaction and self-concept discrepancy may be important correlates of depression across cultures. More research is required with contrasting cultural groups at different levels of depression.

The topic of personality correlates of depression is an important one for understanding the role of culture in depression. Since personality can serve as both a correlate and a cause of depression, it is critical that greater attention be given to the subject. This could certainly be accomplished through a multinational collaborative study of contrasting cultures that included cultural analyses. Currently, cross-cultural studies of personality correlates of depression are too few in number to offer any substantive conclusions. At best, there are some interesting leads that deserve greater inquiry.

Cultural Theories of Depression

Numerous cultural theories of depression have been posited to account for the variations in the rates and expression of depression across cultures. These theories have basically assumed either psychodynamic or social-psychological conceptual frameworks. However, rather than presenting the theories within the context of these frameworks, they will be discussed in terms of the following variables emphasized by the theorists: mourning rituals, family structure, conforming personality, social cohesion, psychological defenses, the expression of aggression, achievement failures, and self-structure.

Family Structure

One of the first cultural theories of depression to be set forth emphasized the role of family structure in the mediation of depression. Quite early, Stainbrook (1954) speculated that depression may occur less often in non-Western cultures because extended family structures serve to minimize early frustrations of life through "multiple mothering" and "generalization of object interest to several family members." Collomb (1967) contended that depression may be lower in non-Western cultures because of close mother-child relationships and long periods of permissiveness, which reduce psychological insecurities in childhood and thus act against the development of personality types sensitive to endogenous depression. Tseng and Hsu (1969) observed that the extended family in Taiwan promotes a feeling of belonging to a group. Further, they noted that the extended family lessens the risk of early loss which predisposes to depression.

Vitols (1967) and Vitols and Prange (1962) concluded that the traditional extended family of the American black in the South acts against depression because it provides a closely knit group that helps share the burdens of death and other losses. Krauss (1968) speculated that the high rates of depression found by Field (1960) among the Ashanti tribe in Ghana could be a function of the fact that childhood experiences are characterized by certain losses. Krauss (1968) stated:

> Childhood was ushered in in a most painful way by the withdrawal of mother and the diffusion of the mothering function to numerous surrogates in the

matrilineage. There was a drastic reduction in the amount and quality of food, a change in attitude on the part of the significant adults in the environment from easy indulgence to harsh demands and often the process was accentuated by being displaced by a younger sibling. (p. 32)

The Conforming Personality

Arieti (1959) and Cohen, Baker, Cohen, Fromm-Reichmann, and Weigart (1954) suggested that depression may be due to child-rearing patterns and family structures that encourage the development of a conforming personality. Both of these formulations posited that the future manic-depressive willingly accepts parental expectations that subsequently lead to "pathological (or exaggerated) introjection." This, in turn, leads to increased feelings of resentment toward parental figures and society for impositions. But, because the individual is highly socialized, the hostility produces the guilt feelings and masochistic tendencies associated with depression. Thus, in brief, these authors contend that depression is more likely to occur among highly socialized individuals who tend to conform to societal and parental pressures. However, experimental investigations of this hypothesis (Marsella, 1975; Marsella & Murray, 1974) failed to confirm the notion. Marsella (1975) stated:

> The speculation that all manic-depressives develop prototypic conformity patterns in youth that generalize to adult behavior is perhaps too broad to be useful to an understanding of the causes of this disorder, especially when there is no reference to gender differences, social class differences, or other ethno-cultural dimensions capable of mediating conformity behavior. (p. 407)

The cross-cultural evidence also conflicts with the "conformity" hypothesis, since depression rates appear to be much lower in those cultural milieus that stress conformity rather than individuality.

Social Cohesion

In one of the first attempts to test a cultural theory of depression, Chance (1964; also see Murphy, Wittkower, & Chance, 1964, 1967) and his colleagues examined the hypothesis that depression may be related to the level of social cohesion in a society. Essentially, social cohesion refers to the extent to which members of a society share value orientations and the extent to which they are highly socialized. Under such conditions, it was speculated that depression rates would be higher among women, members of higher social classes, and members of "highly traditionalized and tightly knit social groupings." A likely mechanism for this would be the internalization of hostile feelings and impulses. These ideas received some support from the Murphy, Wittkower, and Chance investigation and from Hollingshead and Redlich's (1958) classic study, which found higher rates of depression among upper social classes. Yet, the "social cohesion" idea is in conflict with many epidemiological studies of traditional societies in which depression rates are extremely low. One possibility is that the "social cohesion" concept is part of a much larger and complicated equation of variables that must be used to predict depression rates. Further research is needed to better illuminate the complex of variables that mediate social cohesiveness effects on depressive disorders.

Psychological Defenses

Several investigators have speculated that rates of depression may be low in certain non-Western cultures because of the reliance on psychological defenses that are socially sanctioned. For example, Stainbrook (1954) concluded that certain cultures may encourage the use of persecutory delusions that serve to reduce the risk of self-blame. Savage and Prince (1967) contended that the use of projective mechanisms make the risk of depression among the Yoruba tribe in Nigeria quite low. They also observed that there is a heavy reliance on denial, which is bolstered by magical practices, and these also serve to reduce the risks of depression. Vitols (1967) and Vitols and Prange (1962) argued that American blacks living in the South are relatively immune against depression because of tendencies to limit self-expectations and demands. As a result, failures do not occur very often. They also observed that self-esteem is maintained by relatively "simple acts" among Southern blacks.

Mourning Rituals

A number of writers have suggested that the mourning rituals in many non-Western cultures reduce the risks of depression. For example, Tseng and Hsu (1969) claimed that the low depression rates in Taiwan may, in part, be due to the overt expression of grief that occurs in Chinese funeral celebrations. Yamamoto, Okonogi, Iwasaki, and Yoshimura (1969) observed that the practices of ancestor worship in Japan also act against the occurrence of depression because love objects are not considered to be lost through death. Vitols and Prange (1962) and Vitols (1967) concluded that the mourning practices of American blacks also mitigate against depression by the "rich opportunity for adequate grieving" and the fact that death is often perceived to be a relief from life's burdens and a chance to enter heaven. Further, death is "borne by a group rather than by an isolated individual."

The Expression of Aggression

One of the most popular cultural theories of depression to be advanced argues that cultures providing outlets for aggression will experience low levels of depression (e.g., Kendell, 1970). In a test of this hypothesis, Lyons (1972) compared the rates of depression in Belfast, Northern Ireland, and a related peaceful community. Lyons found that the suicide rate dropped by more than 50 percent in Belfast and that depression rates decreased during the period of civil hostilities in Belfast. In contrast, the peaceful neighboring community showed a sharp increase in its rate of depression.

Self-Structure

Marsella, Kinzie, and Gordon (1973) hypothesized that patterns of symptom expression found among different ethnocultural groups may be related to the nature of the self-structure, which is conditioned. They claimed that if a culture conditions a view of self as somatic functioning, somatic symptoms will dominate the picture. In contrast, if a culture conditions a view of self as an existential process, existential complaints will dominate. They stated:

> What emerges is the possibility of interpreting [depression] complaints . . . as reflections of self perceived as somatic functioning, as interaction, as cognitive processes, and as a total entity or existential process. . . . In all these instances, the complaints come to reflect an extension of self which is perceived to be disordered, limited, impaired, or generally inadequate. (p. 449)

Subjective versus Objective Epistemic Orientations

In a recent paper, Marsella (1978) speculated that the expression and experience of depression across cultures may vary as a function of a culture's position on a continuum of subjective versus objective epistemological orientations. He noted that there is close relationship among the self-structure, language, and mode of experiencing reality. In some cultures, an unindividuated self-structure, a metaphorical language structure, and an imagistic mode of experiencing reality are present in an intimate reciprocal relationship. Cultures at this end of the continuum tend to develop subjective epistemic orientations that make it difficult to capture or portray internal effective states like depression in objective lexical terms and experiences. Thus, the reports of subjective mood distress are absent and the experience itself is altered.

In contrast, some cultures are characterized by individuals who have individuated self-structures, abstract languages, and a lexical mode of experiencing reality. These cultures tend to develop objective epistemological orientations in which internal affective states are frequently labeled in abstract terms and in which the affective state is experienced in a more detached manner. In these instances, we find depressive disorders expressed and experienced in ways that are similar to traditional psychiatric representations of depression. These thoughts are displayed in Figure 6-1.

Some Comments on Cultural Theories of Depression

In general, depression appears to be related to both the quantity and quality of stresses present in a culture, especially during critical periods of childhood when object attachments are being formed. Certain types of family structures seem to foster child-rearing patterns that can innoculate individuals against the risk of depression. Further, certain patterns of mourning rituals and aggression outlets seem to be able to reduce the threat of depression that might be precipitated by deaths and other losses. However, these conclusions are based largely on anecdotal material rather than rigorous empirical study. There is great need to examine systematically these thoughts through cross-cultural investigations. But, these investigations would likely be hampered by the current conflicts regarding the definition of depression. Theory may have to wait until conceptual problems are solved.

Conclusions

1. The cross-cultural study of depression offers a valuable approach for clarifying current conceptions regarding the causes, manifestation, measurement, and treatment of depression.

2. There appears to be no universal conception of depression. Indeed, many non-Western cultures do not even have a concept of depression that is conceptually equivalent to that held by Western mental health professionals. However, even among those cultures not having conceptually equivalent terms, it is sometimes possible to find variants of depressive disorders similar to those found in Western cultures. But, because the depressive experience is embedded within an entirely different cultural context, it may assume a different meaning and experience and perhaps should not be labeled as depression.

3. Because of methodological limitations, it is difficult to arrive at any substantive conclusions regarding variations in the distribution rates (epidemiology) of depression around the world. If one is willing to tolerate the methodological limitations for purposes of speculation, depression appears to be less common in non-Western cultures than it is in Western cultures. Further, when it does appear, it seems to manifest itself differently.

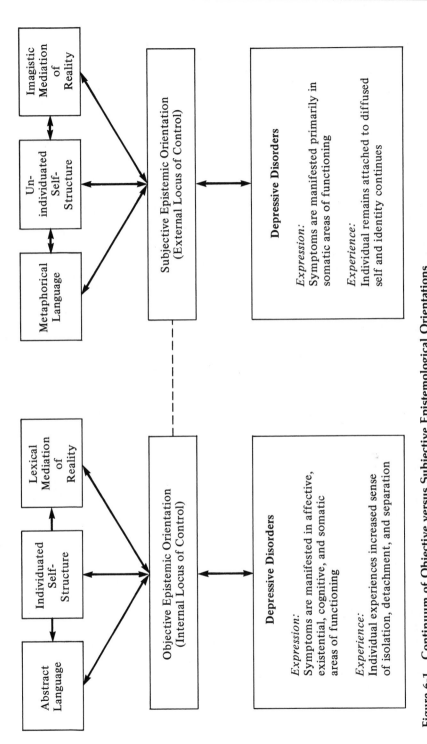

Figure 6-1 Continuum of Objective versus Subjective Epistemological Orientations
From A. J. Marsella, "Toward a Conceptual Framework for Understanding Cross-Cultural Variations in Depressive Affect and Disorder. Address to School of International Studies, University of Washington, Seattle, April 18, 1978.

4. The more Westernized a culture, the more one can expect a picture of depression that includes both somatic and psychological components. In contrast, depression in less Westernized cultures often does not involve psychological components. Among the major differences in depression between Westernized and many non-Westernized cultures are the absence of guilt and self-depreciation. Suicidal attempts and suicidal ideation are also rare in many non-Western cultures. Given these differences, it is questionable whether Western depression can be considered a universal disorder.

5. There may well be many different types of depression and affective dysfunction. Clearly, it is difficult to conclude that a depression manifested solely by somatic components is similar to a depression manifested by both somatic and psychological components. The subjective experience of these two types must of necessity be different to the individual and to the society. The key may be the epistemic orientation of the individual and the culture. Some epistemic orientations emphasize the labeling of psychological experience while others do not. Suicide appears to be associated more with depressive disorders that include psychological dimensions. This may help explain the high rates of suicide in many Westernized countries.

6. A broad typology of depressive disorders that emerges from the cross-cultural literature is based on the presence or absence of the psychological and somatic components and the culture's tendency to label the phenomena as problems. This typology is presented in Figure 6-2.

7. There are many problems in the measurement of depression across cultures including the lack of norms, the inappropriate application of biased norms, inappropriate scale formats, lack of conceptual equivalency, and failure to determine baselines for problem behaviors emically. There is a need for in-depth studies of the shape (i.e., frequency, intensity, duration) of problem behaviors for both normal and clinical populations in different cultures.

8. It is difficult to determine the role of personality factors in depression from existing research. However, there are promising findings regarding the role of hostility in depression across cultures. Guilt appears to play a minor role in depression in many non-Western cultures when compared to the prominence it displays in Western depression. Self-concept discrepancy and body image appear to be valuable areas for further investigation.

9. There are strong theoretical grounds for expecting differences in the frequency and manifestation of depression across cultures. At the present time, most theoretical interpretations are based on psychodynamic and/or social-psychological precepts. But, there is an absence of systematic empirical studies based on these concepts.

Labeling Process

	Indigenous and Professional Definitions Agree	Indigenous and Professional Definitions Disagree
Somatic and Psychological Component Present		
Somatic and Psychological Components Absent		
Somatic Component Present and Psychological Component Absent		
Somatic Component Absent and Psychological Component Present		

Domains of Functioning

Figure 6-2   Typology of Depressive Disorders Generated from Cross-Cultural Research

277

Recommendations for Research

The major problem facing researchers on depression today is one of conceptualization. Investigators are unable to define clearly and to identify "depression" as a syndrome of disorder. As a result, efforts to understand its causes and its prevention are being seriously impeded. According to current thinking, "depression" may well be caused by a number of different independent causes. Further, it appears that these independent causes can be compounded within the same individual, producing either additive or multiplicative effects. When one attempts to understand the causes of depression across cultural boundaries, the difficulties are increased. The display of "depression" is also a complicated problem. It appears to involve numerous individual, situational, and cultural variables operating both independently and in combination with one another.

This state of affairs suggests the need to reconceptualize our thinking about the notion of "depression" as a syndrome or set of syndromes. In the current author's opinion, we need to set aside temporarily existing ideas in favor of careful descriptive research that can provide a foundation for new ideas regarding "depression." The following guidelines for research are commended.

It is necessary to initiate a multinational study of representative world geocultural areas aimed at clarifying the concept of depression. As a first step, ethnoscience methods (e.g., componential analysis, word association methods, semantic differential methods) should be used to identify the categories of psychopathological syndromes and their constituent elements across cultures. Further, it is necessary to determine the connotative meanings and the antecedents and behavioral consequences of various mood states should they emerge as salient dimensions during this stage of research. The key to this phase is the emic perspective it will provide.

Second, once the categories and constituent elements are established for different cultures, efforts should be made to develop baselines for both "normal" and "abnormal" populations in a given culture and across cultures. Baselines should be determined according to the frequency, intensity, and duration of the problem behaviors from the viewpoint of three perspectives for a given individual: self, family member, and professional. This is schematized in Figure 6-3.

Third, patterns should be established through factor analysis for each of the cultures under study based on the scores from the baseline phase. In brief, it would be possible to compare syndromes of disorder between "normal" and "abnormal" populations from the viewpoints of subjects, family members, and professionals and to compare these across cultures.

With this type of data, researchers could then proceed to investigate

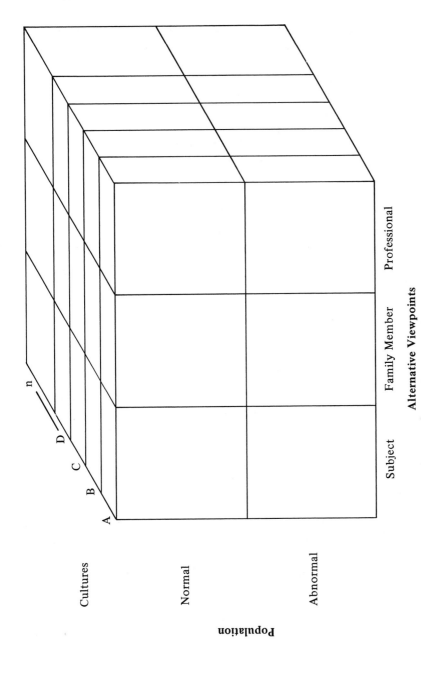

Figure 6-3 Research Design for Investigating Problem Behavior Syndromes across Cultures
NOTE: All respondents rate problem behaviors for frequency, intensity, and duration parameters. Results can then be factor analyzed according to any of the dimensions.

syndrome-by-cause-by-treatment matrices across cultures. This is portrayed in Figure 6-4. These steps could clearly lead to a clarification of the concept of "depression," as well as other forms of psychiatric impairment, by reducing ethnocentric influences. Epidemiological studies would then have a higher probability of success.

If these steps could be taken, it is conceivable that many of the problems surrounding the study of depression could be clarified and resolved. We must set aside our reluctance to give up traditional notions regarding the universality of depression in favor of empirical tests of our beliefs. The suggested procedures may well point out the ethnocentricity of many of our beliefs and, in the process, open new vistas of understanding for one of our most pressing problems.

Note

1. The author wishes to thank Judy Ching for her bibliographical assistance, Shirley Davis for editorial efforts, and Juris Draguns and H. B. M. Murphy for their helpful comments. Portions of this chapter were presented at the Symposium on Cross-Cultural Aspects of Depression, International Association of Cross-Culture Psychology, Tilburg, Netherlands, 1976.

References

AL-ISSA, I. Culture and symptoms. In C. Costello (Ed.), *Symptoms of psychopathology: A handbook.* New York: Wiley, 1970.

ARIETI, S. The manic-depressive psychoses. In S. Arieti (Ed.), *The American handbook of psychiatry.* New York: Basic Books, 1959.

BAGADIA, V., JESTE, D., DAVE, K., DOSHI, S., & SHAH, L. A prospective epidemiological study of 233 cases of depression. *Indian Journal of Psychiatry,* 1973, *15,* 209–231.

BAGLEY, C. Occupational class and symptoms of depression. *Social Science and Medicine,* 1973, *7,* 327–340.

BAZZOUI, W. Affective disorders in Iraq. *British Journal of Psychiatry,* 1970, *117,* 195–203.

BENEDICT, P., & JACKS, I. Mental illness in primitive societies. *Psychiatry,* 1954, *17,* 377–389.

BENOIST, A., ROUSSIN, M., FREDETTE, M., & ROUSSEAU, S. Depression among French Canadians in Montreal. *Transcultural Psychiatric Research Review,* 1965, *2,* 52–54.

BINITIE, A. A factor-analytical study of depression across cultures (African and European). *British Journal of Psychiatry,* 1975, *127,* 559–563.

BÖÖK, J. A genetic and neuropsychiatric investigation of North Swedish population. *Acta Genetica,* 1953, *4,* 345.

BOYER, L. Folk psychiatry of the Apaches of the Mescalero Indian Reservation. In A. Kiev (Ed.), *Magic, faith and healing.* New York: Free Press, 1964.

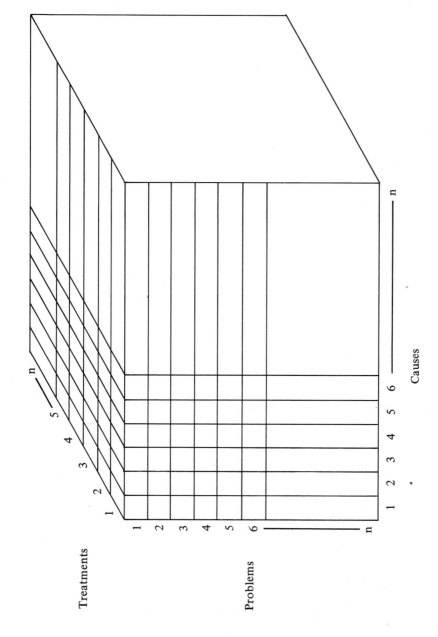

Figure 6-4 Research Matrix for Investigating Problem, Cause, Treatment Interactions

281

BUTCHER, J., & PANCHERI, P. *A handbook of cross-national MMPI research.* Minneapolis: University of Minnesota Press, 1975.

CAROTHERS, J. *The African mind in health and disease: A study in ethnopsychiatry.* Geneva, Switzerland: World Health Organization, 1953, No. 17.

CAUDILL, W., & SCHOOLER, C. Symptom patterns and background characteristics of Japanese psychiatric patients. In W. Caudill & T. Lin (Eds.), *Mental health research in Asia and the Pacific.* Honolulu: East-West Center Press, 1969.

CHANCE, N. A cross-cultural study of social cohesion and depression. *Transcultural Psychiatric Research Review,* 1964, *1,* 19–24.

COHEN, M., BAKER, G., COHEN, R., FROMM-REICHMANN, F., & WEIGART, E. An intensive study of twelve cases of manic-depressive psychosis. *Psychiatry,* 1954, *17,* 103–127.

COLLOMB, H. Methodological problems in cross-cultural research. *International Journal of Psychiatry,* 1967, *3,* 17–19.

COLLOMB, H., & ZWINGELSTEIN, J. Depressive states in an African community (Dakar). In T. Lambo (Ed.), *First Pan-African Psychiatric Conference Report,* Abeokuta, Nigeria, 1961.

CONDE-LOPEZ, V., ESCRIBA, P., IZQUIERDO, T. Evaluación estadística y adaptación castellana de la escala autoaplicada para la depresión de Zung. *Archivos de Neurobiologia,* 1970, *33,* 185–206.

CONDE-LOPEZ, V., & SÁNCHEZ DE VEGA, J. La escala autoaplicada para le depresión de Zung. *Archivos de Neurobiologia,* 1969, *32,* 535–558.

COOPER, J., KENDELL, R., GURLAND, B., SARTORIUS, N., & FARKAS, T. Cross-national study of diagnosis of the mental disorders: Some results from the first comparative investigation. *American Journal of Psychiatry,* 1969, *125,* 21–29. (Supplement)

COOPER, J., KENDELL, R., GURLAND, B., SHARPE, L., COPELAND, J., & SIMON, R. *Psychiatric diagnosis in New York and London: A comparative study of mental hospital admissions.* London: Oxford University Press, 1972.

DAVIS, R. Special aspects of depression in Indian patients. In S. Arieti (Ed.), *World Biennial of Psychiatry and Psychotherapy II.* New York: Basic Books, 1973.

DEVEREUX, G. *Mohave ethnopsychiatry and suicide: The psychiatric knowledge and the psychic disturbance of an Indian tribe.* Washington, D.C.: Smithsonian Institution, Bureau of American Ethnology, No. 1975, 1961.

DEWAR, M., & MacCAMMOND, I. Depressive breakdown in women of the West Highlands. *American Journal of Psychiatry,* 1962, *19,* 217–221.

DIOP, M. La dépression chez le noir Africain. *Psychopathologie Africaine,* 1967, *3,* 183–194.

DOHRENWEND, B. P., & DOHRENWEND, B. S. The problem of validity in field studies of psychological disorder. *Journal of Abnormal Psychology,* 1965, *70,* 52–69.

———. *Social status and psychological disorder.* New York: Wiley, 1969.

———. Social and cultural influences on psychopathology. *Annual Review of Psychology,* 1974, *25,* 417–452.

DRAGUNS, J. G., PHILLIPS, L., BROVERMAN, I. K., CAUDILL, W., & NISHIMAE, S. Symptomatology of hospitalized psychiatric patients in Japan and in the United States: A study of cultural differences. *Journal of Nervous and Mental Diseases,* 1971, *152,* 3–16.

DUBE, K. (Title unavailable). *Indian Journal of Psychiatry*, 1964, *6*, 98. (Cited in Rao, 1966.)

EARLE, A., & EARLE, B. Mental illness in British Guiana. *International Journal of Social Psychiatry*, 1956, *1*, 53–58.

EATON, J., & WEIL, R. *Culture and mental disorders: A comparative study of the Hutterites and other populations.* Glencoe, Ill.: Free Press, 1955.

EDGERTON, R. Conceptions of psychosis in four East-African societies. *American Anthropologist*, 1966, *68*, 408–425.

EL-ISLAM, F. Depression and guilt: A study at an Arab psychiatric centre. *Social Psychiatry*, 1969, *4*, 56–58.

ELSARRAG, M. Psychiatry in the Northern Sudan: A study in comparative psychiatry. *British Journal of Psychiatry*, 1968, *114*, 945–948.

ESSEN-MÖLLER, E. Individual traits and morbidity in a Swedish rural population. *Acta Psychiatrica et Neurologica Scandinavica*, 1956, Supplement *100*, 1–160.

FABREGA, H. Problems inplicit in the cultural and social study of depression. *Psychosomatic Medicine*, 1974, *36*, 377–398.

———. Cultural and social factors in depression. In E. Anthony and T. Benedek (Eds.), *Depression and human existence.* Boston: Little, Brown, 1975.

FALLERS, L., & FALLERS, M. Homicide and suicide in Busoga. In P. Bohannon (Ed.), *African homicide and suicide.* Princeton, N.J.: Princeton University Press, 1960.

FERNANDO, S. Depressive illness in Jews and non-Jews. *British Journal of Psychiatry*, 1966, *112*, 991–996.

———. Cultural differences in the hostility of depressed patients. *British Journal of Medical Psychology*, 1969, *42*, 67–75.

FIELD, M. *Search for security: An ethnopsychiatric study of rural Ghana.* Evanston, Ill.: Northwestern University Press, 1960.

FUNDIA, T., DRAGUNS, J., & PHILLIPS, L. Culture and psychiatric symptomatology: A comparison of Argentine and United States patients. *Social Psychiatry*, 1971, *6*, 11–20.

GAW, A. An integrated approach in the delivery of health care to a Chinese community in America. In A. Kleinman (Ed.), *Medicine in Chinese cultures: Comparative studies of health care in Chinese and other societies.* Bethesda, Md.: NIH, 1976.

GERMAN, A. Aspects of clinical psychiatry in sub-Saharan Africa. *British Journal of Psychiatry*, 1972a, *121*, 461–479.

———. Psychiatric syndromes. In Shaper, L. (Ed.), *Medicine in a tropical environment.* London: British Medical Association, 1972b.

GILLIS, L., LEWIS, J., & SLABBERT, M. Psychiatric disorder amongst the coloured people of the Cape Peninsula: An epidemiologic study. *British Journal of Social Psychiatry*, 1968, *114*, 1575–1587.

GOBEIL, O. El susto: A descriptive analysis. *International Journal of Social Psychiatry*, 1973, *19*, 34–44.

GURLAND, B., FLIESS, J., SHARPE, L., SIMON, R., BARRETT, J., COPELAND, J., COOPER, J., & KENDELL, R. The mislabeling of depressed patients in New York state hospitals. In J. Zubin & F. Freyhan (Eds.), *Disorders of mood.* Baltimore, Md.: Johns Hopkins Press, 1972.

HADLIK, J., & BOJANOVSKY, J. [Incidence of primary depressions in the adult population of the Brno area]. Ĉeskoslovenská Psychiatrie, 1967, 63, 381–388.

HALLSTROM, T. Depressions among women in Gothenberg: An epidemiological
study. Acta Psychiatrica Scandinavica, 1970, Supplement 217, 43, 25–26.

HANSON, B., KLERMAN, G., & TANNER, J. Clinical depression among black and
white women. Unpublished manuscript. Boston State Hospital, Boston,
Mass., 1973.

HELLON, C. P. Mental illness and acculturation in the Canadian aboriginal. Canadian Psychiatric Association Journal, 1970, 15, 135–139.

HELZER, J. Bipolar affective disorder in black and white men. Archives of General Psychiatry, 1975, 32, 1140–1143.

HES, J. Manic-depressive illness in Israel. American Journal of Psychiatry, 1960, 116,
1082–1086.

HOLLINGSHEAD, A., & REDLICH, F. Social class and mental illness: A community study.
New York: Wiley, 1958.

IVANYS, E., DZDKOVA, S., & VANA, J. [Prevalence of psychoses recorded among
psychiatric patients in a part urban population.] Ĉeskoslovenská Psychiatrie,
1964, 60, 152–163.

JOHNSON, D., & JOHNSON, C. Totally discouraged: A depressive syndrome of the
Dakota Sioux. Transcultural Psychiatric Research Review, 1965, 2, 141–143.

JONES, I., & HORNE, D. Psychiatric disorders among aborigines of the Australian
Western desert: Further data and discussion. Social Science and Medicine, 1973,
7, 219–228.

KATO, M. Psychiatric epidemiological surveys in Japan: The problem of case finding. In W. Caudill and T. Lin (Eds.), Mental health research in Asia and the Pacific.
Honolulu: University Press of Hawaii, 1969.

KELLY, R., CAZABON, R., FISHER, C., & LAROUQUE, R. Ethnic origin and psychiatric
disorders in a hospitalized population. Canadian Psychiatric Association Journal,
1970, 15, 177–182.

KENDELL, R. Relationship between aggression and depression: Epidemiological
implications of a hypothesis. Archives of General Psychiatry, 1970, 22, 308–318.

KIEV, A. Curandismo: Mexican-American folk psychiatry. New York: Free Press, 1968.

————.Transcultural psychiatry. New York: Free Press, 1972.

KIMURA, B. Vergleichende Untersuchungen über depressive Erkrankungen in
Japan und in Deutschland. Fortschritte der Neurologie und Psychiatrie, 1965, 33,
202–215.

KLEINMAN, A. Depression, somatization, and the "new cross-cultural psychiatry."
Social Science and Medicine, 1977, 11, 3–9.

KRAUSS, R. Cross-cultural validation of psychoanalytic theories of depression.
Pennsylvania Psychiatric Quarterly, 1968, 8, 24–33.

LAPUZ, L. A study of psychopathology in a group of Filipino patients. In W. Lebra
(Ed.), Transcultural research in mental health Vol. II). Honolulu: University Press
of Hawaii, 1972.

LEFF, J. Culture and the differentiation of emotional states. British Journal of Psychiatry, 1973, 123, 299–306.

LEIGHTON, A., LAMBO, T., HUGHES, C., LEIGHTON, D., MURPHY, J., & MACKLIN, D.
Psychiatric disorder among the Yoruba. Ithaca, N.Y.: Cornell University Press,
1963.

LEIGHTON, D., HARDING, J., MACKLIN, D., MACMILLAN, A., & LEIGHTON, A. *The character of danger: Psychiatric symptoms in selected communities.* New York: Basic Books, 1963.

LEVITT, E., & LUBIN, B. *Depression: Concepts, controversies, and some new facts.* New York: Springer, 1975.

LIN, T. Mental disorders in Chinese and other cultures. *Psychiatry,* 1953, *16,* 313–336.

LIN, T., RIN, H., YEH, E., HSU, C., & CHU, H. Mental disorders in Taiwan fifteen years later: A preliminary report. In W. Caudill and T. Lin (Eds.), *Mental health research in Asia and the Pacific.* Honolulu: University Press of Hawaii, 1969.

LORR, M., & KLETT, J. Major psychotic disorders: A cross-cultural study. *Archives of General Psychiatry,* 1968, *19,* 652–658.

LUBIN, B., & BECHTEL, R. Reporting behavioral science data. *American Journal of Psychiatry,* 1971, *127,* 1701–1702.

LYONS, H. Depressive illness and aggression in Belfast. *British Medical Journal,* 1972, *1,* 342–344.

MALZBERG, B. *New data on mental disease among Negroes in New York State, 1960–1961.* New York: Research Foundation for Mental Hygiene, 1965.

MARSELLA, A. J. Conformity and psychopathology: A comparative study of conformity behavior in manic-depressive, paranoid schizophrenic, and normal populations. *Journal of Clinical Psychology,* 1975, *31,* 402–408.

———. Cross-cultural studies of depression: A review of the literature. *Symposium on Cross-Cultural Aspects of Depression,* International Association of Cross-Cultural Psychology, Tilburg, Netherlands, 1976.

———. Thoughts on cross-cultural studies on the epidemiology of depression. *Culture, Medicine, and Psychiatry,* 1978, *2,* 343–357.

———. Towards a conceptual framework for understanding cross-cultural variations in the experience and expression of depressive affect and disorder. Address to the School of International Studies, University of Washington, Seattle, April, 1978.

MARSELLA, A. J., BRENNAN, J., KAMEOKA, V., & SHIZURU, L. Personality correlates of clinical depression: II. Body image. Unpublished manuscript. University of Hawaii, Honolulu, 1974.

MARSELLA, A. J., ESCUDERO, M., & GORDON, P. Stresses, resources, and symptom patterns in urban Filipino men. In W. Lebra (Ed.), *Transcultural research in mental health,* (Vol. II). Honolulu: University Press of Hawaii, 1972.

MARSELLA, A. J., KAMEOKA, V., SHIZURU, L., & BRENNAN, J. Cross-validation of self-report measures of depression among normal populations of Japanese, Chinese, and Caucasian ancestry. *Journal of Clinical Psychology,* 1975, *31,* 281–287.

MARSELLA, A. J., KINZIE, D., & GORDON, P. Ethnic variations in the expression of depression. *Journal of Cross-Cultural Psychology,* 1973, *4,* 435–458.

MARSELLA, A. J., & MURRAY, M. Diagnostic type, gender, and consistency versus specificity in behavior. *Journal of Clinical Psychology,* 1974, *30,* 484–488.

MARSELLA, A. J., MURRAY, M. & GOLDEN, C. Ethnocultural variations in the phenomenology of emotions: I. Shame. *Journal of Cross-Cultural Psychology,* 1974, *5,* 312–328.

MARSELLA, A. J., & SANBORN, K. *The comprehensive depressive symptom checklist.* Honolulu: Institute of Behavioral Sciences, 1973.

MARSELLA, A. J., SHIRZURU, L., BRENNAN, J., & KAMEOKA, V. Personality correlates of clinical depression in different ethnic groups: I. Self concept. Unpublished manuscript. University of Hawaii, Honolulu, 1974.

MARSELLA, A. J., & TANAKA-MATSUMI, J. Baselines of depressive symptomatology among normal Japanese nationals, Japanese-Americans, and Caucasian-Americans. Unpublished manuscript. University of Hawaii, Honolulu, 1976.

MARSELLA, A. J., WALKER, E., & JOHNSON, F. Personality correlates of depression in college students from different ethnic groups. *International Journal of Social Psychiatry*, 1973, *19*, 77–81.

MEADOW, A., & STOKER, D. Symptomatic behaviors of hospitalized patients. *Archives of General Psychiatry*, 1965, *12*, 267–277.

MURPHY, H., WITTKOWER, E., & CHANCE, N. Cross-cultural inquiry into the symptomatology of depression. *Transcultural Psychiatric Research*, 1964, *1*, 5–21.

MURPHY, H., WITTKOWER, E., & CHANCE, N. Cross-cultural inquiry into the symptomatology of depression: A preliminary report. *International Journal of Psychiatry*, 1967, *3*, 6–15.

OHARA, K. The socio-cultural approach for the manic-depressive psychosis. *Psychiatrica et Neurologica Japonica*, 1973, *75*,263–273.

OKASHA, A., KAMEL, M., & HASSAN, A. Preliminary psychiatric observations in Egypt. *British Journal of Psychiatry*, 1968, *114*, 949–955.

ORLEY, J. *Culture and mental illness: A study from Uganda.* Nairobi, Kenya: East Africa Publishing House, 1970.

PANCHERI, P. *Measurement of emotion: Transcultural aspects.* In L. Levi (Ed.), *Emotions: Their parameters and measurement.* New York: Raven, 1975.

PFEIFFER, W. Psychiatrische Besonderheiten in Indonesien. *Aktuelle Fragen der Psychiatrie und Neurologie*, 1967, *5*, 102–142.

———. The symptomatology of depression viewed transculturally. *Transcultural Psychiatric Research Review*, 1968, *5*, 121–123.

PRINCE, R. Indigenous Yoruba psychiatry. In A. Kiev (Ed.), *Magic, faith, and healing.* New York: Free Press, 1964.

———. The changing picture of depressive syndromes in Africa: Is it fact or diagnostic fashion? *Canadian Journal of African Studies*, 1968, *1*, 177–192.

RACY, J. Psychiatry in the Arab East. *Acta Psychiatrica Scandinavica*, Supplement 21, 1970, 1–171.

RAO, A. Depression: A psychiatric analysis of thirty cases. *Indian Journal of Psychiatry*, 1966, *8*, 143–154.

———. Depressive illness and guilt in Indian culture. *Indian Journal of Psychiatry*, 1973, *15*, 231–236.

———. India. In J. Howells (Ed.), *World history of psychiatry.* New York: Brunner/Mazel, 1975.

RAWNSLEY, K. Epidemiology of affective disorders. In A. Coppen and A. Walk (Eds.), *Recent developments in affective disorders: A symposium.* London: Ashford, Kent, Headley, 1968.

RESNER, G., & HARTOG, J. Concepts and terminology of mental disorder among Malays. *Journal of Cross-Cultural Psychology*, 1970, *1*, 369–381.

RIN, H., & LIN, T. Mental illness among Formosan aboriginals as compared with the Chinese in Taiwan. *Journal of Mental Science*, 1962, *108*, 134–146.

ROSE, A. The prevalence of mental disorders in Italy. *International Journal of Social Psychiatry*, 1964, *10*, 81–101.

ROSEN, G. *Madness in society: Chapters in the historical sociology of mental illness.* New York: Harper, 1968.

RUBEL, A. The epidemiology of a folk illness susto in Hispanic America. *Ethnology*, 1964, *3*, 268–283.

SAENGER, G. Psychiatric outpatients in America and the Netherlands. *Social Psychiatry*, 1968, *3*, 149–164.

SAINSBURY, M. Psychiatry in the People's Republic of China. *Medical Journal of Australia*, 1974, *1*, 669–677.

SARTORIUS, N. Culture and the epidemiology of depression. *Psychiatria, Neurologia, et Neurochirugia*, 1973, *76*, 479–487.

SATHYAVATHY, K., & SUNDARARAJ, N. Transactions of the All India Institute of Mental Health (Bangalore), No. 4, 1964, (cited in Rao, 1966).

SAVAGE, C., & PRINCE, R. Depression among the Yoruba. In W. Muensterberger (Ed.), *The psychoanalytic study of society.* New York: International Universities Press, 1967.

SCHMIDT, K. Folk psychiatry in Sarawak: A tentative system of psychiatry of the Iban. In A. Kiev (Ed.), *Magic, faith, and healing.* New York: Free Press, 1964.

SCHOENFELD, L., & MILLER, S. The Navajo Indian: A descriptive study of the psychiatric population. *International Journal of Social Psychiatry*, 1973, *19*, 31–38.

SECHREST, L. Symptoms of mental disorder in the Philippines. *Philippine Sociological Review*, 1963, *7*, 189–206.

————. Philippine culture, stress, and psychopathology. In W. Caudill and T. Lin (Eds.), *Mental health research in Asia and the Pacific.* Honolulu: University Press of Hawaii, 1969.

SEDIVEC, V. [Analysis of manic-depressive patients hospitalized in the psychiatric hospital in Plzen, 1962–1966.] *Československá Psychiatrie*, 1968, *68*, 49–56.

SEIFERT, J., DRAGUNS, J. G., & CAUDILL, W. Role orientation, sphere dominance, and social competence as bases of psychiatric diagnosis in Japan. *Journal of Abnormal Psychology*, 1971, *78*, 101–106.

SETHI, B., & GUPTA, S. An empirical and cultural study of depression. *Indian Journal of Psychiatry*, 1967, *9*, 230–239.

————. An epidemiological and cultural study of depression. *Indian Journal of Psychiatry*, 1970, *12*, 13–22.

————. A psychiatric survey of 500 rural families. *Indian Journal of Psychiatry*, 1972a, *14*, 183–196.

————. An analysis of 2,000 private and hospital psychiatric patients. *Indian Journal of Psychiatry*, 1972b, *14*, 197–205.

SETHI, B., GUPTA, S., & KUMAR, R. A psychiatric study of 300 urban families. *Indian Journal of Psychiatry*, 1967, *9*, 239–243.

SETHI, B., NATHAWAT, S., & GUPTA, S. Depression in India. *Journal of Social Psychology*, 1973, *91*, 3–13.

SHINFUKU, N., KARASAWA, A., YAMADA, O., TUASAKI, S., KANAI, A., & KAWASHIMA,

K. Changing clinical pictures of depression. *Psychological Medicine*, 1973, *15*, 955–965.

SILVERMAN, C. *The epidemiology of depression.* Baltimore, Md.: Johns Hopkins Press, 1968.

SIMON, R., FLIESS, J., GURLAND, B., STILLER, P., & SHARPE, L. Depression and schizophrenia in hospitalized black and white mental patients. *Archives of General Psychiatry*, 1973, *28*, 509–512.

SINGER, K. Depressive disorders from a transcultural perspective. *Social Science and Medicine*, 1975, *9*, 289–301.

SKEA, S., DRAGUNS, J. G., & PHILLIPS, L. Ethnic characteristics of psychiatric symptomatology within and across regional groupings: A study of an Israeli child guidance clinic population. *Israel Annals of Psychiatry and Related Disciplines*, 1969, *7*, 31–42.

SØRENSEN, A., & STRÖMGREN, E. Frequency of depressive states within geographically delimited population groups (The Samsø Investigation). *Acta Psychiatrica Scandinavica*, 1961, Supplement 162, *37*, 62–68.

SROLE, L., LANGNER, T., MICHAEL, S., OPLER, M. & RENNIE, T. *Mental health in the metropolis: The midtown Manhattan Study.* New York: McGraw-Hill, 1962.

STAINBROOK, E. A cross-cultural evaluation of depressive reactions. In P. Hoch & J. Zubin (Eds.), *Depression.* New York: Grune & Stratton, 1954.

STOKER, D., ZURCHER, L., & FOX, W. Women in psychotherapy: A cross-cultural comparison. *International Journal of Social Psychiatry*, 1968, *14*, 5–22.

SURYA, N., DATTA, S., GOPALAKRISHNA, R., SUNDARAM, D., & JANAKI, K. *Transactions of the All India Institute of Mental Health* (Bangalore), No. 4, 1964, (cited in Rao, 1966).

TAIPALE, V. & TAIPALE, I. Chinese psychiatry: A visit to a Chinese mental hospital. *Archives of General Psychiatry*, 1973, *29*, 313–316.

TANAKA-MATSUMI, J., & MARSELLA, A. J. Cross-cultural variations in the phenomenological experience of depression: Word association. *Journal of Cross-Cultural Psychology*, 1976, *7*, 379–396.

———. Ethnocultural variations in the subjective experience of depression: Semantic differential. Unpublished manuscript. University of Hawaii, Honolulu, 1977.

TEJA, J., & NARANG, R. Pattern of incidence of depression in India. *Indian Journal of Psychiatry*, 1970, *12*, 33–39.

TEJA, J., NARANG, R., & AGGARWAL, A. Depression across cultures. *British Journal of Psychiatry*, 1971, *119*, 253–260.

TERMINSEN, J., & RYAN, J. Health and disease in a British Columbian community. *Canadian Psychiatric Association Journal*, 1970, *15*, 121–127.

TONKS, C., PAYKEL, E., & KLERMAN, G. Clinical depressions among Negroes. *American Journal of Psychiatry*, 1970, *127*, 329–335.

TSENG, W. The nature of somatic complaints among psychiatric patients: The Chinese case. *Comprehensive Psychiatry*, 1975, *16*, 237–245.

TSENG, W., & HSU, J. Chinese culture, personality formation, and mental illness. *International Journal of Social Psychiatry*, 1969, *16*, 5–14.

VITOLS, M. Patterns of mental disturbance in the Negro. Unpublished paper. Cherry Hospital, Goldsboro, N.C., 1967.

VITOLS, M., & PRANGE, A. Cultural aspects of the relatively low incidence of depression in Southern Negroes. *International Journal of Social Psychiatry,* 1962, *6,* 243–253.

WATTS, C. Incidence and prognosis of endogenous depression. *British Medical Journal,* 1956, *1,* 1392–1397.

WAZIRI, R. Symptomatology of depressive illness in Afghanistan. *American Journal of Psychiatry,* 1973, *130,* 213–217.

WEEKE, A., BILLE, M., DUPONT, A., JUEL-NELSON, N., & VIDEBECH, T. Incidence of depressive syndromes in a Danish county: The Aarhus County investigation. *Acta Psychiatrica Scandinavica,* 1970, Supplement No. 217, *43,* 24–25.

WEISSMAN, M., & KLERMAN, G. Sex differences and the epidemiology of depression. *Archives of General Psychiatry,* 1977, *34,* 98–111.

WINTROB, R. Sexual guilt and culturally sanctioned delusions in Liberia, West Africa. *American Journal of Psychiatry,* 1968, *125,* 89–95.

YAMAMOTO, J., OKONOGI, K., IWASAKI, T., & YOSHIMURA, S. Mourning in Japan. *American Journal of Psychiatry,* 1969, *125,* 1660–1665.

YANAGIDA, E., & MARSELLA, A. J. The relationship between self-concept discrepancy and depression among Japanese-American women. *Journal of Clinical Psychology,* 1978, *34,* 654–659.

YAP, P. Phenomenology of affective disorder in Chinese and other cultures. In A. deReuck and R. Porter (Eds.), *Transcultural psychiatry.* Boston: Little, Brown, 1965.

YOO, P. S. Mental disorders in Korean rural communities. *Proceedings, Third World Congress of Psychiatry,* Montreal, 1961, 1305.

YOSHIMITA, T., KAWANO, M., & TAKAYAMA, I. Masked depression in the Department of Internal Medicine. *Journal of the Japanese Psychosomatic Society,* 1971, *11,* 48.

ZILBOORG, G. *A history of medical psychology.* New York: Norton, 1939.

ZUNG, W. A cross-cultural survey of symptoms in depressions. *American Journal of Psychiatry,* 1969, *126,* 116–121.

————. A cross-cultural survey of depressive symptomatology in normal adults. *Journal of Cross-Cultural Psychology,* 1972, *3,* 177–183.

ZUNG, W., & MASTER, R. Cross-national survey of symptoms of depressed and normal adults in India. Unpublished paper, Veterans Administration Hospital, Durham, N.C., 1975.

ZUNG, W., VAN PRAAG, H., DIJKSTRA, P., & VAN WINZUM, C. Cross-cultural survey of symptoms in depressed and normal adults. In T. Itil (Ed.), *Transcultural psychopharmacology.* Istanbul, Turkey: Bozak, 1975.

7

Variations in Psychotherapeutic Procedures[1]

Raymond Prince

Contents

Abstract

Previous approaches to the cross-cultural study of psychotherapies have emphasized the importance of universal features associated with the healer-patient relationship: the shared-world view, labeling and attribution of cause, and the central importance of suggestion. While accepting the therapeutic value of these exogenous factors, in this chapter the focus is upon the commonly neglected endogenous healing mechanisms. These are presented as the organism's self-righting endeavours, which emerge

291

spontaneously under stressful circumstances and take the form of altered states of consciousness, such as dreams, dissociation states, several types of religious experience, and psychoses. It is argued that healers around the world have learned to manipulate and build upon these endogenous mechanisms in a variety of ways to bring about resolution of life problems and alleviation of suffering.

Examination of the relationship between psychoanalysis and other psychotherapeutic techniques suggests that psychoanalysis is a unique and probably superior system for the understanding of psychopathology. As a form of therapy, however, there are severe limitations on its applicability and, indeed, a lack of convincing evidence for its superior therapeutic power where it can be applied. From a worldwide perspective, then, the therapeutic potential of psychoanalysis is much more limited than many other therapeutic forms.

Introduction: Problems of Definition

"I suffer." Psychotherapy may be defined as any psychological procedure that is aimed at relieving an individual with such a complaint. Suffering and psychological methods for the relief of suffering are ubiquitous. But the way individuals experience suffering, the interpretations of the meaning or cause of the suffering, and above all the methods of relieving it vary enormously according to culture. Psychotherapeutic procedures are among the most fascinating and complex of behaviours in the cross-cultural psychologist's territory of study.

The above definition of psychotherapy may be too broad. It would include such practices as the kicking of a stone by a frustrated lover, or his speaking of his heartache to a friend. Yet most previous definitions have been too restricted and do not allow adequate scope for discussion of the field when it is extended beyond our Western perspective. The emphasis on "talk," for example, in Berelson and Steiner's (1964) definition is too narrow: "Any treatment in which the patient or client . . . talks to the doctor, therapist or counsellor . . . during a series of sessions ranging in number from several to several hundred" (p. 287). Frank's (1961) definition is a bit broader: "Treatment always involves a personal relationship between healer and sufferer. Certain types of therapy rely primarily on the healer's ability to mobilize healing forces in the sufferer by psychological means. These forms of treatment may be generically termed psychotherapy" (p.1). But as we will see, "personal relationships" are by no means so universally central as this definition would imply.

Another definitional difficulty has to do with the often hazy boundary between psychological and physical therapies. Electroconvulsive therapy is clearly a physical method of treatment of some kinds of suffering, and psychoanalysis clearly a psychological method, but when a Peruvian healer doses a patient with a psychedelic plant that enables him to "see" the bad object as it is being removed from his body, is the healer using a physical or a psychological treatment? The same question may be raised when a Western physician treats an alcoholic with Antabuse so that he will feel very uncomfortable if he takes a drink.

Another hazy boundary is the one separating activities aimed at preventing suffering from those aimed at treating it. Many cultures employ rituals that seem to have as one of their functions the preservation of emotional equilibrium. Periodic, temporary reversals of sex roles or status reversals, in which the lowly dominate the exalted, are familiar examples (Gluckman, 1959). Sexual license is often permitted at the same time (Beaglehole, 1937). Such prophylactic "blowouts" for groups move by imperceptible degrees into more clearly psychotherapeutic procedures for individuals; to exclude such rituals from definitions of psychotherapy is arbitrarily to amputate procedures that clearly belong to one body.

Such worrisome problems suggest that we should avoid these Procrustean definitions. Indeed we might consider our Western craving for clarity of definition as simply a culture-bound idiosyncrasy. Belief in the possibility of water-tight definitions is largely illusory. As Wittgenstein (1974) has reminded us, contrary to our cultural delusion, our concepts do not cluster items because they share common characteristics but merely because they bear "family resemblances." What definition of the concept "game," asks Wittgenstein, could be sufficiently elastic to include activities as diverse as chess, football, and "I spy"! In the category psychotherapy, then, I will include highly diverse activities that sometimes share only the faintest of family resemblances.

Some Possible Approaches

An important approach to a review of psychotherapy across cultures would be to attempt to link cultural features to psychotherapeutic practices. Several authors have speculated about such linkages (Redlich, 1958; Sanua, 1966; Wittkower & Warnes, 1974). A number of interesting suggestions have emerged: Morita therapy, like Zen Buddhism, emphasizes the acceptance of mental suffering rather than its alleviation, and both are closely linked with Japanese values; autogenic training with its drill-like procedures reflects the cultural values of Germany, where it was invented and where it finds considerable favour as a therapeutic technique. Authoritarian cultures like the Soviet Union, Germany, and Japan have not been enthusiastic about psychoanalysis, which, with its "individualism, rational thinking, scientific idolatry and tolerance of dissent" (Wittkower & Warnes, 1974), has been widely accepted in the United States. Albee (1977) went even further and proposed a relationship between the popularity and growth of psychotherapy in the contemporary United States and the decline of traditional values, rooted in the Protestant ethic as described by Weber (1958). In Albee's analysis, the traditional ethic of self-restraint has succumbed to the affirmation of immediate experience, spontaneous expression, and unbridled self-indulgence. This rise of new hedonism has been accompanied by a frantic search for identity. Verbal psychotherapy, especially in its self-expressive and experiential varieties, has risen to meet this need, together with a variety of nontraditional mystical cults that, as pointed out in this chapter, also perform a number of broadly psychotherapeutic functions.

Other authors have explored such relationships more systematically. Whiting and Child (1953) assembled materials on seventy-five cultures using the Human Relations Area Files and other published accounts. Using a psychoanalytic approach they studied linkages between child-rearing practices, concepts of disease causation, and healing practices. They were able to find significant relationships between oral deprivation or indulgence during childhood and oral ideas of disease etiology and oral healing practices. Less marked relationships were found between aggressive child-rearing practices and aggressive etiological concepts and healing practices. Similar linkages were not found in the areas of anal, genital, or dependency-promoting child-rearing practices.

In an extensive five-year study, Bourguignon (1968, 1973) and her Ohio State University group investigated the sociocultural correlates of the use of altered states of consciousness, which, as we will see, are often employed as psychotherapy. They used Murdock's (1967) *Ethnographic Atlas* from which they drew a sample of 488 societies from all parts of the world. They found that 90 percent of the sample were reported to make use of one or more culturally patterned forms of altered states of consciousness. The frequency of such states varied somewhat according to region and ranged from a high of 97 percent of the societies of aboriginal North America to a low of 80 percent in the circum-Mediterranean area.

The sample of cultures was further divided according to whether the altered states of consciousness involved trance without the idea of "possession" (designated T) and those in which the altered state was linked with the possession interpretation (called PT). Most typically T states were characterized by hallucinations with subsequent recall, whereas PT generally involved impersonation of a specific spirit or deity in speech and behaviour, and there was subsequent amnesia for the period of the altered state. Some cultures employed both T and PT states. Table 7-1 demonstrates that there was again a differential distribution of these phenomena according to geographic area, with T states being more prevalent in North

Table 7-1 Types of Altered States According to Geographic Region

Type of Altered State	Sub-Saharan Africa N = 114	Circum-Mediterranean N = 44	East Eurasia N = 65	Insular Pacific N = 86	South America N = 59	North America N = 120
Trance	16%	23%	22%	29%	54%	72%
Both trance and possession trance	20%	14%	34%	31%	22%	21%
Possession trance	46%	43%	38%	34%	8%	4%
No institutionalized altered states	18%	20%	6%	6%	15%	3%

Source: Adapted from Bourguignon (1973)

295

and South America, PT more prevalent in Africa and circum-Mediterranean areas, and Asia and the Pacific Islands showing a more equal balance.

What accounts for these differences? The investigators examined sixteen social variables and found twelve to correlate at the .05 level of significance or better with the type of altered state. Many of these had to do with social complexity, e.g., size of population, size of the local group, presence of stratification, presence of slavery, and jurisdictional hierarchy above the local level. Possession-trance was more commonly found in highly complex societies. Trance was found in the simplest, while combinations of T and PT were found in societies of intermediate complexity. In a further analysis to account for exceptions to this relationship, Greenbaum (1973) suggests that "societal rigidity in complex societies enhances the likelihood of the presence of possession trance." She feels that possession-trances provide a much needed modicum of elbow room in these highly constrictive systems.

It is possible that systematic statistical approaches such as these will be fruitful in cross-cultural psychotherapeutic studies of the future. The quality of the output, of course, cannot exceed that of the input, and an enormous task awaits the researcher in attempting to draw out the relevant observations even in currently available documents. One of the many important problems would be related to the heterogeneity of contemporary societies, particularly of large urban conglomerates. New York, Ibadan, Calcutta, São Paulo, and Tokyo each provide a surprisingly diverse spectrum of psychotherapeutic endeavours; besides a wide range of Western psychotherapies there is a variety of faith-healing practices, herbalists, dissociation cults, occult practices, and meditation groups, to mention only a few. There are varying degrees of official sanction or prohibition; proportions of the population involved with each practice are largely unknown and might prove surprisingly different from the usually conservative estimates of officialdom.

Most attempts to grapple with the cross-cultural aspects of psychotherapy, however, have been aimed at discovering its universal features (Frank, 1961; Ellenberger, 1970; Kiev, 1964, 1972; Torrey, 1972; Calestro, 1972; Draguns, 1975). These authors have emphasized the healer-patient dyad, verbal communication, the central role of suggestion, and the importance of the shared-world view by healer and patient.

In this chapter, I will also emphasize the common features of psychotherapy. But, while acknowledging the importance of the exogenous influences of the healer upon the patient, I will take a fresh approach by focusing on the importance of endogenous or self-healing mechanisms within the patient. The significance of such mechanisms was brought home to me while observing a healing ceremony in the city of Lucknow in North India. In the ceremony there was no healer! In brief, the ceremony took place in the Anwar Shah graveyard in the centre of the city, before the tomb of an Islamic saint. Every day at twilight a group of thirty or more patients with both physical and psychiatric ills collects before the shrine. Patients believe themselves possessed by one or more evil spirits. Sitting before the tomb, one of the patients (some 80 percent are women) will begin to roll her head and rock her body. This motion increases until the patient's head strikes the ground. Possession rapidly spreads to other patients. Soon the patient begins to rave in a foreign voice, which will speak of how the patient came to be possessed and how long the patient will have to attend the shrine to become free of the spirit. One or more family members are in attendance to hear the communications of the spirit. After perhaps a half hour of strenuous activity the patient falls back on the ground exhausted. Most patients are required to return to the shrine for thirty consecutive evenings. According to local beliefs some half of the patients recover from their illnesses (Asrani, 1973). Healing results from cultural beliefs and endogenous mechanisms. No money is paid and no therapist is involved (apart from the image of the departed saint).

Psychotherapy as the Mobilization of Endogenous Mechanisms

Frank's (1961) definition of psychotherapy, cited previously, referred to the mobilization of the healing forces of the patient. As a jumping-off point for a discussion of cross-cultural psychotherapeutic mechanisms, it is worthwhile to categorize psychotherapeutic forms as they draw upon one or other of the organism's endogenous healing mechanisms. We might ask, what does a suffering person do on his own? He may go to sleep, or take a rest, he may withdraw and try to puzzle out the reason for his suffering, he may socialize or go on a drinking spree, he may buy himself a new horse or, less commonly, he may deprive or otherwise punish himself or commit suicide. On the other hand, involuntary coping mechanisms may come into play. He may dream, or have a religious experience, or go crazy. Suffering individuals, when they have exhausted their own resources, often turn to a specialized healer or healing institution. We will argue here that most of the treatments that the healers offer are simply an exaggeration or extra development of the above-named endogenous mechanisms.

Sleep, Rest, and Social Isolation

Rauwolfia-induced prolonged sleep therapy is used extensively by the Yoruba healers of Nigeria for the treatment of psychoses (Prince, 1960).

Prolonged sleep has also had a long history in European treatment (Palmer, 1937). In modern times it was particularly advocated by Klaesi in Zurich in the early twenties, who used barbiturates to maintain continuous sleep for ten days or more in the treatment of schizophrenics. After an initial flurry of interest, Western psychiatrists soon dropped that method (Diethelm, 1950), except in the Soviet Union where a modified form is still extensively used (Kalinowsky & Hoch, 1961). Caudill and Doi (1963) report that it was introduced into Japan from Europe in the 1920s and continues to be popular there.

Social isolation, relief from responsibility, and rest are the central features of at least two well-developed systems of therapy—Weir Mitchell's "rest cure" and Morita therapy.

Mitchell (1829–1914) was a prominent Philadelphia neurologist who advocated the use of complete bed rest, isolation, a rich diet and, to compensate for physical inactivity, daily massage and electrostimulation as a treatment for neurasthenia and hysteria. Patients were commonly women. The rest cure was characteristically of six to eight weeks' duration (Walter, 1970, and Mitchell, 1877) saw the dynamics as follows:

> To lie abed half the day, and sew a little and read a little, and be interesting and excite sympathy, is all very well, but when they are bidden to stay in bed a month, and neither to read, write, nor sew, and to have one nurse, —who is not a relative, —then rest becomes for some women a rather bitter medicine, and they are glad enough to accept the order to rise and go about when the doctor issues a mandate which has become pleasantly welcome and eagerly looked for. (p. 41)

He also used verbal approaches consisting of long conversations with the patient, eliciting—often in writing—her life history and the circumstances preceding the onset of the illness. Mitchell was well aware of the manipulations and excessive dependencies that might arise from his treatment. He cajoled and coerced patients who did not give up their periods of rest when he felt they were able to. One patient (Burr, 1929, p. 184) refused to get out of bed, and Mitchell threatened to get into bed with her if she did not arise. She finally emerged as Mitchell began to remove his trousers! Although Beard (1884) emphasized the important role of frustrated sexuality in the genesis of neurasthenia, Mitchell never accepted this and regarded Freud's writings, which were beginning to appear in America, as "filthy things" (Veith, 1965, p. 218).

At about the time Mitchell's rest cure was being replaced by psychoanalytic and other forms of psychotherapy in Euro-America (1910 to 1920), a somewhat similar approach made its appearance in Japan.

Morita (1874–1938) developed his therapy in the early twenties as a treatment for a group of psychoneurotic illnesses roughly overlapping those that Mitchell was concerned with. Morita called them *shinkeishitsu* (roughly nervousness or "nervosity" as Ikeda [1971] translated it).

As to the nature of the treatment process itself, there are by now more than a score of publications providing descriptions in the English literature. The most comprehensive are those by Reynolds (1976), Kora (1965), Kondo (1975), Jacobson and Berenberg (1952), Veith (1971), and Caudill and Doi (1963). There are considerable differences in detail in these descriptions, especially as to the degree of isolation imposed, whether the patient chooses or is directed to undertake activities, and the amount of Buddhist philosophy incorporated into the system. The following features seem to be general. As with Mitchell's cure, isolation and rest are central. Morita therapy seems to give a little more prominence to directive verbal psychotherapy delivered through written communications between patient and doctor. An interesting example of the diary exchange is given by Kondo (1953), and the style of the directive lecture to the patient is provided by Caudill and Doi (1963). The duration of Morita therapy is some four to eight weeks and is divided into four stages:

1. Total bed rest and isolation for four to ten days; the patient is totally inactive and not permitted to converse, read, write, or listen to the radio.
2. For the next seven to fourteen days he is out of bed and allowed in the garden where he does light work; the patient begins to write a diary for the doctor but other human contact is forbidden.
3. For a further week or two he is instructed to do heavier work, continue the diary and attend lectures from the doctor on self-control, the evils of egocentricity, and so forth.
4. Finally, the patient gradually returns to full social life and his former occupation; the patient continues contact with the doctor and attends group sessions with other patients on an out-patient basis.

Diet does not receive special attention. Perhaps because of the shorter period of full bed rest in Japan, massage, electrostimulation, or other means to prevent muscular atrophy are not used.

Altered States of Consciousness:
Dreams

Unlike sleep and rest, altered states of consciousness, such as dreams, mystical states, dissociation states, and psychoses, are not so universally accepted as endogenous therapeutic mechanisms. Indeed, most of them are regarded as psychopathological rather than therapeutic. In this section I take the positive view and also show how in some cultures they have been cultivated and elaborated by healers for formal therapeutic purposes.

It is relatively easy to argue in favour of the therapeutic value of dreams, for in our Western tradition this is a well-developed belief (Ellenberger, 1970, pp. 303–311). Freud (1920) thought that dreams were an attempt to preserve sleep, that they provided a safety valve for the discharge of unacceptable impulses of various kinds and, through repetition of traumatic events, they assisted the individual ultimately to master them. Adler saw dreams as adaptive, in that they represented rehearsals of possible future courses of action (Mosak & Dreikurs, 1973). To Jung, dreams were symbolic attempts at problem solving and, like other products of the unconscious, they provided "guiding messages" (Whitmont & Kaufmann, 1973).

In the past twenty years, some progress has been made in transforming these emic beliefs into more etic forms. Aserinsky and Kleitman (1953) discovered that dreams are associated with a special form of sleep (rapid eye movement sleep, REM sleep), and Dement and Kleitman (1957) showed that there are electroencephalographic correlates of REM sleep. More relevant to the question of a therapeutic function for dreams, Dement (1960) provided evidence that individuals deprived of REM sleep show increased REM time during subsequent sleep periods, as well as waking behavioural changes, such as tension, anxiety, and increased appetite. Fisher and Dement (1963) interpreted these findings as supporting the Freudian view of dream functions. But a review by Vogel (1968) indicated that subsequent studies had supported the finding of increased REM time but not that the waking behavioural disturbances resulted from REM deprivation. Vogel believed that the earlier reports of psychological alterations were due to unconscious communication to the subjects of the expectations of the experimenters! However, in a more recent review by Freemon (1972), studies continue to give support to Dement's findings of psychological disturbances of various kinds resulting from REM deprivation both in animals and men. REM-deprived cats, rats, and rabbits show increased motor activity and exploratory behaviour, hypersexuality and reduced seizure thresholds. Hartmann, Baekland, Zwilling, and Hoy (1971), on the basis of their studies of long and short sleepers (those habitually requiring less than six hours sleep or more than nine hours), suggest that REM sleep may be more necessary for introvertive, anxious, and perhaps more creative individuals. It is possible then that the discrepancies regarding the behavioural affects of REM deprivation may have to do with such features as personality type, age, and the presence or absence of significant life stress at the time of the study. REM deprivation might lead to tension states (or psychosis) in vulnerable individuals in times of crisis, but not in other individuals living under more every-day circumstances. In a recent study, Breger, Hunter, and Lane (1971) demonstrated that stressful life events (encounter group, imminent surgery) and alternative attempts at resolution enter dream content. But in their discussion they raise an important issue that we will come back to later in this chapter.

The question is whether dream activity, which goes on continuously for some 20 percent of our sleep time, has any psychotherapeutic effect in itself—apart from whether it can be remembered or, more important, whether the meaning of the dream for the subject is consciously integrated in some way. Breger et al. (1971, p. 191) take the view that "without work directed at integrating the dreams—at breaking down the dissociations that are present both in the dreaming and reporting—the subjects do not learn anything about themselves." Without integration and conscious work the dreams will have no "effect upon the person's life."

Clearly, the field of sleep and dreams is in a state of remarkable ferment, and the outcome impossible to predict. From the point of view of psychotherapy, answers to the following questions would be of interest:

1. Does REM deprivation result in emotional disturbance and, if so, under what circumstances?
2. If REM sleep is important for mental health, is the conscious memory of the dream important in any way?
3. Does insight into the alleged meaning of the remembered dream enhance its therapeutic effect?
4. What factors determine whether or not a dream will be remembered?

Let us now look at the psychotherapeutic use of dreams cross-culturally. It is clear that therapeutic systems making the use of dreams a central feature are relatively rare. Psychoanalysis and many of its derivative systems are well-known examples. We will consider here two other systems that are not so familiar—temple incubation in the ancient world and the Iroquois system as observed in seventeenth century America.

Temple incubation was a widespread healing technique in ancient Babylon and Egypt (Jayne, 1962), but there are much richer descriptions of the procedures from ancient Greece and Rome. Incubation was most used by the cult of Asclepius, a powerful and revered healing deity who was the main rival of Christ during the early spread of Christianity. According to Veith (1965), there were some 300 temples devoted to Asclepius in Greece alone at the time of Alexander the Great (300 B.C.), and many others were scattered over the ancient world. The spiritual healing rites of the Asclepians peacefully coexisted with the secular medical practices of the Hippocratic tradition for many centuries.

The Asclepian system has been exhaustively described by Edelstein and Edelstein (1945) in a two-volume work that includes translations of contemporary descriptions by travelers, historians, and dramatists, as well as the descriptions of healed patients inscribed on stone tablets and steles, which were prominently displayed in the temples.

The patients were largely those who failed to respond to treatment by secular physicians. They would often travel long distances with high expectations of cure, but even the sceptical could be healed. Before the healing began, the patient was required to bathe and offer sacrifices to Asclepius. He was then left to sleep on a pallet in a special room of the temple. During the night he would have a dream in which Asclepius would appear, determine the patient's illness, and either heal him instantly or tell him what to do in order to be healed. For the most part, sufferers themselves made their own incubation, though occasionally a substitute was used. Asclepius commonly appeared as calm and friendly, a bearded man or sometimes a handsome youth; he was never terrifying. He would appear every night. If a patient did not dream, this was interpreted as meaning he was unworthy. Where the cure was instantaneous, it was achieved by a touch, a surgical procedure of some kind, or sometimes by a kiss. When Asclepius prescribed a medicine or a treatment regime, the prescription might follow the current practices of the day, or at times the opposite of these practices. For example, where the secular physician might have ordered the patient to rest, Asclepius would recommend an arduous walk. Occasionally, patients would be cured without a dream. The following case descriptions from the steles of the famous temple of Epidaurus illustrate some of these details (Edelstein & Edelstein, Vol. 1, 1945):

> Ambrosia of Athens, blind of one eye. She came as a suppliant to the god. As she walked about in the Temple she laughed at some of the cures as incredible and impossible, that the lame and the blind should be healed by merely seeing a dream. In her sleep she had a vision. It seemed to her that the god stood by her and said that he would cure her, but that in payment he would ask her to dedicate to the Temple a silver pig as a memorial of her ignorance. After saying this, he cut the diseased eyeball and poured in some drug. When day came she walked out sound. (p. 230)

> A voiceless boy. He came as a suppliant to the Temple for his voice. When he had performed the preliminary sacrifices and fulfilled the usual rites, thereupon the temple servant who brings in the fire for the god, looking at the boy's father, demanded he should promise to bring within a year the thank-offering for the cure if he obtained that for which he had come. But the boy suddenly said, "I promise." His father was startled at this and asked him to repeat it. The boy repeated the words and after that became well. (pp. 230–231)

> Arata, a woman of Lacedaemon, dropsical. For her, while she remained in Lacedaemon, her mother slept in the temple and sees a dream. It seemed to her that the god cut off her daughter's head and hung up her body in such a way that her throat was turned downwards. Out of it came a huge quantity of fluid matter. Then he took down the body and fitted the head back on to the

neck. After she had seen this dream she went back to Lacedaemon, where she found her daughter in good health; she had seen the same dream. (p. 233)*

Almost all the cases described on these votive tablets were alleged to have been cured by a single dream encounter with Asclepius. At least occasionally, however, healing would require much more extended contact with the god. This is exemplified in the remarkable autobiographical account of Aelius Aristedes (A.D. 117–?187). Rosen (1969, pp. 110–120) provides an excellent case summary.

Aristedes was of a wealthy Asia Minor family and was a prominent, widely travelled orator and author. He suffered, among other ailments, from severe asthmatic attacks that turned him into a chronic invalid for about thirteen years, and caused him to organize his life around a relationship with Asclepius. Secular medicine had failed him. He was a hopeless case. Asclepius first appeared to him in a dream. He was seeking relief at the hot springs of Smyrna—he was then twenty-nine years old. In the dream Asclepius commanded him to go to his temple in Pergamum, and Aristedes took up residence there for some ten years. While at the temple he had a host of visitations from Asclepius, upon whom he became totally dependent. The following excerpts indicate some of his experiences, as well as the arduous exercises that Asclepius required:

> Indeed it is the paradoxical which predominates in the cures of the god; for example, one drinks chalk, another hemlock, another one strips off his clothes and takes cold baths, when it is warmth, and not at all cold, that one would think he is in need of. Now myself he has likewise distinguished in this way, stopping catarrhs and colds by baths in rivers and in the sea, healing me through long walks when I was helplessly bed-ridden, administering terrible purgations on top of continuous abstinence from food, prescribing that I should speak and write when I could hardly breathe, so that if any justification for boasting should fall to those who have been healed in such a way, we certainly have our share in this boast. (Rosen, p. 117)

> It [sc., the remedy] was revealed in the clearest way possible, just as countless other things also made the presence of the god manifest. For I seemed almost to touch him and to perceive that he himself was coming, and to be halfway between sleep and waking and to want to get the power of vision and to be anxious lest he depart beforehand, and to have turned my ears to listen, sometimes as in a dream, sometimes as in a waking vision, and my hair was standing on end and tears of joy (came forth), and the weight of knowledge was no burden—what man could even set these things forth in words? (Edelstein & Edelstein, pp. 210–211)

Other dream prescriptions included the requirement that Aristedes should enact a make-believe shipwreck to avoid a real one, and that he should sacrifice a finger to Asclepius so that he would not die. However,

---

* From E. Edelstein and L. Edelstein, Asclepius: A Collection and Interpretation of the Testimonies, Vol. 1 (Baltimore, Md.: Johns Hopkins Press, 1945). Reprinted by permission.

he was finally allowed to substitute a ring instead of his finger! (Rosen, 1969, p. 117)

It is possible that this kind of long-term relationship with the god was more common than the instant cures of the inscriptions, especially among the leisured and wealthy. Whether or not Aristedes eventually regained his health is not clear, but at any rate he lived until he was sixty or seventy years old, years after he had given up permanent residence at the Pergamum temple.

It is interesting that an echo of the temple incubation cure remains in the circum-Mediterranean area today. In his Moroccan study, Crapanzano (1973, p. 174) notes that patients who go on pilgrimage to the tombs of Islamic saints often try to sleep in the mausoleum, hoping to have dreams in which the saint appears and gives them instructions. This is, however, a very peripheral healing technique in the Moroccan system.

A second healing system in which the dream figures prominently is that of the Iroquois of Northeastern America (Wallace, 1958; Ellenberger, 1970). This system astonished the Jesuit fathers at the time of their first contact with the Iroquois in the seventeenth and eighteenth centuries, and frequent mention is made of dream therapy in the famous *Jesuit Relations*, a series of reports from the fathers to their superiors in France between 1611 and 1768.

The basic Iroquois concept was that the soul had concealed, inborn wishes, which if not fulfilled, at least symbolically, would lead to illness and even death. The most important means of identifying the soul's wishes was through dreams, and it was therefore of the utmost importance to monitor them continuously and attempt to fulfill them to remain healthy. If the dream wish was not clear, it might require interpretation by a specialist. Sometimes wishes did not appear in dreams and had to be determined by divination. Various subgroups of Iroquois expressed this basic theory in different ways. The Seneca were regarded as the truest believers:

> The Seneca are more attached to this superstition than any of the others; their Religion in this respect becomes even a matter of scruple; whatever it be that they think they have done in their dreams, they believe themselves absolutely obliged to execute at the earliest moment. The other nations content themselves with observing those of their dreams which are the most important; but this people, which has the reputation of living more religiously than its neighbours, would think itself guilty of a great crime if it failed in its observance of a single dream. The people think only of that, they talk about nothing else, and all their cabins are filled with their dreams. They spare no pains, no industry, to show their attachment thereto, and their folly in this particular goes to such an excess as would be hard to imagine. He who has dreamed during the night that he was bathing, runs immediately as soon as he rises, all naked, to several cabins, in each of which he has a kettleful of water thrown over his body, however cold the weather may be. Another who has dreamed

that he was taken prisoner and burned alive, has found himself bound and burned like a captive on the next day, being persuaded that by thus satisfying his dream, this fidelity will avert from him the pain and infamy of captivity and death, —which, according to what he has learned from his Divinity, he is otherwise bound to suffer among his enemies. Some have been known to go as far as Quebec, travelling a hundred and fifty leagues, for the sake of getting a dog, that they had dreamed of buying there. . . . (Wallace, 1958, p. 235)

Dream fulfillment was important not only for prophylaxis but also for treatment. Inquiries about the patient's dreams by a healer would result in the canvassing of the patient's group to supply the wishes of his soul. When the objects were assembled, a "festival of dreams" would be held, and amid rejoicing and banqueting the patient would receive the wished-for objects and would often not only recover but find himself a wealthy man.

The prescription of illicit sexual activities and self-damage based upon dreams was not uncommon. One report described how a Huron cut off his finger with a seashell because he had dreamed that his enemies had captured him and were performing this amputation. Sometimes the healing ritual would be required not only for the recovery of the individual but for the safety of his group. For example, a warrior who was "wasted, pale, depressed and spat blood" was instructed as follows:

Let there be sacrificed to me ten dogs, ten porcelain beads from each cabin, a collar [belt of wampum] ten rows wide, four measures of sunflower seed, and as many of beans. And, as for thee, let two married women be given thee, to be at thy disposal for five days. If that be not executed item by item I will make thy Nation a prey to all sorts of disaster. (Wallace, 1958, p. 239)

As was the case with Aristedes, the dream wishes could sometimes be fulfilled symbolically. For example, one warrior dreamed that he had killed a Frenchman, but instead of killing a Frenchman in reality he was satisfied to receive the coat of a dead Frenchman.

The above descriptions of the Iroquois' therapeutic system derive from seventeenth century reports, but, according to Wallace (1958) at any rate, the present-day Seneca continue to allow dreams to guide their lives.

Although psychotherapeutic systems employing dreams as extensively as psychoanalysis, temple incubation, and the Iroquois system are unusual, dreams are related to illness and its cure in a variety of peripheral ways in many cultures. Dream events may be regarded as causing illness, or bad dreams may be due to illness, or dreams may indicate that an individual must become a healer to avoid a sickness, and so forth. For example, in Kiev's (1964) volume *Magic, Faith and Healing*, which describes the indigenous psychiatric systems of fifteen widely distributed cultures, dreams are indexed for eight. In only three of these, however, were dreams used directly in the healing process. Turner (1964) mentions in passing that the Ndembu (Rhodesia) diviner may inquire about the dreams of the client in his divination sessions. Berndt (1964) reports that among Australian aborigines, a sick person may dream of a supernatural visitation and be healed. Dawson (1964) describes the use of dreams in the West African diagnostic process. He gives a number of examples in which disturbed women dreamed they had killed their children and were diagnosed as witches who must confess to their witchcraft to be healed of their symptoms. It is interesting that in these eight cultures only one of the authors mentions specifically that dreams are not used in healing. Boyer (1964) states, "Among the Apache today, no shaman inquires about the patient's dreams." This absence of mention of a phenomenon is one of the serious difficulties of the comparative method, for when a phenomenon is not mentioned, the analyst does not know whether it does not occur in that culture or whether the investigator simply wasn't interested in it. In a companion volume to Kiev's, one with a strong anthropological orientation—Middleton's (1967) *Magic, Witchcraft and Curing*—dreams are indexed for only one of the fifteen described cultures. It would appear that this difference between the Kiev and Middleton collections has to do far more with the interests of the authors than with the phenomenon of dreaming and its relation to healing. Similar difficulties exist with such large-scale comparative collections as the Human Relations Area Files.

Mystical States and Meditation

In this section we will consider a second type of altered state of consciousness—the mystical experience—and attempt to show (1) that a significant proportion (of the American population at any rate) have such experiences spontaneously, (2) that these experiences often function as an endogenous healing mechanism, and (3) that attempts to achieve them through meditation are a central feature of a large number of therapeutic systems.

Up until a few years ago, we had very little idea of the frequency of mystical experiences in the population at large. Laski (1961) conducted a pioneer study in England, canvassing her friends, mostly creative intellectuals in the communications field or the arts, using the question: "Do you know a sensation of transcendent ecstasy?" Sixty out of sixty-three responded positively and she went on to elicit further details as to what triggered the experience, its nature, and so forth. She concluded that "the ability to enjoy ecstatic experiences is widespread among intelligent, well-educated and creative people." An American study with more adequate methodology was conducted by the American Institute of Public

Opinion (Back & Bourque, 1970) and included questions on religious experience in Gallup polls in 1962, 1966, and 1967. One of the key questions was: "Would you say that you ever had a religious or mystical experience—that is, a moment of sudden religious insight or awakening?" They found a high proportion of positive responders, which steadily increased from 20 percent to 40 percent over the five years studied. Unlike Laski, they found that the experiences were more commonly reported by low socioeconomic status groups, by residents of small cities, by women, and by Negroes. It is probable that the questions used confounded mystical experiences and conversion experiences, which may have different frequencies according to social class.

More recently, the Chicago-based NORC survey team reported a detailed survey of religious experience involving some 1,400 respondents who were representative of the United States population (Greeley & McCready, 1973). To elicit reports of mystical experiences, the question asked was: "Have you ever felt as though you were very close to a powerful, spiritual force that seemed to lift you out of yourself?" Thirty-five percent answered yes to this question, and seventeen percent stated that they had felt this way "several times" or "often." Those reporting the experience were disproportionately male, black, over forty, college educated, and earned annual incomes of over $10,000. It was also found that the "mystics" reported a state of "psychological well-being substantially higher than the national average." The white mystics were significantly less likely to be racist than the national population.

The finding that those who report mystical experiences are also in better mental health leads on to the question of a causative relationship. Up until recently, the value of spontaneous mystical experiences for the relief of suffering has not been considered; such experiences have been studied for their religious or philosophical implications, if at all (Bucke, 1901; James, 1902). Anecdotal evidence suggests that spontaneous mystical experiences often occur during periods of suffering and difficult life circumstances and that the experience may result in improved attitudes and at least temporary relief of suffering (Owens, 1973). Arthur Koestler (1954) described the positive effects of his own mystical experiences while imprisoned during the Spanish Civil War. He was whiling away his time by working out mathematical formulae on the walls of his cell while waiting to be shot. He suddenly realized that one of these formulae "represented one of the rare cases where a meaningful and comprehensive statement about the infinite is arrived at by precise and finite means." The mystical experience that swept over him left him with a "serene and fear-dispelling after-effect" that lasted for hours and days; he likened it to a massive dose of vitamins injected into his veins. Repetitions of the state occurred two or three times a week during his imprisonment and then at longer intervals subsequently. Koestler could find no way to voluntarily induce the state. The upshot was a conviction of a supernatural order with attendant long-term relief from fears and uncertainties.

The following are two first-hand reports from my own case records:

1. On two occasions these emotions were of such great intensity that I cannot actually explain them. The first was in the mountains of Kootenay Valley, British Columbia, and the second was in Banff. The deepest beauty I have ever experienced in my life was the overwhelming urge to wilfully throw myself into a creek on the mountainside, so that I might become part of it. At the same time I was conscious of my obligations in this life, which held me back. The intensity of happiness and awareness is impossible to justly explain to anyone who has not felt the same flood of life through his body. They are experiences I can bring to mind at any time, as if they only happened moments ago. . . .

The knowledge of these two experiences has given me strength to continue through difficult periods in my life. I am presently 21. After the stunning awareness of this elation in Banff last summer, I found that my atheistic views were instantly replaced by a very strong faith. Accordingly I returned to Vancouver to be confirmed in the church. . . . It is only since my last strong experience that I have been able to lead a socially acceptable and constructive independent life.

2. I would like to mention that at the age of 21 I experienced a period in which I was in a state of ecstasy, lasting about three days, with an acute awareness of everything, and a feeling of unutterable joy and happiness, for which there was no outside reason.

Since I am a very unexcitable, matter-of-fact person, and never subject to either ups or downs in mood, this was a most remarkable experience, almost as if I was one with my Maker. This way of feeling seemed to involve me in a responsibility for everyone which I feared to accept, so I deliberately tuned out. The experience was never repeated.

I am now 52, a working mother of 4 teen-age children, with an alcoholic husband. The experience has helped me all through life.

Religious literature and the lives of holy men suggest that most of the world's religious beliefs represent attempts at formulation of the cognitive content of mystical experiences (Huxley, 1946). Apart from Zoroastrianism (Zaehner, 1957), all of the major world religions prescribe more or less well-developed spiritual exercises or meditation techniques aimed at achieving mystical experiences. There are often special groups within the major religions who devote themselves to the practice of these techniques; Sufis (Islam), Hassids (Judaism), a host of Yoga groups (Hinduism), and the variety of contemplative orders within Christianity are well-known examples. Our argument would hold that these meditation techniques are institutionalized forms of psychotherapy, whose aim is to release the therapeutically potent mystical experience. It should also be noted that some mystics are able to move beyond the occasional mystical experiences of transitory duration to a plateau state (sahaj state, as it is called in Hinduism, unitive state in Christianity) in which the altered state of consciousness is more or less permanent (Asrani, 1967). The differences and similarities of a saint in the *sahaj* state and a successfully psychoanalyzed individual are discussed by Osborne and Prince (1966).

Because this area of study is new in the Western literature, and because it is heavily encrusted with emic beliefs, it is difficult to encompass and generalize the emerging findings. Here we will touch briefly on only three aspects: (1) attempts at categorization of meditation techniques, (2) some examples of techniques, and (3) review of the evidence for therapeutic effects of meditation and the proposed psychological mechanisms involved.

In attempting to come to grips with the psychological aspects of meditation, we are immediately struck by two rather disconcerting features. The first is the remarkable profusion of techniques that have been described, and the second is the inadequacy of most of the descriptions available. This latter problem is no doubt aggravated by the secrecy and cultishness that surrounds many traditions of meditation. Even with Transcendental Meditation, which is said to be stripped of its esoteric trappings in order to adapt it to the needs of the modern world (and indeed which relies heavily on scientific studies to demonstrate its validity), there is still much cultishness involved. At the time of initiation into the practice, the devotee is given a *mantra*—a Sanskrit verbal formula—that is said to be individualized to his or her own needs and must be kept secret. And this secrecy applies even to this most elementary stage of the practice where the broad procedures are well known (e.g., the students close their eyes and dwell upon their *mantra* twice a day for some twenty minutes; they are instructed that when thoughts intrude they are simply to observe them and let their minds come back to the *mantra*). Descriptions of the more advanced stages of the practice have not been published and are transmitted only by personal teaching (Goleman, 1972). Further difficulties associated with the observations at the psychologist's disposal include the fact that many descriptions are rife with culture-bound descriptive words that are often ill-defined. Some descriptions are of important practices that no longer exist, and the psychologist must rely on translations from archaic esoteric manuscripts, whose authors wrote them from a point of view very foreign to the needs of a student of comparative psychology.

In spite of these difficulties, a number of typologies of meditation have already appeared. Naranjo and Ornstein (1971) divided meditation practices into three overlapping types according to the object the meditator is instructed to "dwell upon": (1) *concentrative or absorptive meditation,* which employs externally given symbols such as holy diagrams or *mantras* (verbal formulas); (2) the *way of self-expression,* in which the individual dwells upon material deriving from his own inner fantasy; and (3) the *negative way,* in which the meditator puts his efforts into moving away from all objects and avoiding identification with anything he can conceive of.

These authors cast their net very broadly and include some practices—such as voluntary possession states—that others would no doubt exclude from the concept of meditation. They include possession trances in their category of "expressive meditation," and indeed it must be admitted that there is an almost imperceptible gradation between practices involving physical movements (such as in the Japanese Shingon tradition described by Blacker, 1972) that are clearly meditation practices, through Sufi dances, to the possession trances of West Africa, and these authors may well be right, at least from a psychological point of view, in lumping them all together.

A second attempt at categorization was made by Goleman (1972), who divides meditation practices according to the ultimate state of consciousness achieved rather than by the techniques employed. He tends to reject Ornstein's category of "expressive meditation" on the grounds that it is characterized by a state of consciousness in which discursive thought still occurs—a state that in his view cannot properly be called a meditative state of consciousness. Indeed, Goleman feels that the "expressive way" may actually inhibit genuine meditational states of consciousness, "since by acting out every impulse one may reinforce patterns of thought and desire, strengthening these habits of mind so as to enhance their power to hinder transcending the sphere of thought."

Goleman accepts the other two categories but alters them to relate to the kind of consciousness produced. Concentrative meditation becomes "the way of concentration," which leads to *samadhi* (mind merging with the object of meditation in unity); the negative way becomes the "way of insight," which culminates in *nirvana* (mind watches its own workings until cessation or nothingness). He also points out that there are meditation traditions in which the paths of concentration and of insight are integrated. He therefore again arrives at a threefold but more restrictive typology. The Goleman typology would probably fit better with commonly held ideas about meditation. Naranjo's would include such practices as the imaginative exercises of psychosynthesis (Assagioli, 1965), the directed daydream of Desoille (1965), and Jung's "symbolic realization," as well as the wide variety of possession trances already mentioned. Goleman excludes all these.

Regarding specific meditation techniques, that of Transcendental Meditation has already been noted. Humphreys (1935/1970) describes a variety of others. A common practice is for the meditator to count his breaths with eyes closed; the beginner should count from one to ten, fifty times at a sitting. A second method is the attempt to form clear-cut mental images by gazing at a simple object, such as a two-dimensional diagram, with complete concentration, then closing the eyes and attempting to visualize the diagram in great detail; or he may visualize various colours, again closing the eyes and trying to fill his visual field with a particular colour.

Other techniques call for a more religious orientation. Let us consider the example of the cluster we might designate as the "repetition of the divine name" technique. A very similar pattern exists in widely varying cultures and religious traditions—the Sufi, bhakti yogi, Eastern Christian, and probably in others. The *zikr*, the remembrance or repetition of the divine name is one of the most important meditation techniques in Sufism. Detailed descriptions are provided by Arberry (1950) and Naranjo and Ornstein (1971). In brief, the subject seats himself cross-legged in a dark, private room facing Mecca. While maintaining wakefulness, he repeats frequently and with profound veneration the verbal formula "La Ilaha Illa'llah." He should think in his heart of the meaning of the formula: "I want nothing, seek nothing, love nothing but God." The *zikr* is first repeated aloud as described, but subsequently it becomes lodged in the "heart" and repeats itself ceaselessly of its own accord. As Landolt (1965) expresses it: "the mystic realizes being eternally 'mentioned,' as an existing being, by God."

An interesting description of how this *zikr* technique and its effects appear to an outsider is provided by the nineteenth century French physician and traveller, Jacques Moreau (1845/1973). Travelling up the Nile, he asked his Islamic boatmen to demonstrate their method of prayer:

> Sitting close to one another, legs crossed, they began by repeating the refrain of the hymn that one of them was chanting. I saw their heads move imperceptibly from right to left and from front to back. This movement became faster and faster, and the rest of the body soon followed. Allah, la, la, lah! This invocation, uttered at first in a firm, clear voice, soon degenerated into a kind of growl, a hollow, irregular sound that was painful to the ear. Finally, after more than a half-hour devoted to this increasingly violent and disorderly agitation, one of them, a young man of twenty-three or twenty-four, more excited than his companions, beat his head against the boards of the boat with such force that I thought he would break it. Two other sailors tried to restrain him. The fanatic quickly stood up, as if he had been propelled by a lever. Light convulsive movements appeared, and then he fell exhausted. His face was red and inflamed, the veins of his neck enlarged and bluish, as if ready to burst. His expression was dazed, his head leaned sharply backwards. His eyes were constantly lifted toward the sky. This state lasted nearly two hours! (p. 151)

A highly similar method is practiced in the meditation tradition of the Christian East. Here the verbal formula is "Lord Jesus Christ, Son of God, have mercy on me a sinner." Once again the recitation of the prayer commences during periods of withdrawal in a silent room, and once again there is the progress towards inwardness that Ware (1974) describes as follows: (1) Initially the Jesus Prayer is an oral prayer like any other, repeated with the lips, either aloud or silently. (2) In course of time it grows more inward, until eventually the mind repeats it secretly without any outward movement. (3) Finally the prayer descends from the head into the heart and from there it dominates the entire personality. . . . As it enters the third state it grows increasingly spontaneous, singing within a man of its own accord, its rhythm identifying more and more closely to the movements of his heart.

Finally, let us turn to a brief description of the *japa* tradition—the repetition of the divine name in *bhakti yoga*. We are more familiar with this tradition than with the other two because an example of it—the Hare Krishna movement—was recently introduced into North America by Swami Prabhupada. Groups of devotees dressed in saffron robes may be seen on the streets of many large cities dancing and chanting the divine name.

The verbal formula used in Prabhupada's groups is *Hare Krishna, Hare Krishna, Krishna Krishna, Hare Hare, Hare Rama, Rama Rama, Hare Hare.* The purpose of the *japa* is to revive transcendental or Krishna consciousness that has become buried and adulterated by our involvement with matter (Prabhupada, 1970).

As in the other traditions, there are three levels of *japa*: verbal, silent verbalization, and mental. Each successive form of *japa* is regarded as ten times more efficacious than the preceding one (Poddar, 1965). Aids to accomplishing this constant remembering include gearing the recitation to each breath, or to each pulse. Some suggest that the neophyte practice *japa* for a minimum of six hours a day (Poddar, 1965).

Let us now summarize the techniques and results of this "remembrance of the divine name" cluster of meditation practices. The devotee is instructed to find himself a quiet place and dwell upon the appropriate divine name; he must recite the name aloud while deeply considering its meaning. Special breathing instructions are also included in all three practices, as is the gearing of the recitation to the pulse, though these are aids and not essential according to most texts. In each case, after a variable period of practice, a radical, transitory alteration of consciousness may be experienced. With practice, and in a way that is not well described, a process of internalization occurs so that the divine name becomes implanted, as it were, in the depths of the personality; it "repeats itself" at a subvocal level not only during periods of meditation but during the devotee's entire daily round and during sleep as well. In many texts, it is stated that the devotee often undergoes a profound personality change. "When a person loves the Lord, the whole universe becomes dear to him . . . his whole nature is purified and completely changed" (Vivekananda, 1964).

What evidence is there that there are psychotherapeutic effects from meditation practices and mystical states associated with them? In considering this question, it is clear that although meditation is generally seen as a technique for arriving at mystical experiences, many practitioners achieve this experience only after several years of meditation, or perhaps they never experience it. It is also clear that meditation is often psycho-therapeutic in itself, apart from whether or not a mystical experience is achieved.

As far as the therapeutic effects of meditation alone are concerned, most work has been done on Transcendental Meditation (TM). Earliest reports pointed out its use as an alternative to drug abuse (Robbins, 1969; Benson & Wallace, 1972); it has also been advocated as a means of calming tensions (Peerbolte, 1967; Goleman, 1971). Seeman, Nidich, and Banta (1972) showed its value as a means of self-actualization. More recently, an interesting study by Glueck and Stroebel (1975) provides evidence of its value in the treatment of psychiatric disorders in a hospital setting. Prince, Goodwin, and Engelsmann (1976) report the value of TM in reducing stress and improving ego functions in some 65 percent of meditators, 8 percent reported adverse effects, and the remainder reported no effects.

How do mystical experiences and meditation bring about their thera-peutic effects? There are both psychological and physiological hypotheses. As regards mystical experiences, they have been considered regressions in the service of the ego (Maupin, 1962; Prince & Savage, 1965). Prince (1973) suggested that the therapeutic effect was the result of "the knowledge that the self is part of the All and therefore in some sense immortal; that the fundamental nature of the All is beneficent; and most important, that these beliefs are indubitable because they derive from immediate experi-ence." Another hypothesis holds that mystical experience represents the activation of the mode of consciousness associated with the right cerebral hemisphere (holistic, nonverbal, analogical) as opposed to ordinary left hemisphere consciousness (sequential, verbal, and digital), with the result that the individual has increased adaptive powers through the greater use of all his coping mechanisms (Ornstein, 1972; Fischer, 1972; Prince, 1978). As regards the therapeutic effects of meditation (apart from the mystical experience), Deikman (1963) has argued quite convincingly for the impor-tance of "de-automatization." Automatization was a word coined by Hartmann (1958) to designate the well-known phenomenon that in the building up of motor and perceptual habits, considerable amounts of at-tention energy are first required, but subsequently the process becomes automatic with attendant savings in energy. Gill and Brenman (1959) next developed the concept of de-automatization in connection with their theorizing about hypnosis. "De-automatization is, as it were, a shake-up which can be followed by an advance or a retreat in the level of organiza-tion" (p. 178). They believed that a manipulation of attention upon the psychological structure to be de-automated was necessary. Deikman (1963, 1966a, 1966b) then utilized the concept to explain his observations on changes in perception reported by experimental meditation subjects. He believed that meditation resulted in an inhibition of abstraction and an intensification of perception. He felt that de-automatization did not repre-

sent a regression but rather an undoing in order to permit a new and perhaps more advanced kind of experience. "A crayfish sloughs its rigid shell
when more space is needed for growth" (1963, p. 342).

At the same time it is becoming clear that some meditation techniques
may also result in more or less profound physiological changes. These
changes have been related by some (Fischer, 1971; Benson, Beary, & Carol,
1974) to the physiologically restorative trophotropic response first described by Hess (1957), which is the opposite of Cannon's "flight or fight"
response. The trophotropic response is integrated in the anterior hypo-
thalamus and is characterized by decreased oxygen consumption, heart
rate, respiratory rate, and arterial blood lactate, as well as increased skin
resistance and increased slow-wave activity in the EEG. Benson et al.
(1974) point out that this response may also be elicited by relaxation techniques other than meditation, such as Jacobson's (1938) progressive relaxation methods and autogenic training (Luthe, 1963). These physiological
effects are generally said to be considerably greater than those of sleep
(Wallace, 1970).

Although the concept of meditation and mystical experiences as a
form of psychotherapy is relatively new, the field is rapidly burgeoning.
There are already two journals devoted to the exploration of the field—*R.
M. Bucke Memorial Society Newsletter-Review* and the *Journal of Transpersonal
Psychology*. The American Psychiatric Association set up a special subsec-
tion on Mysticism and Religion in 1974.

Dissociation States

One of the most remarkable features of the human psyche is its ability to
dissociate. In a general way dissociation can be defined by reference to
three characteristics: (1) an altered state of consciousness, (2) the retention
of more or less full control of sensory and motor systems, as well as other
ego functions (memory, judgement, problem solving, and so forth), and
(3) after a return to everyday consciousness, a more or less complete amnesia for the period of alteration. It will be noted that this state is different
from the dreaming state in that in REM sleep there is loss of ego control;
and from mystical states in that memory about the altered state is more
complete in mystical states, as is also true of the hallucinatory states that
we will consider presently. Dream states, mystical states, and hallucinatory states are experiences of one's own ego, whereas in dissociated states,
another ego takes control.

Although dissociated states are found all over the world (Bourguignon, 1968) many questions about them remain unanswered. For example,
we do not know whether dissociation is a part of the psychic repertoire of

the majority of individuals or is a special talent of a few: Belo (1960) reports that all the members of some Bali villages can dissociate, and Bateson and Mead (1942) indeed assume that everyone in Bali has the capacity to do so. Lee (1968) reported that about half of the adult male population of a !Kung bushman community were involved in dissociated behavior. Nor do we know the relationship between hypnotic somnabulistic states, sleep walking, or psychomotor epilepsy and dissociated states (Prince, 1968a). Many questions about dissociation must await neurophysiological studies for clear answers; unlike dream states, hallucinatory states, and mystical states, these dissociated states are virtually virgin territory for physiology (Prince, 1968a).

Among Euro-American cultures at the present time, dissociation states are used in some religious settings such as the snake-handling cults of the American Southeast (La Barre, 1962), spiritualist congregations, and by secular mediums, but for the most part they are used psychopathologically—as a means for an individual to escape from an intolerable personal difficulty. Such phenomena are more common in the lower-class levels of Euro-American society; an individual in difficulty will find himself far from home, having forgotten how he got there and even perhaps who he is. Cases of multiple personality probably represent somewhat similar phenomena.

But dissociation states are widely employed in most other cultures for a variety of reasons, many of which are not related to individual psychopathology. Indeed, quite frequently they are used in psychotherapeutic systems. The outstanding feature of these dissociation states, which gives rise to such heterogenous use, is that they permit fully purposive behaviour without individual responsibility; the locus of control of the behaviour is shifted to other persons or agencies according to situational and cultural needs. We find then that dissociation states can be used by individuals enacting specific roles in culturally or politically important dramas—as among the Calabari (Horton, 1960) or the Dahomians (Herskovits, 1938) or they may be used in cult settings where the roles enacted during dissociation are clearly defined. But there is also considerable leeway for individual improvisation, as in the bori cult (Oesterreich, 1966) among the Hausa, or among a variety of cults of the West African Yoruba (Prince, 1974); or the behaviour of the possessed may be largely individually determined, as in some of the Christian-influenced churches of Accra in Ghana (Kilson, 1968). In other circumstances, as with the !Kung bushmen (Lee, 1968), the dissociated individuals are not seen as acting out roles or speaking with the voice of the Holy Spirit, but merely as working up a special energy within their bodies.

Walker (1972) has suggested that the degree to which dissociated behaviour is institutionalized is related to the length of time required for initiation into the practice and the extent to which the dissociated state is psychotherapeutic. The more formalized and culturally patterned states call for the longest periods of initiation. In Dahomey (Herskovits, 1938), learning to dissociate in an acceptable manner may take several years, and in a variety of Yoruba cults and possession cults in Bahia, initiation may take a number of weeks (Prince, 1974); in less institutionalized forms of possession, there may be no period of initiation. Walker's point that psychotherapeutic effects may be greater in less institutionalized settings, while theoretically interesting, lacks adequate evidence. The least institutionalized kinds of dissociation are of course the spontaneous dissociated states that are often regarded as illness, while some quite highly institutionalized examples are specifically and perhaps exclusively used for psychotherapeutic purposes, as exemplified by the bori cults (Oesterreich, 1966, pp. 253–262; Lombard, 1967; Nicolas, 1970).

In spite of radical differences in usage and setting, dissociated states share a number of characteristics which suggest a common neurophysiological substrate:

1. Dissociation is often achieved through dancing and music that features a pronounced and rapid beat.
2. Dissociation often follows a period of starvation and/or overbreathing.
3. The onset of the state is often marked by a brief collapse, or swoon.
4. In the neophyte, collapse may be followed by a period of hyperactivity; in cults featuring role playing, once initiation has been completed, a controlled, deity-specific behaviour pattern emerges during dissociation.
5. During dissociation there is frequently a fine tremor of the head and limbs; sometimes grosser, convulsive jerks occur. A diminution of sensory acuity may be evident.
6. Return to normal consciousness is followed by a sleep of exhaustion, from which the subject awakens in a state of mild euphoria with more or less complete amnesia for the period of dissociation.

But to turn to dissociated states as they are used specifically for psychotherapy, we find two broad patterns. The first involves the dissociation of the healer himself, while in the second it is the patient who becomes dissociated. In the latter pattern the healer may or may not dissociate. The zar cult exemplifies a psychotherapeutic system in which both healer and patient are dissociated.

The zar cult is widespread in the Middle East. Zar is a term for a variety of illnesses usually suffered by women, as well as a class of spirits who are believed to cause these illnesses through possession. Treatment procedures include diagnosis of the illness as being caused by zar possession, the identification of the particular zar involved by means of a dialogue between the healer and the patient while both are in a dissociated state, and finally the determination of what the zar wants in the way of gifts in order to alleviate the suffering of the patient. In most cases the zar is not exorcised but mollified, and subsequently becomes a kind of guardian angel for the patient. The relationship between the patient and zar may be lifelong and require annual ceremonies and gifts financed by the patient and her husband or family.

According to Oesterreich (1966) zar was described in travelers' accounts in Ethiopia in 1868, in Mecca in 1889, and in Egypt in 1901. More recent accounts have reported the cult as being active in Iran (Modarressi, 1968), Iraq (Bazzoui & Al-Issa, 1966), Kuwait (Kline, 1963), the Sudan (Bassher, 1967) and in Somaliland (Lewis, 1961). The nature of the illnesses caused by zar and the details of its treatment vary somewhat according to region. Kennedy's (1967) account of the cult among the Egyptian Nubians along the upper Nile is perhaps the most detailed. Common symptoms caused by zar in this area are insomnia, anorexia, and behavioural abnormalities such as withdrawal or agitation. Patients involved with zar are usually young married women (which is true in other areas as well with the exception perhaps of Iran and Kuwait). Among the Nubians, the cult leader determines that the illness is due to zar by divination, using special incense; the patient trembles violently if a zar is involved. Once diagnosed as zar sickness the healer calls for a two- to seven-day ceremony. The participants assemble in a large dimly lit room; from thirty to 100 women may attend. The main patient is usually dressed as a bride in white, heavily perfumed, and wearing as much gold jewelry as she can muster. The ceremony begins with drumming and dancing. Each song is specific to a different zar spirit. When a spirit associated with the patient or with some person in the audience is called, the patient makes her way to the central dancing area and dances and trembles until she falls exhausted to the floor. The dissociated healer discusses with the possessing zar the nature of the gift required. This is usually jewelry, new clothing, or exotic foods. It is the duty of the relatives and friends of the subject to gather round and pacify the spirit. During the ceremony, the healer or one of the possessed participants may engage in fortune-telling and prescribing of cures for others in the audience. There are also animal sacrifices; the animal's blood is rubbed over the face and body of the possessed, and the blood may also form part of a potion the patient is required to drink. As a conclusion of the ceremony, the patient leads the other possessed participants to the Nile, where all bathe their faces and bodies. Sometimes the patient is advised to sit for forty days in seclusion, like a bride. Kennedy believes that zar activities relieve symptoms and bring about improvements of social functioning. Most patients who profit are suffering from psychoneuroses, but psychotic patients may also find relief.

In some cultures, the demands of the zar may be satisfied symbolically rather than realistically, as described in the previously mentioned Iroquois dream system. For example, among the Amhara of Ethiopia, Messing (1958) noted that a zar whose symbol was the lion might demand that a tawny-coloured goat be sacrificed at regular intervals, and Modarressi (1968) described an example from South Iran in which a zar demanded a castle of gold and the healer had a model of a golden castle built which he gave to the patient. It is also interesting that in South Iran the zar may demand that he "be beaten with a bamboo stick 100 times." Patients whose zars request such beatings are usually sailors who go to sea for a month or two and return directly to the zar cult for their periodic beatings. These patients are called "addicts to the father of zar's bamboo stick."

The other major pattern in which dissociation is used in psychotherapy is that in which only the healer is dissociated and not the patient. The healer functions as a medium. This pattern is widespread and occurs among the Palau Islanders in Pacific Micronesia (Leonard, 1973), the Azanda of Central Africa (Evans-Pritchard, 1937), in the Kali cult among the Asiatic Indian population of Guyana (Singer, Araneta, and Naidoo, 1975) and in rural villages in Japan (Yoshida, 1967), to mention only a few. To elaborate upon the technique employed, we will give a brief description of the practice in Ghana, where Field (1960) has provided one of the richest accounts available.

Field describes a new type of healing shrine that has mushroomed among the rural Ashanti and other groups during the last forty years in response to the disorganizing effects of Westernization, particularly the growth of the cocoa industry in the area. The shrines are designed to provide supernatural protection and help for "a population increasingly preoccupied with a sense of insecurity." The shrines are involved both in prevention of illness and in healing. The typical pilgrim comes annually, asks the shrine deity for protection for the year, and promises a thank-offering of a sheep and rum. The deity's protection is granted provided the supplicant behaves well, which means that he does not steal or commit adultery, but most of all that he eschew witchcraft or sorcery. If he breaks the rules the deity will punish him with madness or death. This fate can only be avoided by prompt confession and absolution at the shrine.

Each shrine is presided over by a priest who in most cases has been especially selected by the spirit world through the infliction of illness, usually a psychological disturbance. The priest gives his blessing and, in the case of supplicants who are ill, hears their confessions and gives remedial instructions during a dissociated state. Field's description of the possessed priest is worth quoting:

> After a few moments of mounting expectancy the calico curtain at the sanctuary door is suddenly flung aside and out dart the attendants, the *obrafohene* and the two *akyeame*, and lastly the possessed and quivering priest. The latter takes his stand with his back to the sanctuary door and faces the *dua*. He never varies his style: he stands upright on one spot with folded arms but

with his head shaking unceasingly from side to side in furious agitation, his long tassels of *mpese-mpese* hair flicking like whips round his head, his face mask-like, but his expressionless eyes rolling from side to side and his eyebrows flickering up and down as though worked by machinery. The drums redouble their frenzied beating, the gong-gong its iron clatter and the horn its piercing cries. After another minute or so he raises a hand to silence the drums. (pp. 99–100)

The supplicant will approach the possessed priest and tell his story. From time to time the priest may ask for elaborations. He speaks in a low monotone that can be heard by only one of his assistants, who then shouts it aloud to the supplicant. The priest may warn the supplicant that he will die, then an assistant steps forward to beg the spirit to relent. The spirit usually relents and requests the sacrifice of a fowl and prescribes potions, special baths, and perhaps an enema. Many shrines have a steady stream of supplicants and the healings go on all day, several days a week. Field's book provides a wealth of case history material on some 150 patients who visited the shrines in the late fifties.

We must finally raise two important questions: Is dissociation in these contexts actually therapeutic, and, if so, why? Regarding the first question, although evidence of therapeutic effects is pretty much anecdotal at the present time, an increasing number of observers have commented on its value in the therapy both of the neuroses and sometimes the psychoses (Kiev, 1962; Torrey, 1972; Sargant, 1967; Crapanzano, 1973; Wittkower, 1970). A few case studies are scattered through the literature (Kennedy, 1967; Lubchansky, Egri, & Stokes, 1970; Prince, 1974). Finally, the work of Akstein (1973) should be mentioned. On the basis of many years of observing various dissociation cults in Rio de Janeiro, he has attempted to strip trance states of their religious connotations and use them in the treatment of psychiatric patients. Rhythmic music, dance, overbreathing and stimulation of the semicircular canals (by body rotation) are all used to induce dissociation. Most patients are able to enter at least a light level of trance. These secularized trances are used along with more orthodox treatment modalities, such as psychotropic drugs and one-to-one psychotherapy. Although no formal evaluation is reported, Akstein believes that trancing adds an important dimension in the treatment of the neuroses and psychosomatic disorders.

Regarding the question of the therapeutic mechanisms involved, in the case of the healer-as-medium pattern, the answer seems simple enough. The spirit speaking through the medium gives the healing instructions special authority; the power of the healer's suggestions is raised an octave or two when delivered during the dissociated state.

In systems in which the patient himself becomes dissociated, the explanation of the therapeutic effect becomes more complex. Among the first to give thought to such questions, Mischel and Mischel (1958) draw attention to the cathartic effects of acting out otherwise prohibited roles (sadistic, aggressive, cross-sex, masochistic, and so forth), as well as the improved social status that accrues to one who is the mount of the gods. The support provided by group membership is also no doubt important. The extent to which the postdissociation euphoria and peacefulness is a separate effect and unrelated to catharsis is not clear. Certainly Pentecostal glossolalics also report this euphoria, even though they do not undergo very much cathartic release. Sargant (1957) has suggested a physiological explanation. Following a Pavlovian model, he believes that the therapeutic effect of dissociation states is due to excessive sensory stimulation (dancing and drumming), which leads to a state of "transmarginal inhibition" with resulting collapse, loss of former conditioned patterns, and a markedly increased susceptibility to the salubrious suggestions of the healer or priest. He sees the therapeutic effect as due to similar mechanisms as are involved in electroconvulsive therapy, brain-washing practices, and Wesleyan types of evangelical preaching and conversion.

As has been noted, cults featuring dissociation may call for lengthy periods of initiation. In explaining the therapeutic effects of such cults, these initiations have been largely neglected. An early exception was Pierre Verger (1954), whose writings in French have not received the attention they deserve. Verger described in detail the elaborate and lengthy initiation procedures of *orisha* cults in Dahomey and explained them using a conditioned reflex model. He saw initiation as the creation in the subject of a secondary personality through the development of a totally new set of "conditioned reflexes" that were much at variance with his old ones. Initiation occurred during a "state of lethargy" induced by herbal infusions. Since "reflexes" are not in the domain of reason, they can be best inculcated during this period of unconsciousness. Neglected for twenty years, the psychotherapeutic effects of initiation exercises have once more been emphasized by a number of recent authors (Walker, 1972; Henney, 1974; Prince, 1974; Jilek, 1974; Jilek & Todd, 1974).

In reviewing the initiations of a variety of cults among the Yoruba and Yoruba-influenced cults in Brazil, Prince (1974) noted the following general features:

1. There is a period of seclusion lasting from seven to thirty days or even longer. This is followed by several months of vulnerability and reduced social activity during which the individual continued to be closely involved with the cult group.
2. The symbolism of the initiation procedures communicates a sloughing off of the old life or personality and the progressive incorporation of the new personality—the familiar death and rebirth theme.
3. On a psychological level, during initiation there are marked alterations of consciousness generated by drumming and singing, the powerful

suggestive forces of the ritual symbolism, as well as potent herbal substances. The tranquilizer *rauwolfia* may be used in the Yoruba initiations.

4. During the altered state of consciousness the initiate behaves like a young child, during which he is taught a large body or lore associated with the cult. The "child" of the spirit is moulded into the mature cult member by the cult "mother."

5. Some potential exists (in at least some of the cults) for the matching of the secondary personality (the spirit personality) to the psychological needs of the primary personality. (Research into this latter phenomenon is much needed, however.)

One of the best described initiation procedures—as well as evaluations of their therapeutic effect—is that of Salish Indians of British Columbia (Jilek, 1974; Jilek & Todd, 1974). During the winter festival a prospective candidate is "grabbed" by husky ritual aides. He is restrained, blindfolded, and clubbed. Although the clubbing is symbolic, some candidates react as if actually killed and enter a cataleptic state—they become "stiff as a board." Others require extensive treatment to enter the "death state," and this is provided by sensory overload consisting of very loud drumming as well as excessive kinetic, tactile, temperature, and pain stimuli. Resurrected after his "death," the "newborn" initiate is confined to a dark tent for a period of at least four days. No herbal substances are used. Regression is imposed and he is treated like a baby—bathed, fed and dressed, and constantly attended by a "nursemaid." He is also required to fast and not allowed to drink. Such procedures enable the initiate finally to perceive his own spirit dance and song, as well as see his tutelary spirit in an oneiroid vision. A period of "hardening physical training," associated with intensive cultural indoctrination, follows in order "to make the baby strong." After release from incubation, he is dressed in the traditional uniform and engages in strenuous dances spurred by rhythmic drumming, chanting, and clapping of hands. Subjects report intense feelings of bliss during these dances. One of the dancers, a former heroin addict, described this bliss as "closely akin to the thrill he experienced after heroin injection." Once initiated, the devotee continues to dance on frequent occasions each winter festival (from November till April).

Cult leaders consider those suffering from depression, anxiety, and somatic complaints—as well as those with behavioural and alcohol problems—as suitable candidates for initiation. Treatment results of twenty-four initiates are provided by Jilek (1974). In this series two candidates did not improve and one deteriorated; the remainder showed varying degrees of symptomatic or behavioural improvement. Of course, the follow-up period was less than a year in some cases so the final picture may not be so rosy. Five case histories are provided by Jilek and Todd (1974).

Shamanic "Ecstasy"

We turn now to a less clearly defined type of alteration of conscious-ness—the so-called ecstasy associated with the great circum-Pacific sha-manic traditions. The geographic heartland of shamanism[2] seems to be Central and North Eurasia, with widespread diffusion to Southeast Asia, the islands of the Pacific and the Americas. There is some controversy over whether the ecstatic experience was originally generated by psyche-delic substances or by drumming, dancing, asceticisms, and so forth. The scholarly historian of religion, Mircea Eliade (1951) is the most vocal pro-ponent of the nondrug view, while Wasson (1968) has championed the drug-use position.

Fundamental is the belief that during ecstasy the shaman voyages to the upper world of spirits or to the underworld of demons to obtain infor-mation about illness or misfortune or in quest of the kidnapped soul of the patient. An important variant is the belief that during his ecstasy the sha-man may command his spirit assistants to make the voyage. Associated with this supernatural voyage are a cluster of props, beliefs, and symbolic behaviours, including (1) the "world tree" by means of which the shaman travels up or down to the other worlds, (2) the characteristic shallow drum, the beating of which gives the shaman wings for his voyage, (3) the head-dress, which often includes real or symbolic reindeer horns, (4) an altar or sacred enclosure, (5) tobacco smoke, (6) the concept of rebirth from bones, (7) a wide variety of sleight-of-hand or conjuring tricks to demonstrate the shaman's supernatural powers (tent shaking, ventriloquism, breaking out of bonds, and so on), and (8) blood sacrifices (horse, reindeer, human flesh, or other). The extraordinary penetration and survival power of these symbols is illustrated by their highly similar manifestations in areas thou-sands of miles from their presumed Siberian homeland as, for example, among the Huichol of Western Mexico (Furst, 1973), the Mapuche of Chile and Argentina (Faron, 1968), the Warao of the Orinoco delta (Wil-bert, 1973), and among the Himalayan shamans of Nepal (Hitchcock, 1973). Of course, in some specific examples of the tradition the symbols and techniques have undergone extensive transformations. In the more characteristic examples the shaman himself enters ecstasy and his patients do not, the ecstasy is apparently unrelated to drug use, and there is much less likely to be dissociation and the imagery of spirit possession. In some of its transformations, however, the patient as well as the healer enter an altered state of consciousness. The ASC may be a typical dissociated state, in which case the system becomes similar to that of zar possession pre-viously described. Finally, there are numerous examples of drug-induced ecstasy in which both the healer and the patient may be involved.

It should be pointed out that a psychological understanding of shamanism is especially difficult because of ideological suppression in several important geographic areas. Shamanism in the Siberian heartland has been discouraged by the USSR because it is felt that the shamanic system promotes an elitist social structure (Anisimov, 1963). North American Eskimo shamanism has been all but eliminated because of large-scale conversions to Christianity after 1935 (Murphy, 1964; Balikci, 1967). Suppression of Amerindian shamanism has not been so successful, but it commenced in the sixteenth and seventeenth centuries with the arrival of Catholic priests in the New World. Because of these suppressions, the psychologist must often rely upon travelers' accounts or those of nineteenth-century anthropologists and missionaries who were not psychologically oriented.

What is the shamanic ecstasy like? Let us begin with a description of the Evenks of Siberia (Anisimov, 1963).

The ceremony took place in a specially built tent surrounded by wooden figures of the shaman's spirit helpers (ancestral spirits, salmon, reindeer, pike, and so forth). The shamanistic tree—a young larch—was placed in the centre of the tent with its top passing out through the smoke hole. In preparation for the seance the shaman fasted, smoked to excess, and entered "a neurotic sleep accompanied by vivid dreams" in which he sent his spirit helpers to the lower world to get advice from the ancestors regarding how the ceremony should be conducted.

During the ceremony proper, the tent was in semidarkness, and a small fire was lit near the base of the larch tree. A number of clansmen and the patient leaned against the sides of the tent. The atmosphere was of excited expectation. The shaman donned his special robes, breastplate and footwear, and put on a cap and an iron crown that bore representations of reindeer horns. The shaman began slowly beating his drum and singing songs summoning his spirits. "The listeners with bated breath awaited the appearance of the spirit. The ensuing silence was broken by a sharp blow on the drum, changing into a short roll. In the silence following this, the voices of the spirits could be clearly heard: the snorting of beasts, birdcalls, and the whirring of wings . . ." (p. 101). Each of the shaman's helping spirits were summoned in this way in turn.

His spirits assembled, the shaman assigned them to various tasks. One, the *khargi*—his animal double—he instructed to go to the lower world to learn the cause of the illness. This journey to the lower world was then described in songs accompanied by furious drumming during which the shaman passed into ecstasy.

One or two deafening beats were heard and the shaman leaped from his place. Swaying from side to side, bending in a half-circle to the ground and smoothly straightening up again, the shaman let loose such a torrent of sounds that it seemed everything hummed, beginning with the poles of the tent, and ending with the buttons on the clothing. Screaming the last parting words to the spirits, the shaman went further and further into a state of ecstasy, and finally throwing the drum into the hands of his assistant, seized with his hands the thongs connected to the tent pole and began the shamanistic dance—a pantomime illustrating how the *khargi*, accompanied by the group of spirits, rushed on his dangerous journey fulfilling the shaman's commands. . . . The shaman leaped into the air, whirled with [the help of] the tent thongs, imitating the running and flight of his spirits, reached the highest pitch of ecstasy, and fell foaming at the mouth on the rug which had been spread out in the meanwhile. The assistant fanned the fire and bent over the shaman's stiffened, lifeless body. The latter, representing at this moment his *khargi* in the land of the *khergu* (the world of the dead), was outside of this seeming corpse. . . . The shaman began to show signs of life. A weak, half-understandable babble was heard—the barely audible voices of the spirits. This signified that the *khargi* and the spirits accompanying him were returning to the middle world. The shaman's assistant put his ear to the shaman's lips and in a whisper repeated to those present everything that the shaman said was happening at the time to the *khargi* and his spirits. The shaman's weak, barely audible whisper changed into a loud mutter, unconnected snatches of sentences, and wild cries. . . . The shaman leapt up and began to dance the shamanistic pantomime dance symbolizing the return of the *khargi* and his attendant spirits to the middle world (*dulu*). The shaman's dance became more and more peaceful, its movements slow. Finally, its tempo slowed, the dance broke off. The shaman hung on the thongs, swaying from side to side in time with the drum. Then, in recitative, he told the onlookers about the *khargi's* journey to the other world and about the adventures that had happened. Freeing himself from the thongs, the shaman returned to his place. He was given the drum. The shaman's song was again heard. The shaman transmitted the advice of the ancestor-spirits as to how the evil spirit of the disease should be fought, put the drum to one side, and paused. Someone from among the onlookers offered him a lit pipe. Pale and exhausted, the shaman began avidly to smoke pipe after pipe. With this the first part of the performance ended.* (Anisimov, 1963, p. 101)

The performance continued with a variety of attempts to induce the disease spirit to leave the body of the patient. The shaman held a dialogue with the spirit—entreating him, cajoling him, commanding him, bargaining with him. Although it is not made clear in the text, the answering spirit voice was evidently provided by ventriloquism rather than through an altered state of consciousness induced in the patient (as found in the zar cult, for example). During this dialogue with the disease spirit, several trips to the other world were necessary to get advice from the ancestors. Finally, the spirit was induced to leave the body of the patient by inviting him to a meal of reindeer blood. A reindeer was sacrificed in the tent and the patient was smeared with blood. When the spirit was at last wheedled out of the patient to eat the blood, the shaman pounced on the patient,

* Reprinted from *Studies in Siberian Shamanism*, edited by Henry N. Michael, by permission of University of Toronto Press. Copyright, Canada, 1963, by University of Toronto Press.

licked off the blood, and spat it upon a wooden spirit image indicating that the spirit had been mastered and consigned to the lower world. Other parts of the ceremony included the divination of the identity of the enemy who had sent the disease spirit; the sending of a troop of spirits to avenge the wrongdoing, and finally the shaman's voyage to the upper world to beseech the high god's protection of the patient's soul in the future. A wooden effigy of the patient's soul was hung at the top of the larch pole.

Eliade (1951) provides a number of similar descriptions of Siberian shamanic ecstasy. Singing, drumming, excessive smoking, and dancing culminate in the shaman's falling to the ground in an apparently unconscious state. After a few minutes to half an hour he revives and reports his exploits. Similar states are reported from the Hindu Kush (Siiger, 1967) and from some Amerindian groups (Murdock, 1965). The distinction between the shamanic ecstasy and the dissociated state should be noted here. In the ecstasy there is loss of motor power but intense subjective experience of a visionary nature that can subsequently be remembered and reported on by the shaman. On the other hand, in the dissociated state the subject engages in highly coordinated motor activity but has amnesia for the period of the altered state.

But having made his distinction, it is clear that even in the Siberian heartland of shamanism, phenomena occur that sound very much like dissociated states. For example, Eliade (1951, p. 251) describes a seance among the Chukshee of Eastern Siberia in which spirit voices suddenly began to be heard from every direction (presumably by ventriloquism); then a spirit entered the shaman, whose head began to shake, and he spoke with a foreign, high-pitched voice which was regarded as the voice of the spirit. We are not told whether the shaman remembered this period of spirit possession or not. Sometimes the shaman takes on the bodily movements and voice of animal spirits. Murphy (1964) reports the following example of Eskimo shamanic behaviour on Saint Lawrence Island:

> When my brother was sick, my grandmother who was a shamaness tried her best to get him well. She did all her part, acting as though a dog, singing some songs at night, but he died. While she was singing, she fell down so hard on the floor, making a big noise. After about fifteen minutes later we heard the tapping of her fingers and her toes on the floor. Slowly she got up, already she had become like a dog. She looks awful. My grandfather told me that he used to hide his face with his drum just because she looks different, changed and awful like a dog, very scary. She used to crawl back and forth on the floor, making big noises. Even though my brother was afraid of her, he tried not to hide his face, he looked at her so that he would become well. Then my grandmother licked his mouth to try to pull up the cough and to blow it away. Then after half an hour she fell down so hard on the floor again. (p. 59)

When we leave the Siberian heartland there appear to be in fact two streams of shamanic development. In the cultures of Southeast Asia and the West Pacific islands, shamanism is much more likely to take on a mediumistic or spirit possession flavour, which at times is indistinguishable from the dissociation phenomena described in the last section. However, as we move into the Amerindian cultures, especially in Mexico and South America, we are much more apt to find drug-induced shamanic ecstasies. A few examples will demonstrate these trends.

Shamanism in Korea has been described by Kim (1972, 1973). Emotional illnesses are treated during a sixteen- to twenty-four-hour ritual known as *goot*. The shaman enters trance by means of drumming and vigorous jumping. He takes on the voice and manner of a possessing spirit and delivers oracles to the patient during this state. In Taiwan (Tseng, 1972), shamans treat chiefly children's illnesses. They enter trance through drumming and monotonous incantations. Possession is marked by shouting and rhythmic shaking. The spirit identifies himself and conducts his interview with the child's parents in the voice of the spirit. When he comes out of the trance he cannot remember what has transpired during the altered state. Rather similar shamanic behaviour has been reported from Japan (Yoshida, 1967; Sasaki, 1969), Okinawa (Lebra, 1969), Malaya (Kramer, 1970), and Nepal (Hitchcock, 1973).

We turn to the other great area of diffusion of shamanism—the Americas—where there are a few groups that approximate the basic Siberian pattern. Hultkrantz (1967), for example, has described the spirit lodge ceremony of the Arapaho of Wyoming. The ceremony was held in a log cabin where some sixty community members collected to participate in the healing. The patient, the shaman, and four drummers attended. The ceremony began with the shaman smoking a ceremonial pipe. All rubbed their bodies with sweetsage for purification. A rectangular enclosure marked out with string contained an altar on which were feathers, gourds, and tobacco. Two young girls came forward and, during a deafening roll of drums, thin slices of skin and flesh were cut from their arms with a razor and placed in a gourd on the altar as a tribute to the spirits. The shaman was covered with a blanket and bound up with ropes. He called for his guardian spirits and was then placed face down on the floor and the lights extinguished. In darkness the drums were beaten furiously and the participants sang loudly to summon the spirits. Then there was silence except for the moaning of the shaman. The spirits arrived and there were sounds of footfalls, an owl's cry, and a "jingling noise." After the relatives of the patient had loudly prayed for his recovery, the shaman announced that he had been told by the spirits that the patient would recover. When the lights were turned on the shaman was sitting on his blanket and the rope that had bound him was neatly coiled at his feet. The ceremony lasted some five or six hours, terminating in the small hours of the morning. It is not clear from the text whether the shaman was regarded as being in ecstasy during any of this procedure, nor is there any mention of a voyage to other worlds either on the part of the shaman or of his helper spirits. No drugs are mentioned except tobacco smoke. Hultkrantz notes that the patient (his illness is not described) "kept fairly well henceforth; at least he did not get worse."

But clearly the most prevalent and most characteristic pattern of shamanizing among the Amerindians, particularly those in Mexico and further south, involves as a central feature a drug-induced ecstasy. The variety of plants and fungi used as a source of these drugs in truly astonishing. Descriptions of them are many, but perhaps the most comprehensive and most available are by Schultes (1969, 1972). Important hallucinogenic drugs contained in these plants include mescaline, D-lysergic acid, psilocybin, dimethyltryptamine, tetrahydrocannabinol, scopolamine, and harmine.

As an example of the main themes and variations of these drug-induced ecstasies in healing, we will consider the *ayahuasca*-using groups of the upper Amazon area. *Ayahuasca* is a vine of the *Banisteriopsis* genus that contains harmine and other active principles. An infusion of segments of the vine is made with water, often with other plant additives to increase its hallucinogenic potency. Dobkin de Rios (1972) and Rios (1973) have described *ayahuasca* use in psychotherapy in Iquitos, a city on the Amazon in Northeast Peru. From three to thirty patients collect in a clearing in the forest. Sessions start about ten in the evening and may go on till dawn. The cup of *ayahuasca* potion is passed around the circle of patients and is finally taken by the healer himself. The potion takes effect in about a half-hour. The patients sit quietly during their visionary experiences; the healer sings special healing songs and shakes a bundle of dry leaves that makes a soothing, rustling sound. For the most part the patients are left to their own experiences, but from time to time the healer will pass from patient to patient, blowing smoke upon him, inquiring about his visions— perhaps interpreting them—reassuring the patient, and boasting about other patients he has healed. At times, when the patient complains of a localized pain, the healer will suck at the area and sometimes draw out a real thorn or worm, which is regarded as the cause of the pain. Rios (1973) emphasizes that the patient's hallucinatory experience confirms this removal even without the concrete demonstrations; he can see the evil leaving his body without any legerdemain. The patient may also experience a great infusion of strength when the healer blows smoke over him or touches his hands with his finger tips. Another important aspect of the *ayahuasca* experience is that the patient or the healer may get a vision of the person who has damaged the patient by witchcraft. The healer is then able to turn back the damaging influence to its source. The visions may also be of various forest animals, particularly of large snakes—"the mother of *ayahuasca.*" It is believed that if the patient can confront the visionary serpent without fear, the serpent will teach the patient his song, and this is a token that the patient will be healed. Dobkin de Rios (1972) provides brief sketches of the life histories of ten patients, but there is little information about treatment efficacy. Rios (1973) estimated that 75 percent of the patients had psychiatric disorders, and he observed that patients came mainly from lower socioeconomic groups.

These healing sessions in Iquitos are used by culturally mixed populations undergoing rapid culture change, but we have also a number of descriptions of *ayahuasca* use by homogeneous Amerindian groups who occupy the rain forest in adjacent areas. Among the Cashinahua (Kensinger, 1973), the entire male population may use *ayahuasca*, and many partake regularly in the all-night sessions, which occur about every two weeks. Participants find the ecstatic experience frightening and unpleasant, but they believe that on the basis of their visionary experience, they can foresee individual or group problems such as illness and famine and can take steps to avoid them. There are shamans who use *ayahuasca* when other methods of healing fail, but it is not clear from the description what special advantages the shamans have over the layman in this regard. Harner (1968/1973) has given an excellent description of Jivaro *ayahuasca* use. About one in four males are shamans. The shaman's supernatural power is regarded as a kind of concrete substance *tsentsak*, which however can only be seen during *ayahuasca* intoxication. The shaman can use this *tsentsak* in the form of a dart to kill or damage a person, and it is then necessary for another shaman to visualize the dart in the patient and remove it. Only the shaman can see this dart and its removal, but the shaman may use a sleight-of-hand dart to generate conviction in the patient and his relatives. Under *ayahuasca*, the *tsentsak* may appear to the shaman as his spirit helpers under his control and from whom he receives information. These may take the form of huge, gaudy butterflies, snakes, jaguars, and so forth. The patient does not take *ayahuasca*, evidently, nor is it taken in a group by nonshamans. But anyone may become a shaman among the Jivaro through apprenticeship under a practitioner, giving him gifts and submitting to various deprivations. Again, healing songs are an important part of shamanizing. In addition to *ayahuasca*, the healer drinks large amounts of tobacco juice. A somewhat smaller proportion of shamans was found among the neighbouring Sharanahua by Siskind (1973). Three out of the twenty-five village males were shamans. Once again, the shaman sought the cause of illness during an *ayahuasca* vision and cured it through singing. There is a wide variety of songs linked with various plants and animals, and the songs are sung in an esoteric language. It is said that if *ayahuasca* is taken without singing, only snakes will appear. The choice of song for the individual patient depends upon his symptoms and his dreams. In the healing ceremony the shaman and the patient's male kin all drink *ayahuasca*. The men chant, the shaman sings the appropriate healing song, and gradually a vision associated with the patient's dream will appear to him. He then takes up the dream images, controls them, and rescues the patient. The common sucking-out procedure is not used. Unlike the Iquitos healing ceremonies, in none of these three forest-living groups does the patient take *ayahuasca*.

Before proceeding to the possible psychotherapeutic mechanisms incorporated in this great shamanic tradition, two further points warrant brief discussion: the first has to do with what Lowie (1940/1967) has called the "democratization of shamanism"; the second, with the controversial question of the psychiatric illness of the shaman.

Regarding the first point, there is an interesting trend among some Amerindian groups for every individual, particularly every male individual, to seek contact with the spirit world. Each man becomes his own shaman as it were. Contact with the spirit world may be through dreams or through drug- or deprivation-induced ecstasies. We have already discussed the importance of individual dream experiences in the lives of some Iroquois groups. Benedict (1923) drew attention to the importance of the vision quest in many North American Indian cultures: the young man would go off into the wilderness without food or water and wander alone until he attained a vision of his guardian spirit. Jilek (1974, pp. 22–36) has reviewed the literature on the dream/vision quest for British Columbia Indians. Often the literature does not clearly distinguish between visionary experience during waking and dream experiences. In cultures that use psychedelic drugs, the democratization process may become even more pervasive, for anyone can have impressive visions at will with such substances. As we have seen, under these circumstances a large proportion of the population may then be involved in frequent visionary experience. At times, this experience may help with problem solving, as with the Cashinahua (Kensinger, 1973), but sometimes psychedelics seem to be used mostly "for kicks," as for example among the Yanomamo as described by Seitz (1967).

Turning now to the question of the psychiatric disorder of the shaman, there are many reports, particularly in the earlier literature on the shamans of the Siberian heartland, that candidates for shamanism are chosen by the spirits (for review, see Eliade, 1964, pp. 33–144) and that an episode of psychiatric disorder is token of vocation (Kraus, 1970; Silverman, 1967; Sasaki, 1969). This selection by illness is not mentioned as a feature of assuming the role of shaman in the cultures in which psychedelic drugs are used to generate the ecstasy. Dobkin de Rios (1972, pp. 99–107) provides brief life histories of four shamans practising in Iquitos, Peru, and does not mention psychiatric disturbances. Chagnon (1968) doesn't mention such divine selection for shamans among the Yanomamo, where he found about half the adult males to be shamans. There is a popular notion that in many cultures the role of shaman (and indeed other types of healers) is occupied by the psychiatrically disturbed. Even distinguished anthropologists have expressed this view (Wallace, 1967; Linton, 1956), which has, however, been vigorously attacked (Torrey, 1974; Boyer, Klopfer, Brawer, & Kawai, 1964; Fabrega & Silver, 1973; Jilek, 1971). Boyer et al. (1964), as well as Fabrega and Silver (1973), systematically compared projective test protocols of native healers with those of "normal" subjects from the same milieus. While healers differed in greater representation of negatively toned impulse-related material, no support was found for the notion of psychotic decompensation among them. The concept of regression in the service of the ego was invoked to characterize the functioning of healers (Boyer et al., 1964).

It is probable that although illnesses, particularly psychiatric illnesses, may commonly be found in the life histories of healers (including psychiatrists and psychologists), it is only when the initiation or other training procedures result in a cure—or relative containment of the disturbance—that the individual can become an accepted healer.

This concept leads us to the question of the psychosis as an endogenous attempt at healing. This idea was perhaps first expressed by Freud (1953c) in connection with the famous case of the German judge, Daniel Schreber. Freud suggested that Schreber's disturbance and other paranoid psychoses should be looked upon as the shattering of an overly rigid ego and the rebuilding of a more adaptive, if somewhat deformed, ego, and somewhat distorted world view:

> The delusion-formation, which we take to be a pathological product, is in reality an attempt at recovery, a process of reconstruction. Such a reconstruction after the catastrophe is more or less successful, but never wholly so; in Schreber's words, there has been "a profound internal change" in the world. But the man has recaptured a relation, and often a very intense one, to the people and things in the world. . . . (Freud, 1953c, p. 457)

Since Freud, many authors have elaborated this theme (Boisen, 1936; Bateson, 1974; Silverman, 1973; Laing, 1967; Mogar, 1968; Gowan, 1975). Most of these authors have indeed gone beyond Freud, pointing out that at least sometimes the personality that emerges out of the chaos of the psychosis is a more integrated and healthy one than the one that entered it; that is, that psychosis can be a highly successful endogenous healing mechanism. There are of course many parallels in medicine. It is common to regard the fever and weakness associated with infectious illnesses as the disease, but in fact, they are the body's attempts at self-healing—the temperature elevation being helpful in destroying the invading pathogenic organisms and the weakness leading to rest, which allows more successful deployment of bodily defences. The same may be said of the pain and muscular contractions associated with fractures. These are not the problem but the body's attempts at immobilization and splinting to allow the bones to knit. In an analogous way, with the psychotic the real problem is his excessive rigidity and difficult life situation; the psychosis represents the breaking down of the ego, causing temporary withdrawal from the life situation, followed by the remoulding of the ego and attitudes that may prove more adaptive.

It should be pointed out, of course, that this positive view of psychosis is not widely accepted by psychiatrists. They commonly regard the psychosis as an undesirable state to be terminated as quickly as possible.

In any case, the production of a brief hallucinatory episode (ecstatic experience, micropsychosis) is a tactic that is widely employed by psychotherapists of the shamanic tradition. Often the micropsychosis is generated within the shaman himself, who may have previously experienced a "spontaneous" psychosis emically interpreted as a call to the vocation. How could this be therapeutic? On the one hand, we can see the ecstasy as therapeutic for the shaman himself in that by repeating his psychotic experience in a controlled setting he is able to strengthen his own reconstituted world view and heighten his own supportive beliefs in it. Regarding its therapeutic value for his patients, just as the impressive performance of the dissociated healer increases his suggestive power, so the shaman, through his remarkable ecstasy bolstered by sensational tricks, gains enormously in prestige and increases the potency of his suggestions. The ecstasy may be of special value when the shaman is called upon to treat a case of psychosis, for he can provide the patient with a demonstration that it is possible to pass into the dreadful realm of spirits and return unscathed. He can go in and out of this realm at will.

In those cultures where the micropsychosis is generated within the patient, either by psychedelic drugs or other means, the therapeutic effect may parallel that of the naturally occurring psychoses, i.e., the breaking down and reconstitution of an overly rigid ego. Of course the affirmation of the world view of the culture is also important. There is an important difference between intellectually believing in the spirit world and actually entering it, seeing the spirits, and communicating with them. Rios's (1973) observation of the importance of actually seeing the pathogenic object removed from the body during hallucinatory experience is a similarly highly convincing procedure employed in some shamanic traditions.

The Changing Attitudes of Western Medicine

Until recently, Western officialdom including Western medicine has harboured a variety of largely negative attitudes towards the non-Western healers and their practices as described in this chapter. Von Wrangel, the famous German traveller, summarized eighteenth-century attitudes as follows: "Almost all those who up to the present have expressed an opinion on the shamans have represented them as unqualified imposters of a crude and vulgar kind, whose ecstasies are nothing more than an illusion created for base purposes of gain" (quoted in Oesterreich, 1966, p. 296). But as we have seen, Western religious leaders often regarded the practices of indigenous healers more seriously, condemning them as forms of devil worship that should be stamped out. As we have also noted, a more recent and more sophisticated view was that the healers are psychotics or severe neurotics.

These denigrating attitudes were intimately linked with the generally patronizing attitudes towards non-Western cultures during the era of European colonial expansion. But dating back to the 1920s, with the emergence of nationalist independence movements, non-Western cultures began to reevaluate their own indigenous strengths and values, including the values of their indigenous medical systems. This medical reevaluation first appeared in India and China and subsequently in Africa and other areas.

In China there is a well-developed indigenous medical system with sophisticated theoretical underpinnings. Contact with Western medicine, through medical missionaries, dates back to 1800, but significant progress in the introduction of Western medicine occurred only with the founding of the Peking Union Medical College at the turn of the century (Bowers, 1971). By 1949, at the time of the Communist takeover, there were said to be only 15,000 Western physicians in the country as opposed to 500,000 indigenous practitioners (Beau, 1972). Nonetheless, Western medicine enjoyed a high prestige, particularly at the governmental level. With the establishment of the Communist regime, Western medicine has developed remarkably, but at the same time, indigenous medicine was officially afforded equal status with Western medicine and attempts were made to integrate the two systems. Traditional schools teach Western medical principles and Western schools provide courses in traditional medicine, including acupuncture and herbal medicine (Critchley, 1973). Somewhat similar developments have occurred in India; the indigenous *ayurvedic* system receives government support and training schools for *ayurvedic* and Western medicine coexist. Western medicine is, however, afforded higher status (Croizier, 1970). More recently, African governments have become interested in their own indigenous medical systems. Special projects and institutes for the investigation of pharmacological activities of herbal medicines have been set up (Bibeau, 1976), and steps are being taken to provide government support and a measure of control over guilds of indigenous practitioners (Land, 1978). All these developments are very recent and are currently receiving a good deal of attention from the World Health Organization (Bibeau, 1976; Singer, 1977).

Needless to say, these innovations have been looked upon with mixed feeling by Western-type medical practitioners, both inside and outside the affected countries (Prince, 1964). Most support for the use of indigenous practitioners in the health system comes from the psychiatric field, and most progress in this regard has been made in Africa. Official support for indigenous "psychiatry" and cooperative relationships between Western psychiatrists and indigenous healers have been developed in many African countries (Kiev, 1972, pp. 182–186) and, outside of Africa, in British Guiana (Singer, Araneta, & Aarons, 1967) and among the Navaho in the American Southwest (Dick, 1971). Even in the area of psychiatric treatment, however, considerable controversy exists over whether this trend is to be regarded with favour. Arguments supporting the use of indigenous practitioners for the treatment of psychiatric cases include: (1) their effectiveness in the management of psychiatric disorders (as has been documented elsewhere in this chapter), (2) the shortage and expense of Western psychiatric facilities and personnel in many parts of the world, (3) their high prestige in many cultures, which makes them acceptable as treatment resources while Western resources are less acceptable, (4) Western psychotherapies seem to be culture bound and not readily transferred to other cultures. Arguments against their use include (1) indigenous practitioners perpetuate the continued belief in primitive world views (such as witchcraft and sorcery) and retard the thrust towards modernization, (2) some of their treatment practices involve danger to the patient (e.g., some practitioners beat their patients, others use unregulated doses of highly potent herbal medicines), (3) some restrict the freedom of patients arbitrarily because relatives will not pay for treatment. These controversial issues have been debated at length in the literature (Prince, 1963b; Finney, 1969, pp. 307–314; Singer, 1977; Torrey, 1972; Swift & Asuni, 1975, pp. 200–201). The future developments in this area will be most interesting to watch.

Is Psychoanalysis Unique?

Thus far in our analysis, one important question has been left largely in abeyance, namely the relationship between the theories and psychotherapeutic processes of psychoanalysis and these other forms of psychotherapy. In approaching this question it is clear that when psychoanalysis made its appearance at the turn of the century, it provided an enormous stimulus to the study of cross-cultural psychotherapies. Freud (1953a) himself commented on the relationship between psychoanalysis and other therapies in 1904. He pointed out that psychotherapy was the most ancient form of therapy in medicine and was widely practised in classical times and among primitives. He did not denigrate these other psychotherapies: "There are many ways and means of practicing psychotherapy. All that lead to recovery are good." But he believed that psychoanalysis was superior in that it penetrated most deeply, carried furthest, and brought about the most extensive transformations. He also drew attention to the fact that psychoanalysis was the only technique that led to understanding of the origins of the illness; other forms of therapy were merely coverups that prevent "pathogenic ideas from coming to expression" by suggestion. Much of the literature on cross-cultural psychotherapy is frankly polemical and aimed at proving Freud and his followers wrong in their claims to the superiority of psychoanalysis (Frank, 1961; Torrey, 1972).

Strupp (1973) has recently advanced our understanding of this problem by demonstrating the value of dividing a given therapeutic system into its theoretical aspects and its practical therapeutic aspects. For psychoanalysis, Strupp concludes that it has made a major contribution to our understanding of human development and the intelligibility of the whole spectrum of neurotic and psychotic disturbances, but he believes that psychoanalysis as a mode of treatment leaves much to be desired. According to Strupp, Freud made the grave error of believing that the patient's understanding of the causes of his neurosis would automatically result in its cure. On the contrary, Strupp feels that when psychoanalysis does result in therapeutic effects it is due to other factors, such as shaping, suggestion, and coercion on the basis of a powerful personal relationship.

Following Strupp's lead, let us compare psychoanalysis with other therapies along these two lines—the theoretical and the practical. Is there anything unique about psychoanalysis from a theoretical point of view? After anthropology's initial shocked disbelief about the findings of psychoanalysis (La Barre, 1958), one of the early responses was that there was nothing much new in analysis, that other cultures had reached the same conclusions using different symbolic formulations. We have already noted Wallace's (1958) views on the similarity between the Iroquois' dream theory and that of Freud. For both, the dreams represented wishes of the soul, and in both views illness ensued if the wishes were not gratified or come to terms with. Horton (1961) pointed out the similarities between the psychoanalytic view of the unconscious and the beliefs of many West African groups in the contract between the self and his heavenly double. Before a man enters the world (i.e., before birth), he makes a contract with his double as to what his work will be, how long he will live in the world, who he will marry, and so forth. Before he enters the world, he embraces the tree of forgetfulness and thereafter forgets his contract. If he does not live up to the contract, however, he will become ill, and it is therefore necessary through divination to maintain contact with his double to make sure he is doing the right thing in life.

More recently, in her extensive work with the Puerto Rican *Espiritistas* in New York City, Garrison (1977) has shown how many of their concepts parallel those of psychoanalysis. This is a system similar to those described earlier in which the healer dissociates and plays the role of a variety of good and bad spirits. For Garrison, the psychoanalysts' superego is equivalent to the *Espiritistas'* protective spirit, who rewards and punishes and guides; the ego is the "individual spirit"; the id is equivalent to the base or ignorant spirits. The only major difference, she feels, is that for the *Espiritistas* the good and bad spirits exist outside the individual's skin, while for the psychoanalyst all three components—ego, superego, and id—are within the individual. Presumably, one could take many other cosmologies and draw more or less valid parallels with psychoanalytic formulations about the self and the origins of conflict. For me the important and distinguishing aspect of the psychoanalytic formulation is that the unconscious aspects are regarded as the results of the individual's early family relationships. No other system that I know of understands the importance of childhood experiences in the genesis of adult behaviour and illness. For me, such differences are of the order of the difference between alchemy and chemistry, or between astrology and astronomy. Let us consider only one practical consequence, the difference between what the analytic and the *Espiritistas'* theoretical approach might be to prevention of psychiatric ills. If one believes that spirits give rise to such illnesses, one might take steps to coerce, mollify, or gratify the spirits so that they would leave the community alone. Based upon psychoanalytic theory, however, one would take steps to improve family relationships; one would attempt to alleviate the interpersonal, economic, and social factors that have a bearing on family disturbances. For me, this is not simply a shift of symbols or a matter of a play on words, but something rather significant. It is like the difference between a belief in clairvoyance and the invention of television!

Does this mean that psychoanalytic formulations are etic principles of human development and psychopathology? Psychoanalysts certainly believe this to be the case (Fenichel, 1955), but one crucial problem obstructs its verification. To validate psychoanalytic theory, it is necessary to apply the psychoanalytic technique cross-culturally, but this technique is impossible to employ beyond a very limited Western-educated elite (Prince, 1963a; Wohl, 1976). "I know of no evidence indicating that classical analysis is possible in non-Western populations except with urbanized and highly literate individuals whose capacities for abstract thought and self-description along Western lines have already been developed to an extraordinary degree" (LeVine, 1973, p. 208). Here we have a problem akin to Heisenberg's in the realm of subatomic physics—in physics the very act of observation changes the subject. Our problem is that the subject has to be changed before the observations can be made!

The psychoanalytic process requires not only a high degree of psychological mindedness but also access to childhood memories. Based on my own cross-cultural experience, I think there is a more extensive blanket of amnesia over childhood experiences in less affluent societies. This may reflect cultural values or may simply mean that a childhood lived on the borders of starvation is mercifully more completely forgotten.

What about the superiority and uniqueness of psychoanalysis as a therapeutic technique? Here again we enter a highly controversial field. Freud (1953b) himself, as we have seen, believed psychoanalysis to be the most effective kind of psychotherapy and contrasted it to the purely suggestive mechanisms of other approaches. He considered the fundamental and unique therapeutic factor in psychoanalysis to be the therapist's interpretation of the phenomena of transference and resistance.

It is interesting that a number of anthropologists have followed Freud in believing that nonanalytic therapeutic techniques are superficial and work by suggestion. Opler (1936), for example, wrote of the Apache healers he studied: "It is fatuous to suppose that the shaman has delved to the roots of the trouble. . . . We could legitimately say that it entails dealing with symptoms alone by the method of suggestion. . . . What relief the patient experiences . . . is bought at the price of too great dependence upon the shaman." Wallace (1967) has similarly adopted the analytic view. "In the interview, the shaman may directly encounter the patient's unconscious conflicts, help him to verbalize them, and thus, *in the manner of any good psychotherapist*, bring them into a state of consciousness, where the ego can begin to deal with them. *To the extent that he is able to do this, the shaman may be able to accomplish real psychotherapy*" (italics mine).

But many authors disagree. With Strupp (1973) they feel that insight and the analysis of the transference in themselves have very little therapeutic value. They see the fundamental therapeutic factors as being the same in all psychotherapies, including psychoanalysis (Frank, 1961; Kiev, 1964; Torrey, 1972; and Calestro, 1972, to mention only a few). These factors include the shared-world view, the warm personal relationship between healer and patient, the expectant hope of the patient, and the high prestige of the healer, all of which feed into the main therapeutic force, i.e., suggestion. Significant support for such a belief is the considerable literature indicating that a patient's attitudes and behaviour can be changed by covert signals by the healer. A psychoanalyst may think he is taking a neutral and nonsuggestive stance, but covertly, by the focus of his interest, the tone of his voice, and his apparently noncommittal remarks he can play a highly directive role (Shapiro, 1971; Marmor, 1975).

With the awareness of this strong body of opinion that the important therapeutic element is suggestion, in this review I have tried to draw out therapeutic techniques that seem to include important nonsuggestive and self-generated mechanisms in many kinds of psychotherapy. A suffering individual may seek self-healing by withdrawal and sleep, and as a self-righting mechanism his ego may automatically employ a variety of altered states of consciousness, including dreams, dissociation, and a variety of so-called religious experiences and psychoses. As we have seen, psychotherapists around the world have learned to generate and control these mechanisms for the relief of suffering.

In what way are altered states of consciousness psychotherapeutic? Often, of course, dissociation states and shamanic ecstasies, especially when they occur in the healer, merely increase his suggestive power. When a healer is regarded as speaking with the voice of an omniscient spirit, his words gain enormously in potency.

As we have seen, dissociation states also permit powerful cathartic effects resulting from the acting out of otherwise unacceptable roles or impulses. This effect is distinct from suggestion and probably also accounts for some of the therapeutic effects of dreams, shamanic ecstasies, and psychoses. The relationship between these expressive or cathartic effects and psychoanalytic theory is interesting. Psychoanalytic theory would hold that symbolic or real expression of dammed-up unconscious impulses would achieve only temporary therapeutic effects. Permanent release from conflict could only result when the censored impulses are affectively and cognitively linked up with earlier and current life experiences—that is, when insight was achieved. Many of the examples cited in this paper have a bearing on this problem; for example, this theory would hold that Aristedes involved with the Asclepian dream therapy would repeatedly need to express his masochistic drives (cutting off his finger, immersions in freezing baths, and so forth) in order to remain stable, which in fact was the case. Some Iranian sailors need regularly to suffer the beating of the father-of-zar's bamboo stick. In fact, this interpretation does seem to make sense in many of the forms of nonanalytic therapy that we have reviewed. Religious rituals used in healing are characteristically cyclical and periodic as opposed to psychoanalysis, which, in theory at least, provides a way out of the repetition compulsion. Presumably, if life's difficulties are transitory, a few cathartic expressions in dreams or dissociated states may suffice to maintain equilibrium. More deep-seated, or long-term problems, might call for much longer periods of involvement in these cathartic systems. Some become addicted to the zar master's bamboo stick! Some psychoses demonstrate this periodicity. MacLean and Robertson (1976) have reported a striking example of a young schizophrenic Jewish male concerned over his sexual identity. He removed his right eye, after which he felt greatly relieved. But four years later he removed his left eye. Presumably the next term in the series would be auto-castration, or suicide. This example also demonstrates one of the objections to the idea that naturally occurring psychoses are attempts at self-healing. The patient may well have felt better after putting out his eyes, but in fact he was blind. The relief of one kind of suffering by producing another cannot be called healing. But as is sometimes said of surgical procedures, "The operation was a success but the patient died," and not every attempt at healing (either endogenous or exogenous) is successful. In fact, this example suggests another function of the healer or healing institution: the substitution of an innocuous symbolic action for a destructive real action. We have seen a number of examples of this shift to the innocuous in this chapter—a Frenchman's coat was substituted for the death of a Frenchman demanded by the dream (p. 305); a ring was accepted as a substitute for the amputation of a finger in the Asclepian example (p. 304); a mock shipwreck for a real shipwreck (p. 303), and so forth. Had the self-blinded patient been in the care of the Asclepian cult he might have been permitted to substitute the breaking of his glasses for his self-enucleation.

Are remembered dreams and shamanic ecstasies potentially more therapeutic than those that are expressed but remain unconscious? I am aware of no evidence bearing on this question. Pfister (1932) is one of the few analysts who has considered the value of uninterpreted symbol expressions. Commenting on Navaho healing rituals and noting that they seem often to provide cures, he asks, "How is it possible that analytic symbols which remain symbols and into which no clear insight is gained, are able to overcome the resistance to cure?" He suggests that intuitively (through divination) the healer is able to select precise symbolic representations of the patient's important conflicts. In the cure the "unconscious of the medicine man speaks to the unconscious of his patient and circumvents consciousness." In doing this, according to Pfister, resistances are avoided that would have been stirred up, should consciousness have been involved. He also believes that this form of therapy can be much briefer in duration and that "compared with mere suggestion the procedure is of far greater effectiveness, for the inner conflict is reached and a social directive given." However, he believed that such cures must often only be temporary. Uninterpreted symbolic images and behaviours are ubiquitous in nonanalytic therapeutic systems (Prince, 1975).

But there are other more obscure psychotherapeutic mechanisms that seem to come into play during altered states of consciousness. As we have seen, religious experiences such as mystical states, religious conversions, and some psychotic states bring about radical changes in values and attitudes. Whether such transformations are best interpreted as neurophysiological mechanisms akin to brain-washing (Sargant, 1957) or as dissolutions and rebuildings of the ego (Freud, 1953a) remains speculative. In any case healing mechanisms, in addition to suggestion and catharsis, seem to be involved.

If we concede that there is a variety of different psychological mechanisms that can be employed for the relief of suffering, are we in a position to say which ones have superior therapeutic power? Unfortunately, we are not. The evaluation of outcomes of psychotherapy, even of those forms practised in the Western world, remain undeveloped and the results controversial. Eysenck (1969), one of the most strident critics of psycho-analysis, has presented data to show that the majority of psychoneurotics improve spontaneously, and that this improvement does not proceed more swiftly or completely with psychoanalytic therapy. But Kernberg (1972) has shown the considerable value of long-term psychoanalytic treatment. Other authors have pointed out the inadequacy of most evalua-tions of psychotherapy (Luborsky & Spence, 1971) and Fiske, Hunt, Lu-borsky, Orne, Parloff, Reiser, and Tuma (1970) have only recently set down the minimal requirements for valid evaluations. Thus far, then, adequate evaluations of psychotherapy have just begun in the Western world. Evaluations of the non-Western forms discussed in this chapter re-main a distant prospect indeed.

But even if some forms of psychotherapy can be shown to provide better outcomes, or are more economical of therapist time or have other advantages when evaluated in their culture of origin, the question of ap-plicability remains crucial. Raincoats are of little use to desert dwellers. We have already seen, for example, that from today's world perspective, only very limited populations are capable of involving themselves in the psychoanalytic process. On the other hand, trance states, religious experi-ences, and micropsychoses in the service of therapy have a much wider applicability.

Notes

1. An earlier draft of this chapter was presented and discussed at the Conference of the Contributors to the *Handbook of Cross-Cultural Psychology*, organized by the East-West Center in Honolulu, Hawaii, in January 1976. The author gratefully acknowledges the comments of the participants at this meeting and is especially thankful for the helpful critique of the chapter by Liwayway Angeles, Angela Ginorio, and N. Howard Higginbotham.

2. Some authors, of course, use the term "shaman" as a loose generic term to des-ignate any kind of "medicine man" or non-Western healer.

References

AKSTEIN, D. Terpsichoretrancetherapy: A new hypnotherapeutic method. *Interna-tional Journal of Clinical and Experimental Hypnosis*, 1973, *21*, 131–143.

ALBEE, G. W. The Protestant ethic, sex, and psychotherapy. *American Psychologist*, 1977, *32*, 150–161.

ANISIMOV, A. F. The shaman's tent of the Evenks and the origins of the shamanistic rite. In H. N. Michael (Ed.), *Studies in Siberian shamanism.* Toronto: University of Toronto Press, 1963, pp. 84–123.

ARBERRY, A. J. *Sufism. An account of the mystics of Islam.* London: Allen and Unwin, 1950.

ASERINSKY, E., & KLEITMAN, N. Regularly occurring periods of eye motility, and concomitant phenomena, during sleep. *Science,* 1953, *118,* 273–274.

ASRANI, U. A. Comments on modes of transcendent experience. *R. M. Bucke Memorial Society Newsletter-Review,* 1967, *2,* 9–11.

————. Personal communication, 1973.

ASSAGIOLI, R. *Psychosynthesis: A manual of principles and techniques.* New York: Hobbs-Dorman, 1965.

BACK, K. W., & BOURQUE, L. B. Can feelings be enumerated? *Behavioral Science,* 1970, *15,* 487–496.

BALIKCI, A. Shamanistic behaviour among the Netsilik Eskimos. In J. Middleton (Ed.), *Magic, witchcraft and curing.* New York: Natural History Press, 1967, pp. 191–209.

BASSHER, T. A. Traditional psychotherapeutic practices in the Sudan. *Transcultural Psychiatric Research,* 1967, *4,* 158–160.

BATESON, G. (Ed.). *Perceval's narrative: A patient's account of his psychosis, 1830–1832.* New York: Morrow, 1974.

BATESON, G., & MEAD, M. *Balinese character.* New York: New York Academy of Sciences, 1942.

BAZZOUI, W., & AL-ISSA, I. Psychiatry in Iraq. *British Journal of Psychiatry,* 1966, *112,* 827–832.

BEAGLEHOLE, E. Emotional release in a Polynesian community. *Journal of Social and Abnormal Psychology,* 1937, *32,* 319–328.

BEARD, G. M. *Sexual neurasthenia (nervous exhaustion).* New York: Putnam, 1884.

BEAU, G. *Chinese medicine.* New York: Avon, 1972.

BELO, J. *Trance in Bali.* New York: Columbia University Press, 1960.

BENEDICT, R. F. The concept of the guardian spirit in North America. *Memoirs of the American Anthropological Association,* 1923, No. 29.

BENSON, H., BEARY, J. F., & CAROL, M. P. The relaxation response. *Psychiatry,* 1974, *37,* 37–46.

BENSON, H., & WALLACE, R. K. Decreased drug abuse with transcendental meditation. In C. J. D. Zarafonetis (Ed.), *Drug abuse. Proceedings of the International Conference.* New York: Lea & Febiger, 1972.

BERELSON, B., & STEINER, G. A. *Human behavior. An inventory of scientific findings.* New York: Harcourt, Brace & World, 1964.

BERNDT, C. H. The role of native doctors in aboriginal Australia. In A. Kiev (Ed.), *Magic, faith and healing.* New York: Free Press, 1964.

BIBEAU, G. Principales orientations de la politique de L'O.M.S. Face à la médecine traditionnelle africaine. In *Médecine traditionnelle au Zaïre et en Afrique.* Kinshasa, Zaire: Institut de Recherche Scientifique, 1976.

BLACKER, C. Methods of yoga in Japanese Buddhism. In J. Bowman (Ed.), *Comparative religion. The Charles Strong Trust lectures 1961–1970.* Leiden: Brill, 1972.

BOISEN, A. *The exploration of the inner world.* New York: Harper, 1936.

BOURGUIGNON, E. World distribution and patterns of possession states. In R. Prince (Ed.), *Trance and possession states.* Montreal: R. M. Bucke Memorial Society, 1968.

———— (Ed.). *Religion, altered states of consciousness and social change.* Columbus: Ohio State University Press, 1973.

BOWERS, J. Z. Founding of Peking Union Medical College—Politics and personalities. *Bulletin of the History of Medicine,* 1971, *45,* 305–321; 409–429.

BOYER, L. B. Folk psychiatry of the Apaches of the Mescalero Indian reservation. In A. Kiev (Ed.), *Magic, faith and healing.* New York: Free Press, 1964.

BOYER, L. B., KLOPFER, B., BRAWER, F. B., & KAWAI, H. Comparisons of shamans and pseudoshamans of the Apaches of the Mescalero Indian reservation: A Rorschach study. *Journal of Projective Techniques,* 1964, *28,* 173–180.

BREGER, L., HUNTER, I., & LANE, R. W. *The effect of stress on dreams.* New York: International Universities Press, 1971.

BUCKE, R. M. *Cosmic consciousness.* New York: Innes, 1901.

BURR, A. R. *Weir Mitchell. His life and letters.* New York: Duffield, 1929.

CALESTRO, K. M. Psychotherapy, faith healing and suggestions. *International Journal of Psychiatry,* 1972, *10,* 83–113.

CAUDILL, W., & DOI, L. Interrelations of psychiatry, culture and emotion in Japan. In I. Galdston (Ed.), *Man's image in medicine and anthropology.* New York: New York Academy of Medicine, 1963.

CHAGNON, N. A. *Yanomamo: The fierce people.* New York: Holt, Rinehart and Winston, 1968.

CRAPANZANO, V. *The Hamadsha. A study in Moroccan ethnopsychiatry.* Los Angeles: University of California Press, 1973.

CRITCHLEY, J. E. Medical education in China. *Medical Journal of Australia,* 1973, *1,* 1005–1007.

CROIZIER, R. C. Medicine, modernization, and cultural crisis in China and India. *Comparative Studies in Society and History,* 1970, *12,* 275–291.

DAWSON, J. Urbanization and mental health in a West African community. In A. Kiev (Ed.), *Magic, faith and healing.* New York: Free Press, 1964.

DEIKMAN, A. Experimental meditation. *Journal of Nervous Mental Disease,* 1963, *136,* 329–343.

————. Deautomatization and the mystic experience. *Psychiatry,* 1966a, *29,* 324–338.

————. Implications of experimentally induced contemplative meditation. *Journal of Nervous Mental Disease,* 1966b, *142,* 101–116.

DEMENT, W. The effect of dream deprivation. *Science,* 1960, *131,* 1705–1707.

————. Psychophysiology of sleep and dreams. In S. Arieti (Ed.), *American handbook of psychiatry* (Vol. III). New York: Basic Books, 1966.

DEMENT, W., & KLEITMAN, N. Cyclic variations in EEG during sleep and their relation to eye movements, body motility and dreaming. *EEG and Clinical Neurophysiology,* 1957, *9,* 673–690.

DESOILLE, R. Le rêve éveillé dirigé. *Bulletin de Societé de Recherches Psychothérapeutiques de Langue Française,* 1965, *3,* 27–42.

DICK, J. The importance of psychic medicine: Training Navaho medicine men. *Mental Health Program Reports.* Rockville, Md.: Department of Health, Education and Welfare, 1971, 5, 20–43.

DIETHELM, O. *Treatment in psychiatry* (2nd ed.). Springfield,: Ill. Thomas, 1950.

DOBKIN DE RIOS, M. *Visionary vine: Psychedelic healing in the Peruvian Amazon.* San Francisco: Chandler, 1972.

DRAGUNS, J. G. Resocialization into culture: The complexities of taking a world-wide view of psychotherapy. In R. W. Brislin, S. Bochner, & W. J. Lonner (Eds.), *Cross-cultural perspectives on learning.* New York: Wiley, 1975.

EDELSTEIN, E., & EDELSTEIN, L. *Asclepius: A collection and interpretation of the testimonies* (Vols. I & II). Baltimore, Md.: Johns Hopkins Press, 1945.

ELIADE, M. *Le chamanisme et les techniques archaïques de l'extase.* Paris: Payot, 1951. (Revised and enlarged edition in English: Eliade, M. *Shamanism: Archaic techniques of ecstasy* [Willard R. Trask, trans]. New York: Bollingen Foundation, 1964.)

ELLENBERGER, H. F. *The discovery of the unconscious: The history and evolution of dynamic psychiatry.* New York: Basic Books, 1970.

EVANS-PRITCHARD, E. E. *Witchcraft, oracles and magic among the Azande.* London: Oxford University Press, 1937.

EYSENCK, H. J. *The effects of psychotherapy.* New York: Science House, 1969.

FABREGA, H., Jr., & SILVER, D. B. *Illness and shamanistic curing in Zinacantan: An ethno-medical analysis.* Stanford, Calif.: Stanford University Press, 1973.

FARON, L. C. *The Mapuche Indians of Chile.* New York: Holt, Rinehart and Winston, 1968.

FENICHEL, O. Brief psychotherapy. In O. Fenichel, *Collected papers.* London: Routledge, 1955.

FIELD, M. J. *Search for security. An ethno-psychiatric study of rural Ghana.* Evanston, Ill.: Northwestern University Press, 1960.

FINNEY, J. C. *Culture change, mental health, and poverty.* Lexington: University of Kentucky Press, 1969.

FISCHER, R. A cartography of the ecstatic and meditative states. *Science,* 1971, *174,* 897–904.

FISCHER, R. Letter to the editor. *R. M. Bucke Memorial Society Newsletter-Review,* 1972, 5, 42–45.

FISHER, C., & DEMENT, W. Studies on the psychopathology of sleep and dreams. *American Journal of Psychiatry,* 1963, *119,* 1160–1168.

FISKE, D. W., HUNT, H. F., LUBORSKY, L., ORNE, M. T., PARLOFF, M. B., REISER, M. F., & TUMA, A. H. Planning of research on effectiveness of psychotherapy. *American Psychologist,* 1970, *25,* 727–737.

FRANK, J. D. *Persuasion and healing.* Baltimore, Md.: Johns Hopkins Press, 1961.

FREEMON, F. R. *Sleep research: A critical review.* Springfield, Ill.: Thomas, 1972.

FREUD, S. *Beyond the pleasure principle.* London: Hogarth, 1920.

———. On psychotherapy. In S. Freud, *Collected papers* (Vol. I). London: Hogarth, 1953a.

———. On the history of the psychoanalytic movement. In S. Freud, *Collected papers* (Vol. I). London: Hogarth, 1953b.

————. Psychoanalytic notes upon an autobiographical account of a case of paranoia (dementia paranoides). In S. Freud, *Collected papers* (Vol. 3). London: Hogarth, 1953c.

FURST, P. T. To find our life: Peyote among the Huichol Indians of Mexico. In P. T. Furst (Ed.), *Flesh of the gods. The ritual use of hallucinogens.* New York: Praeger, 1973.

GARRISON, V. The "Puerto Rican syndrome" in psychiatry and *Espiritismo.* In V. Crapanzano & V. Garrison (Eds.), *Case studies in spirit possession.* New York: Wiley-Interscience, 1977.

GILL, M., & BRENMAN, M. *Hypnosis and related states.* New York: International Universities Press, 1959.

GLUCKMAN, M. *Custom and conflict in Africa.* Oxford: Blackwell, 1959.

GLUECK, B. C., & STROEBEL, C. F. Biofeedback and meditation in the treatment of psychiatric illness. *Comprehensive Psychiatry,* 1975, *16,* 303–321.

GOLEMAN, D. Meditation as meta-therapy: Hypotheses toward a proposed fifth state of consciousness. *Journal of Transpersonal Psychology,* 1971, *3,* 1–25.

————. The Buddha on meditation and states of consciousness. II: A typology of meditation techniques. *Journal of Transpersonal Psychology,* 1972, *4,* 151–210.

GOWAN, J. G. *Trance, art and creativity,* Buffalo, N. Y.: Creative Education Foundation, 1975.

GREELEY, A. M., & McCREADY, W. C. The sociology of mystical ecstasy: Some preliminary notes. Paper presented at the Society for the Scientific Study of Religion, San Francisco, 1973.

GREENBAUM, L. Possession trance in sub-Saharan Africa: A descriptive analysis of fourteen cultures. In E. Bourguignon (Ed.), *Religion, altered states of consciousness and social change.* Columbus: Ohio State University Press, 1973.

HARNER, M. J. The sound of rushing water. *Natural History,* 1968, *77* (6), 15–27. (Reprinted in M. J. Harner [Ed.], *Hallucinogens and shamanism.* London: Oxford University Press, 1973.)

HARTMANN, E., BAEKLAND, F., ZWILLING, G., & HOY, P. Sleep need: How much and what kind? *American Journal of Psychiatry,* 1971, *127,* 1001–1008.

HARTMANN, H. *Ego psychology and the problem of adaptation.* New York: International Universities Press, 1958.

HENNEY, J. H. Spirit-possession belief and trance behaviour in two fundamentalist groups in St. Vincent. In I. Zaretsky (Ed.), *Trance, healing and hallucination: Three field studies in religious experience.* New York: Wiley-Interscience, 1974.

HERSKOVITS, M. H. *Dahomey: An ancient West African kingdom.* New York: Augustin, 1938.

HESS, W. R. *Functional organization of the diencephalon.* New York: Grune & Stratton, 1957.

HITCHCOCK, J. T. A Nepali shaman's performance as theatre. *Artscanada,* December 1973, 74–80.

HORTON, R. The gods as guests. *Nigeria Magazine* (Lagos), 1960.

————. Destiny and the unconscious in West Africa. *Africa,* 1961, *31,* 110–116.

HULTKRANTZ, A. Spirit lodge, a North American schamanistic seance. In C.-M. Edsman (Ed.), *Studies in shamanism.* Stockholm: Almqvist and Wiksell, 1967.

HUMPHREYS, C. *Concentration and meditation. A manual of mind development.* Baltimore, Md.: Penguin, 1970. (Originally published, 1935)

HUXLEY A. *The perennial philosophy.* London: Chatto & Windus, 1946.

IKEDA, K. Morita's theory of neurosis and its application in Japanese psychotherapy. In J. Howells, (Ed.), *Modern perspectives in world psychiatry.* New York: Brunner/Mazel, 1971.

JACOBSON, A., & BERENBERG, A. N. Japanese psychiatry and psychotherapy. *American Journal of Psychiatry,* 1952, *109,* 321–329.

JACOBSON, E. *Progressive relaxation.* Chicago: University of Chicago Press, 1938.

JAMES, W. *The varieties of religious experience.* New York: Longmans, Green, 1902.

JAYNE, W. A. *The healing gods of ancient civilizations.* New York: University Books, 1962.

JILEK, W. G. From crazy witch doctor to auxiliary psychotherapist—The changing image of the medicine man. *Psychiatria Clinica,* 1971, 4, 200–220.

————. *Salish Indian mental health and culture change: Psychohygenic and therapeutic aspects of the guardian spirit ceremonial.* Toronto: Holt, Rinehart & Winston, 1974.

JILEK, W. G., & TODD, N. Witchdoctors succeed where doctors fail: Psychotherapy among Coast Salish Indians. *Canadian Psychiatric Association Journal,* 1974, *19,* 351–356.

KALINOWSKY, L. B., & HOCH, P. H. *Somatic treatments in psychiatry.* New York: Grune & Stratton, 1961.

KENNEDY, J. K. Nubian zar ceremonies as psychotherapy. *Human Organization,* 1967, *26,* 185–194.

KENSINGER, K. M. Banisteriopsis usage among the Peruvian Cashinahua. In M. J. Harner (Ed.), *Hallucinogens and shamanism.* London: Oxford University Press, 1973.

KERNBERG, O. Final report of the Menninger Clinic's psychotherapy research project. *Menninger Clinic Bulletin,* 1972, *36,* 1–273.

KIEV, A. Psychotherapy in Haitian voodoo. *American Journal of Psychotherapy,* 1962, *16,* 469–476.

————. *Magic, faith and healing: Studies in primitive psychiatry today.* New York: Free Press, 1964.

————. *Transcultural psychiatry.* New York: Free Press, 1972.

KILSON, M. Possession in Ga-Ritual. *Transcultural Psychiatric Research,* 1968, *5,* 67–69.

KIM, K.-I. Psychoanalytic consideration of Korean shamanism. *Korean Neuropsychiatric Association Journal,* 1972, *2,* 121–129. (Abstracted in *Transcultural Psychiatric Research, 11,* 40–42.)

————. Shamanist healing ceremonies in Korea. *Korea Journal,* 1973, *13,* 41–47.

KLINE, N. Psychiatry in Kuwait. *British Journal of Psychiatry,* 1963, *109,* 766–774.

KOESTLER, A. *The invisible writing.* New York: Macmillan, 1954.

KONDO, A. Morita therapy: A Japanese therapy for neurosis. *American Journal of Psychoanalysis,* 1953, *13,* 31–37.

————. Morita therapy: Its sociohistorical context. In S. Arieti & G. Chrzanowski (Eds.), *New dimensions in psychiatry.* New York: Wiley, 1975.

KORA, T. Morita therapy. *International Journal of Psychiatry,* 1965, *1,* 611–640.

KRAMER, B. H. Psychotherapeutic implications of a traditional healing ceremony: The Malaysian Main Puteri. *Transcultural Psychiatric Research,* 1970, *8,* 149–151.

KRAUS, R. F. A psychoanalytic interpretation of shamanism. *Transcultural Psychiatric Research, 1970, 7,* 5–9.

LA BARRE, E. H. *They shall take up serpents: Psychology of the Southern snake-handling cult.* Minneapolis: University of Minnesota Press, 1962.

LA BARRE, W. The influence of Freud on anthropology. *American Imago,* 1958, *15,* 275–328.

LAING, R. D. *The politics of experience.* Harmondsworth: Penguin, 1967.

LAND, T. African witch doctors to get same status as Western-trained MDs. *Medical Post,* February 14, 1978.

LANDOLT, H. Mystical experience in Islam. In R. Prince (Ed.), *Personality change and religious experience.* Montreal: R. M. Bucke Memorial Society, 1965.

LASKI, M. *Ecstasy. A study of some secular and religious experiences.* London: Cresset Press, 1961.

LEBRA, W. P. Shaman and client in Okinawa. In W. Caudill & T. Lin (Eds.), *Mental health research in Asia and the Pacific.* Honolulu: East-West Center Press, 1969.

LEE, R. B. The sociology of !Kung bushman trance performances. In R. Prince (Ed.), *Trance and possession states.* Montreal: R. M. Bucke Memorial Society, 1968.

LEONARD, A. P. Spirit mediums in Paulau: Transformations in a traditional system. In E. Bourguignon (Ed.), *Religion, altered states of consciousness and social change.* Columbus: Ohio State University Press, 1973.

LeVINE, R. *Culture, behavior and personality.* Chicago: Aldine, 1973.

LEWIS, I. M. *A pastoral democracy.* London: Oxford University Press, 1961.

―――. *Ecstatic religion: An anthropological study of spirit possession and shamanism.* Harmondworth: Penguin, 1971.

LINTON, R. *Culture and mental disorders.* Springfield, Ill.: Thomas, 1956.

LOMBARD, J. Les cultes de posséssion en Afrique noire et le Bori Hausa. *Psychopathologie Africaine,* 1967, *3,* 419–439.

LOWIE, R. *An introduction to cultural anthropology.* New York: Farrar & Rinehart, 1940. (Quoted in Hultkrantz, 1967.)

LUBCHANSKY, I., EGRI, G., & STOKES, J. Puerto Rican spiritualists view mental illness: The faith healer as a paraprofessional. *American Journal of Psychiatry,* 1970, *127,* 312–321.

LUBORSKY, L., & SPENCE, D. P. Quantitative research on psychoanalytic therapy. In A. E. Bergin & S. L. Garfield (Eds.), *Handbook of psychotherapy and behavior change.* New York: Wiley, 1971.

LUTHE, W. Autogenic training: Method, research and application in medicine. *American Journal of Psychotherapy,* 1963, *17,* 174–195.

MacLEAN, G., & ROBERTSON, B. M. Self-enucleation and psychosis: Report of two cases and discussion. *Archives of General Psychiatry,* 1976, *33,* 242–249.

MARMOR, J. The nature of the psychotherapeutic process revisited. *Canadian Psychiatric Association Journal,* 1975, *20,* 557–565.

MAUPIN, E. Zen Buddhism: A psychological review. *Journal of Consulting Psychology,* 1962, *26,* 362–378.

MESSING, S. D. Group therapy and social status in the zar cult of Ethiopia. *American Anthropologist*, 1958, *60*, 1120–1126.

MIDDLETON, J. *Magic, witchcraft and curing.* New York: Natural History Press, 1967.

MISCHEL, W., & MISCHEL, F. Psychological aspects of spirit possession. *American Anthropologist*, 1958, *60*, 249–260.

MITCHELL, S. W. *Fat and blood, and how to make them.* Philadelphia: Lippincott, 1877.

MODARRESSI, T. The zar cult in South Iran. In R. Prince (Ed.), *Trance and possession states.* Montreal: R. M. Bucke Memorial Society, 1968.

MOGAR, R. E. Psychedelic states and schizophrenia. *Journal of Existential Psychiatry*, 1968, *6*, 401–420.

MOREAU, J. *Du hachisch et de l'aliénation mentale.* Paris: Libraire de Fortin, Masson et cie., 1845. (The present translation is from the recently published version: Moreau, J. *Hashish and mental illness* (Gordon J. Barnett, trans.). New York: Raven, 1973, p. 151.)

MOSAK, H. H., & DREIKURS, R. Alderian psychotherapy. In R. Corsini (Ed.), *Current psychotherapies.* Itasca, Ill.: Peacock, 1973.

MURDOCK, G. P. Tenino shamanism. *Ethnology*, 1965, *4*, 165–171.

———. *Ethnographic atlas: A summary.* Pittsburgh, Pa.: University of Pittsburgh Press, 1967.

MURPHY, J. M. Psychotherapeutic aspects of shamanism on St. Lawrence Island, Alaska. In A. Kiev (Ed.), *Magic, faith and healing.* New York: Free Press, 1964.

NARANJO, C., & ORNSTEIN, R. E. *On the psychology of meditation.* New York: Viking, 1971.

NICOLAS, J. Culpabilité, somatisation et catharsis au sein d'un culte de posséssion: "Le Bori Hausa." *Psychopathologie Africaine*, 1970, *6*, 147–180.

OESTERREICH, T. K. *Possession: Demoniacal and other among primitive races, in antiquity, the Middle Ages, and modern times.* New York: University Books. 1966.

OPLER, M. K. Some points of comparison and contrast between the treatment of functional disorders by Apache shamans and modern psychiatric practice. *American Journal of Psychiatry*, 1936, *92*, 1371–1387.

ORNSTEIN, R. E. *The psychology of consciousness.* San Francisco: Freeman, 1972.

OSBORNE, A., & PRINCE, R. Exchange of letters. *R. M. Bucke Memorial Society Newsletter-Review*, 1966, *1*, 13–16.

OWENS, C. M. Self-realization—induced and spontaneous. Paper presented at the R. M. Bucke Memorial Society Conference on Transformations of Consciousness, Montreal, October 1973.

PALMER, H. A. The value of continuous narcosis in the treatment of mental disorder. *Journal of Mental Science*, 1937, *83*, 636–678.

PEERBOLTE, M. L. Meditation for school children. *Main Currents*, 1967, *24*, 19–21.

PFISTER, O. Instinctive psychoanalysis among the Navahos. *Journal of Nervous and Mental Disease*, 1932, *76*, 234–254.

PODDAR, H. P. *The divine name and its practice.* Gorakhpur: Gita Press, 1965. (Quoted in Goleman, 1972)

PRABHUPADA, SWAMI. *Krishna consciousness: The topmost yoga system.* New York: Iskon, 1970.

PRINCE, R. H. The use of rauwolfia for the treatment of psychoses by Nigerian native doctors. *American Journal of Psychiatry*, 1960, *118*, 147–149.

———. Western psychiatry and the Yoruba: The problem of insight psychotherapy. *Conference Proceedings, March, 1962, Nigerian Institute of Social and Economic Research*, 1963a, 213–221.

———. Conference report. First Pan-African Psychiatric Conference. *Transcultural Psychiatric Research Review and Newsletter*, 1963b, *15*, 40–44.

———. Indigenous Yoruba psychiatry. In A. Kiev (Ed.), *Magic, faith and healing*. New York: Free Press, 1964.

———. Can the EEG be used in the study of possession states? In R. H. Prince (Ed.), *Trance and possession states*. Montreal: R. M. Bucke Memorial Society, 1968a.

———. Therapeutic process in cross-cultural perspective: A symposium [with A. H. Leighton and Rollo May]. *American Journal of Psychiatry*, 1968b, *124*, 56–69.

———. Psychotherapy and the chronically poor. In J. Finney (Ed.), *Culture change, mental health, and poverty*. Lexington: University of Kentucky Press, 1969.

———. Mystical experience and the certainty of belonging: An alternative to insight and suggestion in psychotherapy. In R. H. Cox (Ed.), *Religious systems and psychotherapy*. Springfield, Ill.: Thomas, 1973.

———. The problem of spirit possession as a treatment for psychiatric disorder. *Ethos*, 1974, *2*, 315–333.

———. Symbols and psychotherapy: The example of Yoruba sacrificial ritual. *Journal of the American Academy of Psychoanalysis*, 1975, *3*, 321–338.

———. Meditation: Some psychological speculations. *Psychiatric Journal of the University of Ottawa*, 1978, *3*, 202–209.

PRINCE, R. H., GOODWIN, A., & ENGELSMANN, F. Meditation and stress: An evaluative study. *R. M. Bucke Memorial Society Newsletter-Review*, 1976, *8*, 19–27.

PRINCE, R. H., & SAVAGE, C. Mystical states and the concept of regression. In R. H. Prince (Ed.), *Personality change and religious experience*. Montreal: R. M. Bucke Memorial Society, 1965.

REDLICH, F. C. Social aspects of psychotherapy. *American Journal of Psychiatry*, 1958, *114*, 800–804.

REYNOLDS, D. K. *Morita psychotherapy*. Berkeley: University of California Press, 1976.

RIOS, O. Ayahuasca: Its religious implications for healing in the Peruvian-Amazon area. Paper presented at the R. M. Bucke Memorial Society Conference on Transformations of Consciousness, Montreal, October 1973.

ROBBINS, T. Eastern mysticism and the resocialization of drug users. *Journal of Scientific Study of Religion*, 1969, *8*, 308–317.

ROSEN, G. *Madness in society. Chapters in the historical sociology of mental illness*. New York: Harper Torchbooks, 1969.

SANUA, V. D. Sociocultural aspects of psychotherapy and treatment: A review of the literature. In L. E. Abt & B. F. Riess (Eds.), *Progress in clinical psychology*. New York: Grune & Stratton, 1966.

SARGANT, W. *Battle for the mind*. New York: Doubleday, 1957.

———. Witch doctoring, zar and Voodoo: Their relation to modern psychiatric treatments. *Proceedings of the Royal Society of Medicine*, 1967, *60*, 1055–1060.

SASAKI, Y. Psychiatric study of the shaman in Japan. In W. Caudill & T. Lin (Eds.), *Mental health research in Asia and the Pacific.* Honolulu: East-West Center Press, 1969.

SCHULTES, R. E. Hallucinogens of plant origin. *Science,* 1969, *163,* 245–254.

———. An overview of hallucinogens in the western hemisphere. In P. Furst (Ed.), *Flesh of the gods.* New York: Praeger, 1972.

SEEMAN, W., NIDICH, S., & BANTA, T. Influence of transcendental meditation on a measure of self–actualization. *Journal of Counseling Psychology,* 1972, *19,* 184–187.

SEITZ, G. J. Epena, the intoxicating snuff powder of the Waika Indians and the Tucano medicine man, Agostino. In D. Efron (Ed.), *Ethnopharmacologic quest for psychoactive drugs.* Washington, D.C.: U.S. Government Printing Office, 1967.

SHAPIRO, A. K. Placebo effects in medicine, psychotherapy and psychoanalysis. In A. E. Bergin & S. L. Garfield (Eds.), *Handbook of psychotherapy and behavior change.* New York: Wiley, 1971.

SIIGER, H. Shamanic ecstasy and supernatural beings. In C.-M. Edsman (Ed.), *Studies in shamanism.* Stockholm: Almqvist and Wiksell, 1967.

SILVERMAN, J. Shamans and acute schizophrenia. *American Anthropologist,* 1967, *69,* 21–31

SILVERMAN, J. A. When schizophrenia helps. *Psychology Today,* September, 1973, pp. 63–65.

SINGER, P. (Ed.). *Traditional healing.* New York: Conch, 1977.

SINGER, P., ARANETA, E., & AARONS, L. Integration of indigenous practices of the Kali cult with western psychiatric modalities in British Guiana. *Transcultural Psychiatric Research Review,* 1967, *4,* 65–67.

SINGER, P., ARANETA, E., & NAIDOO, J. Learning of psychodynamics, history, diagnosis, management, therapy, by a Kali cult indigenous healer in Guyana. *Transcultural Psychiatric Research Review,* 1975, *12,* 71–73.

SISKIND, J. Visions and cures among the Sharanahua. In M. J. Harner (Ed.), *Hallucinogens and shamanism.* London: Oxford University Press, 1973.

STRUPP, H. H. Toward a reformulation of the psychotherapeutic influence. *International Journal of Psychiatry,* 1973, *11,* 263–365.

SWIFT, C. R., & ASUNI, T. *Mental health and disease in Africa.* London: Livingstone, 1975.

TORREY, E. F. *The mind game: Witchdoctors and psychiatrists.* New York: Emerson Hall, 1972.

———. Spiritualists and shamans as psychotherapists: An account of original anthropological sin. In I. Zaretsky & M. Leone (Eds.), *Religious movements in contemporary America.* Princeton, N.J.: Princeton University Press, 1974.

TSENG, W. S. Psychiatric study of shamanism in Taiwan. *Archives of General Psychiatry,* 1972, *26,* 561–565.

TURNER, V. W. The Ndembu doctor in practice. In A. Kiev (Ed.), *Magic, faith and healing.* New York: Free Press, 1964.

VEITH, I. *Hysteria: The history of a disease.* Chicago: University of Chicago Press, 1965.

———. On the "principles of the heart" and the psychiatric insights of Zen. *New England Journal of Medicine,* 1971, *285,* 1458–1460.

VERGER, P. Rôle joué par l'état d'hébétude au cours de l'initiation des novices aux cultes des Orishas et Vodon. *Bulletin de l'Institut Fondamental d'Afrique Noire,* 1954, *16,* 322–340.

VIVEKANANDA, SWAMI. *Bhakti-yoga,* Calcutta: Avaita Ashram, 1964. (Quoted in Goleman, 1972.)

VOGEL, G. W. REM Deprivation: III. Dreaming and psychosis. *Archives of General Psychiatry,* 1968, *18,* 312–329.

WALKER, S. S. *Ceremonial spirit possession in Africa and Afro-America.* Leiden: Brill, 1972.

WALLACE, A. F. C. Dreams and the wishes of the soul: A type of psychoanalytic theory among the seventeenth century Iroquois. *American Anthropologist,* 1958, *60,* 234–248.

———. Anthropology and psychiatry. In A. M. Freedman & H. I. Kaplan (Eds.), *Comprehensive Textbook of Psychiatry.* Baltimore: Williams & Wilkins, 1967.

WALLACE, R. K. Physiological effects of Transcendental Meditation. *Science,* 1970, *167,* 1751–1754.

WALTER, R. D. *S. Weir Mitchell, M. D.—neurologist.* Springfield, Ill.: Thomas, 1970

WARE, K. T. The mystical tradition of the Christian East: Cultural varieties of mysticism. *R. M. Bucke Memorial Society Newsletter-Review,* 1974, *7,* 3–26.

WASSON, R. G. *Soma: Divine mushroom of immortality.* New York: Harcourt, Brace & World, 1968.

WEBER, M. *The Protestant ethic and the spirit of capitalism,* T. Parsons, trans. New York: Scribner, 1958.

WHITING, J. M. M., & CHILD, I. L. *Child training and personality: A cross-cultural study.* New Haven, Conn.: Yale University Press, 1953.

WHITMONT, E. C., & KAUFMANN, Y. Analytic psychotherapy. In R. Corsini (Ed.), *Current psychotherapies,* Itasca, Ill.: Peacock, 1973.

WILBERT, J. Tobacco and shamanistic ecstasy among the Warao Indians of Venezuela. In P. T. Furst (Ed.), *Flesh of the gods.* New York: Praeger, 1973, pp. 55–83.

WITTGENSTEIN, L. *Philosophical investigations.* Oxford: Blackwell, 1974.

WITTKOWER, E. D. Trance and possession states. *International Journal of Social Psychiatry,* 1970, *16,* 153–160.

WITTKOWER, E. D., & WARNES, H. Cultural aspects of psychotherapy. *American Journal of Psychotherapy,* 1974, *28,* 566–573.

WOHL, J. Intercultural psychotherapy: Issues, questions, and reflections. In P. Pedersen, W. J. Lonner, and J. G. Draguns (Eds.), *Counseling across cultures.* Honolulu: University Press of Hawaii, 1976.

YOSHIDA, T. Mystical retribution, spirit possession and social structure in a Japanese village. *Ethnology,* 1967, *6,* 237–262.

ZAEHNER, R. C. *Mysticism: Sacred and profane.* New York: Oxford University Press, 1957.

Name Index

Subject Index

ABA design, 46
Abnormal behavior (*see also* Psychopathology):
axes of, 154–155
borderline states, 4
cultural influences, 2–3, 38, 62–63, 99–100
basic questions, 100–101, 103
cultural recognition of, 5, 63
medical model, 2–3, 101, 112–113
study of, 2, 107–109
issues involved, 102
universal criteria of, 109
Achievement:
disturbance related to, 76, 82–83, 88
study of achievement orientation, 153
Activity-passivity, 153
Adjustment to change, 205–206
minority status and, 200
vs. adaptation, 109
Africa:
depression in, 133, 239, 240, 250, 260, 268, 270–272
disturbed children study, 190
indigenous medicine, 332–333
mental illness in, 217
Aged:
role change, 85, 205
Aggression:
depression and, 267–268, 273
homicides and, 74–75
reinforcement and, 50
in schizophrenic children, 187
Alaska pipeline project, 47
Alcohol:
attitudes toward, 70–71, 203
consumption of native Americans, 26–29
consumption per head, 70
motives for use, 71
social functioning and, 82
Alcoholics:
anxiety and, 71
problems of, 70–71
Alienation, 3–4, 9–59
causes, 10, 38
from cross-cultural perspective, 13–15
definitions, 9–13, 52
effort to clarify, 18–19
deviance and, 29
effect of move to alien society, 46–48
experimental analysis, 48–51
in experimental prison, 48
history of concept, 15–17
implications of studies, 51–52

in industrial society, 19–20, 39, 53
manifestations, 28
Marxist orientation, 13–15, 52
measurement, 20–24, 52–53
discriminant validity, 21–22
response style, 21–23
mental health and social change, 43–46
in migrants, 149–150
multidimensional nature, 22
in non-industrial societies, 24–39
education and, 30
Latin America, 32–34
native American, 26–30
other areas, 34–39
subsaharan Africa, 30–31
in Philippines, 39–43, 53
research, 11, 17–20
shortcomings of, 9–10, 21–23, 30, 32, 39
urbanization effects, 24–25, 37
Alienation and Modernization Scales, 23–24
Altered states of consciousness, 292, 294, 299–331
changing attitudes of Western medicine, 331–333
dissociation states, 314–321
dreams, 299–306
mystical states and meditation, 306–314
shamanic "ecstasy," 322–331
therapeutic factors, 336–338
Amae, 84–85, 203
American Institute of Public Opinion, 306–307
American Psychiatric Association, 314
Amok, 135
Anglo–American Comparative Research Study, 220
Anomia Scale of Srole, 20–22, 35
Anomie (*see also* Alienation), 3, 15–16, 52
causes, 21
industrialization and, 34–35, 37
mental illness and (*see also* Mental illness), 44
social causes, 198
Anthropological research, 103–105, 108, 119, 336
Anxiety, 21
in depression, 252, 255
studies of, 80, 118
Appalachia, 48–49
Arabs:
attitude to women, 210, 211
depression among, 250

363